PASTORAL
COUNSELING

CONTRIBUTORS

Melvin C. Blanchette, S.S., Ph.D.
B.A., Sacred Heart Seminary College
M.A., University of Detroit
Ph.D., United States International University
Licensed Psychologist: Maryland
Member, American Association of Pastoral
  Counselors

Rachel Callahan, C.S.C., Ph.D.
B.A., St. Mary's College
M.A., University of Notre Dame
Ph.D., The Catholic University of America
Licensed Psychologist: Maryland and District
  of Columbia

Joseph W. Ciarrocchi, Ph.D.
B.A., St. Fidelis College
M.A., Capuchin College
Ph.D., The Catholic University of America
Licensed Psychologist: Maryland
Director of Addictions, Taylor Manor Hospital

John R. Compton, D.Min.
B.A., Capital University
B.D., M.Div., Lutheran Theological
  Seminary
S.T.M., New York Theological Seminary
D.Min., Lancaster Theological Seminary
Member, American Association of Pastoral
  Counselors
Counselor Certification: Maryland; NBCC;
  NACCMHC

Kevin G. Culligan, O.C.D., Ph.D.
B.A., M.S., Our Lady of Mt. Carmel
M.S., Marquette University
Ph.D., Boston University
Licensed Psychologist: Maryland

Robert F. Davenport, D.Min.
B.A., University of Florida
M.A., Presbyterian School of Christian
  Education
B.D., Yale University
D.Min., Vanderbilt University
Fellow, American Association of Pastoral
  Counselors
Staff, Pastoral Counseling and Consultation
  Centers of Greater Washington
Counselor Certification: Maryland

Barry K. Estadt, Ph.D.
B.A., St. Fidelis College
M.A., Ph.D., The Catholic University of
  America
Diplomate, American Board of Professional
  Psychology
Licensed Psychologist: Maryland, District of
  Columbia, Pennsylvania, Florida
Diplomate, American Association of Pastoral
  Counselors

James W. Ewing, Ph.D.
B.A., Carleton College
B.D., University of Chicago
S.T.M., Eden Theological Seminary
Ph.D., St. Louis University
Faculty, United States International University

B. John Hagedorn, Ph.D.
B.A., University of Maryland
B.D., Lutheran Theological Seminary
Ph.D., Boston University
Diplomate, American Association of Pastoral
  Counselors
Staff, Pastoral Counseling and Consultation
  Centers of Greater Washington
Counselor Certification: Maryland

William F. Hug, Ph.D.
B.A., Yale University
M.Div., Princeton Theological Seminary
Ph.D., University of Maryland
Licensed Psychologist: Maryland

David L. Luecke, D.Rel.
B.A., Concordia Collegiate Institute
B.D., M.Div., Concordia Seminary
D.Rel., Chicago Theological Seminary
Pastor, St. John's Lutheran Church, Columbia,
  Maryland

Ann Kaiser Stearns, M.Div., Ph.D.
B.A., Oklahoma City University
M.Div., Duke University Divinity School
Ph.D., Union Graduate School
Professor of Psychology, Essex Community
  College
Faculty, Family Practice Residency Program,
  Franklin Square Hospital
Counselor Certification: NACCMHC

SECOND EDITION

PASTORAL COUNSELING

Loyola College Pastoral Counseling Faculty

Barry K. Estadt, Ph.D.
Melvin C. Blanchette, Ph.D.
John R. Compton, D. Min.
EDITORS

PRENTICE HALL, *Englewood Cliffs, New Jersey 07632*

Library of Congress Cataloging in Publication Data
Pastoral counseling / Loyola College Pastoral Counseling Faculty ;
    Barry K. Estadt, Melvin C. Blanchette, John R. Compton, editors —
    2nd ed.
      p.   cm.
    Includes bibliographical references and index.
    ISBN 0-13-652991-7 (casebound).—ISBN 0-13-653007-9 (pbk.)
    1. Pastoral counseling. I. Estadt, Barry K. II. Blanchette, Melvin.
III. Compton, John R. IV. Loyola College in Maryland. Dept. of
Pastoral Counseling.
BV4012.2.P29 1991
253.5—dc20   90-39651
                                            CIP

Acquisitions editor: Ted Bolen
Cover design: Ray Lundgren Graphics, Ltd.
Prepress buyer: Herb Klein
Manufacturing buyer: David Dickey

© 1991, 1983 by Prentice-Hall, Inc.
A Division of Simon & Schuster
Englewood Cliffs, New Jersey 07632

Printed in the United States of America
10 9 8 7 6 5 4 3 2 1

ISBN 0-13-652991-7 {C}
ISBN 0-13-653007-9 {P}

Prentice-Hall International (UK) Limited, *London*
Prentice-Hall of Australia Pty. Limited, *Sydney*
Prentice-Hall Canada Inc., *Toronto*
Prentice-Hall Hispanoamericana, S.A., *Mexico*
Prentice-Hall of India Private Limited, *New Delhi*
Prentice-Hall of Japan, Inc., *Tokyo*
Simon & Schuster Asia Pte. Ltd., *Singapore*
Editora Prentice-Hall do Brasil, Ltda., *Rio de Janeiro*

Contents

PART TWO   ON BECOMING A PASTORAL COUNSELOR

PART THREE   ON DOING PASTORAL COUNSELING

Foreword

Although the advantages of entering the second half of life are problematic and dubious, one possible prize is in the obtaining of a perspective which allows history its rightful place in the evaluation process. Put another way—and in the language of the photographer—growing older *can* mean seeing life and movements through a wide-angle lens. And that can make life different—perhaps even better. Reading *Pastoral Counseling* gave me that sort of experience—an opportunity to see just how far pastoral counseling has come in the thirty years I have been monitoring that movement.

Barry Estadt has gathered together a fascinating group of competent counselors and psychotherapists who demonstrate in their writings his remarkably tantalizing definition of the pastoral counselor as "a religiously integrated person who approaches others with a sense of mystery along with an ability to enter into communion with others in a therapeutic alliance with the goal of reconciliation and personal religious integration."

What is especially refreshing—and what makes in this instance the monitoring of the movement a joy—is the general affirmative stance found throughout this book. Unlike most of the volumes of "the good ol' days," the central tone of this book is one of a confident and gentle assertiveness. Pastoral counseling *is* a ministry! There's hardly any of the old and wearisome apologetics cluttering the pages. There's practically nothing in the way of professional Pollyannaism. And hardly a single note of theological arrogance.

Instead, we discover properly trained persons *doing* such things as psychological testing, premarital counseling, spiritual direction, crisis intervention work, marriage and family counseling, supervision, grief counseling, group therapy, adult development counseling, counseling with alcoholics—all informed and flowing naturally from a stance of religious faith and all being seen clearly and steadily as authentic expressions of ministry.

It seems to me that this sort of demonstration is what "coming of age" is all about. And in this sense, I trust *Pastoral Counseling* will become prototypic of future volumes out to witness to the ways in which counseling and psychotherapy may properly be seen as creative ministry, a ministry which holds firm to old visions, at the same time witnessing to many new possibilities of service.

Orlo Strunk, Jr., Ph.D.
Chair of Editorial Committee and Managing Editor,
Journal of Pastoral Care

Preface

This book is written for all who are searching for meaning and purpose in life. It is written for those who seek a personal integration involving reconciliation with self, with others, and with God. It is written for all who search for meaning beyond the concrete circumstances of daily life and who reach out for spiritual understanding. Those who have a faith which transcends the here and now, and who seek at the same time to explore the richness of their personhood, will find inspiration and direction.

The authors of the book, pastoral counselors, lay and ordained, from many denominations, seek to share their personal lives and work with all who have a sense of "spiritual pilgrimage." They reveal their own intimate personal struggles and share their ongoing counseling work with others as they attempt to combine insights from theology and ministry with those of the contemporary helping professions. The book is not about theory but about the personal lives and ministries of pastoral counselors. It is a book on how pastoral counseling is done.

In communicating their personal experience and the meaning it has had for them, the authors hope to communicate to all religiously concerned people the potential for personal and spiritual growth through the pastoral counseling process. The human person is viewed in a multidimensional manner. Spiritual needs are as integral to the human person as physiological, emotional, and social needs. Healthy emotional and social development frees one for participating more fully in the journey of the spirit.

The authors speak directly to fellow ministers of all kinds: to pastors, associate pastors, chaplains of institutions of all kinds, military chaplains, deacons, vowed religious, lay professional staff ministers, and volunteers. In using the term *pastor* or *counseling minister,* none are excluded. With our colleagues in ministry we share the richness of our own counseling ministry and the variety of applications we have found, hoping in some way our experience will resonate with your own and will in some way enrich your ministry. For candidates in theological schools, seminarians, and laypersons interested in ministry, it is our hope that our shared experience and reflection may open up potential areas of ministry as you seek to identify your own unique ministerial gifts. For students in the social sciences, philosophy, and theology, the book presents a unique attempt of seasoned professionals with roots in these disciplines to integrate their insights as they try to understand more fully the human person. We attempt to integrate the richness that the contemporary sciences and professions have brought to a fuller understanding of the human person with the insights of theology and ministry within the context of our denominational traditions.

Through this book, the authors hope to enter into dialogue with our colleagues in the contemporary helping professions: with counselors, social workers, psychiatric nurses, psychologists, and psychiatrists. We share with our mental health colleagues a concern for the intrapsychic and interpersonal dimension of the human person. What we, as a group, contribute to our colleagues is a sensitive awareness that the human person's full actualization is not complete until the person addresses in some way the "transpersonal dimension" of the human person, that is, our need for a relationship with God.

Pastoral Counseling has been written by faculty members of the Department of Pastoral Counseling at Loyola College in Maryland. The department offers three degree programs: the Master's degree, the Certificate of Advanced Study, and the Doctor of Pastoral Counseling (DPC). Five hundred candidates from forty-five states and twenty-nine countries abroad have enrolled in its programs.

The Loyola faculty is ecumenical and represents pastoral counseling in its broadest perspectives. The faculty members have received their professional training through psychiatry, psychology, schools of religion, theological seminaries, and a wide range of pastoral counseling training institutes and centers. The settings for exercising their counseling ministry include parishes, colleges, universities, theological schools, denominational and ecumenical pastoral counseling centers, private counseling offices, and specialized treatment centers. Although faculty members are diverse in their training, theoretical orientation, denominational affiliation, and settings for counseling, they share in common an abiding belief in the efficacy of the counseling ministry.

The book is organized into three parts: On Pastoral Counseling; On Becoming a Pastoral Counselor; On Doing Pastoral Counseling. In the first chapter, *Profile of a Pastoral Counselor,* I share reflections on my own personal and professional journey. I offer for your consideration a description of the pastoral counselor: "A religiously integrated person who approaches others with a sense of mystery, along with an ability to enter into communion with others in a therapeutic alliance with the goal of reconciliation and personal religious integration." In Chapter 2, the focus shifts somewhat as Blanchette, in *Theological Foundations of Pastoral Counseling*, develops the concept that "to live in God's spirit and to be fully human" are one and the same, presenting pastoral counseling as a process of liberation and transformation. Culligan, in Chapter 3, *The Counseling Ministry and Spiritual Direction*, concentrates on counseling as a means of helping persons deepen their relationship to God. "The spiritual director is a counselor in the Church whose primary focus is helping persons grow in their relationship to God through prayer."

In Part II, the reader is offered three chapters on the process of becoming a pastoral counselor. In Chapter 4, *Supervision: From Technician to Artist*, I reflect on the key role of the supervisory process, offering concrete goals for supervision as one moves from the level of technician to that of artist in the ministry of pastoral counseling. In Chapter 5, *Beyond Theory and Technique: Reflections on the Process of Becoming*, Hug offers a highly personalized account of his own odyssey from the parochial ministry to his present ministry as a specialist in pastoral counseling. In Chapter 6, *Personal and Professional Growth through Psychological Testing*, Blanchette, with a background in both psychology and pastoral counseling, presents a dynamic and developmental vision of the human person, demonstrating how psychological testing can contribute to the personal and professional growth of the pastoral counselor.

In Part III, the chapters focus on the application of pastoral counseling within the parochial and institutional setting. In Chapter 7, *The Counseling Pastor*, I attempt to clarify how I see counseling fitting into the overall role of one who serves a congregation in the role of pastor or chaplain with its multitudinous set of functions and role relationships. This chapter is followed by a series of contributions which focus on specific applications of counseling. Callahan, in Chapter 8, *The Ministry of Crisis Intervention*, reviews the literature on crisis intervention, offers concrete guidelines, and points to the unique role of the counseling minister in assisting people in crisis. Compton, in Chapter 9, *Premarital Preparation and Counseling*, calls upon his thirty years of experience, offering a comprehensive, practical, step-by-step approach to assisting couples in preparing for marriage, suggesting that renewed efforts in this regard are essential to the Church's mission. In Chapter 10, *Counseling with Couples*, Luecke shares his many years of experience in counseling couples as a parish pastor, offering a unique systems approach revolving around issues of compatibility, cooperation, intimacy, and emotional support. Hagedorn, in Chapter 11, *Counseling with Families*, discusses family root systems, systemic family counseling, steps in working with families, and the unique opportunities for counseling ministers to be part of family growth and development. In Chapter 12, *Adult Developmental Counseling*, Davenport calls attention to the need for ministers to "think developmentally," highlighting the special role of the counseling minister in dealing with midlife issues of separation and individuation. Stearns, in Chapter 13, *Counseling the Grieving Person*, vividly describes the steps of the grieving and healing process, pointing to the counseling minister as a valuable partner in the search for healing and new meaning. In Chapter 14, *Counseling with the Recovering Alcoholic,* Ciarrochhi speaks of the spiritual search of the recovering alcoholic and of the counseling minister's potential role in the recovery process. Davenport, in Chapter 15, *Pastoral Group Counseling,* reflects upon his many years of ministry in group counseling. "In my groups, I function as priest, pastor, and prophet, teaching others a ministry of hearing, conversing, and confronting." In Chapter 16, *Professional and Ethical Issues in Pastoral Counseling,* a new chapter for this second edition, Blanchette stresses the need for sensitivity to the highest ethical standards, grounding ethical principles in the special covenant which pastoral counselors enter into with their clients. In the epilogue, *Pastoral Counseling Issues: Current and Future,* Ewing offers assertions which provide a framework from which to extrapolate, project, and guide the future of the profession of pastoral counseling.

Barry K. Estadt

PART ONE
ON PASTORAL COUNSELING

CHAPTER ONE

Profile of a Pastoral Counselor

BARRY K. ESTADT, PH.D.

Over the past twelve years I have read several hundred papers by graduate students in pastoral counseling who were reflecting on personal experiences within the counseling ministry. The students were ordained clergy from a variety of denominations, religious brothers and sisters, advanced-level seminarians, and lay men and women active in ministry within their respective denominations. The papers consisted of a statement of the candidate's theology of ministry, a presentation of the counseling theory which resonated with the candidate's personal experience in the counseling ministry, and a presentation and critique of a typical counseling session. From reflection on this wealth of material and on my personal experience in the ministry of counseling, I have attempted to formulate an answer to the question: "Who is the pastoral counselor?"

It is interesting to me that my work with pastoral-counseling students has led me to formulate that question, using the personal pronoun *who. Who is the pastoral counselor?* This is a far more meaningful question for me than *What is pastoral counseling?* As I have attempted to capture my inner response in words, it has emerged something like this: *A pastoral counselor . . . is a religiously integrated person . . . who approaches others with a sense of mystery . . . along with an ability to enter into communion with others in a therapeutic alliance . . . with the goal of reconciliation and personal religious integration.*

As I reflect on the components of that description, I find each powerfully meaningful to me, calling forth deep feelings about my personal and professional

1

pilgrimage. I share them with the hope that my experience may resonate in some way with your own, realizing full well that my reflections are personal, evolving, and far from a complete statement.

A RELIGIOUSLY INTEGRATED PERSON

Fundamental to religious integration is an awareness of one's *personal finiteness*. As I studied theology in my mid-twenties, I was convinced that I understood my role as creature and was confident in my ability to articulate that role, having at my fingertips a host of theological sources. It was not until I stood at the bedside of my father in my mid-thirties, however, that I experienced the depth of my helplessness and came to understand the highly theoretical nature of my theological formulation.

Standing at the bedside of my father as the days, weeks, and months of his illness dragged on, I experienced an unrelenting powerlessness: I could do nothing to alter the course of his illness.

In the midst of this experience of helplessness, my father gave me a gift that I shall always treasure. I remember very clearly entering his hospital room a few days before he was transferred to a nursing home. I was deeply troubled, having left a conference with the doctors who had disclosed that they had run the full course of treatments. Dad greeted me with a special smile. In a very tender way, unlike his typical open-hearth, pit-foreman style, Dad said: "Thank you, son. I couldn't have made it without you."

It was a profound message for me then, and it continues to affect me today. Although I could do nothing to alter the course of his illness, I was present for him and my presence was a source of strength. It was ironic. To Dad, I made a major difference in his ability to place his trust in God a day at a time, yet my own experience was an increasing sense of helplessness and frustration. As I look back, it seems clear that it was my love expressed in a caring presence that gave strength; it was my unrealistic expectation that I could somehow direct the course of events which led me to helpless anger. Through this experience I came to understand that a lack of control does not equal a lack of potency. Never, perhaps, had I been more potent than when I stood helpless at my dad's bedside.

Since that time, as I have entered into other relationships, I have come repeatedly to experience a similar potency, fully aware of my inability to modify the course of events. Shortly after Dad died, I received a call from a professional colleague, who informed me that his son Timmy was expected to die that night. He asked me if I would be with him and his wife during their home vigil. They had brought Timmy home to die. Here there was clearly no expectation that I had the ability to change the course of the disease. What my friend requested was the strength of my presence. I shall never forget that night: the tangible experience of creature kneeling before Creator, fully aware that the author of life was about to call this young life to Himself. Nor shall I ever forget the experience of reverently carrying Timmy upstairs to his bedroom to fulfill his last request that he be allowed to sleep in his own bed. Shortly thereafter, Timmy fell asleep for the last time.

Special moments with Dad, with Timmy, and with others retain their power to evoke deep feeling as I reflect, in reverence, on the special *awareness of the holy* which I have experienced in the midst of helplessness. I recall many occasions in a five-year supportive counseling relationship with Lori, a struggling mother whose life energies focused on her young son with leukemia. Sometimes toward the end of a session we would leave the counseling office and walk to the hospital chapel. We would stand before the altar: the therapist and the mother. Joining hands, we would stand in reverential awe as we prayed in the words that Jesus taught us: "Hallowed be thy name . . . thy kingdom come . . . thy will be done." Though we did not share denominational traditions, we shared our acknowledged dependence on God. These periodic chapel visits were powerful. I suspect that they symbolized to Lori the fact that God loved her despite her feelings of abandonment and that I cared despite my inability to change the course of events. To me they symbolized our need to work toward an acceptance of the mystery of the divine plan as it unfolds in our lives, full well realizing that it may be necessary for acceptance to precede understanding.

In the early days of my spiritual journey, my experience of God was most tangible during periods of quiet contemplation. These were moments of union with God—a God whom I experienced both outside of me and within. For many years the most meaningful prayer mode for me has been one of simple presence and union with God. It is a presence that has been keenly felt during periods of contemplation in a chapel or church. It is the same presence I have felt in special quiet moments in the mountains or at the shore. The Eucharist, also, has frequently been the occasion for a special *awareness of the holy* in my life as I have shared my faith with friends, colleagues, and family. With increasing frequency in recent years, I have been finding that same kind of presence in my counseling relationships.

There seems to be a close connection between my awareness of God in quiet periods of contemplation and my consciousness of His presence in the counseling relationship. When I experience God's presence in my counseling, I find myself yearning for more moments alone with Him. When I make the space in my life for quiet time with God, I tune in to His presence more readily in my counseling relationships. As a strategy in the midst of days heavily scheduled with teaching, supervision of students, administration, and direct counseling, I find that beginning my day with quiet prayer notably enhances my ability to maintain an active awareness of God's presence as I engage in counseling in His name.

The experience of God in my relationship with Dad, with Timmy and his parents, and with Lori was rooted in a *faith that transcends the here and now* together with a *personal capacity to trust*. When I think of faith and trust, I am reminded of an experience I had while spending a week on the cruise liner *Queen Elizabeth 2*. One afternoon as I stood on deck, I noticed in the distance what appeared to be a mass of dark clouds close to the water. It was puzzling: above, the sun was shining brightly; in fact, the sky was clear in every direction. The water around the ship was tranquil, yet on the horizon was a patch of stormy turbulence. I asked a passerby what it might be. As a cruise veteran, he was pleased to inform me that the turbulence was a tropical squall, common at this time in the Caribbean. He explained that the captain had adjusted course when evidence of the squall was picked up by the ship's electronic equipment. Sailboats, he commented, might enter a squall with little or no warning. The crew would have to hang on for their lives as the wind and waves tested their skill and endurance and the seaworthiness of their vessel. Above the squall, and in every direction, there was the presence of the sun with its bright warming rays; within the squall there was only turbulence.

The similarity with life was striking. How frequently many of us sail along with confidence, even abandon, enjoying the warm brilliance of the sun and the gentle movement of the wind. Then, with no forewarning, we enter upon a squall. Loss, frustration, disappointment—the intensity of personal squalls can strain every sinew of faith and trust, especially when squalls are prolonged and we become exhausted by the struggle. As I reflect on some of my personal squalls and those of individuals who have shared their struggles with me, my thoughts turn to the agonizing darkness and turmoil which Jesus endured in the garden of Gethsemane. His struggle was expressed in a sweat of blood, suggesting that he experienced the human condition in all its deepest turbulence.

In the ministry of pastoral counseling we respond to calls for help from individuals immersed in life's squalls. To understand deeply their experience we inch close enough to the storm so that we can understand the intensity of their struggle and, in turn, can allow them to experience our presence. Without getting caught up in the turmoil, we communicate convincingly, by our way of being: "I care about you, and I will be present to you through this difficult time." We hope the client will hear that message and an implicit deeper message: "God cares about you. He is with you regardless of how alone and abandoned you must feel." If the counselor gets caught up in the client's confusion, hurt, and anger, the counselor can hardly be a confident voice communicating faith and trust.

To be sensitive to the suffering of persons in the midst of intense struggle without being drawn into the struggle itself requires an advanced level of personal religious integration. It requires a sense of personal finiteness, an awareness of the holy, a faith that transcends the here and now, a personal capacity to trust, and what I would term: *a grateful acceptance of one's personal pilgrimage.* For me, this means that we understand our creaturely role and graciously accept our place in the overall plan of God. In effect, we give God permission to be God. Not fighting God's plan, but fully aware that much of life is a mystery, we attempt to discern its meaning as it unfolds in our lives and in the lives of our clients. In a very real way we sign our name to a contract with God without asking to read it in advance, content to allow the terms to emerge over time. I suspect many of us have done this with some ease during peak religious experiences only to find later that the fine print was not at all to our liking.

I found myself very much in this position of protesting God's fine print during the last week of my mother's extended illness. Demonstrated to me was my ongoing struggle with accepting my own personal pilgrimage *gratefully*. In the final year of her illness I spent many quiet hours at Mother's bedside: sometimes in the hospital, at other times at my sister's home. Although we were not accustomed to speaking an explicit language of love at home, I was determined to use these days to express my deepest feelings. Through hours of reminiscing, I held my mother's hand and repeatedly said: "Mum, I love you. You have been a wonderful mother." She would respond: "I know. I love you too." As Mother's Day approached, I knew that her time was short. I tried to capture my feelings in a card. Two of the paragraphs read as follows:

> Mum, I want to be with you as much as possible as you prepare to move from this life to the next. I want you to share both your fears and your hopes. I pray that I will be with you as you pass from the chains of sickness and pain to the freedom that you deserve forever and ever.
>
> Mum, may God bless you. May He give you joyful and peaceful days as you realize that we all love you deeply, each in our own way. As the front of this card says, "A mother like you is a *True Gift of God.*"

As I approached the last weeks, I had envisioned Mother's death as something of a quiet sunset. Instead, the last week was a terrifying time of darkness in which her pain, for days, seemed to keep out of reach of the medication. I will never forget one night when Mother awoke from a semi-coma, jolted spasmodically with pain. She looked up at me, confused, pleading: "Why don't you help me? Please help me! You won't help me!" Those words, like scalpels, cut to my innermost core. The physician's promise of "keeping Mother comfortable" seemed like cruel deceit.

I yielded my vigil to my brother-in-law and sister, who were awakened. I spent some hours alone, walking, expressing my rage at a God who had the audacity to call Himself merciful. I refused to curb or repress the intensity of my anger and expressed it in direct personal affront. I knew that I would later be able to put this experience in perspective, but I refused to deny my inner rage.

A few days later, in my funeral eulogy, I concluded with the analogy of the turbulent storm at sea. I praised God that He allowed us to be with Mother during her final squall. "She knew that we were near. There were many tender moments. Perhaps, stepping back, we will come to understand and appreciate how we were the vehicles of God's love as we stuck with her to the last breath. We had ordered a sunset, but God chose to welcome Mother after a squall. She was surely ready to hear the words of Jesus: 'Come . . . I will refresh you . . . your soul will find rest.' "

It took a full six months to be able to step back. My acceptance came unexpectedly during a meditative morning walk in a little woods outside my apartment. With no premonition, I found myself on Calvary, standing with Mary and John at the foot of the cross. It was suddenly clear: Jesus died on the *cross;* Dad died on the *cross;* now Mother died on the *cross.* I was allowed to stand at the foot of the cross! I wept tears of acceptance as the dammed-up anger flowed out of me. I felt at the center of the mystery of life, death, and resurrection. I understood and accepted, in that moment, the fact that I will also die on the cross. I thanked God for what had been and what is. I realized clearly what I had so often preached: that Jesus came, not to change the human condition but to embrace it. He came, not to take away human suffering but to give it meaning in terms of the resurrection.

Slowly I began to feel unweighted. I felt free to mourn the loss of Mother without the contamination of my anger. I felt the empty numbness, characteristic of my relationship with God in recent months, giving way to feelings of joy, love, and peace. A renewed inner spirit of resurrection, life, and lightness seemed to replace the heavy prodding steps of grief. I seemed to be emerging from the squall into the sunlight. With cautious hopefulness, I looked forward to the possibility that I might soon be moving with full sail, powered by the steady breeze of God's grace and warmed by the brilliance of the unobstructed sun. I was feeling grateful again. Knowing full well that I will also die, I began to treasure being alive.

WHO APPROACHES OTHERS WITH A SENSE OF MYSTERY

As pastoral counselors, we approach clients with wide-angle lenses and attempt to scan the mystery of the human person in all its complexity. We are interested in the intrapsychic processes of our clients and in their successes and failures in relating to others. We are concerned with their ability to function with effectiveness in meeting life's goals. In pursuing these interests, we borrow constructs from any number of schools of thought, and we follow one or a variety of therapeutic approaches or styles in understanding and relating to our clients. What is unique in pastoral counseling, however, is the fact that we are instinctively interested in and sensitive to the transcendent strivings of our clients. Pannenberg (1970) addresses these strivings of the human person as follows:

> Man is dependent not just on particular conditions of his surroundings but beyond that, on something that escapes as often as he reaches fulfillment. Man's chronic need, his infinite dependence, presupposes something outside of himself that is beyond every experience of the world. . . . Man is infinitely dependent. Thus in everything that he does in life he presupposes a being beyond everything finite, a vis-à-vis upon which he is dependent. . . . Our language has the word

"God" for this entity upon which man is dependent in his infinite strivings. (p. 10)

To summarize Pannenberg, it belongs to the nature of the human person to be open to the world. This openness pushes us beyond every experience, every horizon, and, in fact, creates in us a dependence on the infinite. To crave infinity is to be dependent on "the infinite," whatever that may be or however it may be understood. For the Christian, the fulfillment of this human desire reached its climax historically in the person of Jesus. The most fundamental desire for a relationship to the infinite is made possible through the life, teaching, and person of Jesus of Nazareth.

As a pastoral counselor, I am privileged to deal with people over a broad range of the developmental life cycle. My clients struggle with intrapersonal and interpersonal issues which run the full gamut of human concerns. Meeting people at their respective stages of development, I find personal satisfaction when the counseling relationship can facilitate growth in a way that is consistent with the goals of the person. I must admit, however, that I am most completely engaged as a pastoral counselor when the client moves into the mysterious areas that transcend the present experience. When clients deal with issues of forgiveness, conversion, surrender, faith, trust, love, and commitment, I am in deep but familiar waters. Being a copilgrim with the client in these waters is uniquely pastoral.

The pastoral counselor, in touch with the historical reality of Jesus and the richness of the entire Christian tradition, has a special opportunity within the counseling relationship. Touching as it does the inner core of the client's being, the counseling relationship gives us the opportunity to witness the marvel of God revealing Himself anew. Over and over again we witness the Scriptures come alive as clients deal with issues of suffering, death, resurrection, and an acceptance of the divine plan. The experience of God working within the counseling relationship has led me to view my office as a sanctuary. When I enter that office sanctuary, I do so with a sense of *awe, respect,* and *mystery* as I prepare myself to witness God's activity, hoping to utilize my professional training in order to enter more fully into the mystery of the client's personal pilgrimage.

Recently, in a session with Sister Margaret, a religious leader suffering from administrative burnout, I commented: "What you feel now must be very close to what Jesus felt in the garden of Gethsemane. He pleaded: 'Father, let this chalice pass from me.' " Sister Margaret looked at me appreciatively: "That's exactly how I feel, but I can't bring myself to say: 'Thy will be done.' " She stayed with those feelings for a long time: "All I feel now is abandonment." After a period of time, Sister Margaret remembered a profound retreat experience at the beginning of her term as superior. She had prayed that she might share not only in the public ministry of Jesus, but also in His passion. "My God," she sighed, "He has taken me up on that offer!"

This insight did not change the intensity of Margaret's personal anguish as she went through the steps of resigning her position. It did, however, give her a renewed sense of meaning and purpose. It was a moment of special grace in which she gained a sense of perspective even in the midst of her struggle.

The religious perspective, in this case and many others, need not cloud basic underlying issues. Sister Margaret realized that she needed a sabbatical experience away from the daily pressure of administrative role expectations. She needed both time and space for herself. She recognized that she should continue with therapy, initially to deal with frustration and depression and eventually with her desire to chart a new course in ministry. She clearly needed to learn how to incorporate recreation and space for personal renewal into her lifestyle. Sister Margaret's religious perspective does not deny the human but adds a further dimension as she deals with the meaning and purpose of life events.

The concept of *copilgrimage* does not give me a "cover" for interjecting my own issues upon the client, nor does it give me license to impose my own set of values through subtle forms of proselytizing. As copilgrim, I fully acknowledge the separateness of my client and am keenly aware that the client's journey is unique, involving the mystery of the interaction of God and the individual human person. I understand "copilgrim" to mean that Providence, in some way, has allowed or caused our paths to cross at a particular point, perhaps to run parallel for a while: sometimes for a short walk, other times for an extended period. As copilgrim, I do not relinquish the professionalism which I bring to my counseling relationships; I am very much the copilgrim with professional expertise in the field of counseling and psychotherapy. Attitudinally, however, I regard my clients as fellow pilgrims on a journey, for in the ultimate analysis that is the reality. The client needs assistance at a particular phase of the journey. I, at times, need assistance in my journey.

ALONG WITH AN ABILITY
TO ENTER INTO COMMUNION WITH OTHERS
IN A THERAPEUTIC ALLIANCE

There have been many routes into the pastoral counseling ministry. My own route was to follow up four years of theological study and ministerial training with a doctoral program in counseling and clinical psychology. Others have studied in schools of psychiatry or social work or in departments of education, religion, or theology. Many have approached their education as pastoral counselors through the tutorial route in programs associated with the Association of Clinical Pastoral Education (ACPE) and the American Association of Pastoral Counselors (AAPC). All programs deal, in varying degrees and each from its own perspective, with personality theory, developmental psychology, interpersonal relations, marriage and family dynamics, group dynamics, psychopathology, theories of counseling, and the like. The critical issue in all programs is that they lead to our personal and professional integration as pastoral counselors.

Carl Rogers (1961, Ch. 2), in discussing the necessary and sufficient conditions for personality growth to occur within the counseling relationship, pointed to the person of the counselor as a key element. The counselor, according to Rogers, must have the capacity for entering into a warm, accepting, empathic relationship characterized by unconditional positive regard. In addition, the counselor must have the ability to communicate acceptance and understanding to the client. Only if such capacities and skills exist will positive growth take place.

This same point has been underscored by Carkuff (1969), well known for his systematic work in training counselors in specific skills. He stressed the importance of the person of the counselor:

> If the helper cannot actualize his own potentials he cannot enable another to do so. The focus of training, as the focus of treatment then, is upon the change or gain of the trainee himself. This is most critical, for without an effective person in the helping role, all else is futile. (p. xii)

Weiner, in *Principles of Psychotherapy* (1975), summarizes the thinking in the field as follows:

> Some approaches to psychotherapy have focused largely on technical skills with little attention to the personal qualities of the therapist. Others have stressed the personal interest and warmth of the therapist as the major agent of change in psychotherapy and have minimized the importance of technique. Yet most psychotherapy practitioners and researchers concur that effective psychotherapy requires a balanced combination of personality and technical skills. (pp. 34–35)

As pastoral counselors, we share with other counseling professionals the above concern for personal integration in our preparation for the counseling ministry. In addition, however, the pastoral counselor, being a minister of the Church, is expected to have achieved a level of personal *religious integration*.

In its comprehensive study, *Readiness for Ministry,* the Association of Theological Schools in the United States and Canada assessed the most significant characteristics that people across denominational lines look for in their ministers (Schuler et al., 1975). The study found that people expected a broad range of competencies in the various areas of ministry. In addition to competence, however, people expected that their ministers have a deep commitment to the Gospel which, in fact, permeates and informs each of the activities of ministry. The variables: "service without regard for acclaim," "personal integrity," and "Christian example" were rated the highest.

Characteristics most criticized in clergy were the following: "self-serving ministry," "undisciplined living," and "emotional immaturity." In applying these findings to ourselves as pastoral counselors, it is clear that people expect a personal integration involving *knowledge, personal maturity,* and *a religious way of being.*

WITH THE GOAL OF RECONCILIATION AND PERSONAL RELIGIOUS INTEGRATION

In attempting to conceptualize the goals of pastoral counseling, I have settled, for the time being, on the broad concept of reconciliation. Webster gives three distinct nuances to the word *reconcile:* to restore to friendship, harmony, and communion; to adjust or settle differences; and to make congruous. As I reflect on these meanings, it seems to me that my work in counseling has involved a threefold reconciliation. At times the focus has been on inner congruity; sometimes the task has involved settling differences with others; frequently enough, the underlying need has been for a restoration to harmony with God. As I see it, then, a threefold reconciliation—with self, with others, and with God—is sufficiently broad to include the goals of the clients with whom I have journeyed over the years.

Reconciliation with Self

Many of the clients who have sought me out as a pastoral counselor have come because they experienced a degree of disharmony and a lack of congruence within themselves. In the earlier years of my ministry with young adults at the college and preprofessional level, I found a keen interest in the process of self-discovery and personal growth. Many of those who sought counseling yearned for a self-conscious awareness of their underlying feelings regarding basic developmental questions: Who am I? What do I want from life? Are my goals realistic? What do I believe? How can I better meet my needs for friendship and intimacy? To what extent is God important to me? How can I grow spiritually? Am I called to minister to others?

In recent years, having worked more extensively with clients dealing with midlife concerns, I have observed less emphasis on exploration and experimentation and more concentration on a reevaluation and renewal of purpose. Those who come for help ask: at forty, who am I? Where have I been going with my life? What do I want for the years ahead? Do I need to modify my goals? How do I redefine myself occupationally? What values have I come to affirm? Where am I on my spiritual journey? What do I have to offer others in continued ministry?

In my counseling with young adults and with clients in the middle years, it has been a profound personal source of satisfaction to see them move in the direction of a greater openness and freedom as they begin to listen to the experience that is going on within. It is a precious therapeutic moment when a client is able to own negative feelings, previously denied, as part of oneself. Over and over I see the counseling process lead clients to an ongoing, honest self-assessment as they are able to recognize and to accept even the "shadow side" of self. The suggestion attributed to Jung, that one's journey into the unconscious usually results in discovering that the contents are 90 percent gold, is verified repeatedly. Sometimes with clients, I compare the journey inward to riding a raft into the rapids of an underground river. It is both exhilarating and frightening. Eventually, one hopes to reach a deep inner lake of tranquility and beauty.

A movement toward greater freedom follows upon increased openness. I have seen clients shift from a near total dependence on the opinions and perceived expectations of others to a genuine reliance on the inner self. Some ongoing reflections, written by a thirty-year-old client of mine, speak to these movements:

As a priest who has been in psychotherapy for a year, following upon severe anxiety attacks, I am intrigued by the process evolving within me during this year. When I began therapy, I considered myself open to new experiences; as I look back, I realize it was more of an intellectual exercise in which I isolated feelings from myself and categorized them as good feelings or bad feelings. Bad feelings such as anger, frustration, aggression were denied. When angry, I smiled; when frustrated, I smiled; when my impulse was to strike out, I smiled. Eventually the lack of harmony between my inner experience and my understanding of that experience erupted in severe anxiety reactions. I could not continue . . . I needed help.

Over the year of counseling I have made notable headway in recognizing and owning feelings. Regardless of whether they are positive or negative, they are my feelings and I have a right to them. In fact, it's something like a birth experience as I daily risk expressing feelings as they are experienced. I have experienced anger and expressed it only to find acceptance of my right to be angry. I have experienced feelings of anxiety and self-doubt only to find a closer bond through my openness. I have shared, through sermons, my perceptions of my handicaps and have found that I touch responsive cords. Each week as I risk being true to myself and honest with others, I find my own sense of self enriched. I am feeling an increasing reverence toward myself along with a sense of mystery and discovery.

Something else has been emerging which is still somewhat frightening—I am discovering through therapy that I must be the focal point for any future direction—what others say and think is becoming less critical as I claim responsibility for my life. That is both frightening and exhilarating. My life is becoming more and more my own and that has become an exciting discovery.

This client's excitement at his taste of inner freedom is a familiar one in counseling. Frequently, clients come to realize that they are not determined by their past, only influenced by it. As they come to view strengths and limitations as their personal legacy, they are enabled to understand their personal potency in the present and in the future. Maslow (1962) describes this process of self-actualization as follows:

> a development of personality which frees the person from the deficiency problems of youth, and from the neurotic (or infantile, or fantasy, or unnecessary, or "unreal") problems of life, so that he is able to face, endure, grapple with the "real" problems, the unavoidable, the "existential" problems to which there is no perfect solution. (p. 109)

As pastoral counselors, we help to free our clients so that they can enter more fully and more authentically into the process of living. This may mean, at times, that we contribute to making their lives more difficult. Increased freedom carries with it both risk and responsibility. Each step forward is a step into the unfamiliar. Growth often means giving up a simpler, easier, and more effortless life in exchange for a more demanding, more responsible, and more difficult life. Growth forward requires courage, will, and choice. As pastoral counselors, we serve as copilgrims, urging our clients onward toward ever increasing personal growth and responsibility.

Reconciliation with Others

Although much of my counseling over the years has been with individuals, I would estimate that about 20 percent of it has been with couples. Some come expecting the pastoral counselor to salvage the marriage; others come unconsciously looking for permission to separate. I make it clear that I can do neither. What I do offer is an attempt to facilitate a process of communication. I work toward an atmosphere in which husband and wife can reexamine their present and past relationships with a view to discovering the possibilities of the future. If they decide on renewed commitment together, I will celebrate with them. If they decide that the marriage is, in fact, shipwrecked, then I am interested that they both make it safely to shore. In the later case, my approach has been to work with one of the spouses, referring the other for appropriate help elsewhere.

Sometimes in dealing with couples I use the analogy of a precious and beautiful mosaic buried beneath the accumulated rubble of many years. From all external appearances the mosaic does not exist; the memory of the mosaic, however, endures. To find out whether the mosaic is still intact, or is irreparably damaged, I recommend that we dig away at the layers of debris, a shovelful at a time, being careful not to damage or destroy the mosaic in the process. I find the analogy helpful in communicating the reality that the counseling process takes time, requires careful effort, and demands the willingness to look at painful experiences from the past. Over a period of months partners need to air deep resentments, frustrations, and disappointments if they are to clear the way to the mystery of love which brought them together. The wounds inflicted over the years need to be healed. There is the need for each partner to ask for and to offer forgiveness for past hurts.

I sense a copilgrimage with clients as I offer to help them clear the rubble away so that they can get to the core of their relationship. Recently, working with a couple led to a rediscovery and reaffirmation of their love for one another. Married nineteen years, financially successful, with children aged fifteen, sixteen, and eighteen, they had both concluded that they could not continue in the marriage unless they could learn to communicate and to relate to one another in a more positive manner. They consulted me as a last resort before moving toward separation. They were skeptical at the prospect of counseling being helpful but were committed to making the attempt. After a year of hard work, they found the mosaic of love intact. Currently, they are experiencing a renewed interest in each other and a growing confidence in one another's love. They are beginning to have fun together and to see humor in situations that previously would have led to conflict. Although the mosaic has been found intact, it is my intuition that there will have to be some polishing of a number of the pieces over the months to come.

Sometimes the reconciliation deals with significant persons who are deceased. Some years ago I worked with a woman in her early fifties who had suffered from severe house phobia for twenty-eight years. She could not leave the block on which her house was located without suffering a severe anxiety attack. She had contacted the mental health center where I counseled one day each week on the occasion of her youngest son's heart attack. Her son lived out of state; she loved him dearly, yet she could not leave her home to be with him. Although her son recovered, she felt that he needed her. Moreover, since her husband had died three years previously, she was getting more and more restless at home; yet she could not leave it. The center insisted that she take the first step by coming across town (a six- to seven-minute drive), assuring her that she could be helped. Somehow, she was assigned to me.

We established a rapport from the first session: she liked me and said so; I liked her and was committed to whatever it took to get her well. The director of the center gave me freedom to use my intuition and to give her whatever time was required. Each Monday she was brought to the center by her older son; at the end of each session I drove her home, but not directly. Each week the drive home was more circuitous. With me, she felt safe as we gradually increased the range of distance from the home. One day, she surprised me at the beginning of a session. "I want to go to the cemetery. I want to see my husband's grave." I acceded without hesitation; we drove in silence. When we found the grave, I witnessed the unleashing of the rage of three decades: she spat on the grave, kicked at it, trampled it, tore at it with her hands: "Turn over in your grave . . . go ahead, turn over . . . See if I care. You are not going to control me anymore. You can burn in hell, but I am going to live again." Tears of gratitude trickled down my cheeks as I witnessed this miracle of God's grace. When she was finished, I drove her home in silence. There were no appropriate words to be said.

At the next session she began to speak of her husband's virtues. "George had many good qualities," she said. "He was a very good man but he didn't understand how to treat a pretty young wife. He was good for everyone, but he was bad for me. He treated me well, he gave me everything, but he did not allow me to be free. He did not understand."

Over the weeks to follow we met one intermediate goal after another until one day I drove her sixty miles to the airport and saw her board a plane to visit her son over a thousand miles away. I treasure the pictures she sent back: a proud and free mother enjoying the company of her adult son. We terminated when I left the area for a sabbatical; I was pleased to hear through friends in the area that she sold the house which had been her prison for so many years. She had made her peace and was moving on.

Most counseling sessions involving reconciliation with others are not so dramatic, but many involve intense emotion as angers are released. I sometimes find it helpful, at a key point in the therapy, to have the client imagine that the person being dealt with has joined us in the room. I invite the client to get in touch with underlying feelings and to express them without fear of reprisal and without fear of hurting the party involved. Recently, I invited a young man to bring his mother into the room with us. He reacted immediately: "Get out . . . get out . . . I don't want you in the same room!" This spontaneous response surprised my client and led to an exploration of his unrecognized need to put emotional space between himself and his mother as a condition for his own emotional growth.

Sometimes having the client take the role of the other party is enlightening: a parent whom the client portrays as totally rejecting has often enough sounded fairly "mellow" in the portrayal. It helps not only the therapist but also the client to move from generalized suppressed feelings to a more realistic assessment of significant others. I have found various types of "empty chair" techniques and role-playing most helpful in working toward reconciliation with significant others. Frequently, the client can subsequently move beyond the office to work toward a more complete reconciliation, freed from the emotionality connected with real or perceived past hurts.

Reconciliation with God

One of the most moving experiences I have had in therapy dealt with the anger that a young man experienced toward God because of his mother's illness and death. One day Bill was talking about the unfairness of it all. Bill's mother had dedicated herself to the family, attempting to make up for the long absences by his father, a career navy enlisted man. She was vivacious, outgoing, and generous. Just as Bill turned seventeen, old enough to begin to show his appreciation to his mother and to enjoy her as the dynamic person that she was, his mother suffered a heart attack. The physical recovery process was slow. Her personality had changed: she was anxious, fearful, and withdrawn. After many months she received an optimistic medical report about her physical condition and she decided, against Bill's advice, to resume her walk to daily Mass. Three days after that report she died suddenly from a heart attack. In Bill's judgment the precipitating cause was his mother's overexertion in walking up the long hill to Mass.

Bill recounted, for the first time, the details of the final moments with his mother as she died in his arms. For months he had been in something of a twilight state of shock. Today, anger and rage surfaced as he looked out the window to a life-sized cross which stood in the church cemetery. His gaze moved toward the crucifix on my wall. It was a solid wood cross with a ceramic corpus. Bill turned to me, his eyes searching mine. My eyes searched his in return. It was a moment of profound contact. I said to Bill firmly: "Do whatever you need to do." Bill reached for the crucifix, removed it from the wall, raised it over his head, and smashed it against the floor over and over again until the ceramic figure was broken into bits.

Bill quietly dropped the cross on the floor and collapsed into the couch next to me. I held him as he poured out his grief in deep, powerful, unrestrained sobs. His grief seemed to be bottomless as quiet moments gave way to successive waves of emotion. At the end, Bill was exhausted. He was limp but peaceful.

Bill replaced the corpusless cross on the wall. Together, we knelt before that cross as copilgrims praying for strength and new life. For both of us that prayer was answered over the weeks and months to follow. Bill reentered the process of living. I came to a deeper appreciation of what it meant to me to be a pastoral counselor.

Sometimes anger at God is coupled with deep religious questioning. God's apparent lack of concern about human suffering leads people to question the very existence of God. For weeks, Jean, a beautiful young woman in her early thirties, had been using the phrase: "If God exists." Two years before, she had lost her first child at birth. A year later, after a precarious pregnancy, Jean gave birth to a healthy baby girl. On the christening day, while the family gathered in celebration, Jean's father committed suicide.

For Jean, the suicide was especially problematic. She had been close to her father through his many years of psychiatric treatment. She felt that she understood him better than any of the family. Throughout the christening preparations she felt apprehensive about some strange comments which her father had made. She sensed that he might be thinking about ending his life. When she expressed her concerns to members of the family, they dismissed her fears as "nonsense." The next day her father was found dead from an overdose of medication.

Jean came to me after ten months of grieving. She reported that she knew exactly how her dad had felt. She, too, wanted to end it all. For Jean, life had no meaning. She did not want to bring up her child in a world of suffering. As she poured out her feelings of despair, she described God as a huge giant sitting on a throne, whose chief delight was squashing unsuspecting little people with His big toe. I was stunned by her analogy. After three months, I understood her concept of God. I responded: "God squashes people with His big toe, and you don't like it. He's not going to squash you! In fact, you've decided to fight back by squashing God with your big toe."

Jean looked at me with grateful surprise: "That's what I've been doing, isn't it, when I say: "If God exists." She sighed deeply as she opened the floodgates to allow her anger to drain quickly and quietly. She spoke of experiencing a deep inner peace. She surely did not understand God's ways, but she no longer wanted to fight Him. We ended the session in prayer for continued healing. As we rose to leave, our arms met in an embrace of peace.

CONCLUDING REFLECTIONS

The pastoral counselor . . . a religiously integrated person . . . who approaches others with a sense of mystery . . . along with an ability to enter into communion with others in a therapeutic alliance . . . with the goal of reconciliation and personal religious integration. As I reflect on this description, looking back on some three decades of the counseling ministry, I realize that I have been alternately congruent and incongruent with it. When my own religious integration has been operational, I sense that I have been more effective as a counselor. My personal and professional life seem to be closely interwoven. As I attend to the spiritual dimension in my life, I am more effective as a pastoral counselor.

Reflecting on my personal and professional journey at this point, I sense a power in the concept of copilgrimage that I have never before experienced. It is awe-inspiring for me to realize how deeply my life has been affected by my clients. As I have entered into communion with clients in a therapeutic alliance, communicating my care and understanding, I have found a deeper self-acceptance. As I have worked with others toward the goal of reconciliation, I have found myself more reconciled within, more at peace with others, and more at one with God.

It seems to me that today I have less of a need to be a caregiver than ever before, but I suspect that I am giving better care. I am able to acknowledge my vulnerability in ways not previously imagined and find myself able to be a source of strength to increasing numbers. I look forward, over the decades to come, to my copilgrimage with clients, but also with colleagues and friends. I do not find myself looking far ahead: today, tomorrow, this week, have assumed an increasingly greater importance.

I am intrigued by the open-endedness of the future. I yearn to sink deeper spiritual roots. At the same time, I experience the urging to use my gifts within the broad context of the counseling ministry: teaching, supervising, counseling. I recognize a need to do this within an atmosphere of collegiality and mutual support. I am grateful to my faculty colleagues and to the students at Loyola College. I offer my personal reflections to them and to all my colleagues in ministry.

REFERENCES

Carkuff, R. R. *Helping and Human Relations.* New York: Holt, 1969.
Maslow, A. H. *Toward a Psychology of Being.* New York: Van Nostrand, 1962.
Pannenberg, W. *What Is Man?* Philadelphia: Fortress, 1970.
Rogers, C. *On Becoming a Person.* Boston: Houghton, 1961.
Schuler, D., M. Brekke, and M. Strommen. *Readiness for Ministry.* Vandalia: Ohio: Association of Theological Schools in the United States and Canada, 1975.
Weiner, I. *Principles of Psychotherapy.* New York: Wiley, 1975.

RECOMMENDED READINGS

Bulka, R. *The Quest for Ultimate Meaning.* New York: Philosophical Library, 1979.
Clinebell, H. *Contemporary Growth Therapies.* Nashville: Abingdon, 1981.
Corey, G. *Theory and Practice of Counseling and Psychotherapy,* 2nd ed. Fullerton: Brooks-Cole, 1982.
Hiltner, S. *Preface to Pastoral Theology.* Nashville: Abingdon, 1958.
Kelsey, M. T. *Prophetic Ministry.* New York: Crossroad, 1982.
Leech, K. *Soul Friend.* San Francisco: Harper, 1977.
May, G. *Care of Mind/Care of Spirit.* San Francisco: Harper, 1982.
May, R. *The Art of Counseling.* Nashville: Abingdon, 1967.
Maslow, A. H. *The Farther Reaches of Human Nature.* New York: Viking, 1971.
McNeill, D. R., D. A. Morrison, and H. J. Nouwen. *Compassion.* Garden City, N. Y.: Doubleday, 1982.
Niklas, G. R. *The Making of a Pastoral Person.* New York: Alba House, 1980.
Nouwen, H. J. *The Wounded Healer.* Garden City, N. Y.: Doubleday, 1972.
Pruyser, P. *The Minister as Diagnostician.* Philadelphia: Westminister Press, 1976.
Rogers, C. *On Becoming a Person.* Boston: Houghton, 1961.
————. *A Way of Being.* Boston: Houghton Mifflin, 1980.
Schillebeeckx, E. *Ministry.* New York: Crossland, 1981.
Wimberly, E. P. *Pastoral Counseling and Spiritual Values: A Black Point of View.* Nashville: Abingdon, 1982.

CHAPTER TWO

Theological Foundations of Pastoral Counseling

MELVIN C. BLANCHETTE, PH.D.

INTRODUCTION

This chapter will offer an initial orientation of the theological foundation for the ministry of pastoral counseling. It will be maintained that pastoral counseling needs, for its identity as a science and art, the justification that comes from a theological foundation. Without this grounding, pastoral counseling is deprived of its uniqueness as a distinctive form of counseling. The methodology employed to accomplish this task will be to do an analysis of what practitioners of pastoral counseling do. This approach will be largely experiential: the stories of two people will be used to illustrate certain major understandings and to underscore the functions of pastoral counseling.

It is suggested that by doing a functional analysis of pastoral counseling, the theological foundations that give it form and that shape its identity will emerge. Accordingly, this chapter will consist of three sections. First, reasons supporting a functional analysis will be given. Second, a functional analysis will lead to an answer to the question: What is the function of pastoral counseling? Third, the theological underpinnings will surface from this exploration, answering the over-arching question: What is/are the theological foundation(s) for the ministry of pastoral counseling?

RATIONALE

Before addressing these various questions, it might be useful to outline the reasons for this approach. Other authors have advanced the theological foundations for pastoral counseling starting from an *a priori* base. It is my belief—and I choose the word *belief* purposely—that the first reason for this experiential approach is that the foundation for pastoral counseling should evolve from the practice or experience of pastoral counseling. What is in the experience that makes pastoral counseling pastoral?

A second reason for this experiential approach is the result of a statement that had a powerful impact on me. The theologian Roy Eckhardt (quoted in O'Collins, *Foundations of Theology,* 1971, p. 1) maintains that "a sensible way to discover what an enterprise means is to look at what its practitioners do." A few years ago, in the *Journal of Pastoral Psychology,* various professionals were asked how they interpreted the following questions relative to pastoral counseling. The questions were designed to uncover the pastoral dimension in counseling and psychotherapy.

1. Is pastoral counseling a defined term to you? How?
2. Are all counselors pastoral? To what degree?
3. How pastoral is counseling and psychotherapy?
4. What is the pastoral factor in (a) the clergyman and (b) the psychotherapist?
5. Is pastoral something to grow from, toward, or through?

What will follow is a representative sampling of quotations dealing with the what and how of pastoral counseling. Walter E. O'Connell, Clinical Associate Professor of Psychology, Baylor College of Medicine wrote:

Today I no longer view the person or process marked "pastoral" as being inherently inferior. In fact, pastoral activities might be seen as the end stage of a humanizing process which hopefully progresses through such stages as establishing positive encouraging relationships, uncovering social goals and life styles, and practicing more socially constructive behaviors. Ideally, I would like to think of "pastoral" as connected to a process by which one tries to communicate hope in good works and a loving God.

The Rev. James E. Sullivan, Director, Religious Consultation Center, Brooklyn, New York, answers the question: Are all counselors pastoral?

All counselors are pastoral in the sense that all are concerned for the suffering, the depressed, and confused. However, the pastoral counselor approaches his work from a framework and a value system that is God-oriented. He doesn't force his value system on his clients but his particular value system gives him (1) a greater sense of the dignity of the person as a child of God, a brother (or sister) in Christ as well as (2) a greater motivation to reach the client with the redeeming love of Christ. In a word the *what* of all counseling is pastoral. Perhaps also the *how*. It is the *why*—the personal framework value system and motivation of the pastoral counselors that makes pastoral counseling different from other counseling.

J. B. Rhine, Ph.D., Director, Foundation for Research on the Nature of Man, College Station, North Carolina, answers as to what he thinks the adjective *pastoral* means and what the practitioners do.

The term *pastoral* suggests to me an attitude on the part of one person to share in another's attempt to understand himself and to meet the problems of his life. It connotes a protective, sympathetic identification with the individual in need of friendship and assistance. A counselor would seem to be pastoral to the extent that he is thoughtfully concerned with the individual client as a fellow man, one who has a genuine claim upon his care and interest.

Finally, Sidney Jourard, Ph.D., Professor of Psychology, University of Florida, indicates how he thinks counseling psychotherapy is pastoral:

To speak of a "pastoral" counselor is to speak a redundancy. A pastor is a shepherd, a guide, one who leads his flock along paths where they will flourish and prosper. A counselor, likewise, is a guide to the good life. Like any guide he leads by stepping ahead, serving as living exemplar of the path.

Seen from this vantage point, all counseling and psychotherapy is pastoral counseling, but not all counselors and psychotherapists serve as exemplars of viable lives. Those who seek their work as the practice of technique are pastoral counselor manqués: yet in spite of their intent, their clients likely emulate the way that they live, not the way they profess.

Psychotherapists and clergymen alike can serve as mouthpieces for pious phrases—in which they are not properly pastoral—or they can themselves be seekers, and in being such, likely function as guides.

In these various descriptions of what is done through pastoral counseling, what is noteworthy can be arranged around three terms: process, product, and person. Through the process of pastoral counseling a person is enabled to become free of those obstacles preventing growth and differentiation. Accordingly, this is a process of humanization: a person becoming fully functioning, free, consciously aware, responsible, and loving is the product of the process. To enable another to reach this level of mature development, the practitioner of pastoral counseling must be a person who has reached a certain level of personal and professional integration on many levels. What is needed for the pastoral counselor would include a knowledge of normal as well as abnormal behavior, technical skill and competence derived from study and supervision, and an in-depth appreciation of the theological, philosophical, and psychological issues involved in the *mystery* of becoming human.

A third reason for the experiential approach is my conviction that it is necessary for the pastoral counselor to be a certain kind of person if help is to be communicated and felt by people experiencing difficulties in living. The most important quality of the pastoral counselor is to be a person who can be with others. It is not necessary to do anything for another. In fact, as will be related in the story of Carol, her parents kept her in bondage by always doing for her rather than enabling Carol to live her own life. Many times people might be confused when they visit a pastoral counselor, but deep down they know what they must do. The effective pastoral counselor facilitates and motivates a person to make choices and exercise the freedom that is within. For some reason this freedom has become frozen or nonfunctional. The pastoral counselor's privilege is to help liberate a person in the process of becoming fully human. The beautiful but unfinished sculpture of Michelangelo provides us with an excellent illustration. These unfinished pieces are called the Captives. They remain unfinished because Michelangelo saw the sculptor's role as that of a divine genius who liberates artistic conceptions from the imprisoning stone, and thus his unfinished captives struggle within the massive blocks that seem to be drawing their human spirit back into a state of formless chaos. The pastoral counselor is no divine genius, but, one hopes, a human person who can be with another who struggles with the unfinished business of becoming human.

A fourth reason supporting this process approach is that the pastoral counselor does not make decisions for the person. To do so would be to enter into the pathology of the client. Rather, the pastoral counselor helps the person discern what is really healthy, assisting in the process of making decisions that will enhance life. The issue is how do I make a good decision when faced with choices and options. What is really the best one, or the one from which the most good will flow? The poet Robert Frost has captured the anguish and ambiguity of making a good decision as well as the challenge that risk demands in "The Road Not Taken" (1944):*

> *Two roads diverged in a yellow wood,*
> *And sorry I could not travel both*
> *And be one traveler, long I stood*
> *And looked down one as far as I could*
> *To where it bent in the undergrowth;*

Then took the other, just as fair,
And having perhaps the better claim,
Because it was grassy and wanted wear;
Though as for the passing there
Had worn them really about the same,

And both that morning equally lay
In leaves no step had trodden black.
Oh, I kept the first for another day!
Yet knowing how way leads on to way
I doubted if I should ever come back.

I shall be telling this with a sigh
Somewhere ages and ages hence:
Two roads diverged in a wood, and I—
I took the one less traveled by,
And that has made all the difference.

Frost writes in literary terms what many of us have felt in living. We have all heard stories of how people make decisions. Some throw a coin in the air and call either heads or tails. Others consult various magical formulas. Still others open the Scripture, hoping that God will speak to them through the passage chosen by chance. It is ironic that people who want a definitive answer to life's problems would accept a message chosen in so arbitrary a fashion. Perhaps this is a sign indicating how burdensome making a good decision can be and signifying that people grow tired struggling and will accept an inadequate solution rather than searching through the various alternatives to find the proper solution.

Each of us makes decisions in our own way. A basic conviction of mine is that we know what decision should be made. What becomes problematic, however, is our inability to feel right about a difficult decision. There is a tug of war going on inside the person faced with demanding issues. There is likewise within society a crisis of anxiety because of its reluctance, refusal, or inability to make decisions that will free it from the burden of unnecessary anxiety. We live in an age of critical issues that agonize the heart and mind. There is the anxiety of war: how much blood may a human being shed for the sake of injustice? There is the anxiety of race: where does a human being draw a color line? There is the anxiety of interpersonal relationships: what may two persons do in the name of love? There is the anxiety of poverty: how long must two-fifths of the world go hungry? There is the anxiety of religion: at what point does a form of worship become heresy or idolatry? The issues of war and peace, white and black, man and woman, rich and poor, Catholic, Jew, Protestant—these are indeed the anxieties of our age. They are felt and realized on both a personal and societal level.

The pastoral counselor's task is to help persons formulate and test out the validity of their decisions. This process will demand great resources of moral and ethical standards. Perhaps a guiding question could be: If this action is held up to public scrutiny, will I still feel that it is what I should have done and how I should have done it? The statement of Gerard Piel, the recent editor of *Scientific American,* does not answer the question in a way that results in peace of mind, but it does give a perspective permitting a context of understanding: "It was a cowardly and costly truce in the academics of the nineteenth century, at the close of the great Darwinian scandal, that set up the false dichotomy between the sciences and humanities as if truth can be sought in the absence of concern for values, or values cherished without courage to face the truth." (1972, p. 21) There is something alike about sin, falsehood, unlawfulness, and ugliness as understood in theology, philosophy, psychology, and the humanities—that any solution to a person's or society's problems must be undertaken with a clear view toward the importance of values. These values are the silent and hidden potentials of behavior which take the form of questions we ask of life. Through the dialogic process of pastoral counseling, the person is helped to frame and understand the question so that the answer might be realized not in the abstract but in the day-to-day existence of life.

In summary, the reasons supporting a functional analysis of pastoral counseling are: that the foundation for pastoral counseling should evolve from the practice and experience, that what an enterprise means is ascertained through what its practitioners do, that a pastoral counselor places a high priority on being a relational person, and last, that a pastoral counselor motivates and facilitates people to take risks and to make decisions which enable them to become what they are meant to be.

Thus far this chapter has isolated two distinct questions: What is the function of pastoral counseling? These questions are interrelated but will be explored in sequence. First we will turn our attention to the first question and explore the function of pastoral counseling.

THE FUNCTION OF PASTORAL COUNSELING

There are reasons, many and compelling, why a person experiencing difficulties in living enters into a pastoral counseling relationship. Two functions that pastoral counseling can fulfill are (1) to enable a person to become free in order to be responsible, and (2) to enable a person to deal with pain.

Many times a person is told to do the responsible thing. Parents are quick to urge children to act responsibly. However, it has been my experience that before a person can be responsible, he or she must first experience what it means to be free. In teaching pastoral counseling to students for the past several years, I have used the metaphor that when people come for counseling it seems they are imprisoned within a box. They fear there is no exit. I cannot emphasize enough how important the counseling relationship is, for once it has been established and the process begun, a person comes to freedom. After a time, a boxed-in quality no longer exists, but rather the person has found openings in the box—windows are raised and doors are opened to possibilities and alternatives.

The second function of pastoral counseling is to enable a person to deal with the pain generated by existence. Pain is caused by our reaction to the expectations placed upon us because we exist—both those expectations we place on ourselves and those we allow others to place on us. Growth is the result of dealing with the stresses involved in living. The noted Jewish philosopher Rabbi Abraham Heschel (1975) states the issue very pointedly:

> We are concerned with the problem of man because he is being afflicted with contradictions and perplexities, because he is not completely a part of his environment. A good horse, properly cared for, lives as a part of his habitat and is unencumbered by problems. In sharp contrast, man is a problem intrinsically and under all circumstances. To be human is to be a problem, and the problem expresses itself in anguish, in the mental suffering of man. Every human being has at least a vague notion, image or dream of what humanity ought to be, of how human nature ought to act. The problem of man is occasioned by our coming upon a conflict or contradiction between existence and expectation, between what man is and what is expected of him. It is in anguish that man becomes a problem to himself. What he has long disregarded suddenly erupts in painful awareness. (p. 2)

It is this painful awareness that motivates a person to enter into a pastoral counseling relationship. A person does this not necessarily to solve problems but rather to experience growth through the relationship established with a pastoral counselor, to relate more appropriately to the struggles and pain life invites all of us to grapple with and respond to. Hence, the most fundamental function of pastoral counseling, in addition to enabling a person to become free to be responsible, is to relieve pain. Pain comes with problems and tensions in living. It is unfortunate that until only recently pain was seen in negative terms. However, when one comes to the appreciation that something is wrong with the way his or her life is going and pain is experienced, then pain takes on a positive quality. It becomes a signal, a warning. To this end, pain becomes a strong motivation for change. There are many ways that a person might experience pain. A person might perceive pain as a conflict keeping or holding the individual in a state of bondage. Sometimes this conflict prohibiting happiness and joy might be severe. At other times, it might be caused by the inability to communicate well. There are many varieties of pain and conflict-causing situations.

Perhaps the two biggest barriers blocking happiness and causing pain are anxiety and depression. There are many definitions of anxiety and depression and the causative factors are well outlined in many textbooks. What is clear about anxiety is that it is unpleasant, and we want relief from its burden. The everyday experience of depression is known to us all. It might begin as a disappointment, sadness, disillusionment, or despair. Each of us knows what it means to become depressed over a loss of some kind. We have felt the immobilizing hold depression can have, and the resulting sense of powerlessness.

The pastoral counselor reaches out to the community of those who bear the marks of pain—the dispossessed, lonely, alienated, unwanted, divorced, those suffering because of sexuality issues, and so on, to serve them in the struggle to become free and responsible and to enable them to grow from and through their pain. Pain becomes an all-important call to growth. It is the tension element in life, the situation in which a person comes face to face with the power of life and power of love. In these confrontations the pastoral counselor invites the person to act in a way that will promote personal growth and the growth of humanity—for it is only at the cost of pain that one becomes the best.

In the pastoral counselor's office the drama of life is seen in all its complexity and variety. Shakespeare has Hamlet say that the player's vocation is to be a mirror to show each age its form and feature. It would seem that the pastoral counselor's task would be to make sure that the image reflected is sound, sincere, and real. Images seen by pastoral counselors run the whole range of mental illness. This complexity of images and variety of forms brings out clearly the need of diagnosis—which helps us to clarify our thinking about a given case and to communicate effectively about what treatment procedures might be appropriate. Paul Pruyser, in his book, *The Minister as Diagnostician* (1976), writes with clarity about the pastoral implication of diagnosis:

> To diagnose means grasping things as they really are, so as to do the right thing. Hence, in medicine, diagnosis at the best entails etiology, for the penetrating view arrives at causes and deals with patterns of cause-and-effect relations in the course of illness. (p. 30)

It is extremely important for us to grasp things as they really are. In making a diagnosis we literally come to know people through the experience of their story—as the etymology of the word suggests. Images seen and diagnosed by pastoral counselors include those of neurotic and psychotic persons. The image seen most frequently is that of a person with a character disorder. In all of these images reflected in humanity's mirror, there is a failure of the individual to deal with a given reality; they thus represent a failure to find socially acceptable gratification for needs. The suffering of these individuals stems from the person's distorted view of self, faulty communication with others, and views held about the meaning of existence.

At this point, it might be useful not only to deal with images, but to illustrate the major functions of pastoral counseling. These examples are taken from my own practice. Former clients have been contacted and their permission has been obtained to use this material.

THE CASE OF CAROL: FROM BONDAGE TO FREEDOM

Carol first entered pastoral counseling to become free to be a richer, fuller, and more mature person. In the first interview she was very fearful, and later told me she almost didn't come back. What convinced her of the advantage of pastoral counseling was the fact that she found someone who did not judge her but accepted her as she was. Carol was imprisoned by her fear, and she failed to make choices, to accept the consequences of her decisions. She was approaching middle age but still acted and responded to others as a child. She had a characterological sweetness about her, but beneath this veneer was a great deal of unresolved hostility directed against her parents, former teachers, employers at work. In addition, she lived out her relationship with God in dread of offending him.

As the weeks and months of counseling continued, she faced these fears and found a creative force to deal with these important people and relationships. It was painful but she came to realize that she had been setting herself up for many of her own conflicts. She replaced inappropriate behavior with actions more in keeping for a woman of her years. This gave her a great deal of satisfaction. In the course of counseling, she discerned why she disliked her parents so much. They constantly did things for her and thus kept her a child. They had never enabled her to feel free. It must be said that they did this out of love, but it was, in the long run, cruel. Trying to protect her, they never explained to her what should be told a child regarding sexuality and healthy human functioning. Encouraged through the counseling sessions, she read books on human sexuality and asked many questions until she began to act and feel like a woman. At this point, I felt ready to ask her about her body. She disliked her body, and she hated herself. She was overweight and dressed in clothes appropriate for an older woman. Frequently, I have found in my work that when persons hate their bodies they end up hating themselves. This observation is in keeping with Freud's statement that the ego is first and foremost a body ego: it is not merely a surface entity but is itself the projection of a surface. As changes happened in Carol's body and she began to lose weight, she dressed more and more in keeping with her chronological age. She became an attractive person and began to like and love the person she was becoming. No longer did she treat her body as a barrier keeping herself imprisoned and alone. She readily accepted my encouragement to do nice things for herself. Through this experience, she came to realize she was a good person and one loved by God.

Counseling continued for almost two years, as she unraveled all the reasons why teachers in school disliked her, why employers were fearful of her. Our biggest breakthrough to freedom occurred, however, during the Holy Week of her last year in counseling. It was at that time that she accepted the truth that she could not earn God's love. Until then she had tried to keep herself always in God's grace. However, she did this not because she loved God but rather because she feared him as one would a despotic and arbitrary ruler. During this season of hope, Carol learned the lesson Anne Sexton writes about Jesus Christ: "His love was the greatest thing about him—not his death."

Coming to the profound awareness that God loved her through Jesus, Carol experienced growth and reconciliation. At last, she was free to be herself and no longer had to endure the frustration of trying to be someone else.

Carol came to freedom through awareness. This process always involves grappling with oneself. It is a painful experience to deal with oneself, with one's parents, and with relationships with other important people. However, there is no substitute if one desires to become free.

This story brings out how little I did in the process of Carol's reaching freedom. Acting as her guide, I would ask questions, make comments, provide a gentle and challenging presence, but I never told her what she should do. Carol serves as a paradigm of all those people with whom I've worked who became free.

THE CASE OF BRIAN: FROM PAIN THROUGH AWARENESS

Accepting the exacting terms of one's own existence. . . .

Sisyphus was a legendary king of Corinth; he was condemned in Tartarus to roll a big rock up a hill, and each time it reached the top, it rolled down again. In some ways he is a good example to us that we must accept the rock of the human condition and find our happiness in dealing with it. In addition, he is a reminder to me of Brian, a person who never really accepted himself or the exacting expectations of his life which caused him so much pain. Life, as Camus maintains, can be absurd and as frustrating as rolling a rock up a hill only to have it roll down again. What preserves us from this maddening experience is awareness which creates meaning and presence.

Brian was middle-aged when he first came for counseling. He was late, had been drinking to get up his courage to face the counselor. He was experiencing anxiety to a high degree, and the source of his anxiety was problems with sexuality. When he began to tell me the story of his life, he was very upset because he was facing financial disaster. He was leading two lives—one by day, another at night. Brian was a homosexual who never integrated this dimension of his life into his total personality. It was always for him a problem to be solved, never something to be accepted, to be understood and dealt with appropriately. He had never stopped rolling the rock up the hill to stop and ask what the meaning of his life was. It took outside forces to get Brian into pastoral counseling to look inside himself for the causes of his difficulties. Brian was a professional person, and his work was suffering terribly because he stayed out all night. During the day he was never sure of the relationships he sought in futile fashion at night. Brian knew very well the expectations that come with existence, and was aware that he used alcohol to avoid confronting the demands of his life.

I shall never forget the day he came to the clinic for help. He looked like a man who had exhausted all his energy and wealth. I asked him if he was willing to work on his problems as he saw them and if he was willing to change. He had had other counselors, been in and out of treatment centers, but never accepted the reality of having a problem. He came to realize that having a problem does not equate with being a bad person. As counseling progressed and we explored the dynamics of his life, the truth of his life emerged as an impression on a photostatic plate. The image reflected was a person who had never loved himself. He sought love as a young person until he realized he was different. For the rest of his life he defended against his homosexuality and pretended, at great cost, to be someone he was not. He was clearly a man who did not know how to confront the demands of his life. No therapist or psychiatrist ever talked to him about facing the truth of his life. It must be said that I also cite this case out of my respect for and profound appreciation of Brian, who responded to God's grace through the instrument of my ministry. It was through our conversations that Brian came to understand his uniqueness and his limitations. The theoretical background for the preceding statement is something I had read in Adrian van Kaam's book, *Religion and Personality* (1964).

> The first mark of the experience of being a personality is this self-awareness in its uniqueness and unity; a second characteristic is the consciousness of one's own limitations, which is the necessary counterpart of the awareness of uniqueness and unity. In self-awareness, a man knows what he can do, the assignment of his existence, the task of his life. In knowing his limits he realizes what he is not. (p. 45)

Coming to terms with his uniqueness meant to Brian that he was a good person in spite of his homosexuality, that God loved him because he was. When Brian began to realize that he was a good person, as was true with Carol and many other people with whom I have worked, he began to dress better and take care of himself. Responding to my gentle challenge not to waste so much energy on defending, Brian began to test out certain people with whom he could share the heavy burden of his life. Until then, Brian knew only the hater's bombs and not the real lover's balm. It is only through self-revelation that he received the awareness of being loved as he is. The process of risking opened up to Brian the possibility of being loved, and this was transforming. Lastly, Brian affirmed the awareness that if he was to be a professional person, he would have to do the work of a professional. This meant accepting the limitations of his life, and particularly how he chose to use time.

From these three levels—sexuality and the goodness of himself, truthfulness and the risk of revelation, and unity of his life and work—Brian came to freedom. This awareness motivated him to change. At this time, Brian is still a homosexual and a much healthier person. He has stopped the life-threatening behaviors associated with drinking and promiscuity. He is trying to answer his normal need for closeness and intimacy in more appropriate ways. He is a happy person working as a professional in his area of competence. In working with Brian, I helped him look at his own feelings and inclinations. He came to appreciate that feelings are neither good nor bad but they have great meaning. Working very diligently, he began to recognize what inner forces were pulling him in directions that were not life affirming. At this point in the counseling, he began to establish long-range goals that were realistic and meaningful.

In sum, we have examined the functions of pastoral counseling. The two main functions were identified as enabling a person to become free so as to be responsible, and helping another deal with the pain caused by the tension between expectation and existence. Certainly, other functions might be included, but I suggest that in some way they would be subsumed under the functions already mentioned. Now we will turn our attention to the second question and explore the foundations supporting these functions of pastoral counseling.

THE FOUNDATIONS OF PASTORAL COUNSELING

With images, poetry, and human history, Scripture recounts the story of a people's struggle to become free, to wrestle from both captivity and guilt. With the Exodus, this people celebrates an important moment as they make the shift from a captive people to a free people, living in the land promised to them. In various degrees and with new personalities, the Exodus story is told over and over again as people become bound in guilt and then are invited to return to their God to grow in a deeper covenant relationship.

Their experience is the experience of a very ordinary group of people, and yet the experience has a theological ground as manifesting the process of salvation. The story of these people is not unlike the story of Brian or Carol, for in each case these two individuals wrestle with painful issues in order to participate in a new and more human way of living.

In the previous section the methodological principles of pastoral counseling were explained and two important stories were summarized. They are important because they are the vehicle through which the process of salvation may again be discerned. The purpose of this section is to treat more explicitly the theological foundations that support the work of the pastoral counselor. In fact, these foundations give pastoral counseling its meaning as a work of ministry, a work done in faith.

Narrative has become a significant tool in the work of Christian ministers. Its significance lies in the fact that the stories of ordinary human experience have the capacity to draw others into the process of that experience. The proclamation of the Word of God is just such an event; through a proclamation that narrates ordinary events, human persons are summoned to share in the extraordinary. They begin to see the reign of God present in their own lives. Consequently, I have narrated my own experience by summarizing some important principles that have become a part of my life and practice; second, I have shared the stories of Brian and Carol. It is hoped that the reader will be drawn to identify with my experiences.

In that identification the theological value of pastoral counseling may also be felt.

This final section will attempt to draw out the theological foundations by asking three significant questions: the first two dealing with *persons* and the third with *process:*

1. What characterizes the personality of a pastor? Can the pastoral counselor be identified as such a person?
2. What are the qualities that mark the client, before, during, and after the pastoral counseling process?
3. In what sense can the process of pastoral counseling be designated as a ministry?

The Pastor

The original discourse of Christian faith makes a connection between the pastor and the shepherd. The shepherd serves as one who cares deeply for the sheep; the most popular of psalms draws such great attention because through the remembrance of the shepherd, people meet a God, a pastor, who brings comfort, who refreshes the sheep by leading them to green pastures and cool waters. The Hebrew people meet their God as a shepherd. He assumes the pastorate of the people by leading them from exile (Ezek. 34:11–16; Isa. 40:10–11). As pastor/shepherd, God stands as a sign of strength, one who can battle against evil (the lions) and lead the nation to its grazing land (Ps. 2:9; Isa. 40:1–11). In their experience of captivity, God promises to the people that they will have a new shepherd, a new David, who will establish a lasting covenant of peace (Ezek. 34:23–27).

As an individual grows in his or her identification with the Spirit of God, Jesus is portrayed as that new David. He assumes the title of the Shepherd, who loves his flock as they love him. The common experience of finding the lost sheep becomes an indication of what it is like to experience the reign of God. Jesus, the Shepherd, serves as pastor to those for whom he cares, promising to bring comfort to them and to ease the burdens and sorrows that they experience.

The texts of Scripture shed light on what it means to be a genuine pastor by taking an understandable image and associating it with God's care. Perhaps the image of the pastoral counselor is just such an image.

What kind of person do Brian or Carol meet in their experience of pastoral counseling? Like the Hebrew people held in bondage by false pastors, they meet a person whose work is primarily concerned with letting them know they are loved, with alleviating the tension and pain they feel. The pastoral counselor whom they meet is one who clearly walks with them to a place of freedom, where they will be enabled to make healthy decisions in regard to their own lives.

The genuine pastoral counselor can be said to be a pastor in every sense of that word. In careful listening, through sensitive responses, and with compassionate understanding, the pastoral counselor shepherds persons into a new grazing land, leads people to cooler waters. As the shepherd cannot do the grazing or the drinking for the sheep, so too pastoral counselors are limited in what they can do for their clients; they can only be with and walk with those who have entrusted to them the depths of their lives. The journey of the pastor stands as another moment of Exodus; the life of the pastoral counselor engages one in the very same journey.

Yet it is not enough simply to identify in images the work of the pastoral counselor with the work of the pastor or the shepherd. The images remain only a facade unless they are matched by a faith that guides the work of the pastoral counselor. For this work flows from the life of the pastoral counselor, a life rooted in faith. Consequently, Brian and Carol do not seem surprised if the experience of God's love is equated with what it means to be fully human, fully free.

The viewpoints of those who have been quoted regarding the pastoral dimension of counseling support this idea that pastoral counseling goes beyond images in order that a person may experience the depth of God's love. Rev. Sullivan notes that the pastoral dimension of counseling comes from a value system that is God-oriented; that internalized value system makes pastoral counseling different from other forms of counseling. In a similar vein, Dr. Jourard, adopting the image of the pastor/shepherd, notes that the pastoral counselor may be viewed as a "living exemplar" of the path on which individuals journey in their lives.

This does not mean that pastoral counselors are without their own tensions of points of suffering. Through critical self-examination, however, they have come to grips with their own lives because of the faith stance which they share. They themselves have been able to experience the healing of God and they have come to know the positive meaning of suffering. They too are still on the way to becoming fully human. When the client comes in contact with the pastoral counselor, the client meets one who stands as a partner in the event of life, yet a partner who is able to use advantageously the resources that life provides for decision making.

A primary resource for the pastoral counselor is the faith which enlivens the counseling dialogue. Just as the relationship between the pastor and the flock, between God and His people, is marked by both compassion and challenge, the relationship between pastoral counselor and client is marked by similar characteristics of growth. If, through the person of the pastoral counselor, a person meets a God who is with His people in their joys and in their sufferings, the client is on a path toward experiencing the freedom which counselors see as the goal.

The faith stance of the pastoral counselor enables the counselor to understand self as an image of God to those encountered; it also enables the counselor to approach clients with the awareness that the clients, too, live in the very same likeness of God. As a living exemplar, the counselor may be understood as a brother or sister who serves another so that the other may experience life to the fullest. Hearing clearly the words of Jesus, the counselor knows that one does not stand among people as a master but as a friend.

The friendship of the pastoral counselor comes as a gift to the Christian community. In the appropriate use of the skills and qualities which pastoral counselors have developed, their work with individuals enables those people to live as members of the community and of society. In that sense, the pastoral counselor has a secondary role as one who builds the community so that its members are able to live fully as human persons, freely choosing to express their care and love for others in valuable ways.

This secondary foundational role takes a back seat, however, to the primary role of relating to an individual client. The love of the shepherd is both personal and concrete; similarly, clients meet a counselor whose attention and concern are given totally to the individual client. It is when that client has personally experienced the renewing event of the Exodus that he or she may join the community to become a full participant in its journey.

The Client

Descriptions of the client are as many as there are clients; each one comes to the pastoral counseling process with a unique question or set of questions regarding the situation of his or her life. The cases of Brian and Carol obviate the unique character that individual clients possess. At the same time, these two serve as models for the type of situation and process which clients of pastoral counseling will experience. They typify, as has already been noted, the event of the Exodus as it is experienced in a deeply personal way.

Prior to the pastoral counseling process, the client may be bound in a way that hinders personal growth. Carol is controlled by a lack of self-acceptance, most obviously expressed by her physical appearance, and Brian is blinded by a judgmentalism which deceives him into believing he cannot make worthwhile human choices. Like many clients, neither of them is free; like the people before the Exodus separated from God, both are alienated from themselves and from other people. In fact, they too are alienated from God.

The Christian community and the pastoral counseling process together affirm that the situation of these people is not hopeless. The proclamation of reconciliation by people of faith goes hand in hand with pastoral counseling, which gives concrete form to the process of reconciliation. For those individuals who lack the experience of God's love, the faith stance of the pastoral counselor provides an opening to that experience.

Current theology from South and Central America reminds us that it is in the experience of the poor and the oppressed that the presence of God may be most keenly felt. This theology points us in the direction of those scriptural events where God, through Jesus, extends himself to those who suffer and who are separated.

In his own time, for example, Jesus related to people held in slavery because through him they realized that they were human beings, even when they were being treated like property. He broke into their history and helped them to see that they possessed a quality of human life that could not be destroyed by others' lack of love and concern. In like manner, Jesus relates to people today through the ministry of pastoral counseling, helping them to maintain the value of human life and freedom in situations of oppression. The Jesus who relates to us today is a fully human person who is the paradigm for what it means to live as a human being. People who focus on the Exodus event understand Jesus is the figure who, in a very pointed and personal way, expressed the desire for all who are burdened to be free from their captivity and to share in the fullness of human life. In the persons to whom Jesus reaches out, the pastoral counselor may see Brian or Carol or other clients. In short, the people who enter into the pastoral counseling process need that love of God to touch them. If a person makes the initial approach, that person is probably ready for that experience to begin; the ground is fallow, and the possibility for new life looms brilliantly.

This is the person of the client prior to the pastoral counseling process. Throughout the process, the client may be understood to have begun a journey, which leads to freedom and an alleviation of pain. Again, the client is very much like those who walked through desert and wilderness for forty years. For the Hebrew people, the journey had its own set of challenges and beliefs; it helped to constitute them as chosen people directed primarily to God. The client in pastoral counseling similarly faces a set of challenges and beliefs. By getting in touch with the love of God, the client is assisted in making loving choices for himself or herself; the developing love of self is itself a freeing experience.

In the beginning of the process the client may often appear to be defensive, much as Brian began the process by defending against his own homosexual tendencies. Yet, in the faith context, the defensive client faces the same consistent acceptance and love which the unfaithful Israelites met in the words of the prophet Hosea (Hos. 11:9). Through an ability to be with others in a compassionate and caring way, the counselor stands in gentle opposition to the client who has been surrounded with notions of unacceptance.

When the goal of the counseling process has been met, the client is a transformed person. This is not to say that the client will engage in the life process without any tension or difficulties. It does mean that a client will have a new set of resources from which to make positive and loving choices. Whereas prior to counseling we may identify these people with those in the Scripture who were most in need of God's love, we may see in the transformed client those individuals who have been clearly changed through the ministry of Jesus. The change in the disciples, from a group fearfully locked in a room to a community vibrantly proclaiming God's message, dramatically underscores the difference. The goal of pastoral counseling is founded upon the counselor's desire to see clients whose enthusiasm for life and whose ability to make sound choices is greatly enhanced. Breaking out of the locked room of one's myopic existence opens a horizon of new life with new possibilities.

The Process

Looking at the client before, during, and after the pastoral counseling process provides clues as to what that process is. It is a process of liberation based on the ministry of Jesus.

If the Exodus event serves as an adequate paradigm for framing the counseling process, the same Exodus motif finds its fulfillment in Jesus as the new Exodus. He is the one sent from God, to live as one like us and then return to God; He is the one who gathers us up with Himself to make our identification, our oneness with God complete. The ministry of Jesus enables people to live in the freedom of God's Spirit, to live anew as a people consecrated to God. Those who accept the challenge of faith find themselves surrounded by the comforting and awakening love of God; it is a love concretely experienced through the ministry of Jesus and through those who choose to be his disciples.

Pastoral counseling is one form which that ministry of Jesus takes in this age; it is a genuine ministry to the members of the Christian community. It follows upon the announcement that the reign of God will bring freedom to those held captive, joy to those in sorrow, sight to those who are blinded. It is shaped by counselors who identify their work with the work of Jesus, who has called people to Himself that their sorrows may be comforted and their burdens eased.

For each individual, the sources of captivity, pain, blindness, and sorrow take a unique concrete form. To these forms of evil, sin, or ugliness, the pastoral counseling process holds up the values of the Gospel. For it is from the Gospel and the life of Jesus that flow the ethical and moral standards which are integral for sound decision making. Where the client enters into the process aware of the concrete forms that ugliness has taken in his or her life, the process enhances vision so that Gospel-related values may be seen as viable alternatives in the day-to-day process of living. The pastoral counseling process serves to personalize the liberation of Jesus through its one-on-one relationship between the counselor and client. It personalizes the Gospel further by opening up possibilities for living through the specific application of these integral values.

As a dialogic process, pastoral counseling follows upon the patterns of ongoing relationship which can be discerned in the dialogue that continues through history between God and His people. Consequently, pastoral counseling is marked by compassion and gentleness, by an invitation to see more in existence than is evident with a superficial glance. Understanding new possibilities takes the place of coercion to behave in particular ways; such freedom to say yes or no to God's love undergirds every beckoning which God addresses to the people whom he has chosen.

If perhaps it appears that to live in God's Spirit and to be fully human are one and the same, then the pastoral counseling process has been successful. Even prior to the second century, when Irenaeus wrote that the glory of God is the human person fully alive, the followers of Jesus understood that the reign of God had already broken upon them, to be shared and to live among them as human persons. God's will and the good of the human family are co-terminous; this principle founds the process of pastoral counseling as a Christian ministry. Liberation means that human persons are freed to see themselves as a people who share in a new life; the radical transformation of the world which the Gospel envisions begins now with the transformation of individuals who are willing and ready to make healthy and loving decisions. In such transformation, the process of pastoral counseling finds its roots.

REFERENCES

Frost, Robert. *The Poetry of Robert Frost,* ed. Edward Connery Latham. New York: Henry Holt and Company, 1969.
Heschel, Abraham, J. *Who Is Man?* Stanford, Calif.: Stanford University Press, 1975.
Irenaeus, Adversus Haereses, Bk. IV, 20.7 (Sources Chrctiennes), Vol. 100, p. 648.
Journal of Pastoral Psychology, "Pastoral Dimensions in Counseling," 5, No. 1, 1970, 4–27.
Metz, Johann Baptist. *Faith in History and Society,* trans. David Smith. New York: Seabury, 1980.
O'Collins, Gerald. *Foundations of Theology.* Chicago: Loyola University Press, 1971.
Piel, Gerald. *The Acceleration of History.* New York: Knopf, 1972.
Pruyser, Paul W. *The Minister as Diagnostician.* Philadelphia: Westminster, 1976.
Van Kaam, Adrian. *Religion and Personality.* Englewood Cliffs, N.J.: Prentice Hall, 1964.

RECOMMENDED READINGS

Becker, Ernest. *The Denial of Death.* New York: Free Press, 1973.
Brown, R.E. *The Gospel According to John.* New York: Anchor Bible 29 & 29A, 1966, 1970.
————. *Jesus God and Man.* New York: Macmillan, 1967.
Brueggmann, Walter. *The Bible Makes Sense.* Winona, Minn.: St. Mary's College Press, 1977.
Duncan, Elmer H. *Søren Kierkegaard.* Waco, Tex.: Word Books, 1967.
Gilkey, L. B. *Naming the Whirlwind: The Renewal of God Language.* New York: Bobbs-Merrill, 1969.
Kung, Hans. *On Being a Christian.* Garden City, N.Y.: Doubleday, 1974.
Macquarie, John. *Principles of Christian Theology.* New York: Scribner, 1977.
McBrien, Richard P. *Catholicism.* Oak Grove, Minn.: Winston Press, 1980.
Niebuhr, H. Richard. *The Purpose of the Church and Its Ministry.* New York: Harper, 1956.
Rahner, Karl, and Wilhelm Thüsing. *A New Christology.* New York: Seabury, 1980.
Schillebeeckx, Edward. *Ministry.* New York: Crossroad, 1981.
————. *Christ: The Experience of Jesus as Lord.* New York: Seabury, 1980.
Segundo, Juan. *The Community Called Church.* Volume I: *A Theology for Artisans of a New Humanity,* trans. John Drury. Maryknoll, N.Y.: Orbis Books, 1973.

CHAPTER THREE

The Counseling Ministry and Spiritual Direction

KEVIN G. CULLIGAN, PH.D.

The chapters in this book reveal that counseling in the Church is all about relationships—with God, one's own self, other people, family, things, and events. In this chapter I will concentrate on counseling as a means of helping persons deepen their relationship with God. I call this kind of counseling *spiritual direction,* although it often goes by other names such as religious counseling, prayer counseling, or spiritual guidance. By spiritual direction, I mean that form of counseling in the Church which helps persons grow in their relationship with God through prayer.

Spiritual direction arises out of the Church's long spiritual and mystical tradition. As early as the fourth century, Christians sought out the holy hermits in the deserts of Palestine, Syria, and Egypt to learn how to live entirely for God. Succeeding generations continued the search for reliable guides in prayer. In each century, spiritual masters like Saint Jerome, Saint Catherine of Siena, Saint Ignatius of Loyola, Saint John of the Cross, Saint Teresa of Avila, and Saint Francis de Sales, to name but a very few, have guided this longing in Christian hearts for intimate union with God. The writings of these and other Christian masters remain a valuable source of spiritual guidance. Today, we in the counseling ministry recognize the increasing relevance of our Christian mystical and spiritual tradition as more of our clients seek our help in deepening their relationship with God and as we recognize that our ability to respond effectively to such requests is a distinctive resource of the Church's counseling ministry.

Although its name and methods derive from the past, spiritual direction harmonizes with newer forms of counseling which have emerged in the Church following the advent of modern therapeutic psychology. If we view our counseling ministry as the Church's attempt to help all her people grow in all their relationships, then spiritual direction, which concentrates on the person's relationship with God, coordinates with other specialities such as psychotherapy, group therapy, marriage and family counseling, crisis counseling, and career guidance where the focus is on the person's relationship with self, others, things, or events. In this view, the spiritual director is a counselor in the Church whose primary focus is helping persons grow in their relationship with God through prayer. This is not to exclude other relationships from spiritual direction, for our relationship with God involves these other relationships; however, the focus in spiritual direction is upon the person's relationship with God just as, for example, marriage counseling, without excluding the couple's relationship with God, concentrates primarily on their relationship with one another.

BASIC ASSUMPTIONS UNDERLYING
SPIRITUAL DIRECTION

I approach spiritual direction with some very specific assumptions drawn from my own experience of God, the mystical tradition of the Church, and modern theology. I believe that God lives fully within each of us, not only as the Cause of our existence and the Ground of our being, but also offering to reveal Himself totally to us and waiting to be known and loved by us in return. God reveals more than knowledge about Himself; He communicates to us His very Self. This divine Self-communication completely satisfies our longing for human fulfillment and transforms us entirely in God, enabling us to transcend human modes of knowledge and love to assume God's ways of knowing and loving.

This intimate Self-revelation of God differs from the revelation of Himself in the created universe around us or in His public Self-revelation in the Bible and the Church's traditions in that it is made known in our own unique experience of life and can exist without thoughts or images; it is a direct communication from the Spirit of God to our own spirit. Because it is so intimately a part of our own daily experience, God's Self-revelation is the basis of our own personal values, our direction in life, and our unique individuation as persons. We best attune ourselves to this revelation through interior prayer and respond to it with ever-increasing faith. Spiritual direction helps us become increasingly aware of God's presence in our lives through prayer and more disposed to accept God's gift of Himself in greater faith, hope, and love.

In spiritual direction I thus assume the possibility of an intimate interpersonal relationship between ourselves and God. This is the most important relationship in our lives, for it ultimately determines what kind of persons we become. In this assumption, God is our real Spiritual Director who guides us to union with Himself through His own Self-revelation: the human spiritual director simply helps us become more open and responsive to God's transforming self-communication in our daily experience.

My assumptions about God, the human person, and their relationship may differ markedly from those held by other directors. While all directors need not share the same assumptions, we ought to be clear in our beliefs about the human person's relationship with God, for these determine our practice of this ministry. I have stated my own assumptions as clearly as possible because they are the foundation of my own approach to spiritual direction.

THE PROCESS OF SPIRITUAL DIRECTION

When someone approaches me with the request for spiritual direction, I never take for granted that the person is asking me for help in his or her relationship with God. When translated, the request may mean: "I want someone to talk to," or "My religious order requires that I have a spiritual director," or "I want someone I can go to regularly for confession," or "Help me become a saint," or indeed, "I want to deepen my relationship with God." Obviously, my first task is to determine exactly what people want when they ask for spiritual direction.

To do this, I find out as soon as possible why they are coming to me, why they are coming at this particular time, and what they expect will happen in spiritual direction. The answer to the "why me" question allows me to see whether I am perceived as someone who can help with prayer and spiritual growth or whether I am looked to for some other kind of help such as psychotherapy or supportive counseling. The answer to the "why now" question gives me an understanding of the motivation for spiritual direction and where the person is in his or her relationship with God. For example, one may come on a referral from a therapist colleague to explore the religious questions in his or her life but without much awareness of what that means or where it will lead; another may come following a recent conversion experience, requesting support and guidance in responding to this new awakening; a third may simply state: "I have been receiving spiritual direction regularly for years, but my director has recently been moved to another part of the country. I value the direction process as an aid to my faith life and I'd like to continue it with you." Finally, the hopes people express for spiritual direction reveal whether it is spiritual direction or some other form of counseling they are seeking. For example, "I expect that this will help me be more open to what God is doing in my life" is clearly a request for spiritual direction, whereas, "I hope I can better cope with my wife and children" suggests family counseling as a more appropriate form of help.

The answers to the above questions enable me to ascertain whether the person is truly a candidate for spiritual direction as I understand it or whether I should recommend some other form of counseling. What people ask for and what they want are not always the same; nor is what they want always what they need. To accept a person for spiritual direction, I look for two things: (1) Is the person truly aware of God in his or her life and committed to a deeper relationship with Him? and (2) Is the person sufficiently free from major psychopathology to pursue a sustained life of prayer? Both qualities must be present together: some may seriously intend to love and serve God but be too psychotic to pray in a way that I can help them; others may be relatively free of psychopathology but have no deep commitment to God or prayer.

Because I am both a priest and a psychologist and because it is still easier for most people to ask a priest for spiritual direction than a psychologist for psychotherapy, I explore the psychopathology possibility very carefully. When people ask me for spiritual direction because I am a priest with training in psychology, I suspect they may really be requesting psychotherapy or some other form of psychological counseling rather than spiritual direction.

When this suspicion proves correct, I next decide whether to continue working with the person but adjusting our focus from spiritual direction to psychotherapy or bereavement counseling or crisis intervention or whatever form of assistance the person's real problem calls for. This may be done in the understanding that we will move into spiritual direction once that problem is resolved. Or we may simply agree to concentrate on the resolution of that problem, leaving aside altogether the initial request for spiritual direction.

Or a referral may be in order. If the problem is one I am not prepared to work with, I will refer the person to another counselor or therapist outright. In some cases we may arrange for concurrent counseling where I continue to see the person in spiritual direction focusing on the person's relationship with God in prayer while the other counselor focuses on the resolution of other problems, such as marital conflict or endogenous depression or alcoholism.

Once we have agreed that spiritual direction is the preferred mode of counseling, I attend more closely to questions affecting the person's relationship with God. I strive first to grasp something of the uniqueness of the person before me. Believing that each person is unique and that God deals uniquely with each person, I try to accept this person as different from any other I have ever known. To arrive at this understanding, I pay attention to people's age, sex, state in life, sociocultural background, intelligence, and educational experience. I observe their level of self-acceptance, whether their religious ideals permit them to accept or cause them to deny or distort basic human experiences, especially sex or anger; their level of faith as it relates to their psychosocial development, whether quite independent of their chronological age their faith appears more characteristic of one developmental stage than another; the level of their strongest motivating needs, whether it be for approval, security, acceptance, or self-transcendence. These factors—age, sex, vocation, culture, intelligence, education, self-acceptance, psychosocial development, motivating needs—provide insights into both the uniqueness of each person and the unique way God works in his or her life.

I also assess their relationship with God. How do they experience God? As a merciless judge? A loving father? An impersonal force? An intimate friend? What about prayer? How often do they pray? In what ways? Is personal prayer more active or passive, more meditative or contemplative, more talking or listening, more verbal or nonverbal? How do they use spiritual disciplines or ascetical practices? As a denial of or defense against human experience in an effort to please God or as a means of openness to human experience to hear God speaking in every event of life?

I also notice how they speak about God. If they are explicit and detailed, I suspect that their relationship with God may be more intellectual and cognitive; if they speak devotionally, I suspect more emotion in their relationship; and if they have difficulty expressing their relationship or can speak only in general terms, I suspect the possibility of ineffable or "peak" experiences of God. I observe their relationship to me for an insight into their relationship with God. If they keep me at a safe distance psychologically and emotionally, I suspect they may do the same with God. If there is more warmth and spontaneity with me, I would look for this to be true also with God. I ask for their "salvation history" or a description of how they have seen God working in them throughout their entire life. I ask them to describe their most significant religious experiences. Through questions such as these I form an idea of where people are with God in order to know how best to help: persons just beginning to pray seriously following a religious conversion require a different kind of help from me than persons who have been praying contemplatively for years.

In the beginning I usually recommend to individuals that we meet first for no more than ten sessions. This permits enough time for us to decide not only whether they are truly candidates for spiritual direction and what the nature of their relationship is with God, but also whether we can work together. In these initial sessions we also settle such questions as our working goals, the frequency and length of our meetings, and whether fees will be involved.

Once we have committed ourselves to work together in spiritual direction, we begin to concentrate more on God's Self-revelation in their life, their prayer as openness to this revelation, and their response to this revelation through increasing faith, hope, and love. With those who have undergone a recent conversion or who are relatively new to the spiritual life, my work is often to teach them how to pray and to recommend spiritual reading which will enlighten them about the "new way" they have begun. Frequently, I must help beginners regulate their enthusiasm for religious activity with reason and the spirit of the Gospel, for while sincere in their new attachment to God, they are generally still strongly motivated by the pleasure principle and subtly seek their own satisfaction in these activities. The attempt to bring order into their enthusiasm can be met with resistance and hostility, which must be accepted and worked through. Often, I become the object of their positive, sometimes amorous, transference feelings which must be explored and resolved in a manner that leads them to a deeper attachment to God.

With persons further along in the spiritual life and more experienced in prayer, spiritual direction has a different emphasis. We attend to their experience of God in prayer and its effects in their daily life. As God becomes more central in their life, they change. Some change vocations and careers as God leads them in totally new directions. Others become more socially or politically active as they perceive God calling them to a more prophetic response to life. Most continue their regular daily activities and relationships but with a heightened awareness of God's presence there. To discern these movements in spiritual direction, we explore the entire range of their relationships and activities, but always in relation to their experience of God. Carefully, I remind persons never to consider any understanding or experience of God as final so that they may always remain open to God's continual Self-revelation and the Spirit's moving them in new directions and to deeper levels of understanding.

One of my most crucial functions as a spiritual director is to assist persons in times of spiritual crisis which result from the psychological effects of God's increasing Self-communication as He gradually transforms them from self-centeredness to God-centeredness. Usually, the first such crisis, appearing relatively soon after they have begun to pray seriously, is one of emotional dryness. Up to this point, persons have found intense pleasure in their prayer and spiritual works. Suddenly, the pleasure vanishes and discursive meditation becomes almost impossible. Because they still long intensely for God, these persons become confused by the loss of pleasure and the inability to meditate, sometimes believing their new religious commitment to be all self-delusion. Actually, God is now beginning to reveal Himself more directly to the deeper, spiritual levels of their being and less through their senses, imagination, emotions, and feelings. In this crisis, God draws persons away from excessive attachment to the personal satisfaction derived from prayer and religious activities and leads them toward a more disinterested love and service of Himself in deeper faith; accompanying this movement, God leads them from a meditative way of praying to a greater experience of Himself in contemplation.

As a director, I attempt to discern whether the dryness results from God's Self-communication or from some other cause such as sickness (which could account for the inability to meditate) or a person's abandoning the spiritual quest (which could account for the loss of pleasure in prayer). When I discover all three phenomena present simultaneously—loss of pleasure, inability to meditate, yet an intense longing for God—I conclude that God is revealing Himself at deeper levels of their life. In this case, I help persons to understand the crisis taking place within them, encourage them not to abandon their spiritual life but to trust their longing for God, allowing their prayer now to be a quiet expression of that longing. In short, I help them change from a discursive, meditative form of prayer to a contemplative way of praying.

As God continues to reveal Himself more fully to persons in prayer, other crises come, periods more like depression and bereavement than dryness, caused by the gradual death to self that occurs as one lives more completely for God. In the light of God's increasing Self-communication, one not only understands God more as He really is, but sees oneself more truly. At times this light causes painful insight into the self, allowing one to see clearly, for example, the self-seeking motives in one's altruistic behavior or the subtle manipulation of others to meet one's own neurotic needs. These insights may cause deep feelings of grief as one's earlier, cherished but deluded, self-images die. Similarly, one's deeper understanding of God sometimes causes a painful loss of earlier, devoutly held but distorted, images of God. Or one may simultaneously intensely long for a loving union with God yet fear His loss because of one's unworthiness. These periods of loss and grief, anguish and dread, guilt and unworthiness accompany the gradual transformation being effected in persons by God's ever-deepening Self-revelation, a transformation involving a switch of one's psychological energies from attachment to self to attachment to God, a transformation in which one dies to an old self in order to arise a new person in God.

My function as a spiritual director during these critical periods is, once again, to discern whether the person's experiences result from an intensification of God's Self-revelation or from some other natural cause, like the death of a loved one or involutional depression. While death to self is intensely felt, it is not ordinarily accompanied by the marked mood and behavior changes and altered social and occupational functioning usually seen in bereavement and clinical depression. The reason for this difference is that God's Self-communication, which often causes a distressful knowledge of one's true self when seen in relationship to God, also fills a person with the strengthening power of His love, enabling one to perform daily responsibilities effectively. When it is clear that persons are in a time of spiritual crisis, I try to support them by conveying as accurately as possible an empathic understanding of what they see and feel about themselves and God, yet without attempting to relieve their pain or deny their experience with false reassurances: these purifying periods are necessary to free them of inordinate attachments to false images of God and self that prevent their total transformation in God and the fullest realization of their human potential.

But people's relationship with God is not all dryness and pain. Long periods of inner peace often pervade their relationships and activities; these are times when I as a director simply remain available to discern with them the way God is revealing Himself in their lives and to encourage their response in greater faith, hope, and love. There are sometimes moments when God will flood them with Himself, causing ecstatic joy. Though such an experience is ineffable, I encourage persons to describe it to me as best they can to help them more fully appreciate the experience and its personal meaning.

Few persons actually attain such complete union with God in this life that they are totally transformed in Him, viewing life as He sees it, knowing and loving His creation as He knows and loves it. For those who do, I simply try to be present to them as a spiritual friend with whom they may always share their experience of God. Because God is truly their Spiritual Director, my one rule is never to interfere with His work in them.

Reviewing the process of spiritual direction, one may readily see it as primarily a faith process. It assumes that the person and I both believe that God is present in the person's depths, revealing Himself. I can never predict how God will guide any one person until He reveals Himself in the person's experience. Rather than having a predetermined plan for each person, I must rather wait in faith with the person to hear what God is revealing in his or her experience, to discern the meaning and significance of that revelation, and to support the person's own unique response to it.

As distinct from other forms of counseling, which are usually limited in time to weeks, months, or sometimes years depending on the nature of the counseling issue, spiritual direction is, at least in principle, a lifelong process. One's relationship with God, the focus in spiritual direction, is itself lifelong, moving always to newer levels, each with its own distinct challenges as God communicates Himself in new and different ways. Although the duration of a spiritual direction relationship varies with such factors as the director's availability or ability to meet a person's special needs at a particular stage of the spiritual journey, it is not unusual for a person to meet with the same spiritual director regularly—say, once a month—for over twenty-five years. In the earlier stages of people's relationship with God, I am far more active, determining their needs, teaching them how to pray and what the principles of the spiritual life are, working through transference and countertransference issues, helping them with decisions, and supporting them in crises. As their relationship with God grows, I become less active and more supportive, helping them through an empathic understanding of their experiences to discern and respond to God's action in their lives.

To facilitate God's truly becoming the person's real Spiritual Director, I endeavor throughout the entire process to remove the obstacles in a person's life that interfere with his or her receiving God's Self-communication. My working principle for this is continually to hold before them, regardless of their stage of spiritual development, the example of Jesus Christ and His constant openness to the Father. Jesus emptied Himself of every obstacle preventing His hearing and responding to the Father's will in His life, culminating in the cross, which represents Jesus' complete openness to His Father's will and the perfect fulfillment of His human destiny as Reconciler of the human race with God. Similarly, I encourage persons to free themselves of the obstacles preventing them from receiving God's Self-revelation so that they may be led by the Father to their own particular human fulfillment. Centering on Jesus Christ simplifies the spiritual life and allows the spiritual direction process to maintain its proper focus.

Although spiritual direction has traditionally taken place within the one-to-one helping relationship, new developments with group spiritual direction promise an enriching development in this ministry. In group spiritual direction I find that not only are persons able to explore fruitfully their relationships with God and its consequences for their lives as they do in individual direction, but they also profit from the unique growth-producing factors inherent in the small group process. Persons involved in group spiritual direction learn from one another, challenge one another, and support one another in their common desire to grow in their relationship with God. Group spiritual direction will gradually come to have a greater part in the ministry of spiritual direction, not simply because it can make spiritual guidance available to more persons, but also because of the unique contributions groups can have in helping their members become more open to God's Self-communication in human experience.

PREPARATION FOR SPIRITUAL DIRECTION

From what we have seen of the process of spiritual direction, it is clear that one ought to have a special preparation for this ministry. The first area of preparation is personal experience. To guide others along the road of faith and prayer to a deeper union with God, a director must know that road from experience. This involves cultivating the awareness of God's presence in one's own life and opening oneself in prayer to receive God's Self-communication. As I listen to God in the depths of my own experience, I am better able to hear Him in the experience of others. From experience, I know the problem of being faithful to prayer, the darkness of faith, the resistance of human nature to surrendering completely to God's guidance; yet I also know from experience that God never abandons me in my darkest moments and is always present in each daily event, transforming my life into His. These experiences enable me to be with others in their own trials of faith and prayer to assure them that God has not abandoned them but is drawing them ever more deeply into the mystery of His own life.

A second area of preparation for spiritual direction is academic learning, especially in those disciplines that illuminate the human's relationship with God. I find, for example, that the theology of grace and the philosophy of knowledge have significant implications for understanding the ministry of spiritual direction. The theology of grace enables us to conceive of God as present within the human person, freely revealing Himself to the person, and the philosophy of human knowledge enables us to comprehend that the human person can receive this divine Self-communication directly and immediately, without formal images or logical concepts. These two understandings imply that God, who is Spirit, may communicate Himself to the human spirit in an infinite variety of ways, and that for me as a spiritual director, my challenge is to help persons become more open to these infinite possibilities within themselves. By thus expanding my understanding of the relationship between God and the human person, theology and philosophy enable me to be more alert to and supportive of the infinite number of ways God can reveal Himself to a human person.

Knowledge of Sacred Scripture is another valuable resource for the spiritual director. The biblical record of God's relationship with His people Israel is the paradigm of His relationship with each individual in the spiritual life. The story of Israel is the story of each person with God. Moreover, Scripture reveals Jesus' relationship with His Father, the model of each person's openness to the Self-communication of the Father. The more familiar the spiritual director is with the history of

Israel and the life of Jesus, the better equipped he or she will be to help persons grow in their relationship with God.

Another important source of knowledge for the spiritual director are the classics of Christian spirituality, such as the writings of Saint John of the Cross, Saint Ignatius, and Saint Teresa of Avila. Rather than abstract treatises on the spiritual life, these are more often personal accounts of men and women who have tried to live fully their relationship with God and who have experienced the many effects of His Self-revelation in their lives. Familiarity with these recorded experiences of God in the lives of earlier Christians prepares the spiritual director to discern God's guiding action in the lives of spiritual pilgrims today.

Finally, psychology provides valuable information for the spiritual director. Spiritual direction constantly deals with three mysteries: God, the human person, and their relationship. Through psychology the spiritual director may gain a deeper insight into human development, motivation, and psychopathology, which will aid in understanding the person's relationship with God.

Theology, philosophy, biblical studies, spirituality, and psychology: these may be considered the basic sciences upon which the practice of spiritual direction rests. The more thorough the knowledge in these areas, the better prepared will the spiritual director be for this ministry.

Attaining skills in helping relationships is the final area of preparation for the spiritual director. The helping relationship distinguishes spiritual direction from other forms of spiritual guidance such as spiritual reading or participation in liturgy. The relationship with another human being in spiritual direction provides a person with help in the spiritual journey that comes from no other source. Consequently, a spiritual director must be able to appreciate and understand the powerful influence which interpersonal dynamics have in helping persons grow in their relationship with God. He or she must be able to recognize and work with the phenomena of transference and countertransference, collusion, and unconscious communication of attitudes. More important, a director, through his or her own genuineness, caring, and understanding, must be able to create an interpersonal atmosphere of trust which enables persons to speak openly about their relationship with God, for it is in openly sharing their experience of God with another human being that persons gradually come to perceive, understand, and accept God's Self-revelation in their own lives. No matter what model one chooses in order to understand the ministry of spiritual direction (for example, a healing model, or a prophetic model, or a charismatic model), it is primarily the quality of the relationship between the director and the person that makes spiritual direction an effective means for deepening one's relationship with God.

Upon reviewing the areas of preparation for spiritual direction, one might become discouraged from entering this ministry, believing that it requires a special charism or grace. However, one need not view spiritual direction as any more specialized or charismatic than other forms of counseling in the Church. If one is committed to growing in a relationship with God through faith and prayer, to studying the basic intellectual disciplines, and to acquiring skills in helping relations, one may develop the necessary qualities to help others deepen their union with God.

RESEARCH AND TRAINING

Research in spiritual direction today is limited primarily to clarifying theories and approaches to spiritual direction found in the literature of Christian spirituality, the application of new psychotherapeutic modes to spiritual direction, and some empirical investigations of the results of spiritual direction. More research is needed to enhance the effectiveness of this ministry within the Church. With the help of research tools drawn from therapeutic psychology, we can fruitfully examine the factors affecting the director-directee relationship and the process and outcome of that relationship as well as develop testable hypotheses regarding the human person's relationship with God as these emerge within the direction process itself.

The growth of spiritual direction as a modern counseling ministry will also depend upon the wise selection and training of future spiritual directors. Based on the approach to spiritual direction discussed in this chapter, such training programs should include: (1) a training atmosphere created by the training staff that facilitates the growth of persons who are able to be in genuine, caring, and understanding helping relationships with others; (2) opportunities for personal and spiritual growth experiences, including private prayer and meditation, retreats and spiritual exercises, common worship and liturgical celebrations, journal keeping, spiritual reading, and psychotherapy and/or spiritual direction on a group or individual basis; (3) academic studies in theology, Sacred Scripture, philosophy, spirituality, and psychology as these apply to the ministry of spiritual direction; and (4) opportunities to provide spiritual direction for others, both individually and in groups, under the supervision of qualified staff members.

SUMMARY

In this chapter I have attempted to define spiritual direction and to indicate its place within the Church's counseling ministry, to state the assumptions that underlie my approach to spiritual direction and to describe my role as a spiritual director in helping others grow in their relationship with God, to indicate the areas of preparation for entering the spiritual direction ministry, and to suggest approaches to research and training that will enhance the quality of this ministry today. My hope is that this chapter will hasten the day when the venerable tradition of spiritual direction will be seen as an integral part of the counseling ministry in the Church.

REFERENCES

Culligan, K. G. "Toward a Model of Spiritual Direction Based on the Writings of Saint John of the Cross and Carl R. Rogers." Doctoral dissertation, Boston University, 1979. University Microfilms No. 79-23923.

Galvin, J. P. "The Invitation of Grace." In L. J. O'Donovan (Ed.), *A World of Grace: An Introduction to the Themes and Foundations of Karl Rahner's Theology*. New York: Seabury, 1980.

RECOMMENDED READINGS

Barnhouse, Ruth Tiffany. "Spiritual Direction and Psychotherapy," *The Journal of Pastoral Care*, September 1979, 33, 149–63.

Barry, William A., and William J. Connolly. *The Practice of Spiritual Direction*. New York: Seabury, 1982.

Barry, William A., and Mary C. Guy. "The Practice of Supervision in Spiritual Direction," *Review for Religious*, November 1978, 37, 834–42.

Bouchaud, C. "The Spiritual Director of a Subject in Psychotherapy," *Insight*, Winter 1968, 6, 38–42.

Cameli, Louis John. *Stories of Paradise: The Study of Classical and Modern Autobiographies of Faith*. New York: Paulist Press, 1978.

Coburn, John B. "Contemporary Non-Catholic Spirituality and the Guidance of Souls," *Worship*, December 1965, 39, 619–34.

Culligan, Kevin G. (Ed.). *Spiritual Direction: Contemporary Readings*. Locust Valley, N.Y.: Living Flame Press, 1983.

———. "Toward a Contemporary Model of Spiritual Direction: A Comparative Study of Saint John of the Cross and Carl R. Rogers," *Carmelite Studies*, 1982, 2, 95–166.

Dyckman, Katherine M., and L. Patrick Carroll. *Inviting the Mystic, Supporting the Prophet: An Introduction to Spiritual Direction*. New York: Paulist Press, 1981.

Edwards, Tilden H. *Spiritual Friend: Reclaiming the Gift of Spiritual Direction*. New York: Paulist Press, 1980.

English, John. *Choosing Life: Significance of Personal History in Decision-Making*. New York: Paulist Press, 1978.

Gratton, Carolyn. *Guidelines for Spiritual Direction*. Denville, N.J.: Dimension Books, 1980.

Hakenewerth, Quentin. "Group Methods in Spiritual Direction," *Review for Religious*, January 1968, 27, 71–79.

LaPlace, Jean. *Preparing for Spiritual Direction*, trans. John C. Guinness. Chicago: Franciscan Herald Press, 1975.

Leech, Kenneth. *Soul Friend: The Practice of Christian Spirituality*, intro. Henri Nouwen. San Francisco: Harper, 1980.

May, Gerald. *Pilgrimage Home: The Conduct of Contemplative Practice in Groups*. New York: Paulist Press, 1979.

Merton, Thomas. *Spiritual Direction and Meditation*. Collegeville, Minn.: Liturgical Press, 1960.

Rogers, Carl R. "The Interpersonal Relationship: The Core of Guidance," *Harvard Educational Review*, Fall 1962, 32, 416–29.

Tyrrell, Bernard J. *Christotherapy: Healing Through Enlightenment*. New York: Seabury, 1975.

Van Kaam, Adrian. *The Dynamics of Spiritual Self-Direction.* Denville, N.J.: Dimension Books, 1976.
Walsh, William. "Reality Therapy and Spiritual Direction," *Review for Religious,* May 1976, 35, 372–85.
Ware, Kallistos. "The Spiritual Father in Orthodox Christianity," *Cross Currents,* Summer-Fall 1974, 24, 296–320.

Tapes

Barry, William, Anne Harvey, Paul Lucey, and Bill Connolly. *Initiating Spiritual Direction.* 3 tapes. Cleveland: Audio Communications Center, n.d.
Goergen, Donald. *The Christian Counselor: A Guide to the Art of Spiritual Direction.* 6 tapes. Kansas City, Mo.: NCR Cassettes, n.d.

PART TWO
ON BECOMING A PASTORAL COUNSELOR

CHAPTER FOUR

Supervision: From Technician to Artist

BARRY K. ESTADT, PH.D.

The art of counseling is not something we can be taught; it can only be learned. Erich Fromm, in his widely read work *The Art of Loving* (1956), discusses the necessary steps in learning any art. He writes:

> The process of learning an art can be divided conveniently into two parts: one, the mastery of the theory; the other, the mastery of the practice. If I want to learn the art of medicine, I must first know the facts about the human body, and about various diseases. When I have all this theoretical knowledge, I am by no means competent in the art of medicine. I shall become a master in this art only after a great deal of practice, until eventually the results of my theoretical knowledge and the results of my practice are blended into one—my intuition, the essence of the mastery of any art. (p. 4)

The process of acquiring an art, according to Fromm, requires discipline, concentration, patience, and supreme concern. "If one wishes to become a master in any art, one's whole life must be devoted to it, or at least related to it." (1956, p. 93) Within the pastoral counseling field, the supervision of the student's ongoing counseling experience has come to be regarded as the primary catalyst in facilitating an integration which includes: (1) an incorporation of the body of knowledge common to the field of counseling theory and practice; (2) the development of specific

49

counseling skills and a general way of being toward clients that facilitates personal growth in the client; and (3) a formulation of one's personal theological understanding of ministry. The goal of supervision, within pastoral counseling, is to assist individuals as they seek to become knowledgeable and competent practitioners committed to the counseling ministry.

In an issue of *The Counseling Psychologist* devoted entirely to the topic of supervision, Hennessy (1982, p. 52) defined supervision as "an intensive, interpersonally focused, professional function in which one person is designated to facilitate appropriate, professional competence in the other person." Hennessy defines three global interrelated functions of the supervisor: monitoring client welfare, promoting the supervisee's professional growth, and evaluating the supervisee. In most of the supervisory relationships with Loyola students I do not have the primary responsibility for monitoring client welfare since most students are involved in clinical settings where immediate supervision is provided. This frees me from the pragmatic need to focus on crisis management and other areas of immediate concern thereby allowing me greater freedom to deal with the needs of the student as counselor without changing, however, the focus of supervision to therapy. Accordingly, in this chapter I will concentrate on the growth issues of the counselor and on the process of evaluation as it has evolved in the master's program at Loyola College. In so doing, attention to the welfare of the client is assumed.

SUPERVISION: A LEARNING ALLIANCE

Supervision, within the Loyola program, is a special kind of tutorial relationship in which a person with less experience presents his or her work for the scrutiny and critique of a person with more experience. The point of departure for the supervisory session is the work sample, along with the variety of issues that the work sample generates. The focus of supervision varies with the level of training of the counselor: the beginning counselor versus the near graduate. Needs of counselors-in-training also vary widely because of diverse backgrounds and varying degrees of prior ministerial experience. For some the supervisory hour focuses on the acquisition of basic skills; for others the "growing edge" is an integration of basic skills with theoretical formulations; at times the task at hand is an understanding of one's pastoral role in relationship to clients.

Although supervisors within the Loyola program share the same basic goals, they vary widely in their personal styles and techniques, ranging from client-centered approaches to supervision to more directive styles. The overall philosophy of supervision, however, might be characterized by the long-treasured medical dictum: *primum non nocere,* loosely translated as "the cardinal rule is not to inflict pain unnecessarily." The Loyola approach is a gentle one in keeping with a quotation attributed to Saint Francis of Assisi: "Nothing is so strong as gentleness; nothing is so gentle as real strength." At the core of the Loyola approach to supervision is the understanding that faculty and supervisors should model a pastoral way of being to students, *attempting to relate to students as they would have students relate to their clients.*

My personal supervisory philosophy and style are very similar to my counseling approach. I am interested in establishing a relationship with counseling candidates which will facilitate their professional growth. I approach candidates with a basic acceptance of their current level of experience in counseling, attempting to create a learning atmosphere of trust and safety wherein threat is kept to a minimum. When I succeed in doing this, I find that students become progressively nondefensive in looking at their work with clients. Initial anxiety, reflected in an effort to impress the supervisor, gives way to candor and openness in the supervisory session.

My initial strategy in most supervisory sessions is to draw out what the counselor already knows about the client. I am especially interested in how the counselor *feels* toward the client, for in focusing on a total feeling response to the client, a counselor often discovers from within a wealth of knowledge about the client and about the client's interaction with other persons. It is a way of affirming the counselor as a person with important inner resources and of inviting the counselor to begin to call upon these resources.

Frequently enough my focus on how the counselor feels toward the client brings to light countertransference issues within the counselor which affect the counselor's ability to offer a relationship characterized by unconditional acceptance. I am especially attuned to the counselor's underlying feelings and attitudes when the lifestyle of the client is at variance with the values of the counselor. In each of the past ten years, for example, I have supervised clergy and religious who were dealing for the first time with homosexual clients. Part of the supervisory process involved an exploration of the counselor's underlying attitudes and theological assumptions regarding sexuality insofar as they related to working with the given client.

Focusing on the counselor's feelings toward a particular client can lead to reflection on how one relates to other similar clients and to clients in general. A few years ago I was supervising a young man whose client was an aggressive, outspoken fifty-year-old woman, adept in the use of colorful profanity. The client's style of relating was in marked contrast to the soft-spoken, gentle, polite, and deferential manner of the counselor. During the course of supervision the counselor became aware of wanting his client to be less spontaneous in the expression of her aggressive feelings, implying that she should exercise a "proper control" more in line with his own style. As the counselor examined these feelings, he became aware that he had never dealt with what he termed the "shadow side" of himself. For this reason, he entered into therapy to deal with the largely repressed aggressive components of his own personality. As he began to understand and to accept this long-denied side of himself, he was amazed at how quickly his various clients began to deal with similar feelings. The counselor was profoundly moved as he came to realize how his personal lack of spontaneity had served to inhibit his clients. As he came to a fuller experience of his personal world of feeling, he was able to facilitate an expression of similar feelings by his clients. He continued in therapy for some time with a view to continued personal growth but with the further realization that his personal growth would positively impact his professional work as a counselor.

As issues for personal therapy emerge within the context of the supervisory process, I find it important to keep clear the respective roles of supervision and therapy. Supervision is a "working alliance" which focuses on a person's *functioning as a counselor;* therapy is a "working alliance" which focuses on one's *functioning as a person.* When personal therapeutic issues arise within supervision, I work with the counselor in understanding the impact of these issues on the counseling relationship. This exploration, within supervision, is done in direct relationship to the work sample presented. Frequently, it results in the counselor's realization that personal therapy would be a valuable adjunct for fostering both personal and professional growth.

When I am able to establish a supervisory relationship characterized by an atmosphere of acceptance and trust, students are deeply grateful, for in the process of uncovering their limitations in relationship to clients, they find themselves accepted and affirmed as counselors who have much to bring to the counseling relationship. I am most pleased with my supervision when I am able to communicate a deep respect for a counselor's strengths and, at the same time, invite the counselor to deal effectively with areas needing growth and development, that is, with one's professional "growing edges."

SPECIFIC GOALS OF THE SUPERVISORY PROCESS

Over the course of years an attempt has been made at Loyola to make explicit and concrete the goals of supervision within the context of the master's program. Guidelines have been developed for beginning students and for more advanced students under five basic headings: (1) Basic Helping Skills; (2) Knowledge of the Client; (3) Personal Qualities of the Counselor Relating to Personal Growth; (4) Skillfulness in the Counseling Relationship; and (5) Sensitivity to Pastoral Concerns and Ethical Issues. The items utilized for more advanced counselors are listed after the items for beginning counselors to highlight the gradual progression in expectations through the training program. While no list of items can capture the total gestalt, these do help to keep in focus, for counselor and supervisor, some of the expectations of the learning process.

BASIC HELPING SKILLS

Beginning Counselor

____ a.   An ability to accept clients in a nonjudgmental way.

____ b.   An ability to attend to the client's internal world of feeling.

___ c.   An ability to respond empathically to the client.

More Advanced Counselor

___ a.   Attending, responding, and initiating skills (à la Egan, Carkuff) are a relatively effortless part of the counselor's repertoire.

___ b.   The above skills manifested in a consistent way within the context of the counselor's personal theoretical orientation.

The helping skills of attending and responding with accurate empathy to the client's internal world of feelings are basic counseling skills irrespective of one's theoretical orientation to the counseling process. The work of Carkuff (1969), Ivey (1971), Kagan (1967), Egan (1975), and others has demonstrated the fact that basic counseling skills can be taught by isolating and illustrating discrete components of effective counseling, followed by appropriate practicum experiences. In the Loyola program counselors are expected to move from an initial, self-conscious awareness and demonstration of basic counseling skills to a level of proficiency where attending and responding skills have become a consistent and effortless part of the counselor's way of being with clients.

KNOWLEDGE OF THE CLIENT

Beginning Counselor

___ a.   An ability to elicit essential data from the client.

___ b.   Some understanding of the significance of essential data.

___ c.   An understanding that there may be a difference between the presenting problem and the underlying problem.

___ d.   A beginning ability to assess the strengths and weaknesses of the client.

More Advanced Counselor

___ a.   An ability to formulate a "working diagnosis" based on an assessment of the facts.

___ b.   An ability to assess one's own professional readiness to deal effectively with the client.

___ c.   Facility in making referrals to other professionals when appropriate.

___ d.   An ability to modify one's "working diagnosis" as new facts emerge or as one's understanding increases.

Basic counseling skills are the precondition for creating an atmosphere in which clients feel free to reveal the details of their inner experience. The professional counselor's role, however, goes far beyond the empathic response. It includes an ability to differentiate the essential from the peripheral in what the client reports and to move beneath the surface to an understanding of the underlying dynamics of the client. The skilled counselor's grasp of personality theory, developmental psychology, and psychopathology allows him or her to assess the strengths and weaknesses of the client, formulating in a relatively short time a "working diagnosis." The counselor's awareness of personal competency, professional experience, and the realities of the counseling setting enter into an assessment of the appropriateness of working with a client personally as opposed to facilitating a referral. In the development of these abilities and skills, the input of courses and private study are foundational. It is in the supervision of one's ongoing counseling work, however, that one has the opportunity of integrating the cognitive data with one's ongoing experience in the counseling relationship.

PERSONAL QUALITIES OF THE COUNSELOR
RELATING TO PROFESSIONAL GROWTH

Beginning Counselor

___ a. An openness to presenting one's work for critique in a variety of supervisory settings (individual, small group, case conferences).

___ b. An ability to "hear" both positive and negative feedback from supervisors and peers.

___ c. An indication that one has the ability to incorporate feedback by appropriate follow-through on supervisory recommendations.

___ d. A willingness to learn through active participation in individual, small group, and other supervisory situations.

More Advanced Counselor

___ a. An ability to initiate pertinent discussion in supervisory sessions.

___ b. An increasing ability to offer an objective analysis of one's performance including both positive and negative observations.

___ c. An ability to identify one's own "growing edge" with respect to specific clients and clients in general.

___ d. An ability to utilize the supervisory process to gain insight into transference and countertransference issues.

Beginning students are not expected to be skilled; they are expected, however, to be *supervisable*. This includes an ability to risk criticism by presenting one's work for critique by peers and supervisors in a variety of formats. More critically, it involves the ability to incorporate the positive and negative aspects of feedback received. Implicit is an acceptance of oneself as a "counselor-in-process" with a capacity to learn about one's strengths and "growing edges," and a willingness to modify attitudes and performance. As experience in supervision proceeds, the more advanced counselor is expected to take more initiative in the critique of his or her counseling work, actively identifying strengths and weaknesses in a given work sample. The advanced counselor is expected to identify needs and to utilize the supervisory process as a means for facilitating personal and professional growth.

SKILLFULNESS IN THE COUNSELING RELATIONSHIP

Beginning Counselor

____ a. Respect for the rights of the client.
____ b. Appropriateness of one's own emotional responses.
____ c. Capacity for empathic response.
____ d. Ability to enter into an empathic, nonpossessive helping relationship.
____ e. An emerging awareness of and trust in the therapeutic process.
____ f. An ability to maintain a professional helping relationship adhering to the concept of the "working alliance."
____ g. An ability to accept the responsibilities inherent in a professional helping relationship.

More Advanced Counselor

____ a. An ability to formulate counseling goals in the light of working diagnosis.
____ b. An understanding of the psychodynamics of the client.
____ c. Skillfulness in dealing with issues of interpretation, resistance, transference, and countertransference within the context of one's theoretical orientation.
____ d. An ability to deal responsibly with termination and/or referral.

A degree of self-knowledge, self-acceptance, and understanding of one's own inner dynamics is required if one is to enter effectively into a counseling relationship dealing with the inner life of another person. The counselor must understand the individuality of the client with experiences, needs, interests, values, and goals that are unique. Counseling involves a professional "working alliance" focused on the needs of the client.

The emotional capacity to enter into an effective counseling relationship is something that course work cannot supply. Frequently enough, personal therapy can help a counselor-in-training to overcome specific "blocks" which interfere with effective counseling. The advanced counselor is expected to be especially sensitive to the dynamics of the counselor-client interaction and to be active in utilizing the supervisory process in guaranteeing the professionalism of the working alliance.

SENSITIVITY TO PASTORAL CONCERNS AND ETHICAL ISSUES

Beginning Counselor

____ a. An understanding of the counseling contract: its limits and responsibilities.
____ b. Respect for the confidential nature of the counseling relationship.
____ c. Sensitivity to the client's pastoral concerns.
____ d. An emerging ability to reflect theologically on one's ministerial (counseling) experience.

More Advanced Counselor

___ a.   Familiarity with ethical issues as outlined in the handbooks of the American Association of Pastoral Counselors and the American Psychological Association.

___ b.   An experiential grasp of one's role as a professional counselor with an understanding of the ethical issues involved in general as well as the special issues involved in one's own counseling setting.

___ c.   An ability to reflect theologically on one's ministerial (counseling) experience.

"Pastoral Counselors are committed to a belief in God and in the dignity and worth of each individual. They accept and maintain in their own personal lives the highest ethical standards, but do not judge others by these standards." These opening sentences set the tone of the Code of Professional Ethics of the American Association of Pastoral Counselors. (For a more complete statement of ethical principles and practices, counselors are referred to the classic work of the American Psychological Association, begun in 1952 and revised and enlarged through the years.) It is assumed that pastoral counseling candidates have a sense of the ethical; these codes make explicit what is regarded as ethical in a wide variety of situations involving professional counselors. Moving beyond the ethical, it is expected that the pastoral counselor will come to view the work of counseling within the framework of the ministry of the Church, developing a keen understanding of counseling as ministry.

FORMATS FOR SUPERVISION

The Loyola program uses three formats for supervision: individual supervision, small-group supervision, and interdisciplinary case seminars. The rationale behind a variety of formats has been to benefit from the advantages of the three different learning modalities.

Individual supervision, based on a dyadic tutorial model, is deeply personal. It allows the supervisor to give consistent, ongoing, uninterrupted attention to the work of the counselor at the counselor's own pace in a noncompetitive setting. The counselor is responsible for setting the agenda for the individual session. It is an hour to utilize the supervisor for ongoing professional growth. Typically, in the Loyola format, individual supervisors require a brief write-up of a case along with a tape recording of a session as the work sample for the supervisory hour, being open to adjustment as the needs of the counselor suggest.

Small-group supervision is based on the premise that participants can learn a great deal from one another as well as from the group supervisor. Making presentations to the group strengthens one's ability to conceptualize the client's problems in clear and concise terms. It also allows for response from a variety of persons, thereby giving the student a broader-based feedback. Frequently, small groups, because of the personal nature of the interaction, develop into strong support groups in which students become increasingly comfortable responding to one another with both positive and negative feedback. The major focus in the Loyola small group is on the counselor's taped session. A two- to three-page summary addressing the following elements, as appropriate, is also required:

I.   *Identifying Information*
     (Name, age, sex, religion, etc.)
II. *Initial Clinical Impression*
     (Description of appearance, behavior, speech, etc.)
III. *Presenting Problem*
IV. *Relevant History and Background*
     (History of presenting problem; brief psychosocial, family, developmental, medical history)
V.   *Initial Assessment*
     a. Clinical and/or diagnostic impressions
     b. Cause of the problem (etiology)
VI. *Summary of Counseling Process to Date*
VII. *Counseling Goals and Recommendations*
VIII. *Critique of Counseling Technique*
     a. What responses were most helpful? (Explain)
     b. What responses would you change? (Explain)
IX. *Pastoral Perspectives*
     (Reflections on theological presuppositions of client; identification of theological themes; formulation of pastoral goals)
X.   *Requests of the Group*
     In what ways can the group be helpful? (Be specific.)

The interdisciplinary case conference has been designed to allow the student the opportunity to present a counseling case in depth, demonstrating to supervisors and peers a level of competence in the total management of a case and at the same time utilizing the group for consultation. A detailed grasp and organization of the case are required: the demonstration of clinical skills, a theoretical grasp of the psychodynamics of the client and the counselor-client interaction, and an understanding of one's own pastoral identity. Participants have the opportunity of learning about a variety of clients through the in-depth presentations of their peers.

A typical case conference takes seventy-five minutes. Prior reading of the report is required, and the first ten minutes are devoted to questions for clarification by members of the group. This is followed by a fifteen- to twenty-minute selection from the taped counseling session. The presenter initiates the forty-minute group discussion by commenting briefly on the session. In the last five to ten minutes the presenter summarizes the input received from the group. The format for the written report is presented below.

INTERDISCIPLINARY CASE CONFERENCES

I. *Identifying Information*
   (Name, age, sex, religion, etc.)

II. *Initial Clinical Impression*
   (Description of appearance, behavior, speech, etc.)

III. *Chief Complaints*
   (Problems as patient sees them, and patient's thoughts as to why they are present; recent crises, if any)

IV. *Personal History and Background*
   a. Childhood, adolescence, adulthood (succinctly!)
   b. Marriage? Description!
   c. Relations to others, e.g., interpersonal, sexual

V. *Mental Status*
   a. Symptoms: e.g., depression, anxiety, phobias, compulsions, rituals
   b. Any psychosis: Hallucinating, delusions, ideas of reference, sensorium, memory, insight, and judgment

VI. *Medical History*
   a. Serious illnesses, operations, head injuries
   b. On medication now? What kind, dosage?
   c. Seeing a psychologist, psychiatrist, counselor now? In the past? How often, how long?

VII. *Psychodynamic Formulation*
   Overall statement of problems, defenses, using material at hand. Comment briefly on transference, countertransference, and resistance issues.

VIII. *Diagnosis, Prognosis, and Recommendations*
   (If counseling is recommended, what goals, how often will client be seen, what kind of counseling?)

IX. *Pastoral Perspectives*
   (Reflections on theological presuppositions of client; identification of theological themes; formulation of pastoral goals)

X. *Requests of the Group*
   In what ways can the group be helpful? (Be specific.)

In the Loyola program the ongoing counseling work is formally evaluated at the end of each semester. The small-group supervisor serves as the clinical director of five to six students, collating reports from individual and agency supervisors and the student's self-evaluation with the candidate's work as presented in the small group. Small-group supervisors discuss their tentative evaluation of students in a collegial setting with a view to keeping some uniformity of expectations regarding students at a given stage of development. This meeting of supervisors also helps to deal with personal issues which might arise in the process of supervision between the supervisor and the candidate. The final step of the evaluation process involves an individual interview of the candidate with the small-group supervisor to discuss the summary written report and any recommendations from the core faculty of supervisors. With a focus on affirming strengths and identifying "growing edges," the evaluation component of supervision serves as a catalyst for professional growth.

In evaluating the supervisory process, pastoral counseling students completing the master's program highlight the relative contribution of the various formats for supervision. One student writes:

> The various forms of supervision have contributed differentially to my growth. Individual supervision has been most helpful in terms of learning the overall process in counseling a client and in checking my diagnoses and therapeutic strategies with each client. Small group was helpful in dealing with particular issues and problems with a client, and in receiving constructive criticism from varying points of view. Both small and large group expanded my "experience" of various types of clients and showed me that there are many different and valid ways to deal with a given client (and that a consideration of those approaches enriches one's approach).

Another candidate focuses on the overall atmosphere of acceptance and support within the supervisory process:

> The gentle approach of the interdisciplinary supervisors in both affirmation and constructive criticisms invites the students to be willing to risk sharing sessions that are less than perfect. There is also the tendency on the part of students to reflect and emulate this same gentleness with each other. The use of two supervisors gives most often concurrence in evaluations and the added view from a different approach.
>
> The small-group setting has all the advantages of large group plus stronger personal relationships and the freedom that those give for confrontation in the airing of issues that do not belong in the larger group. It is a more intimate, relaxed setting. M. B. has been informative, insightful, and honest.
>
> Individual supervision has been a joy from the start. D. L. has been insightful, a good listener, and a supportive counselor. His knowledge and experience are mixed with a healthy sense of humor. There have been occasions when personal issues have arisen which I know are more properly part of therapy. He has been open to that in small doses and that has helped me understand them for grinding in therapy. D. not only listens to my hypotheses; it has been an enjoyable give-and-take experience and I will miss these sessions when it is time to leave.

A number of students point out the growth in *self-knowledge* through the supervisory process, and their *growing ability to assess personal strengths and "growing edges"* in relationship to their counseling work. The following quotations are typical:

> In the various types of supervision I am receiving this year, I have found that I have gotten to know myself much better, because I have had to reveal much of myself in the whole process. I have to look at myself as much as at my client to understand what is going on in the counseling. My strengths and weaknesses are pointed out, so I can see what I bring to the counseling process and which "rough edges" I need to smooth out. I have felt a growing confidence in my own abilities as a result of this experience.

> Supervision has been an excellent opportunity for my own growth as a person. The process has led me to a heightened awareness of my own gifts and limitations, and through discussion with supervisors has left me with a more realistic picture of myself coupled with more realistic expectations. Working with a supervisor on some of my clients' issues that are similar to my own issues has given me new insights, and the acceptance experienced has helped me to better accept myself.

THE SUPERVISORY RELATIONSHIP

Throughout the evaluation of the supervisory process, students stressed the importance of the personal qualities of the supervisor in creating an atmosphere for facilitating their personal and professional growth. From their comments it is clear that they perceive the *modeling of the supervisor* to be an important part of the learning process. The following quotation is representative:

> One of the most gratifying parts of my small-group supervision has been to experience J.C.'s ability to stress the positive aspects in each one of our presentations. He combines this with some very helpful and constructive criticism, so that I leave the class feeling both affirmed and instructed in the whole process.
> J.C. sets the stage where we perform creatively and without pressure. He is affirming, challenging, and nonthreatening. He is a model to students of what a counselor is to be to his clients.

A study of student responses to the supervisory process has led to the formulation of Guidelines for the Evaluation of Supervisors. Although it is used as a rating scale at the end of each semester, the twenty-seven statements also serve as a list of the expectations of supervisors within the program. Although supervisors vary widely in theoretical orientation and in personal styles, the items clearly reflect the "counselor-centered" attitude characteristic of the Loyola program. A study of the items, printed below, also speaks to some of the goals of the supervisory process to be formally discussed in the section to follow:

1. Shows an interest in my personal and professional growth.
2. Accepts and respects me as a person.
3. Recognizes and encourages further development of my strengths and capabilities.
4. Gives me useful feedback when I do something well.
5. Provides me the freedom to develop flexible and effective counseling styles.
6. Encourages and listens to my ideas and suggestions for developing my counseling skills.
7. Provides suggestions for developing my counseling skills.
8. Helps me to understand the implications and dynamics of the counseling approaches I use.
9. Encourages me to use new and different techniques when appropriate.
10. Is spontaneous and flexible in the supervisory sessions.
11. Helps me to define and achieve specific concrete goals for myself during the practicum experience.
12. Gives me useful feedback when I do something wrong.
13. Allows me to discuss problems I encounter in my practicum setting.
14. Pays an adequate amount of attention to both me and my clients.
15. Deals with both content and affect when supervising.
16. Helps me define and maintain ethical behavior in counseling and case management.
17. Encourages me to engage in professional behavior.
18. Helps me to reflect theologically on my counseling.
19. Helps me to deal with my identity as a *pastoral* counselor.
20. Helps me organize relevant case data in planning goals and strategies with my client.
21. Helps me to improve my diagnostic skills.
22. Helps me to formulate a theoretically sound rationale of human behavior.
23. Offers resource information when I request or need it.
24. Helps me develop increased skill in critiquing and gaining insight from my counseling tapes.
25. Allows and encourages me to evaluate myself.
26. Applies his/her criteria fairly in evaluating my counseling performance.
27. Models a "pastoral way of being" as a supervisor.

This checklist suggests notable similarities between the prerequisite characteristics for quality counseling and effective supervision, pointing to the critical importance of the "relationship" between supervisor and supervisee. A recent article
(Loganbill, Hardy, and Delworth 1982, p. 29) suggests that this relationship be viewed
through two perspectives: first as a vehicle through which essential knowledge can be
given in terms of a flow of information, and second in terms of the learning experience
to be derived from the experiencing of the relationship itself. Although a trusting
relationship is essential, "no significant relationship progresses without conflict,
without stress, without stalemates. These conflicts within the relationship, rather than
seen as barriers, can themselves serve as a focus for promoting growth in the
supervisee."

Kell and Mueller (1966) speak about the beginning phase, the developing phase,
and the terminating phase of the supervisory relationship. The beginning phase is
characterized by the development of trust; the second phase begins when the central
issue moves from trust to some other issue. Ekstein and Wallerstein (1972) speak of
the beginning phase, the "middle-game," using a chess analogy, and the end phase.
They characterize the beginning phase in terms of the supervisee's need to make this
new and unfamiliar experience a familiar one. During the first stage the more salient
and *conscious* expectations of both parties are identified and defined. During the
second stage the more *unconscious* and unarticulated expectations are played out
within the relationship.

The termination phase of supervision ought to be one of relative integration in
which the counselor has the opportunity of assimilating the learnings of a given
supervisory relationship. A successful termination process should allow the counselor
to emerge from the supervisory relationship with a "reorganization, integration, a new
cognitive understanding, flexibility, personal security based on awareness of insecur-
ity and an ongoing monitoring of the important issues of supervision." (Loganbill,
Hardy, and Delworth, 1982, p. 19)

IN CONCLUSION

It takes time, trial and error, and years of openness to the supervisory process to move
from technician to artist in the pastoral counseling ministry. Theoretical constructs and
counseling techniques are the brushes and the colors of the pastoral counselor. Each
school of thought offers to the pastoral counselor a variety of constructs which are
helpful for understanding the complexities of the human condition. Each school has
its unique techniques for facilitating the personal growth of the client. Human behavior
and experience are so richly varied, however, that no single school of counseling is
adequate to embrace it all. Though each can point to a measure of therapeutic success,
none is complete in itself. Openness to the insights of all schools of thought is
recommended within the Loyola program as each pastoral counselor develops a style

that is consistent with his or her own way of being and theological understanding of the human person.

REFERENCES

Carkuff, R. R. *Helping and Human Relations,* Vols. 1 and 2. New York: Holt, 1969.

Egan, G. *The Skilled Helper: A Model for Systematic Helping and Interpersonal Relating.* Monterey, Calif.: Brooks/Cole, 1975.

Ekstein, R., and R. S. Wallerstein. *The Teaching and Learning of Psychotherapy,* 2nd ed. New York: International Universities Press, 1972.

"Ethical Principles of Psychologists." Washington, D.C.: APA, 1981.

Fromm, Erich. *The Art of Loving.* New York: Bantam, 1956.

Hennessy, Thomas C. "Reaction," *The Counseling Psychologist,* 10, 1982, 10, 49–52.

Ivey, A. E. *Microcounseling: Innovations in Interviewer Training.* Springfield, Ill.: Charles C Thomas, 1971.

Kagan, N., et al. *Studies in Human Interaction: Interpersonal Process Recall Stimulated by Videotape.* Lansing, Mich.: Educational Publication Services, Michigan State University, December 1967.

Kell, B. L., and W. J. Mueller. *Impact and Change: A Study of Counseling Relationships.* Englewood Cliffs, N.J.: Prentice Hall, 1966.

Loganbill, C., E. Hardy, and U. Delworth. "Supervision: A Conceptual Model," *Counseling Psychologist,* 10, 1982, 3–42.

RECOMMENDED READINGS

Accreditation Procedures Manual for Counselor Education. Washington, D.C.: American Personnel and Guidance Association, 1978.

Cogan, M. L. *Clinical Supervision.* Boston: Houghton, 1973.

Corey, G. *Theory and Practice of Counseling and Psychotherapy,* 2nd ed. Monterey, Calif.: Brooks/Cole, 1982.

Cormier, W. H., and L. S. Cormier. *Interviewing Strategies for Helpers: A Guide to Assessment, Treatment, and Evaluation.* Monterey, Calif.: Brooks/Cole, 1979.

Diagnostic and Statistical Manual of Mental Disorders, 3rd ed. revised. Washington, D.C.: American Psychiatric Association, 1987.

Estadt, B., M. Blanchette, and J. Compton. *The Art of Clinical Supervision: A Pastoral Counseling Perspective.* New York: Paulist Press, 1988.

Frank, J. D. *Persuasion and Healing.* Baltimore: Johns Hopkins Press, 1973.

Gazda, G. M. *Human Relations Development: A Manual for Educators.* Boston: Allyn & Bacon, 1973.

Goldhammer, R. *Clinical Supervision.* New York: Holt, 1977.

Guggenbuhl-Craig, A. *Power in the Helping Professions.* New York: Spring Publication, 1971.

Hess, A. K. (Ed.). *Psychotherapy Supervision: Theory, Research, and Practice.* New York: Wiley, 1980.

Hora, T. "Contribution to the Phenomenology of the Supervisory Process," *American Journal of Psychotherapy,* 1957, 11, 769–73.

Ivey, A., and J. Authier. *Microcounseling: Innovations in Interviewing, Counseling, Psychotherapy, and Psychoeducation,* 2nd ed. Springfield, Ill.: Charles C Thomas, 1978.

Kadushin, A. *Supervision in Social Work.* New York: Columbia University Press, 1976.
Kaslow, F. W., et al. *Issues in Human Service: A Sourcebook in Supervision and Staff Development.* Washington, D.C.: Jossey-Bass, 1972.
MacKinnon, R. A., and R. Michels. *The Psychiatric Interview in Clinical Practice.* Philadelphia: Saunders, 1971.
Mueller, W. J., and B. L. Kell. *Coping with Conflict: Supervising Counselors and Psychotherapists.* Englewood Cliffs, N.J.: Prentice Hall, 1972.
Rogers, C. R. *Freedom to Learn.* Columbus, Ohio: Chas. E. Merrill, 1969.
Schuster, D. B., J. J. Sandt, and O. F. Thaler. *Clinical Supervision of the Psychiatric Resident.* New York: Bruner & Mazel, 1972.
Truax, C. B., and R. R. Carkuff. *Towards Effective Counseling and Psychotherapy.* Chicago: Aldine, 1967.
Whitehead, J. D., and E. E. Whitehead. *Method in Ministry: Theological Reflection and Christian Ministry.* New York: Seabury, 1980.
Williamson, M. *Supervision: New Patterns and Processes.* New York: Association Press, 1961.

CHAPTER FIVE

Beyond Theory and Technique: Reflections on the Process of Becoming

WILLIAM F. HUG, PH.D.

INTRODUCTION

A person becomes a pastoral counselor through many experiences. The pastoral counselor undergoes rigorous theological and psychological training. There has to be a good blend of the theoretical and the experiential. There has to be a mastery of certain basic technical counseling skills. The education of a pastoral counselor includes, however, more than just those components that can be taught didactically. There has to be an emphasis on the personal growth and development of the counselor as well. This chapter will look at the evolutionary process whereby the pastoral counselor integrates varied life experiences into becoming a winsome human being capable of helping others. The education of the best pastoral counselor is as much a matter of the heart as of the head.

Other chapters in this book detail the various theoretical and technical components that are part of the formation of a pastoral counselor. My chapter will focus on those aspects that lie beyond the theoretical and technical: the maturation of the person who is a pastoral counselor. It emphasizes a more intangible process by which the person who counsels is continuing in the process of becoming whole. I will examine how this formation of the individual is aided by interaction with significant others: therapists, mentors, colleagues, and clients.

I will make this chapter a personal narrative. I believe the nature of this chapter requires self-disclosure and I am most at home writing in this vein. I will share facets of my own formation as a pastoral counselor in hopes that my story will serve as a catalyst for the reader. My story is uniquely mine. My journey is not *the* way. It is but one of many ways. I invite the reader to consider the personal nature of the reader's own pilgrimage.

I will discuss four sources of individual maturation. First, I will look at the impact of therapy on the pastoral counselor. I believe that every pastoral counselor should undergo therapy. It is through the very process that we offer to others that we ourselves achieve self-understanding and acceptance. I believe it is only upon experiencing the personal integration that comes through therapy that the pastoral counselor can offer healing to others. Second, I will examine the process whereby the pastoral counselor learns the craft of counseling. I believe that the pastoral counselor must find a unique style. To arrive at such an individual style the pastoral counselor needs the supervision of more experienced clinicians who serve as mentors. Third, I will affirm the importance of colleagues. I believe the pastoral counselor needs a lot of emotional support. The pastoral counselor is obliged to find such support by establishing a network with other therapists. Fourth, I will underscore how much we learn from those we help. I believe that our clients are often our best teachers. They let us know what is most helpful. They show us a clear path to an effective ministry.

My purpose in this chapter, then, is to stress the ways in which we mature as pastoral counselors. As important as theory and technique are, they alone cannot form a competent pastoral counselor. Only by being receptive to the influence of therapists, mentors, colleagues, and clients can the pastoral counselor attain the necessary personal maturation to do the craft of counseling well. Only the pastoral counselor who continues a personal journey toward wholeness can offer to others a ministry of wholeness.

THE PROCESS OF PERSONAL THERAPY: ENHANCING THE SELF

After graduating from seminary in 1962, I was eager to become involved in the realities of parish life. Having spent four years in college and three in seminary, I was aching to move from the theoretical to the practical. I was intrigued with knowing about the daily lives of people beyond the cocoon of the academic world.

The parish I was called to was located in a rural setting, but its 150 members were an eclectic lot. They came from every walk of life and all socioeconomic levels. Nearby was an old factory village of forty houses. The church had been built ninety years previously by the factory owner so that his workers would have a church. The factory had long since disappeared and only a few of the inhabitants of the village attended the church any longer. However, there was an expectation that the minister serve as a quasi-chaplain to the various crises arising in the village.

My ministry, then, was to a varied group of parishioners and to the inhabitants of the village. My first years in the parish I was filled with enthusiasm for the myriad challenges I faced as a pastor—especially as a pastoral counselor. I liked being "involved."

What happened eventually, though, was that I became overwhelmed. I felt inadequate to do the various kinds of crisis intervention counseling I was asked to do. I felt helpless in the face of the complexities of family and marital counseling that came my way. I felt lost. I had no sense of a formal discipline with which to engage people's problems professionally. I didn't know the first thing about setting a counseling contract and working within cleanly defined parameters. Often I became too involved personally, trying to "rescue" people from life's dilemmas.

In my fifth year in the parish I decided to attend a four-day workshop on pastoral counseling at my former seminary. One of the two persons leading the seminar had taught us briefly as seniors about pastoral counseling. New to the seminary himself, he told us frankly that our seminary curriculum had not prepared us adequately for the ministry of pastoral counseling. He had advised us to get further training while in our parishes.

I went to the workshop expecting to have a "fix-it" course in counseling. I was looking for a "how-to" approach from the two leaders. The second leader was a clinical pastoral educator in a hospital setting. I knew he had a reputation for being confrontational. As it turned out, he and I had an intense exchange during the four days. He refused to give me a neat set of guidelines with which to return to my parish as a skillful practitioner. Instead, he invited me to explore my own feelings. Since I was mainly angry at him and since I had a hard time coping with my anger, I experienced the invitation as though given in a strange language. But, in the aftermath of that conference, I began to pay attention to all sorts of feelings I had been repressing: anger, lust, disappointment, envy, fear, depression, dependency, and so on.

In sum, after five years of throwing myself into the external realities of my parish, I began to explore more gingerly the scarier inner realities of my own life. Parallel with this I began to think about leaving that parish. I decided that before I accepted a call to another parish, I needed to get further training in pastoral counseling. At a deeper level I also recognized a need for individual psychotherapy. However, I was scared by that need. I didn't know how to say straight to myself, "I need some therapy," let alone tell the officers of my church that.

In retrospect I arrived at a fairly creative compromise. I asked my church officers for a three months' sabbatical to take a quarter of clinical pastoral education in a nearby state mental hospital. The chaplain supervisor of that program required his students to be engaged in personal therapy as a prerequisite for being accepted into his CPE program.

I share this aspect of my personal pilgrimage to emphasize the integrality of my need for increased pastoral counseling skills with my need for increased self-knowledge through therapy. I had reached a point of professional *and* personal anxiety for which the only appropriate response was a combination of clinical training and personal therapy. The two together offered me the opportunity to grow professionally and personally. This tandem approach offered me a chance to integrate and appropriate aspects of my own life in service to other lives. I was to come to value myself as my primary resource in helping others. For that I needed to know and accept myself in a way I never had allowed. For that I needed the skills of a professional psychotherapist. At that time my chaplain supervisor suggested several psychiatrists who had good reputations as clinicians and who were known to have worked supportively with clergymen as clients. I would make the point that today I might have gone as easily to a pastoral counselor as to a psychiatrist (or to a psychologist, social worker, or lay person) so great has been the proliferation of good therapists in the mental health discipline in twenty years.

I also share this aspect of my personal pilgrimage to make the point that we pastoral counselors are ourselves always in the process of our own growth. Periodically, it behooves us to be in some form of psychotherapy ourselves—and particularly so at the outset of our training as pastoral counselors. There is no substitute for therapy for the therapist. In the beginning of my teaching I used to advise students to get their own therapy. Then I implored them to. Now I state categorically that no one can be a pastoral counselor without having had personal therapy. This helper of others needs to see life as an organic process in which the counselor has to receive nurturance in order to nurture others. This minister has to accept ministry. This therapist has to have had, and always be open to, personal therapy. It would be a travesty to conceive of a therapist as one who has finished growing, who is through wrestling with shadows, who is above the trauma that assails all who live. I can only help insofar as I acknowledge my own recurring need for help. All of us who aspire to treat the wounds of others do so with the greatest authenticity when we have faced our own.

The step I took in entering therapy and clinical pastoral education was a big one for me. I was entering a dual process, which might lead in any number of directions: continuing as a parish pastor; becoming a clinical pastoral educator; specializing as a pastoral counselor; or finding myself called to some vocation I could not at that point anticipate. The step I took was scary for other reasons. I was about to let another human being, my therapist, know me better than I had allowed anyone else to. I was about to allow someone else to minister to me. I was preparing to admit my sense of personal and professional inadequacy. Also I was readying myself to let one other human being in on some shadows that terrified me (I had years to go before I would know that much of my potency lies in those same scary shadows!).

Of course, it was a "growth" step. Up until that point in my ministry I had not integrated into my concept of ministry a sense of the minister's needing help. I had not allowed myself to conceive of my need for personal therapy as evolutionary, as part of my continued growth as a person, a pastor. And I had not seen the potential of role modeling for my parishioners: I had a need for counseling and I would get counseling. I had devised a view of pastoral ministry which allowed no room for growth, for seeking to be ministered to as well as ministering, for unfinishedness. There was no room for "becoming" in my theology and psychology.

The most important discovery I made in my first round of therapy was that I am my own best authority on me. My therapist kept telling me that I could continue forever my pilgrimage in search of "the one who knows." Over time I came to realize that such an odyssey was demeaning. I had to accept what I knew. I had to authenticate my own experience of reality. I could have so much more power if I stopped mortgaging my energy in this pointless search for others wiser than me. To this day I still get tempted to defer to others as more knowledgeable. I bring myself up short and remember how many hours I've wasted in that futile pursuit. I can now celebrate my own hard-won wisdom about life. I can now reflect on life as I experience it and not discount what my own senses tell me.

Being in therapy also taught me from "the inside out" all of the subtle nuances of feelings that a client feels toward a therapist. I know firsthand my resistance: I have gone and not gone to therapy on days when I felt tired, depressed, broke, confused, stuck. I know from experience what it is to love/hate this other one who has heard from my lips things no one else knows about me. I know what it means to accept/test a therapist's parameter. I know how demanding I was that my therapist pay rapt attention to everything I said and did. I know the narcissistic aspects of self-exploration.

Over the years I have always allowed myself the freedom to go back into therapy whenever I needed it. I like the sense I have that there is never a time when I can't use therapy. Recently one of my students brought in a client she has been seeing for two years. Her client is now ninety-one years old. And *her* first experience of therapy was in New York with one of the first lay analysts to come to this country from Vienna. This ninety-one-year-old woman's most exciting new venture: she's learning to swim! "I think yesterday for the first time I got the breathing part right." I like that. I like her commitment to continued growth—physical, emotional, intellectual, and spiritual.

In their classic *The Roots of Psychotherapy,* Whitaker and Malone (1953, p. 166) suggested that in order to do effective work a therapist needs to have certain "slivers" of the client's pathology. These "slivers" enable the therapist to help the client. While working with the client's pathology, the therapist copes with comparable pathology in the therapist's own life. However, at times these "slivers" become telephone poles. And before they reach that magnitude, I need to get to my own therapy.

Therapy is also important for any pastoral counselor in order to sort out all the feelings generated by parents and siblings during the formative years. We pastoral counselors spend a lot of time helping our clients understand their families of origin. It is essential that we understand our own. When I first entered therapy, I made a special trip to reassure my parents that my being in therapy had nothing to do with *them!* That was, of course, nonsense. In all my times of being in therapy I have dealt at some point with my parents. Today I am grateful for that synthesizing process. I claim and value the many contributions my father and mother have made. I realize the sense in which my being a pastoral counselor is an outgrowth of their love and example. Among my earliest memories are long conversations I had with my mother. With her I first experienced the grace of being listened to, understood, and encouraged. I am convinced that her caring attitude is the primal model for the kind of caring I seek to offer others as a pastoral counselor. I learned the value of intuition, of risk, and of making claims on life from my father. I am sure that many of the ways I conduct my practice of pastoral counseling are based on his model of seizing life and enjoying it.

In my own most recent therapy I chose a woman as my therapist. For some time I knew that I wanted to counterbalance the male dominance of my training and previous therapies. Also, for some time I have worked with a female cotherapist, doing therapy with couples, families, and groups and conducting supervisory seminars for burgeoning pastoral counselors. I have been envious of the good things my cotherapist gives to our clients and students, and I have wanted to nurture my own anima. Therefore, I began again the scary/exciting process of therapy.

This time around I allowed myself the "luxury" of support. I found out how neat it was to focus not so much on growth or change but just on being. After several months I told my therapist: "I chose you because you have a reputation for being surgical. So far I haven't experienced much of that side of you. I like what I *am* getting—your support, your caring, your acceptance of me mean very much to me. I'm just surprised I haven't experienced your surgical side much."

My therapist's response was a compassionate statement I treasure: "Maybe you've had enough surgery."

I cried. And in my tears was born a deeper appreciation than ever before that therapy doesn't have to be an adversarial experience to be profoundly liberating. In my therapy this time I got a new respect for the importance of just *being with* my clients. We helping-relations professionals feel helpless if we can't be helpful! Our quandary, however, is how to be, not do. People seek our "help" because their "being" has been interrupted. We fail *their* curative process when we start *doing* for them instead of *being* with them.

In this section I have spoken about enhancing the self of the therapist through personal therapy. I feel there is a lot to be received also through the process of spiritual direction. When I began teaching in the Loyola program, I didn't know what the term *spiritual direction* meant. Now for several years I have been a "directee." I meet with my spiritual director, a Roman Catholic sister, about every six weeks. She skillfully and winsomely monitors my journey with God. She suggests certain Scripture passages or new ways of approaching prayer. She has helped me see the value of keeping a journal.

Through this process my spirituality has deepened. Consequently, my work as a therapist has been affected. I have discovered that I pray silently to God during most therapy sessions. This has evolved naturally over time. It was not something I set out to do intentionally. These prayers of my heart are that God will help me to be present to the client. These are prayers that I may discern what to say—or not say—that will be helpful. These are prayers that come out of my sense of inadequacy: "God, help me. I'm not sure what this person needs. Show me Your way through to the core." These are prayers for recognition: "Lord, help me to see You in this one before me."

If my therapy helped me to take myself seriously as a person and professional, my spiritual direction has helped me to take seriously that what I do as a therapist is ministry. And as a minister, I need God's help continually to offer healing, affirmation, confrontation, and forgiveness to my clients. As a minister, I need to set aside times for spiritual renewal and reflection. I go for a day or two at a time to spiritual retreat centers. I need to do this about six times a year. Because I'm engaged in the "talking cure," I need times of solitude and silence. I relish in those times the purging of all the pain I've heard and the infilling of the Spirit. I find the Eucharist most meaningful at such times.

I think the best of all possible worlds for the maturation of any pastoral counselor is to combine personal therapy with spiritual direction. One is not a substitute for the other.

We pastoral counselors do our best work when we pay attention to our own becomingness. We do our best therapy when we conceive of ministry in a way that allows for our own neediness. Any other approach smacks of superiority to those who come to us in need. The superior stance is not only not helpful—it can be dangerous. The pastoral counselors who are unaware of their own inner conflicts may inflict their clients with projections of their own unclaimed shadows. We demonstrate our belief in the healing aspects of therapy by submitting our own lives to the process. The ultimate resource I have to work with is myself—and the clearer I am about this complex being I am, the more useful I am as a "resource person." The knowledge of myself I gain in therapy is to me the most precious possession I have to offer my clients.

THE PROCESS OF MENTORING: LEARNING THE CRAFT

After my initial quarter of clinical pastoral education I decided to enter a two-year residency in the same hospital. I left my parish after seven years with mixed emotions. I had grown fond of my parishioners and felt a personal loss in leaving them. I also knew I had to leave in order to pursue my own growth. I was both scared and excited about that. I left with my congregation's blessing: they recognized and supported my need to further my pastoral counseling skills. They had taught me all they could. Now I needed the honing skills of experienced clinicians.

During the next seven years I was engaged intensively in "retooling" myself as a specialist in the ministry of pastoral counseling. I completed the two-year clinical pastoral education residency in a state mental hospital. Concurrent with the second year I was also involved in a one-year training program in pastoral counseling. This program, offered by a pastoral counseling agency, prepared me more directly for work with persons on an outpatient basis. In that same year I began working as a pastoral counselor for the agency. In succeeding years I was to complete my doctorate in human development, amass a lot of supervised clinical experience, and continue my own therapy in a variety of modalities: personal, marital, and group.

In this "retooling" process I was influenced by a series of clinical supervisors. These included a psychoanalyst, psychiatrists, psychologists, and pastoral counselors. Each made an impact on my evolving personal style as a therapist. Each was able to hone my skills. All of them I acknowledge as supervisors. Only a few of them, however, were what I call mentors. A mentor is someone special, someone whose impact on one's life transcends supervision. A mentor is a combination of wise counselor, trusted teacher, guru, and spiritual guide. Not all supervisors are mentors. More precisely, a supervisor may be experienced as a mentor by one student and not by another. Mentoring involves a sense of being singled out. A supervisor may create an aura in which a student feels summoned to become the best there is to be. Or, a student may single out one supervisor above all others and through a mixture of transference and idolatry allow that supervisor to make a more profound impact than others. Either way something special happens to the student. The student experiences a quantum leap in personal and professional growth. The stakes are suddenly higher than they have ever been: life is perceived as deadly serious. And the subject the student seeks to learn from the mentor takes on the mystique of an art, a craft. The mentor challenges the student to take this craft very seriously. The mentor models for the student what being a craftsman is all about. The mentor imparts to the student much more than theory and technique. The mentor calls forth in the student a love for the nuances of his craft. The mentor models "involvement," an intense commitment to doing the best work.

In the preceding chapter Barry Estadt discusses the important role of supervision in our training as pastoral counselors. In this section I want to take a slightly different (and, I hope, complementary) tack. I want to focus on the *mentoring* aspects of my retooling process, and I want to suggest that for every pastoral counseling student there can be the very special experience of encountering a supervisor who challenges the student to become an artisan, a craftsman: to enter a realm of ministry that lies beyond theory and technique.

Though there are several mentors I could cite, the limitations of space suggest I focus on the one mentoring experience that was most catalytic for me. During the time I was in graduate school and working for a pastoral counseling agency, I participated for two years in a weekly supervisory seminar conducted by Sheldon B. Kopp, a Washington, D.C., psychologist. Shelly's seminar included psychologists, pastoral counselors, and laywomen. Each therapist was responsible for presenting to the seminar samples of clinical work. Unlike other supervisory seminars in which I have participated, however, we did not utilize verbatims or tapes of our work. Instead, we invited persons who were currently or recently our clients to be present. The supervision focused on the therapeutic alliance between the client and therapist. Shelly zeroed in on both the transference and countertransference aspects of the therapeutic relationship. The therapist usually felt more "on the spot" than the client. Shelly helped us confront the unclaimed or unaccepted shadows in ourselves which contributed to impasses with our clients. It was at times a painful, searing exposure of our own hidden selves. More than once I left Shelly's office knowing more than I wanted to about my own darker side—and about how my refusal to own my "darker brother" got in the way of being an effective therapist.

Being with Shelly Kopp is a unique event. One of my colleagues describes Shelly's mentoring technique as that of a Marine boot camp drill sergeant: "While you're at Paris Island, he's the meanest S.O.B. you ever want to be around. But when you get in actual combat and hit the beaches, you're damned glad you had him as your drill instructor!"

Shelly is very intense in his commitment as a mentor. He has a religious zeal for teaching his students how to be therapists. "I only want to teach you all I know about this work," he would say. Shelly talked a lot about doing *impeccable* work. I was impressed by the phrase. To do *impeccable* work means to pay strict attention to the process of therapy. It means setting parameters with clients and sticking to them. It means following the client's lead, going where the client needs to go. It means being vulnerable with the client while never neglecting the professional stance needed to serve the client. To do *impeccable* work requires clinical judgments as to when to stay in the here and now with the client and when to delve into personal/family history, when to utilize dreams and when to invoke fantasy, when to share out of my own life and when to allow silence to work its way in the room.

As I have brooded upon Shelly's call to do impeccable work, I realize it invokes two facets of being a pastoral counselor which are essential to any training paradigm. One is competence, the other is passion. First I will discuss how Shelly's mentoring summoned me to competence.

When I was under supervision with Shelly, I found myself wanting to get on with the business of learning how to do this work well. I became dissatisfied with half measures. I wanted to master a craft which I could then count on in any given situation. I remember once when I was floundering all over the place on a given case, Shelly asked me if I had read a key book on the subject. I answered lamely that I always wanted to but had not. He shot back, "Why don't you stop hanging around the fringes and become a first-rate therapist?" It stung! It helped. I was being invited—exhorted— to competence of the first order. One of the things for which I am most grateful to Shelly and my other mentors is that they always expected me to be their peer. I could not hide very long under some mantle of apprentice. I was to become their equal— nothing less. That is a true gift from the mentor to the pastoral counseling student. If I am to do this craft, let me do it competently.

Dr. Ernest T. Campbell conveyed exactly this point to the graduating class in his 1978 commencement address at Princeton Theological Seminary:

I stand in awe of the memory and agility of the short-order cook. Frequently I find occasion to have breakfast in one of the many luncheonettes that dot the island of Manhattan. My order is usually the same: "Two eggs over light, whole wheat toast, butter on the side, coffee with the eggs." You wouldn't believe the number of ways in which that order can be fouled up!

Now, if upon receipt of that order the cook resorts to a manual on food preparation and commences to take two hands to break a single egg, I don't relax and read *The New York Times*. If, however, as is usually the case, the cook cracks and empties the eggs with a nonchalant flip of the wrist without looking, and backhand yet, while moving gingerly to flip pancakes here, butter a bagel there and slice a few potatoes in the meantime, my mind is at ease and I enjoy the paper. I am in the hands of a professional! *I have been ministered to by competence!* (p. 6)

The whole point dealing with competence is this: the burgeoning pastoral counselor aspires to a professional competence that can be relied on in all situations. The pastoral counselor needs to arrive at that level of ability where the counselor feels in charge of the craft. Not that the counselor has all the answers—far from it—but the counselor knows how the best work is done, and is committed not to depart from that level of skillfulness. What I value about how my mentors introduced me to competence is that they showed it working in their own lives and challenged/invited me to have it work for me.

The first thing I learned from Shelly Kopp was that ours is a craft, that I am privileged to be part of a guild that takes this work seriously, that there are ways to do therapy and ways not to do it, that to become the best that I can I seize the reins, set limits, recognize boundaries, carve out parameters—and stay within them. What I value about Shelly's call to competence is that he invited me to get at it from "within," to find my own style which would work for *me*. The best mentoring is not being taught someone else's way to do a craft, but being given a chance to discover your own way.

The second facet I recognized in Shelly's call to do impeccable work is passion. By passion I mean a total involvement of the self of the therapist with the self of the client. There is for me a sense of privilege when a client begins to share from the core. I feel like I am treading on holy ground. I recall the Psalmist's words "deep calling unto deep" when my heart is touched by what comes to me from the client's heart. My passion in doing pastoral counseling is a recognition that I am dealing with the most sacred aspects of another person's life. I am moved when a client tells me something and then adds, "I have never told anybody else that." I feel touched, humbled, and in awe of such trust.

I speak of passion because we live in a technological age. We live in an era that values theory and technique, the rational approach, problem solving. We pastoral counselors are tempted to sell our souls for a "mess of pottage," a potpourri of quick fixes. We are tempted to treat our clients as problems and to see what we offer as solutions. I feel strongly that in such an age we are called to be craftsmen who deeply honor the individuality of the persons who seek our help. We are called to join their pilgrimage, not to give them a map.

What I liked about Shelly Kopp's call to do impeccable work was its intensity. I felt summoned to join a craftsmen's guild and to respect what we handle as sacred. In years since when others have looked to me as a mentor, I have felt it incumbent upon myself to convey more than mere didactic information. I am responsible for conveying no less than a contagion, an excitement about what we do.

I recall a phrase from a poem by James Dickey when he spoke at the 1976 presidential inaugural festivities: "Lord, let me shake with purpose!" I like that. Ours is a calling to something more than merely being technicians. In fact, we as pastoral counselors can call on a rich heritage captured in the phrase, "the cure of souls." Ours *is* more than a "fix-it" enterprise. There ought to be about us more than an automobile body shop repair mentality. It is a travesty to call ourselves pastoral counselors and not feel the privilege of grappling with the very stuff of the human heart.

Apropos of passion in our counseling, for some years now I have admired the artistry of Fred Begun, the timpanist of the National Symphony Orchestra. He goes about his playing with an intensity which is compelling. Even his quiet, unobtrusive grace notes in a score exude passion. Fred brings to each note the best he is. So, too, our work as pastoral counselors can display an artistry as we touch each counselee's life.

I have always liked to think of what I do as a kind of art form more than a science or a technique. Early in my own formation process, I wrote the following (1973):

> It is helpful to me to conceive of myself as an artist. That frees me from the confinements of our technical society, of modules, of dogmas, of rote theories. I do my best work when I follow my intuition. I have apprenticed myself to "senior artists." And there is always the ambivalence for me as an apprentice—I want to learn their way, yet my own yearns to be born. And for a while longer I will be an apprentice. In the end, though, what I want is a discipline, a dance, a celebration!

Aubernon Waugh, emphasizing the author's privilege to write about the private side of public characters, tells this vignette (Koenig, 1980):

> There is a famous story about Lord Curzon, when he was Viceroy of India, arriving in the hall of a great house. A little child was watching him from the top of the stairs, and he saw Lord Curzon, who thought he was alone, lift up the tails of his dress coat and do a little dance before the fire. That is what we write about, the dance before the fire. (p. 89)

What we have to do, then, is treat with a sense of reverence what our clients choose to reveal to us. And to do so without passion is unthinkable.

To complete this section on the mentoring process, I want to emphasize that it is just as important to leave a mentor as to find that person in the first place. It is in our leaving that we claim our own style. It is in our leaving that we claim our own potency. It is in our leaving that we fully become who we set out to be. A large part of maturing in this field has to do with giving up mentors. It's hard. It's frightening. I remember telling a colleague about my struggle to leave Shelly's seminar. My colleague listened and then caringly said, "It's hard to give up a daddy, especially when you're getting good stuff."

We leave our mentors and become ourselves. Otherwise, there is no closure to our formation, to our apprentice stage. One way to get clear how important it is to leave our mentors is to think about what we would be like if we didn't. I have been in the presence of "third-generation types." These are people who continue to copy the mannerisms of their mentors' mentors. At a conference once I was talking with a pastoral counselor I hardly knew. Suddenly, I felt an eerie echo of someone else. I was haunted by the familiarity of certain mannerisms: the way this person cocked his head; the clipped cadence of his words; a certain macho, menacing stance; the way he held his cigar. I thought, "My God, that's two generations removed! He got this from his supervisor, who in turn copied an original!" The "tragedy" here, of course, is that the pastoral counselor wasn't free to become himself. He hadn't worked away from another's style. He was so mesmerized by the outward trappings of his mentor that he failed to take his own inner trip to maturity.

I have written elsewhere (Hug 1976) of the freedom which comes in "moving on":

> My best day is when I stop apprenticing myself to any "master." When I forget how Jarvis or Chuck or Joe or Shelly "do" it. When I allow myself to make my own "mistakes." When I allow the playful side to overcome the cautious side. When I don't seek refuge in preconceptions of how I should be in the hour. On such a day there is a flow in my work uninhibited by the ghosts of the "masters" with which I sometimes people my office. (pp. 16-17)

Recently one of my students presented an excellent tape of his work. I commented on how much he had changed since the last time I had heard his work. I told him I liked how he had risked himself with the client. He smiled and said, "I felt like I threw away all I learned from my supervisors! I was just me."

Mentors are people we sometimes desperately want to imitate—that *is* part of our becoming. Later what we realize is so compelling about a mentor is that the mentor is resolutely a unique person. The real travesty would be ending as a carbon copy of someone else. What we aspire to is not the mentor but that person's freedom to be a distinct self. It is the ultimate gift of a mentor to set us free to be ourselves. I don't mean to suggest the process is ever complete. We go on becoming ourselves.

THE PROCESS OF COLLEGIALITY:
ESTABLISHING A SUPPORT NETWORK

The art of pastoral counseling is a draining craft. We constantly need to replenish ourselves in this work. Collegiality is the oxygen we breathe. Without it we become exhausted, disoriented, useless. It is commonplace to recognize the perils of isolation for the parish pastor; loneliness is the number-one enemy of the parish clergy. It is not always as clearly articulated that loneliness is the enemy of the pastoral counselor. To do this work well requires a network of supportive colleagues. I need fellow therapists to laugh and cry with. I need them to brag about my brilliance and to bemoan my stupidity. I need colleagues with whom to celebrate my victories and to mourn my defeats. Most of all, I need them to help me keep centered, to stay honest with myself about my own best work.

In this section I want to make a brief for the importance of a support network for the pastoral counselor. As before, I will cite my own experience in hopes that it will be catalytic for the reader to think about the ways in which the reader personally establishes collegiality. There are many ways to do this. I will suggest a few I have found essential.

I speak so adamantly about the necessity for collegiality because as a private practitioner I know its importance to me. While I was in the supervisory seminar with Shelly Kopp, I got the "bug" to be in my own practice. I had spent seven years as a parish pastor and seven as a staff member of two pastoral counseling agencies. The next step seemed to be in my own office. Moreover, I longed to have an office of my own where I could surround myself with my own furnishings, books, and personal trappings. In the process of entering private practice I became certified by the state as a psychologist. I resolved to surround myself with a support network made up of clinicians from various mental health disciplines so that my private practice would rest on a firm foundation of collegiality.

I have found that I need three sources of collegiality: consultants upon whom I can call to help me with difficulties encountered in my clinical case work; individual friends and colleagues who nourish me as I seek to nurture others; and small groups of peers with whom to share an ongoing sense of support. (Note: there are also larger realms of collegiality we all need, like national accrediting associations; I choose in this section to detail the more immediate and personal sources I have found helpful.)

The kind of consultant I need is a person with whom I can talk as openly about myself as about my client. I want to be able to talk about being stuck. I want to disclose my lack of knowledge without feeling defensive. I need to be able to speak as openly about countertransference issues as those of transference. I utilize psychiatrists, psychologists, social workers, and pastoral counselors as consultants. The common denominator is this: I need to be able to share all my crazy places with a consultant. If a consultation is to be really helpful, some healing has to occur in me, for that I have to feel comfortable enough to confess my blunders, to own my side of whatever impasse has developed with my client.

Sometimes I need only talk to a consultant by phone. More often I need to see the consultant in person. Sometimes I need to have the consultant see my client. Sometimes my client and I find it useful to see the consultant together. Because the last model cited is the one with which most pastoral counselors are least familiar, I will spend some time elaborating on the three-way consultation.

I was introduced to the three-way consultation in my own formation process. In the traditional consultation two counselors often talk about an absent counselee. In the three-way consultation the counselor and counselee seek the one-time services of a second counselor as a consultant and the focus is on the therapeutic relationship. Counselor and counselee talk about their relationship: the consultant is a catalyst for them to discover and work through any impasse.

I did my doctoral dissertation in this area (Hug, 1975) and I have utilized three-way consultations in my work with clients. I have often served in the role of consultant for colleagues who want to avail themselves of the potency of this type of consultation.

To me the key is that the counselor must have a high degree of trust in the person who serves as consultant. I have to feel cared for by that person in order to become vulnerable in the presence of consultant and client. I have to know that I am valued as a person and as a professional to expose myself to the critique of my work, which inevitably comes out of a three-way talk.

In an article entitled "Partners in Psychotherapy" John Warkentin (1967, p. 7) suggested that it is the secrecy, the aloneness, the isolation of the therapist in this work which causes the therapist stress and eventually causes stress in the client-therapist relationship. Warkentin pointed out that most schools of psychotherapy are based on the medical model, yet at a very critical juncture, namely, the utilization of consultants for situations that the therapist cannot solve alone, many therapists fail to follow this model. Warkentin proposed that therapists, precisely because they become involved emotionally (I would say passionately) with clients in the process of trying to help them, need to employ consultants. Warkentin furthermore advocated the use of the three-way consultation at these junctures of therapy: during the intake phase; at one-year intervals; whenever an impasse occurs; before changing the mode of therapy (say, from individual to group); and during the termination phase of therapy.

Whenever I utilize the three-way consultation with a client, I insist on paying half of the consultant's fee. By doing this I say to my client that I have as much to learn from the consultation as the client does. When our presenting problem to the consultant is that we have reached a therapeutic impasse, I also am telling my client that I am as much responsible as the client is. In effect, we are seeking "marriage counseling" on our troubled therapeutic alliance. I need to own my part. Splitting the consultant's fee is one way I admit to parity in the impasse.

In addition to the on-call use of consultants, I also experience collegiality through my association with other therapists. I need both one-on-one and small-group experiences of support.

When I entered private practice, I was warned by many about the perils of loneliness. People told me I could really miss the colleagueship of an agency or clinic setting. The truth is, however, that I have enjoyed more collegiality in these recent years than in the previous seven years working for an agency or the seven years before that in the parish. The reason is that from the start of my practice I built into my schedule some time to be with colleagues. I meet with a pastoral counseling colleague, and he and I have evolved a friendship which is precious to us both. Our time together is sacrosanct. Only our families have prior claims to interrupt us from our discipline of friendship. We have reached a point of intimacy where we can talk about whatever we need to: our marriages, our parenting, our victories and defeats as therapists, our "stuck" points with clients, our spiritual journeys, our aging—whatever we need to. I also meet with a cotherapist. She and I have worked together in a variety of therapeutic and supervisory modes. We reserve the time not only to discuss cases we are currently working on conjointly, but also to present cases out of our individual practices.

In addition to these experiences of collegiality, I have been meeting monthly with four other psychologists. We have developed a level of intimacy where our case presentations involve a high degree of personal disclosure and vulnerability. Prior to this group I used to meet monthly with three pastoral counselors. The same dynamics pertained. The key is developing a level of trust where we can drop the *persona* masks and be persons who need each other. Most recently I have begun to meet with a small group whose function is to support one another in our common spiritual pilgrimages. I find that we are combining spiritual, psychological, and theological themes into a rich experience of mutuality.

In addition to the above I meet at least twice a month with other pastors and therapists for lunch just to sustain and nourish my personal life. I look forward to talking theology, therapy, and current reading. I do not believe any pastoral counselor can do this demanding, draining work without receiving a lot of encouragement and self-nourishment. There is a need for collegiality whether the pastoral counselor's setting is a parish, an agency, or private practice. We can serve others' growth only when we tend well to our own.

THE PROCESS OF COPILGRIMAGE: BEING TAUGHT BY THOSE WE SEEK TO HELP

To this point I have shared how my formation as a pastoral counselor has been influenced by certain significant others: those who have had me as a client in therapy, those who have supervised and mentored me, and those who are my colleagues. I want to speak now of those who know my clinical work most intimately and who have shaped my style most directly: my clients. All the personal therapy, mentoring, collegiality, not to mention theory and technique, come to fruition when I take my place as therapist opposite this person who is seeking my help. What I do as a pastoral counselor when the door is shut and it is just me and my client is the real test of my ability as a therapist. Over the years I have come to have a profound respect for my clients as my teachers.

One of the privileges of being a *pastoral counselor* is that we belong to a tradition that values the two-wayness of ministry. We know deep in our soul that the one who ministers to a congregation is also ministered to by them. The whole concept of the Church as *koinonea,* a fellowship of kindred spirits who bring healing and support to each other, undergirds the pastoral nature of our work. We pastoral counselors know that our counselees help us get on with our becoming even as we help them. We know they often keep us sane. They give us courage. They inspire us to get on with our own developmental tasks. They humble us, anger us, make us think, touch us, and keep us growing. They can move us to tears, to laughter, to shared silence. They meet us where we are and we are transformed in the meeting.

We hear a lot about copilgrimage in pastoral counseling today. It is the notion that we as counselors do not have all the answers. Rather, we seek to share a journey with our clients. Ours is a mutual pilgrimage. I sometimes picture what I do with a client this way: we have been up in the hills prospecting all day. Now it is night. We are gathered about the intimacy of a fire. The two of us take turns rummaging about in each other's knapsacks. I pick out a nugget the client has trucked down from the hills. I hold it up to the firelight and ask: "I wonder what this could be? I wonder what ore is in this piece?" Sometimes the client holds up to the light a nugget from my knapsack and I suddenly see something I hadn't seen up in the hills.

I relish the two-wayness of the work I do. I am grateful to each client who has been part of my formation as a therapist and a person. My clients have been and continue to be my teachers. Often the friendly ghosts of former clients inhabit my room and inform my work with current clients.

I think of Jane, who taught me once and for all that it is all right for me to be supportive of my clients. I had been in a phase where I felt the most helpful therapy was to leave *everything* up to the clients. Let them discover their own strengths. I was not in any way going to reassure them or reinforce their discoveries. It was an excess of a good thing: previously, I had been overly supportive, overly concerned about clients' welfare, so I had cut back, but to absurd lengths.

One day when Jane seemed floundering, I recalled her strengths. I reminded her of some progress she had made to take better care of herself. I let her know I valued her and felt supportive of her. Then I asked her how she felt about my "new" attitude. She grinned impishly and said, "Taking care of people is no sin!" I felt absolved and I resolved to be more flexible in my use of supportive therapy.

I think of David, a client who struggled with self-esteem. I was in supervision at the time and was aping one of my supervisor's characteristics—his clever use of one-liners to go to the core of an issue. The trouble was that I lacked a sense of appropriateness in using "zingers," and mine came out as venomous sarcasm, unredeemed by any sense of humor or compassion. After enduring this treatment from me for a few sessions, David confronted me: "Look, I grew up with a father who put me down every chance he had. I don't appreciate that same treatment from you. The next time you get sarcastic with me, I'm leaving. I didn't come here for that."

I can now use one-liners with flair—and care. I have a sense of when they are suitable and when they only serve to hurt someone who wouldn't be seeing me in the first place if there wasn't already too much hurt in life. I am grateful to David. I don't think any supervisor could have brought home that point as he did. It came out of our being together, out of his pain and my sense of how I was only adding to it. And, of course, it came when I was threatened with a client's walking out on me!

I think of Nancy. I was in one of my self-disclosing phases. Almost anything a client told me triggered an anecdote out of my own life. I was sharing as fast as I lived. One day after Nancy told me something that triggered a memory of my own, I said, "Have I told you about . . . ?" I got that far before she interrupted me with "Probably!" We spent the rest of that session exploring her feelings about my using her time to talk about myself. I now know that self-disclosure is a more powerful therapeutic tool when used sparingly, discreetly. I am grateful that Nancy brought me up short on this key point.

I also feel profound respect for what clients teach my students. When a student brings a client to one of my seminars, I often end up marveling at just how right that client is for that student at that point in the latter's formation.

In one of my seminars, Dick, a parish pastor seeking to improve his skills as a counselor, played an audio tape. We listened, and we told him he sounded patronizing. The next time Dick presented, the other students told him the same thing. He sounded like a critical parent speaking to his client. He was stuffy. There was no sense of his presence with his client.

I asked Dick to invite this client to come with him the next time he presented. I have great trust in this three-way consultation model, especially for its leveling effect on the counselor: in the absence of the client, the counselor may pontificate and posture, whereas in the client's presence the same counselor has to come to grips with how the client is affected by the counselor's style.

On the day Dick brought in his client, he seemed even more uptight than usual. Dick began by telling the seminar how long he had been seeing Carole in therapy. He rambled on about his concern for Carole's lack of progress in therapy. He documented Carole's "deficiencies" as a client: she still seemed as depressed as when she began therapy eight months before; she hadn't resolved her separation from her husband; one of her children still acted up in school. And so on.

All this while Carole was looking down at the floor. She seemed to have tuned out Dick. Eventually I interrupted Dick and said: "Carole, how does it feel to disappoint your therapist? How does it feel not to measure up to his expectations?" Her eyes filling with tears, Carole looked at me appreciatively and said, "Sometimes I feel like I get in the way of what he wants to do to me—no, I mean for me."

I told Carole, "No, the slip of the tongue is important. *To* you is what it feels like!"

Carole laughed.

I asked, "How do you feel about Dick when he tries to *do* therapy to you?"

Thoughtfully, Carole looked at Dick and said: "I feel like you are pushy. It's like you can't wait for me to find my own way. And when you're pushy, you get in my way!"

Dick responded: "I guess a lot of people have been trying to tell me that. I haven't wanted to hear it. What hurts most is that I could never stand to see a parish pastor push his flock instead of being with them, and now I'm doing that very thing myself."

That three-way consultation wasn't a magical cure-all. Dick still struggles with his tendency to push his clients. His tapes still give off that old patronizing hum now and then. But the point is that Dick first was willing to look at his pushy style when Carole confronted him. What he wouldn't hear from his supervisor or his colleagues, Dick did finally hear from Carole. His client became an important part of his formation: she became his teacher.

A review of current introductory texts on the conduct of psychotherapy reveals a surprising lack of reference to the role of the client in the formation of the therapist. This is a glaring omission, pertaining across all the lines of mental health disciplines and all schools of therapy, even though all the various disciplines and schools of therapy are heavily dependent on the role of the client as teacher. All our educational efforts come to fruition when the counselor is alone with a client. There is the real test of what the therapist knows. There is the real proof of how the therapist can be helpful. And there the real shaping process occurs. The blending of the therapist's personal, didactic, and supervised clinical experience occurs in the presence of a client. Some texts talk about how the therapist gives subtle reinforcements to certain client behaviors, but none speaks about the process in reverse. Our clients are constantly shaping and reinforcing our behaviors. They let us know what works. They tell us when we are on target. They teach us what *is* warm, empathic, and unconditional positive regard—*for them*. They show us the way to help them with whatever concerns brought them in our door to begin with.

Most of us owe a lot to our clients, especially the ones we "practiced on" during our training. Often our clients made real what our training only hinted at. Our clients continue to offer us the unique opportunity to learn by doing. They knock off some of the rough edges. They bring us back full circle to the raw core of our own existence which underlies all we have accrued in our formal learning. Beyond theory and technique, thank God, sits the real live client. As much as our own therapists, mentors, and colleagues, our clients teach us to do pastoral counseling.

CONCLUSION

Mentors, clients, therapists, family, colleagues—all have been part of my becoming. And the process, once begun, continues. I come to trust it, interrupt it, lose it, and then stumble back, as though tracking an overgrown trail through the woods.

Now those who influence my becoming are a diverse lot. They include writers (Lillian Hellman, Irene Claremont de Castillejo, Henri Nouwen, Morton Kelsey, John Fowles), musical composers (Berlioz, Dvořák, Shostakovich, Willie Nelson), artists (Goya, El Greco), movies, plays, family, and friends. I find I read fewer books on psychotherapy, more on literature, theology, poetry. I am turned off by the proliferation of *psychobabble* in our culture. I would rather read the experiences of a few human beings who have created valued words out of their anguish and grace. Essentially, what I seek is that with which I started out on this pilgrimage: the raw core of myself. What I crave in whatever book, friend, piece of music, or dream I come across is that which helps me become the person I was born to be. I want a congruence between my inner and outer selves.

As I write this, I am sitting at the table in the home of a cousin who lives in a small New England town. I have come here to renew a relationship which goes back to our mutual childhoods. This weekend we have gone to the graves of our grandparents, a cherished uncle, and a close family friend. We have wept together, laughed, and retraced familiar ancestral paths. We have honored our similar journeys to finding our individual identities. We have claimed each other again as spiritual kin, as fellow pilgrims. We have renewed our deep trust in the mystery of family, blood, love. And I find again that wholeness which comes whenever I experience intimacy with myself and those I love.

What I know is that whenever I follow my intuitive side, I feel my best and do my best work. I do my best when I have paid attention to my own process of becoming. The image I have in mind is that of descending a mountain. It is a descent with the effort of an ascent! Effort because I have to let go of more and more to reach the core of my being. Descent because I have to come down from all those idealisms which entrap me. I have to let go of what I insist life be in order to touch life as it is. I am aware of becoming more lonely and more connected at the same time! Lonely because I let go of my pretensions. Connected because along the way I *meet* others who have done the same.

I find my new posture with myself allows a new stance toward my clients. I no longer feel a need to do magic, to cure, to dazzle! *I* am no longer the focus of the therapy I do. I am drawn to my clients as they grant me the privilege of knowing them.

It is enough for me to be touched by their struggles and triumphs. Their journeys whet my appetite to continue my own. As I allow them to become new persons, I continue to become my own new person. As I allow them to know both their darker and lighter sides, so I know mine. As I allow them to follow the deep urgings of their dreams, so I become what I too am dreaming. And the process goes on!

REFERENCES

Campbell, E. T. "They Also Serve Who Lead," *The Princeton Seminary Bulletin*, II, no. 1, New Series (1978).

Hug, W. F. Personal Journal, 1973.

———."A Comparison of Two Psychiatric Consultation Processes Involving the Participation or Nonparticipation of the Female Client." Unpublished doctoral dissertation, University of Maryland, 1975.

———."Reflections on Goya's 'Black Paintings,' " *Voices: The Art and Science of Psychotherapy*, 11, no. 4 (1976).

Koenig, R. "A Handful of Mud: Aubernon Waugh's War on Manners," *Harper's*, 261, no. 1567 (December 1980).

Warkentin, J. "Partners in Psychotherapy," *Voices: The Art and Science of Psychotherapy*, 3, no. 2 (1967).

Whitaker, C. A., and T. P. Malone. *The Roots of Psychotherapy*. New York: Blakiston Co., 1953.

RECOMMENDED READINGS

Buechner, Frederick. *The Sacred Journey*. San Francisco: Harper, 1982.

Campbell, Will. *Brother to a Dragonfly*. New York: Seabury, 1977.

Castillejo, Irene C. De. *Knowing Woman*. New York: Harper, 1974.

Fowles, John. *A Maggot*. Boston: Little, Brown, 1985.

Hellman, Lillian. *Three: An Unfinished Woman, Pentimento, Scoundrel Time*. New York: Little, Brown, 1979.

Heschel, Abraham Joshua. *A Passion for Truth*. New York: Farrar, Straus & Giroux, 1973.

Jung, Carl. *Memories, Dreams, Reflections*, rev. ed. Recorded and edited by Amelia Jaffé. New York: Vintage Books, 1965.

Kopp, Sheldon. *An End to Innocence*. New York: Macmillan, 1978.

Rako, Susan and Harvey Mazer (Eds.). *Semrad: The Heart of a Therapist*. New York: Jason Aronson, 1983.

Sarton, May. *Journal of a Solitude*. New York: Norton, 1973.

CHAPTER SIX

Personal and Professional Growth Through Psychological Testing

MELVIN C. BLANCHETTE, PH.D.

Several years ago when I was a student at the University of Detroit studying clinical psychology and marriage and pastoral counseling, I took my first course in psychological testing. That experience was to have a lasting impact on my life and my practice as a psychologist. It is only now, with the perspective that time and distance give, that I am beginning to realize the power of that activity and the depth of understanding which I came to appreciate as a result of my participation in the course. It was the *experience* that had a profound influence on my life, not the professor or the interaction with other students. The experience—as William James says in his *Psychology,* that molds us every hour and makes of our minds a mirror of the time-and-space connections between the things in the world—was transforming. The connection, made that day in early September, was the truth realized between my consciousness and the depths of my personality functioning and relational style.

No teacher in school, no friend ever told me what this simple projective test was to point out with such precision and clarity. To this day, I believe the precision came through the instrument—the clarity became mine because I participated in the experience. Someone could have told me what the test meant; however, the truth realized was all the more gripping because I came to it myself. I suggest that when we arrive at such moments of truth we are faced with many questions. Do we want to own this reality? Is this fact really true? Could we not go on hiding from, evading what this really tells us? What will it mean if we accept this truth about ourselves? It is at this moment of experience that life reaches out to us and gives us a challenge. That challenge, which rings with all the fear of the unknown that comes from being on seas uncharted, is the invitation to change. It is not easy to recognize that there are things keeping us from being the unique, never-to-be-repeated act of creation we are. Change is a wrenching experience. After all, it has taken years to become what and who we are. Now, this experience is revealing that what we have been doing might not be the best way to live. Therefore, we are faced with the challenge to change. Seeing how personality functioning kept areas of freedom and spontaneity frozen—at least in my case—was a threatening experience.

Another form of this same challenge is to integrate. Integration is a noble word in my vocabulary. Basically, when a person comes to integration or begins to deal with the struggle that integration demands, he or she is no longer denying certain unpleasant realities about oneself. It also means that one agrees to become one with oneself—to affirm the shadow side of one's personality, to use a Jungian term, and to see how this negative personality characteristic or trait might be adapted, integrated, and transformed so as to become a positive and life-giving force. It was the insight received that day which enabled me to change and integrate what was a negative and life-denying set of attitudes, behaviors, and feelings.

At this point let me share with you that experience which so influenced my life and taught me that conflict has its own career, that what is important is that we face any fear, that by looking into the face of fear we find the answer, the resolution, and the force of transformation.

As a graduate student I began my studies with all the enthusiasm and energy of an athlete. I realized very early in the process that I needed to know myself better. Hence, I decided to take a course in projectives. I had already taken individual testing and could administer, interpret, and write up evaluations dealing with intelligence testing. What I wanted now was something that would go deeper. My wish was granted when a certain professor allowed me to take his course on the Hutt Adaptation of the Bender-Gestalt. The first day of class arrived and I was ready for insight! The professor was well regarded, and I was sure it was only a matter of time before pearls of wisdom would become mine. What happened was the farthest from my mind.

He came into class and greeted us with the request: "Please clear your desk. Take out a clean sheet of paper. You will need a pencil. A pen will not do. If you want to learn about projectives, you will have to take one." He went on to say that the test was a series of gestalts which we would have to draw as well as we could. I said to myself, "That will be no problem." He told us further what we in turn would say many years later to our students: "There is no wrong or right answer." That was reassuring! Standing in front of the class so that all could see, he held certain cards in his hand. He told us that we would have to draw nine designs. It was at this point that my personality style began to surface. Nine cards—no problem, I said to myself. They will all fit on one sheet of paper. I folded the paper as one would a letter and then folded the sides to the center, forming nine perfect blocks. After this I decided, since there were nine figures to be drawn, I should number the blocks appropriately. The first figure was shown, and I placed it in the upper left-hand corner in the middle of the block—neat, tidy, and perfectly drawn! The professor presented the second, and so on until we finished the entire exercise. I was very proud of myself. After all, other students were using a single sheet of paper for each figure or they were placing the figures all over the page. It was obvious to me they lacked order, regularity, perception, and certainly the ability to reproduce these cards as well as possible.

Next the professor asked us to put these drawings away. Then we were told to draw the figures again, but this time we could modify the figures to suit our taste. We could change them, make them pleasing to ourselves. True to form, I again folded my paper as I described earlier. When the cards were presented, I decided there must be a catch—so I drew the cards exactly the same as the first time, but this time tried to draw them even better. I counted the dots with mathematical accuracy, made the points of intersection sharper, and in general reproduced the cards. After this phase I thought we would be finished with the exercise. This was not the case. A second time he asked us to clear our desks, and this time he asked us to make associations, to say anything that came to mind regarding the first set of drawings and then the second set of drawings. I made the associations with the first set and recorded them on a separate sheet of paper. But, alas, my second set of drawings were exactly as the first! Now, truth and insight were beginning to form.

The class ended, and we were told to take our drawings home and reflect further on the meaning and interpretation of our work. We were not told to read the textbook, *The Hutt Adaptation of the Bender-Gestalt* (1969), but you can bank on the fact that I went home and devoured that book. In particular, I read Chapters 5 and 6, "Specific Test Factors and Their Interpretation" and "Principles of Inferential and Configurational Analysis." Page after page, the truth began to emerge. I was one of the world's most controlling persons, unfree, lacking spontaneity, distrustful, and rigid. It took days for me to comprehend fully what this meant. After all, I was a successful graduate student mostly because of these characteristics. My work was well done, punctual—but what were these aspects of my personality doing to my life? I began to understand why I wanted to study psychology in the first place, and why I think most graduate students in psychology begin their studies—to solve their own problems, or at least find a way to deal with them constructively. After these many years, I accept that fact about myself and rejoice that I had wonderful professors who were enablers of my personal and professional growth through their courses and their conversations, and most important, that they provided models to guide me in the process of integration. Most of all, I am grateful for the insight that growth begins only when one accepts his or her unique starting point and that the greatest struggle in life is not with outside forces but with inside feelings which must be brought to awareness, understood, and hopefully worked through to insight and acceptance. Once we have come to such a point in our personal lives, our professional activities as psychologists, pastoral counselors, social workers, or mental health professionals will certainly afford us greater happiness, and better care to our clients.

It is reasonable for the reader to ask why I have chosen to be so autobiographical in introducing this chapter on personal and professional growth through the use of psychological testing. One reason that prompts this approach is my belief that we are much more alike than different, and my struggles are not at all dissimilar to those of others. There is a commonality among those who share the human condition. If this chapter is to have an impact on you, it must be authentic and ring true with your observations and feelings. Hence, I have chosen a conversational tone, inviting participation and reflection.

This chapter will focus on the process through which psychological testing enhances personal and professional growth in the life and ministry of the pastoral counselor. Before describing the process, I will try to present important philosophical principles from which an understanding of human existence is derived. Second, a list of psychological criteria for sound and mature personality functioning will be presented. The list will be by no means exhaustive and is intended only as a guide to help us appreciate what the psychological characteristics of the well-integrated person are. After this initial presentation, each procedure contained in a typical battery of psychological testing will be explained. This explanation must remain on an introductory level for the purpose of this chapter. To present each procedure in great detail would necessitate an entire book. The reader whose interest is only in the clinical use of psychological testing is advised to consult the very fine chapter in Nicoli's *The Harvard Guide to Modern Psychiatry* (1978). For an overview of the field of psychological testing, it is suggested that the reader consult the work of Anne Anastasi, *Psychological Testing* (1982), which is thorough and complete. The various procedures will be introduced under the headings of intelligence testing, self-rating tests of personality, and projectives. Finally, the values that accrue to the pastoral counselor who participates in the process of psychological testing will be highlighted through a representative sampling of statements made by former students. These statements were elicited to determine what value the experience of psychological testing had for them in their personal and professional lives.

PHILOSOPHICAL PRINCIPLES

From the experience of having completed a great number of psychological testing batteries, and from my interaction with people from many different walks of life, the following philosophical principles and psychological characteristics have become convictions. These convictions take the form of philosophical principles from which certain understandings of human behavior and existence are maintained. The psychological characteristics became convictions as the result of my years of practice as a psychologist, and they represent what I consider to be the criteria of the mature, well-integrated person.

The first and guiding principle is that each human person is a unique individual. At first sight, this might seem like an understatement; however, there are those forces at work in life and science whereby the individual is not considered to be unique. There is a drive to treat everyone the same rather than as an individual. This is true in psychology, wherein we have broad classification schema and nosological categories in which almost everyone should fit. However, it is not sufficient merely to come up with a psychiatric label that fits the person. Psychiatric labels refer only to the broad categories of human behavior. If psychological testing is to facilitate personal and professional growth, it must answer the specific question: What kind of person is this? As a result of testing, an idiosyncratic evaluation of a particular individual is made, identifying the issues, struggles, unconscious conflicts, and concerns. It does little good to diagnose a person as a hysteric, an obsessive-compulsive, or a paranoid. Psychological testing has the responsibility and the challenge to answer the question: What kind of a hysteric is this person? What kind of an obsessive-compulsive is this? What kind of a paranoid is this? The process of integration deals with how this person is handling both the problem and mystery of being and becoming human. What this person did in the past is subjected to critical analysis so as to understand the reasons for behavior in the present. The goals of human behavior, and the way this individual is attempting to solve the solution to the problem of being human, should also be encompassed. Various authors have advanced what they consider to be the answer to this search. William Glasser (1965) says it this way:

> Being human for each individual means that a person has found his/her real self and has the courage to be that self, that a person has the cheerfulness to accept his/her social responsibility, is free of the compulsion to his/her inferiority feeling, is striving towards socially constructive ends, and finally, is free of morbid guilt feelings, and accepts and affirms the religious tension inherent in human nature. (p. 5)

The existential-humanistic psychologist Rollo May (1967) states what he considers to be the objective of the growth or integration process:

> Being human means that a person has experienced authentic love in a dependable relationship, has a sense of one's own worth, lives responsibly, has an inner freedom (owns oneself), has a sense of meaning and a loving, trustful relationship with the sacred. (p. 192)

Through the experience of psychological testing, the skilled clinician attempts to locate the obstacles to one's becoming fully human. As the Greeks said so many years ago, knowledge is power—if we can come to know why we do certain things, what needs are being answered through our behavior, what are the developmental lags in our process of becoming human, then psychological testing is fulfilling its function.

A second philosophical principle, arising from a phenomenological viewpoint, is that the human person is a spirit-in-the-world existence. A person is not just spirit; this would lead to a kind of idealism. Nor is a person just a body; this would lead to a kind of reductionism. Nor again should the person be thought of as a combination of body and spirit functioning together as two independent but related parts. Rather, a person is essentially spirit-in-the-world, open to transcendence and meaning that go beyond the here and now. This causes problems for us all, for if we live only for the here and now, one dimension of our life is cut off. This dimension could represent the life that is without boundaries. On the other hand, if we live only for the spiritual, we avoid the happiness and the joy that come with struggling to be both human and divine. Ernest Becker (1973) deals with this conflict in his seminal book, *The Denial of Death:*

> Man's body is a *problem* to him that has to be explained. Not only his body is strange, but also its inner landscape, the memories and dreams. Man's very insides—his self—are foreign to him. He doesn't know who he is, why he was born, what he is doing on the planet, what he is supposed to do, what he can expect. His own existence is incomprehensible to him, a miracle just like the rest of creation, closer to him, right near his pounding heart, but for that reason all the more strange. Each thing is a problem, and man can shut out nothing. As Maslow has well said, "It is precisely the god-like in ourselves that we are ambivalent about, fascinated by and fearful of, motivated to and defensive against. This is one aspect of the basic human predicament, that we simultaneously are worms and gods." There it is again, gods with anuses. (p. 51)

Thus, on one hand we must deal with those issues that call us forth to live in the spirit. On the other, we must accept and make sense out of the fact that we have a bodily existence. The self is the result of integrating these two forces.

> The assumption is that as each individual develops he has the difficult task of meaningfully organizing the sensations from his body—which is one of the most important and complex phenomena in his total perceptual field. It is a phenomenon relatively more complex and difficult to organize perceptually than other phenomena "out there" because of its unique simultaneous role as a participant in the perceptual process and also as the object of this same perceptual process. (Fisher and Cleveland, 1958:420)

In sum, both dimensions are equally important for human existence. Remove one and you no longer have human existence. Psychological testing deals with the hopes and aspirations of people trying to live within boundaries. It likewise enables us to deal with the struggle to integrate the human and divine.

A third philosophical principle is that human existence is an outright gift as well as being limited. Because human existence is an in-the-world existence, it is a limited existence with limited capabilities. However, experience shows that existence is also a gift, that life is not an earned reward but a gift graciously and gratuitously given. It is in the process of living that we come to the awareness of what this principle means, that there are two marks of the experience of being a personality.

> The first mark of the experience of being a personality is thus self-awareness in its uniqueness and unity; a second characteristic is the consciousness of one's own limitations, which is the necessary counterpart of the awareness of uniqueness and unity. In self-awareness, a man knows what he can do, the assignment of his existence, the task of his life. In knowing his limits he realizes what he is not. (Van Kaam, 1964:45)

As was the case with the second philosophical principle, so too with the principle of limited and unlimited existence, both ends of the spectrum must be maintained. The tension that comes from uniqueness and being limited must be resolved through acceptance of being oneself and living freely within limitations.

A fourth principle which merits attention and reflection is that human existence is a self-conscious existence. A person is capable of being self-conscious of his or her world and participation in that world. Consciousness of one's world and of oneself can take various forms, including perceiving, understanding, knowing, reflecting, loving, and hating. This consciousness of one's world and of oneself is not restricted to collecting data but rather to the task of discerning meaning. To put this in another perspective, whenever a person is conscious of a phenomenon, that person is simultaneously conscious of some meaning of the phenomenon. The opposite to this conscious mode of existence is the drifter. The drifter has not yet found himself; he has not yet discovered his own need and so is content to do what everyone else is doing. He has not yet discovered his own will and so is content to choose what everyone else is choosing. He has not yet discovered a mind of his own and so is content to think and say what everyone else is thinking and saying, and the others too are apt to be drifters—each of them doing, choosing, thinking, and saying what others happen to be doing, choosing, thinking, and saying. To discover meaning and to become conscious of this force in our lives is to unlock possibilities for change and differentiation.

A fifth principle that describes human existence is that human existence is a process existence. A person is a dynamic process capable of growth, never static. There is an ongoing process of equilibration, of maintaining itself in the midst of and despite interactions with the environment and with others. Becoming oneself is the result of a shared experience. There is no possibility of attaining self-actualization if one does not do it in the company of other human beings. We can do it only as we react to others who share the human condition. Only as the interaction is terminated in the transaction are we fulfilled. Only through the process of sharing with other human beings in uplifting the human condition are we uplifted and understood.

A sixth principle of human existence is that it is a holistic existence. To understand and appreciate human existence, one must view it from a holistic viewpoint. To fragment a person into parts is not to see a person as a person. In considering human existence, however, it is very important to be aware of the interconnectedness of the cognitive, affective, behavioral, physical, and spiritual aspects that make up the whole of the human person. Finally, it is important to understand that the whole of the human person is more than the sum of the various parts or aspects comprising the person.

A seventh principle of human existence is that it is free. Freedom is a meaningless concept unless there are choices to be made. In becoming human, we make choices that determine the quality of person we become. In doing so, we deal with the fact that human freedom is not an unlimited freedom. To be free, one is to act, to make decisions in conformity with reality and not according to nonexistent alternatives. This reality might not be satisfying all the time, but freedom demands that we learn to accept life with such imperfection. Later, we may be able to evoke the vision of a different alternative into a concrete choice. However, the prospect of a valid cause of action for the future does not relieve us of the responsible freedom of making a choice with respect to present reality. Many times a person prefers to undergo anxiety rather than make a decision that will free that person from the anxiety. To be free is human, and to be human is a difficult task.

An eighth principle of human existence is that it is a relational existence. Human existence involves relationships with objects and subjects. A person enters into various such relationships from the moment of birth until death. These relationships are vitally important if the person is to grow and become. Without relationships, a person suffers and fails to realize the fullness of life.

This is by no means an exhaustive list. These principles of human existence are important to me because they speak to the reality of the situation and provide a framework within which psychological testing can be done without doing violence to the person. These principles have given us a point from where we can begin, and a background against which the activity of psychological testing can be placed appropriately. The psychological characteristics, which we will now consider, will provide us with at least an outline of the mature and well-integrated person.

PSYCHOLOGICAL CHARACTERISTICS

As was said earlier, the psychological characteristics that will be discussed in this section are certainly not the result of empirical research. They are the fruit of my own reflection, what emerged from the psychological profiles of people tested and from discussion with many graduate students. In some strange way they point out the wisdom contained in this quotation of the character played by the actress Sylvia Sidney in a conversation with her daughter (played by Joanne Woodward) in Gilbert Gates's movie *Summer Wishes, Winter Dreams* (quoted in Haun, 1980):

> *Growing up is harder to do*
> *Than learning how to fly.*
> *The former requires truth at every turn—*
> *The latter only fairy dust.*

This metaphorical insight is true as we grow up; it is equally true as we attempt to integrate various and sometimes conflicting drives and impulses. The quotation also serves as a ready introduction to what I consider the most important characteristic of the healthy, well-integrated person. That person is healthy, mature, and well integrated who is reality oriented. This means that the individual lives to a greater degree in terms of reality, of the actual facts of life, than in terms of fantasies, wishes, and fears. To this end, the question always needs to be answered: What is the reality of the situation? How can I live my life in keeping with reality? Maslow (1963) captured this insight of Freudian psychology in this remark:

> Freud's greatest discovery, the one which lies at the root of psychodynamics, is that the great cause of much psychological illness is the fear of knowledge of oneself—of one's emotions, impulses, memories, capacities, potentialities, of one's destiny. We have discovered that fear of knowledge of oneself is very often isomorphic with, and parallel with, fear of the outside world. In general this kind of fear is defensive, in the sense that it is protective of our self-esteem, of our love and respect for ourselves. We tend to be afraid of any knowledge that could cause us to despise ourselves or to make us feel inferior, weak, worthless, evil, shameful. We protect ourselves and our ideal image of ourselves by repression and similar defenses which are essentially techniques by which we avoid becoming conscious of unpleasant or dangerous truths. (p. 119)

I shall never forget a few years ago talking with a graduate student who was a Ph.D. candidate but was transferring to a new school in a field of knowledge requiring very different skills than did his previous course of study. He came into my study feeling disappointed and ready to leave his new field of interest. He was embarrassed because he had received a failing grade on his first test. I asked him if he didn't feel he was overreacting. After all, this was the first month of school. There is always a period of adjustment. He responded that the test was unfair, that the professor did not know how to test graduate students. (This could have been true, incidentally!) What he failed to realize was that he placed his total reason for being, his level of competence of being a human person, on one examination. He had fused himself with his failing grade! In time, however, once he was freed from the distortions of the situation, he came to appreciate that he was fearful of failing. Facing this fear within himself, he went on to become a very successful student and is now practicing in his field of interest.

What would have happened if he hadn't faced the reality of the situation? One thing is certain—his life would have been very different.

The second psychological characteristic of integration and growth is the capacity to live well in terms of long-term values instead of short-term values. What is at stake here is that as we grow older, we must make adaptations to life and to other people. Sometimes we must give up certain temporary pleasures for the sake of more lasting happiness. We may have to defer immediate gratification when those satisfactions would frustrate the more lasting satisfaction in life. This is one of the hallmarks of the mature and well-integrated person.

A third characteristic is that the mature individual should have a grown-up conscience instead of a childhood variety of conscience. We are individuals of a community, and we are very much what we were. However, there must be a moment of discontinuity when we leave the trappings of childhood behind and move forward to accept adult responsibilities. It might be well to highlight the difference between an infantile conscience and a mature conscience. Generally speaking, an infantile conscience is based on threats, fear, guilt, and the distorted ideas and fancies of childhood. The adult conscience, on the other hand, is based on real dangers and possibilities and standards.

The childhood conscience holds the adult back from enjoying the rightful pleasures to which he or she is entitled. It is a sad fact of life that many adults are still operating from an inadequate and ill-formed conscience. They refuse to accept the responsibility that comes with making decisions in keeping with grown-up standards and ideals. They want someone to tell them what to do, what they can enjoy, and how they should go about the task. In short, we can derive a sound appreciation of how free people are when we know on what level they are responding to their conscience.

A fourth characteristic of the well-integrated, growth-filled person is the ability to be independent. What this means is that this person can stand on his or her own feet, that the individual is no longer tied to parents' apron strings nor dependent upon others for guidance. Being independent, however, does not mean having an attitude of blustering defiance, feeling that one does not need anyone, that one can go through life entirely on one's own—in short, that one is self-sufficient. To be independent is to accept the risk of taking hold of one's life and living it. Any clinician could give example after example of people who come for therapy who are still living a caricature of life. By this I mean the kind of person who is still unfree and unable to take hold of the gifted nature of his or her life. Unfortunately, many times, and this is perfectly understandable, this kind of person is often filled with hostility well concealed under layers of depression.

A fifth characteristic to which we should turn attention is the ability to be dependent. This might appear contradictory to what has just been presented. However, there is a difference, namely, the ability to be reasonably dependent on others. We have all seen examples of the inappropriately dependent person: the clinging-vine type, the husband who expects to be babied, the person who cannot make any kind of decision without consulting many people. These are good examples of very passive people who are still living out a need for the gratification that comes with being dependent. To compare this type of dependent person with someone who is appropriately dependent, I would suggest that the latter has the capacity to take advice when it is consistent and contributory to one's decision and responsibility. It should also be said that the appropriately dependent person can receive love and affection from others. The ability to receive from others as well as to give to others is an important dimension of maturity and integration. The ramifications are very far reaching. Some people can never receive a gift from another because this would hurt their pride. Some men in a love relationship cannot be seen to be dependent because this might mean a lack of masculinity. Therapy is a good example of mature dependence because an adult seeks a solution through a relationship that is transient, current, and nonneurotic.

To be mature and well integrated means to have a balance regarding the continuum upon which is placed the tension to be independent as well as dependent. Once again the use of questions might serve to underline the difference. In what ways and to what extent are the person's present wishes, drives, and impulses in the real world influenced and directed by the persistent longing for the dependent and passive pleasures of childhood? On the other hand, to what extent and in what ways does the person give up dependent or passive pleasures that are appropriate in adult functioning? In short, we must decide when it is appropriate to be independent and when to be dependent. If we are reasonably comfortable within ourselves, reasonably self-sustaining, and therefore free of undue demands of others for satisfaction, the tension between the two poles is relaxed and our response is appropriate to the situation.

A sixth characteristic of sound and mature functioning is the capacity to love someone, to be in a relationship where the interests and satisfactions of the other are preferred to one's own. I am indebted to the great American psychiatrist, Harry S. Sullivan, for this definition of love. "When the satisfaction or the security of another person becomes as significant to one as is one's own satisfaction or security, then the state of love exists." (1953:42–43) This definition is perhaps one of the least romantic I have ever read; however, it relates the state of love to the reality of the situation. To love someone is not easy, and high levels of maturity are required. Along with the capacity to love, the mature person must not fear the power to hate, or to feel the aggressive urges in our human condition. What is being asked is that we integrate the power of anger and the force of aggressiveness in the service of socially appropriate responses. Frequently, opposing forces are at work in the lives of us all. Where there is love, there is the lurking eventuality of hatred. Where there is ambition, there is the uncanny hope for failure. The mature person accepts the shadow side of life and attempts to integrate that force into the totality of personality functioning.

A seventh characteristic that gives evidence of healthy emotional functioning and integration is the capacity to accept ourselves as we really are. This acceptance comes about very gradually and is the result of having been already accepted and affirmed by others. It seems to me that if we accept ourselves, we do so to the depths of our being—where we are most of all ourselves. This acceptance includes the individual's acceptance of his or her own gender. At present there is a heated debate regarding many aspects of sexual functioning and identity. Part of the discussion concerns role expectation, and we know that roles have changed and will continue to change. What is necessary for us to remember in this controversy is that we really cannot change who we are essentially, that if we are to make sense out of life, we do so as either man or woman. The mature attitude is to understand that there is no general superiority of men over women or of women over men, that men have certain strengths and assets that women do not have, and women have certain strengths and assets that men do not have. Mature sexuality is seen as a dimension of personality functioning that makes one male or female, capable of loving and giving life; it is a way of being that involves closeness and distance among persons. Sexuality is the gift given to us by which we love others. It is an aspect of persons, and it is between persons, *not* between organs. If sexuality is the latter only, it is inhuman. If we are to be emotionally healthy humans, we accept ourselves as we are, and we love others by means of the vitality and energy grounded in our sexuality.

To accept oneself as one really is, is the final characteristic of the present listing. There are other aspects of emotional growth and integration that might be discussed. These include having a sense of God/universe, a sense of humor, ability to forgive oneself, ability to affirm others, ability to gain insight from experience, and ability to be generative, but these are essentially variations of the seven characteristics already listed.

Thus far the stage has been set to introduce psychological testing within the context of growth and integration. Certain philosophical principles have been stated from which an understanding of human existence is derived. Likewise, psychological characteristics which typify the healthy and well-integrated person have been presented. These criteria are by no means absolute, but reflect my view of what authentic growth and development entail. These convictions, while theoretical, are also grounded in experience. Psychological testing is undertaken within the context of growth and differentiation, and we will turn our attention to those psychological procedures used to discern and facilitate personal and professional growth.

PSYCHOLOGICAL PROCEDURES

At this time it is necessary to make an important distinction or clarification. Throughout this chapter we have been discussing the importance of psychological testing as a means through which one can determine both the presence and lack of personal and professional growth. However, since we are at the point of meeting the person in the testing situation, I want to suggest how I introduce psychological testing. In doing this,

I never use the word *test*. As soon as the clinician says "test," the anxiety level increases. Accordingly, when I introduce the activity of psychological testing I will invariably say, "These are some procedures that will be used to help you understand yourself better. They are means to be used to gather important information." I thus attempt to engage the person as participant in the process rather than treating the person as an object—something to be examined and about whom a report is written. To the extent that good rapport is established and an optimal level of interaction maintained, the results of psychological testing are more useful and even more valid. My recommendation is that the clinician who wants to create this relationship spend at least one hour with the person. It is an important time to gather background on the individual and to do a social history. What this interaction accomplishes is to decrease unnecessary anxiety and to create a working partnership. A natural situation is furthered by answering pertinent questions and explaining in understandable terms what is to be expected. This kind of sensitive relating should ensure that the testing is a positive experience for the person and will allow the clinician to formulate hypotheses about many levels of human functioning and behavior. What follows is an example of a clinical interview in which important data are gathered.

Background Information and Social History

Background information is used in writing the psychological profile of the person. It is important to gather information in as natural a fashion as possible. The usual items are listed: date of birth, referred by, evaluated by, and date of the report. The reason for the testing is next determined through the interview method. After this part is completed, an inquiry is made concerning the parents of the person to be tested. I usually ask: Are your parents living? Are they in good health? How do you feel about them? Even if a parent is deceased, I ask the question about how the person feels about them. This conviction came to me as a result of seeing a movie which left a lasting impression. The movie was *I Never Sang for My Father* (1970) starring Gene Hackman and Melvyn Douglas. It began with these lines: "Death ends a life but does not end a relationship, which struggles on in the survivor's mind toward some resolution which it may never find. It continues on in the lives of the survivors." (Haun, 1980:56) One's parents might be dead, but unless that relationship is worked through, the person is bound to have deep and lasting feelings. This interview also includes ascertaining any illnesses the person might have had during developmental stages. In addition, I like to discern how this person is regarding some recreational interests, and how he or she has fun. I usually ask about hobbies, sports, music, and favorite authors. After deriving this information, I ask the person to give a self-description. For example, one person, named Bill, described himself as "intelligent, self-reliant, happy, observant, quick-tempered, and confident. The quality I would like others to think I have is that I am easygoing. I like to take things in stride and not worry." Through the course of the testing, these attitudes and values are examined to see what level of insight the person has and whether the person fits the self-description. Since parents are so important, I usually ask how their parents would describe them. Bill had his parents describing him as "intelligent and happy" and indicated that they would say that he doesn't like physical labor and likes to sleep late. In addition, they would say how much he likes sports. Since we live our lives in relation to others, the question is asked: How would a close friend describe you? This process yields important information about oneself, one's parents, and what perception a person has about how others feel about him.

Sometime later in the interview, other questions might be given such as the following: What three experiences were the most important in shaping your life? If you were to receive a telegram right now, what would it say? If you had a chance to stand on a platform and shout out your pet peeves, what would they be? What three wishes might you ask of a "fairy godmother"? What three persons might you like to interview? What would you like to see included in your eulogy? What was the best thing ever to happen to you? What is your greatest strength and also your weakness? These are sample questions designed to elicit information as well as to discern one's relational style. It does not take long to find out if this person can engage in fantasy. Nor does it take long to realize if this is an open or closed person. As a result of these questions and the interaction, the clinician is made aware of important data. After the interview, the clinician must judge whether or not the person is ready to continue the next portion of the process. If the answer is yes, the clinician introduces the various procedures, beginning with the least threatening and going toward the most complex. If the answer is no, then the clinician must spend more time with the person to allay fears and to establish an atmosphere in which testing might be profitable.

To gain a dynamic and developmental understanding of the person, the clinician needs various procedures to tap both conscious concerns and unconscious conflicts. This is usually done by means of a battery of tests, including intelligence tests, self-rating tests of personality, and projective procedures, which are designed to identify attitudes, needs, level of insight, defenses, anxieties, relational styles, impulse control, and basically how a person interprets, understands, and copes with reality. What follows is a description of the various procedures used in a typical testing battery.

Intelligence Testing

The most common and comprehensive procedure used to discern adult intelligence functioning is the Wechsler Adult Intelligence Scale. Since this procedure taps various functions, it has a number of subtests which survey the range and depth of intelligence. These subtests are arranged under two major scales—the Verbal and the Performance. The Verbal contains subtests on information, comprehension, arithmetic, similarities, digit span, and vocabulary. The Performance includes digit symbol, picture completion, block design, picture arrangement, and object assembly. Table 6.1 also has a description of the Verbal and Performance Scales indicating what functions are being ascertained through each subtest.

Table 6.1　Diagnostic Categories of the Wechsler Adult Intelligence Scale

DIAGNOSTIC CATEGORY	I.Q. SCORE
Mentally Retarded	69 + Below
Borderline	70–79
Low Average	80–89
Average	90–109
High Average	110–119
Superior	120–129
Very Superior	130 + Above

Name　　　　　　　　　　　　　　　Full Scale I.Q. Score

Date Tested　　　　　　　　　　　　Verbal-Performance I.Q.

VERBAL AND PERFORMANCE SUBTEST SCALE SCORES

SCALE
SCORE

_____ INFORMATION: Information gained from experiences and education; intellectual effort; alertness to the world around us.

_____ COMPREHENSION: Practical knowledge and social judgment; anticipation and judging consequences. (Poor verbalizers often score low.)

_____ ARITHMETIC: Concentration and arithmetic reasoning; specific school learning; mental alertness.

_____ SIMILARITIES: Ability to recognize and describe essential relations between objects or ideas; verbal concept formation; concrete versus abstract kinds of thinking.

_____ DIGIT SPAN: Attention and auditory memory; self-control. (Low score may indicate anxiety.)

_____ VOCABULARY: Best single measure of verbal intelligence and learning ability; cultural environment reflected; potentiality for dealing with symbols; quality and character of thought processes.

_____ DIGIT SYMBOL: Visual motor reaction and association of symbols; ability to learn an unfamiliar task.

_____ PICTURE COMPLETION: Visual alertness and organization of symbols; ability to recognize essential details; contact with reality.

_____ BLOCK DESIGN: Best single nonlanguage test; analysis of reproduction of abstract designs; logical insight into space relationships; visual motor perception and coordination; best test of potential, general intelligence.

_____ PICTURE ARRANGEMENT: Nonverbal judgment, anticipation and planning (through use of essential pictured clues); responsiveness to interpersonal relationships.

_____ OBJECT ASSEMBLY: Seeing relationships of parts to the whole in a familiar configuration; carefulness and persistence at a task; critical appraisal of small details.

Self-Rating Tests of Personality

Like intelligence tests, self-rating tests of personality are objective tests, in contrast to projectives which will be discussed in the next section. These self-rating tests include the Minnesota Multiphasic Personality Inventory, Strong-Campbell Interest Inventory, and the Edwards Personal Preference Scale, as well as the Myers-Briggs Type Indicator.

Minnesota Multiphasic Personality Inventory. This test was designed to help diagnose mental dysfunction by reflecting the type of disorder and the intensity of the problem. In the construction of the test, subjects were chosen who, on the basis of consensus among clinical workers, were representative of specific types or intensities of disorders to be investigated. Then 550 test items were given to this group and to a control group of normal subjects.

The 550 test items were divided into twenty-six subset items which asked the subjects to tell about their general health, neurologic symptoms, motor movements and coordination, habits, family and marital relationships, and various psychological characteristics. Scales were obtained by ascertaining which items discriminated subjects with specific types of psychological disturbances from those with other psychopathologies and from normal subjects.

On the basis of weights assigned to test items, various scales of personality characteristics have been developed. Nine of these scales have been used widely:

1. *Hypochondria* (Hs) Subject reports being worried about bodily functions. Often associated with past history of exaggerated physical complaints.
2. *Depression* (D) Subject reports being in depths of depression, discouraged, and without self-confidence.
3. *Hysteria* (Hy) Subject reports being worried about paralyses, gastric or intestinal complaints, attacks of weakness, fainting, or even epileptic attacks.
4. *Psychopathic deviation* (Pd) The subject's responses reflect an absence of deep emotionality. Nothing seems to matter. He may be intelligent but likely to lie, to cheat, or to be addicted to drugs. Crimes may be undertaken without interest in personal gain.
5. *Masculinity-Femininity* (Mf) This scale tends to differentiate masculine-feminine psychological characteristics between men and women in the normal group of subjects.
6. *Paranoia* (Pa) Subject is suspicious, is oversensitive, and has delusions of persecution.
7. *Psychasthenia* (Pt) Subject's responses are typical of those with phobic or compulsive behaviors. Subject may have strange thoughts or ideas from which he cannot escape.

8. *Schizophrenia* (Sc) Subjects who give responses scored as unusual and bizarre are high on this scale. Generally these responses reflect a dissociation of the subjective life of the individual from reality.

9. *Hypomania* (Ma) The subject reports he is overproductive in both thought and action. Often this may go along with trouble resulting from attempting too much and from a disregard of social conventions.

A number of other scales have been developed and found useful in clinical practice. Three of these are especially important in the routine analysis of this test's results. One is the Question Score (?). Since subjects are asked to respond to each item of the test in terms of "yes," "no," or "cannot say," it is possible to summate the number of "?" scores of "cannot say" scores. Tests with abnormally high "cannot say" scores are considered invalid since they cannot properly be compared with the standardization group. Another score is the Lie Score (L), which indicates the number of improbable answers given by the subject. These are answers that indicate denial of symptoms or behaviors that are so ubiquitous that denial is indicative of evasion. Finally, there is a False Score (F), which indicates that the subject gave far more than the usual number of extremely rare responses and thus was careless, or was trying to fake the answers, or was otherwise responding invalidly.

The MMPI is the most frequently used objective personality test in current clinical practice. It has also been used widely in research, and special scales such as those purporting to measure "social desirability," "anxiety," and the like have been devised from responses to the items. Nevertheless, the validity of the test has been questioned sharply. For one thing, there are a number of studies which indicate that the test fails to correlate as well with psychiatric judgment as is claimed. For another, the test scores do not give much information about the nature of the personality problems or their psychodynamics, beyond a label of type or types of psychopathology.

The authors of the test are well aware of its limitations and have made various efforts to provide more meaningful and detailed analyses. In their *Atlas* they provide many methods for analyzing this test, presenting clinical examples of sophisticated analyses of the test results. Some research studies have shown the value of some of its original or derived scales in predicting significant behavioral correlates.

Strong-Campbell Interest Inventory. The Strong-Campbell Interest Inventory (SCII) provides a means for measuring interest patterns. It is a thoroughly tested instrument which has been under constant revision since its publication in 1927 and in which new scales have been developed or old ones replicated. There has been extensive research leading to the construction of the various scales. The Strong consists of forty-one vocational scales as well as the interest maturity, masculinity-femininity, occupational level, and academic orientation scales. The test has been described by Horst (1968) in these words:

Perhaps one of the most familiar personality type tests is the interest test, best exemplified by the Strong Vocational Interest Blank. This test consists of a great variety of items that indicate things one might be interested in. Perhaps the chief justification for grouping in one test a collection of stimulus elements, each of which calls for a response as to one's interest in the object or activity specified by the term, is the general agreement that the term "interest" is relatively unambiguous and familiar to the layman. (p. 22)

There are, however, limitations to the use of the Strong. These are basically twofold. One minor drawback is the effort required in a complete scoring and interpretation. However, today most clinicians make use of computerized scoring services. A second weakness is the possibility that the person may fake an interest score to give what is considered a desirable response. This is unimportant if the person is earnestly searching for an interest pattern or direction in life. A beneficial addition to the Strong would be the development of a "lie" scale similar to that of the MMPI. However, there are no "lie" scales, no "validity" scales, and no "good impression" scales for the Strong Vocational Interest Blank, and none is planned. The reason for this position is supported by the following philosophical posture by Campbell (1974).

When a person is asked, or required, to take an interest inventory, the examiner is entering into an implicit agreement with him to find out something about his interests. If the person—for any reason whatsoever—does not wish to provide straightforward information, that is his right. If he wishes to modify his answers in directions that he believes will make him appear more favorable, he would be foolish not to do so, and he should be no more penalized for that than for other attempts to make a good impression, such as showing up for an interview in a clean shirt and fresh haircut. (p. 23)

Professor Campbell states the case well that persons are to be respected and their integrity safeguarded. There have been a host of studies on the ability of persons to fake answers. This research is summarized as follows.

1. People can and do raise their SCII scores on specific scales when instructed to do so in experimental studies.
2. When instructed to fake, individuals generally increase their scores by roughly one to two standard deviations (10 to 20 standard points).
3. When instructed to fake in a specified direction, say, "like a man," individuals exaggerate their answers; in a sense, they answer much more "like a man" than does the average man.
4. In real-life situations, some people sometime give different answers when they are applying for a job or advanced training than when they are seeking counsel-

ing, but the differences are mild, usually about one-third of a standard deviation (3 or 4 standard score points). (p. 23)

Regarding the reliability and validity of the Strong-Campbell Interest Inventory, there are extensive data in the *Handbook* on the stability over time. It is noted that scores on the occupational scales are stable over short time spans, such as a few weeks; for adults, the same stability holds over much longer intervals, up to several years. It is reported that test-retest correlations over thirty days average slightly over .90, dropping to about .75 over twenty years for adults and to .55 over thirty-five years for those tested at age sixteen. Published accounts certify that correlations over the four years of college average in the .60's. Two variables which influence the size of these test-retest correlations are age when first tested, and the retest interval. Of the two, the former is more important. It is concluded that when the Strong is used for those below the age of twenty-one, the possibility of future change must be acknowledged. In conclusion, the reliability of the occupational scales is .80. The literature supports the claim that the stability over time of the Strong is certainly high enough for adults. Consequently, the inventory can be used without undue concern for change.

It should be remembered that there are two different kinds of scales—occupational and nonoccupational. The occupational scales were developed by contrasting the Strong responses of persons in a specified occupation with a group of persons in general. Each scale is reported to discriminate between the interests of these two groups. Accordingly, a person's score provides an index of the similarity between the score obtained by the individual and the interests and characteristics of people in that designated occupation. On the Strong, the occupational scales are grouped into clusters of related occupations, employing the scale intercorrelations and similar data to identify similarity. The theory behind the test is that if one scores high in a given occupation, his or her interests are the same as a person who is successful and happy in that occupation, so the individual tested would be more likely to be successful and happy in that occupation than in one for which interests were dissimilar. The test does not indicate whether or not one possesses the ability or aptitude to pursue a specific occupation.

The research associated with the Strong testifies to its recognition as one of the best procedures available for measuring interest patterns. Segal (1955) concluded that the findings on the Strong validate the idea that personality theory can lead to a more complete understanding of the role of personality factors as determinants of vocational choice. In this vein, I use the Strong to gather important data on the individual, and I attempt to use that data to establish collaborative evidence that someone has indeed made a good vocational choice.

Edwards Personal Preference Schedule.   The Edwards Personal Preference Schedule is the result of the research on the concept of personality done by Henry Murray and his colleagues at the Harvard Psychological Clinic in 1938. Their work will be noted again in the section on projectives when the Thematic Apperception Test is discussed. Murray is a giant in the area of understanding the functions of the personality. He sees personality as an organizing and integrating force:

> [T]he general functions of personality are to exercise its processes, to express itself, to learn to generate and reduce insistent need-tension, to form serial programs for the attainment of distant goals, and finally, to lessen or resolve conflicts by forming schedules which more nearly permit the frictionless appeasement of its major needs. (Murray and Kluckhohn 1953, p. 39)

From this theory Edwards developed the more thorough inventory to assess the strength of need-tension. Edwards drew fifteen needs from the research of Murray, and he prepared sets of items whose domain or content appeared to fit each of those needs. The inventory is made up of 210 pairs of statements; items from each of the fifteen scales are paired with items from the other fourteen. The person must make a choice, selecting one statement which is more characteristic of his/her need-tension. Examples chosen by Anastasi in her book *Psychological Testing* (1968) are:

> A. I like to talk about myself to others.
> B. I like to work toward some goal that I have set for myself.
> A. I feel depressed when I fail at something.
> B. I feel nervous when giving a talk before a group. (p. 452)

Two important features of the Edwards Personal Preference Schedule must be highlighted. First of all, this is an excellent procedure to ascertain what needs are motivating behavior. The procedure has an internal check of consistency, because fifteen pairs of statements are repeated in identical form, giving us an index of responding consistency. If the consistency raw score is less than nine, the scores on the variables may be in question. This scale is similar to the "Lie" on the Minnesota Multiphasic Personality Inventory. Second, the results of this inventory are expressed in what are known as ipsative scores. Hence, the strength of each need is expressed not in absolute terms but in relation to the strength of the person's other needs. The person, not the normative sample, becomes the focus of interpretation and reference. It is thus possible for two persons to obtain identical scores on the Edwards but still differ significantly in the absolute strength of the needs. The reader is referred to the *Edwards Personal Preference Schedule Manual.*

To conclude this section, two important clinical insights are offered. First, all of us have needs, based originally on our biological requirements. As we mature, we find more complex and more socially relevant ways of satisfying our needs. When we are frustrated, we may seek neurotic ways of satisfying the needs. These ways may be abnormal, but the needs themselves never are. All needs are normal. Second, we must remember that our attitudes are related to our values, and our values originate in our deep and insistent needs. Using the Edwards Personal Preference Schedule permits us to discern what needs are motivating behavior and influencing a person's life.

Myers-Briggs Type Indicator. The Myers-Briggs Type Indicator was developed by Isabel Briggs Myers during two distinct phases of construction. The first phase, lasting from 1942 to 1944, resulted in the adult form of the procedure. The test construction followed the classical norms, and a 60 percent item-consistency analysis was reached. During the second period, from 1956 to 1958, two hundred new items were added, including word pairs. From this latter analysis resulted the present form of the Indicator known as a Form E and F. These are identical except that F includes unscored experimental items and requires more time to complete. Form F may be given from the eleventh grade up whereas Form E is adapted to fit into a high school class period and may be given to students from the seventh grade up.

Typical items included on the Myers-Briggs are:

When you go somewhere for the day, would you rather

(a) plan what you will do and when

(b) just go

Typical word pairs which reflect a person are:

Which word in each pair appeals to you more?

(a) literal   figurative (b)

(a) gentle   firm (b)

From questions such as these, the Indicator points out certain preferences of the person. What is important, and reassuring, is that there is no right or wrong preference. The answers simply indicate how a given person perceives reality. There are basically two ways to interpret reality: perception and judgment. *To find out* is an example of perception. *To decide* is an example of judgment. According to the theory that supports the Myers-Briggs, there are two basic ways of finding out and two ways of deciding. One way to find out is through *sensing*—using the eyes and ears to discern what is actually going on. As a result of sensing, facts are learned and stated. The other way to find out is through *intuition,* which goes beyond the limitations of the senses and meanings relationships to where possibilities are felt or intuited. In the course of finding out, both sensing and intuition are used, but not at the same time and frequently in different degrees.

The two ways of deciding are *thinking* and *feeling.* Thinking is a process through which an action is taken as a result of logical deduction based on cause and effect. Feeling, on the other hand, takes into consideration whatever is important to the person, and the decision is made on the basis of personal values. On the basis of the way the person decides, either a thinking or feeling preference results.

If these two ways are put together, four permutations are possible: sensing plus thinking, sensing plus feeling, intuition plus feeling, and intuition plus thinking.

Thus far the Indicator has enabled us to understand how people interpret reality through perception and judgment. Two ways of perceiving, or finding out, are sensing and intuition. Two ways of deciding are thinking and feeling. The remaining terms to be explained are introversion and extraversion. These are Jungian terms which describe how a person relates to perception and judgment. The introvert is happy relating to the inner world of concepts and ideas whereas the extravert delights in working in the world of people and things.

The Myers-Briggs has resulted in a feeling of peace and well-being for many people. This is particularly true of those who live in a community environment such as religious orders. It is very reassuring to know, and consequently to expect, how another person interprets reality. This procedure has been used to help those working in small groups to understand differences. Basically, what this procedure gives evidence of is that differences need not divide. There is a richness which can be enhancing to our lives when we can respect the individuality of another person. The Myers-Briggs brings out well the idiosyncratic nature of each of us.

Projective Tests

Projective techniques discussed in this section are the Sentence Completion, Hutt Adaptation of the Bender Gestalt, Thematic Apperception Test, and the Rorschach Inkblots. Before reviewing these procedures, it might be well to establish the principle from which any interpretation of these projectives is predicated. The projectives are based in large part on the ego defense of projection. The theoretical framework is Freudian, and through the theory we understand that projection is a defense operating outside of and beyond conscious awareness. Consciously disowned or rejected aspects of the self are thrown outward and imputed to others. Accordingly, through the use of projectives we are enabled to tap the less conscious aspects of the personality.

Sentence Completion.   Perhaps the simplest procedure in the entire battery is the sentence completion. The opening words of a sentence, or sometimes only a single word, are given, and the person is asked to complete the sentence and express his or her real feelings. The values of this procedure are many. It permits a great deal of flexibility because the procedure can be changed quickly, or new stem sentences developed for a particular reason. The range of stem sentences or items to be explored is limited only by the imagination of the clinician. There are various forms of the Sentence Completion, the most famous being the Rotter Incomplete Sentence Blank. Though the Sentence Completion appears on the surface to be a simple device, it does yield a rich harvest clinically through comparing and contrasting of the data from the other tests in the battery.

    Bender Gestalt Test. The Bender Gestalt Test is perhaps one of the most fascinating procedures in the battery of psychological tests. It is fascinating because of the experience required to accomplish it and the many ways in which it can be administered. I have already described my own experience of taking the Bender and what the results meant to me. Through the years I have given this procedure to any number of students, only to have my own experience replicated in the lives of others. The reason for this phenomenon is the strikingly simple task required by the Bender. When one is asked to draw simple geometric designs, many reactions are possible. My reaction was to plan exactly how this task would be accomplished, and my anticipatory style of relating was well documented through the drawings. Others take this procedure with a grain of salt, and their lack of interest and uninvolvement become significant issues as the battery progresses. What is perhaps most noteworthy with this procedure is that it is a protest to the verbal style of most of us. Since the procedure is one of copying and elaborating, few words are needed. Only in the association phase are words really required. Hence, the defense mechanisms are given an opportunity to be expressed in writing through the drawings. What is demanded is a skilled clinician with an intuitive sense to discern the deeper and more uncommon aspects of the personality. Because of its nonverbal nature, the Bender can be the most significant instrument in the whole battery.

    The reader will be quick to ask why Bender, and why the Hutt adaptation? Basically, the answer is that both have done extensive research using the original drawings of Wertheimer, who based his work on the theoretical framework of Gestalt psychology. Lauretta Bender was the first person to introduce the procedure in this country. Her particular technique was to ask the person to describe the drawings, and she made some modifications from the work of Wertheimer. Hutt, who later became interested in the procedure and wanted to preserve the integrity of the original Wertheimer cards, had them reproduced through the help of F. L. Wells of Harvard University so that the cards could not contain any irregularities.

    To administer the Hutt Adaptation of the Bender Gestalt Test (HABGT), the clinician invites the person to copy the cards. The reader will recall how I first was introduced to this procedure. The Hutt Adaptation can be used in many ways. In addition to the original copy phase, elaboration phase, and association phase, the clinician may also ask the person to draw the cards from memory, or perhaps to draw what their favorite card was and explain it. Accordingly, there are many "tests" or procedures contained in this one technique. I am personally grateful to Professor Hutt, who generated my personal and professional growth and integration.

    Thematic Apperception Test. The Thematic Apperception Test is a most relevant instrument today because of the importance given to the concept of storytelling and getting in touch with one's own story. The literature is filled with books on the importance of the story. Perhaps the most widely read is John Shea's *Stories of God*.

The Thematic Apperception Test was first developed by Henry Murray and his colleagues at Harvard in 1938. It consists of nineteen cards on which there is a picture in black and white, plus one blank card. The person is asked to make up a story using the card as a stimulus. He or she is instructed to tell what led up to the experience of the moment contained in the picture, what is happening at the moment, what the characters in the picture are feeling and thinking, and finally what the outcome of the story will be. For the blank card, they are invited to imagine something on the card, describe it, and tell a story about it. The stories are interpreted in terms of the hero of the story, who is usually the one the person identifies with. After the hero of the story is isolated, a content analysis of the story is made using Murray's list of needs. Special attention is given to the intensity, duration, and frequency of what is talked about in the story. The Thematic Apperception demands a great deal from the person, because to tell a story is difficult. There must be a definite beginning, middle, and end. Consequently, this procedure demands complex and well-organized verbal responses. From these responses, the clinician gathers some idea of the present motivational and emotional functioning of the person and the way the person relates to a very unstructured situation.

As we have noted, the Edwards Personal Preference Schedule, based on the personality research of Henry Murray, gives us a good index of a person's needs. The Thematic Apperception Test, on the other hand, gives us the process—through the action of the storytelling, the person makes sense out of a situation. Accordingly, the use of these two procedures enables us to compare and contrast the data obtained both in the form of content responses on the Edwards and the process approach of the Thematic Apperception Test.

Rorschach Inkblots. The Rorschach perhaps requires the greatest sophistication to administer, to understand, and to interpret. It was created more than sixty years ago by Hermann Rorschach. Today it is regarded as a powerful instrument for predicting suicide attempts, formulating treatment plans, and evaluating the progress of therapy. The Rorschach is receiving more and more attention because it enables a clinician in one hour to gather information that would take hours or weeks of ordinary interviews. The test and its interpretation are based on the psychoanalytic teachings of Freud and Jung. However, the procedure may be used by clinicians of any theoretical orientation.

The Rorschach consists of ten cards designed in ink. A person is asked to consider each of the ten cards and describe what he or she sees. The clinician writes down everything the person says using a shorthand technique. The number of responses varies from person to person. What is constant in the relational style revealed by the person is far more important than the creatures and plots they see. Examples of what people see in the Rorschach include bats and butterflies; human faces and futuristic paintings; landscapes, maps, fire, blood, and many more items. These responses may be taken as a whole, or focus on this or that detail. Whether or not the person is aware of color is regarded as very important information. Likewise, if a person perceives human movement, this is considered significant in the overall analysis of the results. Putting all this information together in a report requires a great deal of effort, time, and training. Most clinicians take at least three courses in their preparation to give and interpret the Rorschach.

Thus far, the procedure for making an assessment of one's intellectual functioning has been described. The Wechsler Adult Intelligence Scale can be used as a clinical instrument, and much can be ascertained of the person's style of relating from the rapport established between the two persons. The clinician must be sensitive to the person, and observant of behavioral signals of anxiety and depression, as well as interactional and anecdotal comments made during the testing situation. The self-rating tests of personality were presented and the various scales explained. It should be noted that on these procedures faking good or bad is possible. Hence, it is all the more necessary for the skilled clinician to discover convergent as well as divergent data to support hypotheses which will be developed as a result of the testing. The projectives, used in a typical battery, enable unconscious material to surface. These procedures were described less fully because the nature of these instruments requires the element of surprise and novelty. To explain their functioning and methodology too completely is to contaminate their effectiveness.

Each procedure in the battery has now been explained. The Wechsler Adult Intelligence Scale was presented as the most common and comprehensive test used to discern the person's ability to learn from experience. Each of the self-rating tests of personality was reviewed. The Minnesota Multiphasic Personality Inventory was used in the diagnosis of mental dysfunction reflecting both the type and the intensity of the problem. The Strong-Campbell Interest Inventory isolates a person's interest pattern and gives collaborative evidence to someone who desires to know if his or her vocational choice still obtains. The Edwards Personal Preference Schedule examines a person's needs; from this index of needs, we can come to appreciate what motivates a person to behavior. The Sentence Completion provides a broad range of items for the individual to respond to, and from these responses the clinician is given knowledge about important relationships in the person's life, emotions, fears, attitudes, wishes. The Hutt Adaptation of the Bender Gestalt provides us with the opportunity to observe both the product and process of personality functioning. The Thematic Apperception Test enables us to understand how a person makes sense out of an unstructured situation by telling a story about it. Finally, the Rorschach permits us to observe the relational style of the person. Next, we will explore the values derived from psychological testing from those who have participated in this experience.

PERSONAL AND PROFESSIONAL GROWTH

For the past five years I have requested pastoral counseling students taking my course in psychological testing to answer two questions: (1) Of what value has this experience been in your personal life? (2) Of what value has this experience been in your professional life as a pastoral counselor? What follows is the testimony of students whose personal and professional lives have been enriched through the use of psychological testing.

I think what the procedures have done for me is that they have affirmed and made more concrete some of the insights others and myself have raised concerning myself. I really didn't learn anything that I hadn't already suspected. However, the procedures ratified these suspicions in such a way that I can no longer say "Well, maybe this is true but . . ." and instead now look at them and deal with them. The procedures further provided a framework on which to base further work in dealing with the basic and important issues in my life. The series of procedures helped me reduce anxiety in taking such tests and viewing them as something which is threatening rather than helpful. Now I feel more that the results are threatening only if I choose to ignore or fight them. The course and the taking of the procedures taught me a greater respect for being more precise in my own work as a counselor and also the uniqueness and frailty of the human person. Underlying all of this is the possibility of growth.

Psychological testing has helped me to pull together a large body of factual information about myself: my values, my needs, my fears, the places where I seem to be stuck and perhaps need some help, and best of all, it has helped me to see more clearly my growing edge.

First of all, psychological testing has helped me in my work because I know myself more precisely and I am less likely to allow my own issues to intrude into the therapeutic process. Second, it has given me a much clearer understanding of and appreciation for the value of psychological testing. Third, it has given me at least one procedure that I can administer myself, the Sentence Completion procedure. And fourth, it has helped me to understand what to look for when reviewing psychological test results and what to ask for when requesting a battery to be given to a client.

I feel the most help obtained from psychological testing was to take time to look at the person I am according to what I put on paper. In the beginning, I blocked out any positive help the experience could be. I just felt there would be too many negatives and limitations and I would not be able to deal with them. However, after examining all the procedures, I came to the conclusion that even though negatives do exist, the positive aspects are factors I should keep in mind and build on rather than be overly concerned about the negatives. Working through all the procedures has affirmed me in the woman I am and the woman I hope to become.

I have not yet administered any of the procedures to any client. I work with a priest who uses several of the projective procedures and I feel more comfortable in understanding their use and meaning. I feel particularly interested in the TAT procedure and the Sentence Completion. If I were to use any, I would probably start with them. However, I do feel I would need more experience in interpreting the meanings of the procedures before I would use them comfortably. I understand how these and other procedures could help when an impasse happens in a therapy process. Although the course was intended to teach us about psychological testing, I believe I learned more about how to develop a comfortable and trusting relationship with the client before any amount of therapeutic work can be done.

Psychological testing has helped me personally by providing procedures which helped me to gain greater insight into myself: my skills, my talents, interests, strengths, needs, and weaknesses of character. It allayed some of the fears and fantasies that I had of discovering "skeletons" in the closet. Essentially what it did was provide a singularly worthwhile opportunity to get a comprehensive picture of my strengths and weaknesses. I feel that in drawing up my psychological profile, I actually went through a process of self-acceptance and, beyond that, of celebrating self and the marvel of God's work in me.

Psychological testing has helped me become familiar with some of the basic psychological testing procedures, how they were formulated, what they are designed to measure, and the basic principles for interpreting the data that result from these testing procedures. I had heard of most of the procedures presented in the course and even taken some of them before. However, the course gave me a close-up familiarity I had not had before. Learning about the tests in an experiential manner proved a valuable experience both because it gave me an appreciation of what clients go through when they take the tests and because it provided valuable information for my own understanding. For example, I became more aware of my dependency needs and how I tend to express aggression covertly. Although I do not feel qualified to administer the testing procedures or make definitive interpretations on their results, I do feel confident about drawing tentative conclusions from the test data. I also feel confident that I can read with understanding a psychologist's report based on the test data. As a result of the course I think I could ask intelligent questions about the testing procedures and how interpretative conclusions were reached from the data. The course has whetted my appetite for more reading in the area of psychological testing and planted the idea of becoming credentialized some day to administer the testing procedures.

Psychological testing has had no immediate payoff in my clinical work but I expect it will down the road. My familiarity with the tests and their value make it likely that I will refer clients to a psychologist for testing when such seems indicated. This could prove beneficial both to client and myself in the process of therapy.

Psychological testing has helped me to begin to integrate the different learning experiences that have been part of my life. It has helped me to sum up my life, and to assimilate especially the learning experiences of this past year; to confront my life issues and to meet myself as I truly am. It also gave me an opportunity to see where I have been stifling my creativity, blocking myself from the depth, width, and breadth of who I can be. I am less arrogant, more vulnerable, hopefully more patient, more accepting of self, and am a wiser person than when I decided to take this course. I did not expect the outcome of this course to affect me so personally; I thought it would be something useful for the others and therefore I thought it would be good to take. I *know* now so much less and I have experienced my faith in a new way. It is a frightening experience to see myself as I really am, to risk becoming the person that I have not been and to leave the future of how it will work out for me in God's hands. This course had a resurrection impact on me and has helped me to face issues that would have taken years to face. The different tests that I took engaged me in living and have challenged my creativity. I do not see how without this experience I could have been fruitfully and creatively engaged in helping others to become whole and to be able to do that through my life experiences. The latter is a necessary ingredient to be a faith-filled pastoral counselor, who in my book should be understanding, caring and wise—a person who knows how to be self-actualizing and hopeful.

CONCLUSION

In this chapter various procedures were explained through which a dynamic and developmental vision of the human person is obtained. These included various dimensions of the personality expressed through intelligence, emotional affectivity, relational style, interest patterns, needs analysis, and behavioral manifestations. Providing the background for the activity of psychological testing, certain philosophical principles were advanced from which the "given" nature of human existence and the human person might be understood. The foreground, or goal directedness, was expressed in certain psychological criteria befitting the growth-oriented individual. It must be clearly stated that the growth process is never completed. Rather, a call to further and more differentiated growth is always being signaled by the questions life asks of the individual. The context of the chapter was authentic growth, which is necessarily expressive of the individual pastoral counselor. Only through a free and open involvement in the process do growth, direction, awareness, acceptance, insight, and depth of self-understanding result. These are the beneficial results of psychological testing. After these issues have surfaced, a sensitive dialogue must occur between the clinician and person for the purpose of isolating important questions through which the person can grow to a higher and more integrated self. This is accomplished when the person can understand areas that need remediation, or can receive help to work through conflicts, which can become possibilities for change and growth. Psychological testing can be a tremendous help to someone engaged in therapy.

In closing, psychological testing can, and does, enable personal and professional growth of the life and ministry of the pastoral counselor. The context for this activity is seen within the framework of growth. What is of paramount importance is for the clinician to approach the activity of psychological testing with reverence, awe, and dignity because of the human person. This is accomplished when the human person is related to as subject rather than dehumanized as object. It is likewise important for the clinician to be aware of his or her own needs, woundedness, brokenness, and vulnerability as the unique struggle of another person is discovered through psychological testing. There is indeed a commonality among those who share the human condition.

REFERENCES

Anastasi, A. *Psychological Testing*. London: Macmillan, 1982.

Becker, E. *The Denial of Death*. New York: Free Press, 1973.

Bender, L. *A Visual Motor Gestalt Test and Its Clinical Use*. American Orthopsychiatric Association Research Monographs, No. 3. New York: American Orthopsychiatric Association, 1938.

Campbell, D. P. *Handbook for the Strong Vocational Interest Blank*. Stanford, Calif.: Stanford University Press, 1974.

Edwards, Allen L. *Edwards Personal Preference Schedule Manual*. The Psychological Corporation, 1954, revised 1959.

Fisher, S., and S. Cleveland. *Body Image and Personality*. New York: Van Nostrand, 1958.

Glasser, W. *Reality Therapy*. New York: Harper, 1965.

Haun, H. *Movie Quote Book*. New York: Lippincott & Cromwell, 1980. *I Never Sang for My Father*, Columbia, 1970. Screenplay by Robert Anderson; based on his play, directed by Gilbert Cates.

————. *Movie Quote Book*. New York: Lippincott & Cromwell, 1980. *Summer Wishes, Winter Dreams*, Columbia, 1973. Original screenplay by Stewart Stern, directed by Gilbert Cates.

Horst, P. *Personality: Measurement of Dimension*. San Francisco: Jossey-Bass, 1968.

Hutt, M. L. *The Hutt Adaptation of the Bender-Gestalt.* New York: Greene and Stratten, 1969.
Maslow, A. "The Need to Know," *Journal of General Psychology,* 68, 1963, 111–125.
May, R. *The Art of Counseling.* Nashville: Abingdon, 1967.
Murray, H. A., and C. Kluckhohn. "Outline of a Conception of Personality." In C. Kluckhohn, H. A. Murray, and D. Schneider (Eds.), *Personality in Nature, Society, and Culture,* 2nd ed. New York: Knopf, 1953.
Nicoli, A. M., Jr. (Ed.). *The Harvard Guide to Modern Psychiatry.* Cambridge: Belknap Press of Harvard University Press, 1978.
Segal, S. J. "The Role of Personality Factors in Vocational Choice," *American Psychologist,* 10, 1955, 365–66.
Shea, John. *Stories of God.* Chicago: Thomas More Press, 1978.
Sullivan, H. S. *Conception of Modern Psychiatry.* New York: Norton, 1953.
Van Kaam, A. *Religion and Personality.* Englewood Cliffs, N.J.: Prentice Hall, 1964.
Wertheimer, M. "Studies in the Theory of Gestalt Psychology," *Psychol. Forsch.,* 4, 1923, 301–350.

RECOMMENDED READINGS

General References

Anastasi, Anne. *Psychological Testing.* New York: Macmillan, 1968.
Anderson, H. H., and G. L. Anderson. (Eds.). *An Introduction to Projective Techniques.* Englewood Cliffs, N.J.: Prentice Hall, 1951.
Cronbach, L. J. *Essentials of Psychological Testing,* 2nd ed. New York: Harper, 1960.
Cronbach, L. J., and P. E. Meehl. "Construct Validity in Psychological Tests." *Psychological Bulletin* 52, 1955, 281–302.
Harrower, M. *Appraising Personality: An Introduction to the Projective Techniques.* New York: F. Watts, 1964.
Lindzey, G. "On the Classification of Projective Techniques," *Psychological Bulletin, 56, 1959, 158–68.*
Meehl, P. E. *Clinical Versus Statistical Prediction.* Minneapolis: University of Minnesota Press, 1054.
Ogdon, Donald. *Psychodiagnostics and Personality Assessment: A Handbook,* 2nd ed. Norfolk, Va.: Western Psychological Services, 1979.
Rabin, A. I., and M. R. Haworth (Eds.). *Projective Techniques with Children.* New York: Grune & Stratton, 1960.
Rapaport, D., M. Gill, and R. Schafer. *Diagnostic Psychological Testing,* rev. ed. New York: International Universities Press, 1968.
Schafer, R. *The Clinical Application of Psychological Tests.* New York: International Universities Press, 1948.

References to Specific Techniques

RORSCHACH AND OTHER INKBLOT TECHNIQUES

Beck, S. J. *Rorschach's Test: Vol. I. Basic Processes.* New York: Grune & Stratton, 1944.
————. *Rorschach's Test: Vol. II. A Variety of Personality Pictures.* New York: Grune & Stratton, 1945.

————. *Rorschach's Test: Vol. III. Advances in Interpretation.* New York: Grune & Stratton, 1952.

Exner, J. L., Jr. *The Rorschach Systems.* New York: Grune & Stratton, 1969.

Holtzman, W. H. *Inkblot Perception and Personality: Holtzman Inkblot Technique.* Austin, Tex.: University of Texas Press, 1961.

Klopfer, B., M. D. Ainsworth, W. F. Klopfer, and R. R. Holt. *Developments in the Rorschach Technique.* Vol. I: *Techniques and Theory.* New York: Harcourt, 1954.

Klopfer, B., et al. *Developments in the Rorschach Technique.* Vol. II: *Fields of Application.* New York: Harcourt, 1956.

Phillips, L., and J. G. Smith. *Rorschach Interpretation: Advanced Technique.* New York: Grune & Stratton, 1953.

Piotrowski, Z. *Perceptanalysis.* New York: Macmillan, 1957.

Rickers-Ovsiankina, M. A. (Ed.). *Rorschach Psychology.* New York: Wiley, 1960.

Schafer, R. *Psychoanalytic Interpretation in Rorschach Testing.* New York: Grune & Stratton, 1954.

THEMATIC APPERCEPTION TEST

Bellak, L. *The Thematic Apperception Test and Children's Apperception Test in Clinical Use.* New York: Grune & Stratton, 1954.

Henry, W. E. *The Analysis of Fantasy.* New York: Wiley, 1956.

Lindzey, G. "Thematic Apperception Test: Interpretive Assumptions and Related Empirical Evidence," *Psychological Bulletin,* 49, 1952, 1–25.

Murray, H. *Explorations in Personality.* New York: Oxford University Press, 1938.

————. *Thematic Apperception Test Manual.* Cambridge, Mass.: Harvard University Press, 1943.

DRAW-A-PERSON TEST (DAP)

Goodenough, F. R. *Measurement of Intelligence by Drawings.* New York: World, 1926.

Hammer, E. F. *The Clinical Application of Projective Drawings.* Springfield, Ill.: Charles C Thomas, 1958.

Harris, D. B. *Children's Drawings as Measures of Intellectual Maturity.* New York: Harcourt, 1963.

Machover, Karen. *Personality Projection in the Drawing of the Human Figure.* Springfield, Ill.: Charles C Thomas, 1948.

BENDER VISUAL-MOTOR GESTALT TEST

Bender, L. A. *A Visual Motor Gestalt Test and Its Clinical Use. Res. Monogr.* No. 3. New York: American Orthopsychiatric Association, 1938.

————. *Instructions for the Use of the Visual Motor Gestalt Test.* New York: American Orthopsychiatric Association, 1946.

Hutt, M. L. *The Hutt Adaptation of the Bender-Gestalt Test.* New York: Grune & Stratton, 1969.

Koppitz, E. *The Bender-Gestalt Test for Young Children.* New York: Grune & Stratton, 1964.

HOUSE-TREE-PERSON TEST

Buck, J. N. "The H-T-P Technique: A Qualitative and Quantitative Scoring Manual. I," *Journal of Clinical Psychology,* 4, 1948, 319–96.

————. "The H-T-P Technique: a Qualitative and Quantitative Scoring Manual. II," *Journal of Clinical Psychology,* 1949, 37–76.

————. "The H-T-P Test," *Journal of Clinical Psychology,* 4, 1948, 151–59.

SENTENCE COMPLETION TECHNIQUES

Forer, B. R. "A Structured Sentence Completion Test," *Journal of Projective Techniques,* 14, 1950, 15–30.

Rotter, J. B., and J. E. Rafferty. *Manual for the Rotter Incomplete Sentences Blank, College Form.* New York: Psychological Corporation, 1950.

Tendler, A. D. "A Preliminary Report on a Test for Emotional Insight," *Journal of Applied Psychology,* 14, 1930, 123–36.

MINNESOTA MULTIPHASIC PERSONALITY INVENTORY

Dahlstrom, W., Welsh and Dahlstrom. *An MMPI Handbook.* Minneapolis: University of Minnesota Press, 1979.

Gough, H. D. "Diagnostic Patterns on the MMPI," *Journal of Clinical Psychology,* 2, 1946, 23–27.

Graham, John R. *The MMPI: A Practical Guide.* New York: Oxford University Press, 1977.

Hathaway, S. R., and J. C. McKinley. *Minnesota Multiphasic Personality Inventory.* Minneapolis: University of Minnesota Press, 1942.

Hathaway, S. R., and P. E. Meehl. *An Atlas for the Clinical Use of the MMPI.* Minneapolis: University of Minnesota Press, 1951.

Hathaway, S. R., and E. D. Monachesi. *Analyzing and Predicting Juvenile Delinquency with the MMPI.* Minneapolis: University of Minnesota Press, 1952.

———. *An Atlas of Juvenile MMPI Profiles.* Minneapolis: University of Minnesota Press, 1961.

———. *Adolescent Personality and Behavior: MMPI Patterns of Normal Delinquent, Drop-out and Other Outcomes.* Minneapolis: University of Minnesota Press, 1963.

Meehl, P. E. "Profile Analysis of the MMPI in Differential Diagnosis," *Journal of Applied Psychology,* 30, 1946, 517–24.

———. "Configural Scoring," *Journal of Consulting Psychology,* 14, 1950, 165–71.

Meehl, P. E., and S. R. Hathaway. "The K Factor as a Suppressor Variable in the MMPI," *Journal of Applied Psychology,* 30, 1946, 525–64.

Welsh, G. S. "An Extension of Hathaway's MMPI Coding," *Journal of Consulting Psychology,* 12, 1948, 343–44.

Wiener, D. N. "Subtle and Obvious Keys for the MMPI," *Journal of Consulting Psychology,* 12, 1948, 164–70.

PART THREE
ON DOING PASTORAL COUNSELING

CHAPTER SEVEN

The Counseling Pastor

BARRY K. ESTADT, PH.D.

Pastors and their associates in ministry have rich opportunities for entering into a counseling relationship with a wide range of people at the precise time that they most need it. Studies have consistently pointed to the fact that religiously involved people turn first to their ministers when they need help.

Henderson (1990) in a doctoral dissertation at Loyola College studied the question "Who sees a pastoral counselor?" In his literature review, the pattern for individuals seeking out the clergyperson for initial assistance continues to be consistent. Among the studies cited by Henderson are the following:

In 1960, based on a 1957 study, Gurin, Veroff, and Feld reported in *Americans View Their Mental Health* that the source of help used by people who have sought professional guidance for a personal problem are: clergy, 42 percent; doctor, 29 percent; psychiatrist or psychologist in private practice, 12 percent; psychiatrist or psychologist in a clinic or hospital, 6 percent; and marriage counselor, 3 percent; with 8 percent listing some other source.

In their 1976 study, Veroff, Douvan, and Kulka (1981) found that 39.2 percent of those studied said that they would first go to the clergy. Henderson summarizes the studies of Arnold and Schick (1979) who reviewed the previous twenty years of research on clergy and pastoral care: "Clergy are sought out first or exclusively by many who decide they require formal help."

Henderson points to an interesting disparity which, I am convinced, is critical to understanding the role of the pastoral counselor. He points to research that reveals that 96.25 percent of Americans acknowledge a belief in God, while only 42 percent of psychiatrists and psychologists profess to be believers. Henderson also cites research that indicates that counselors are resistant to discussing spiritual values.

The results of Henderson's personal research is directly pertinent to the role of the counseling pastor. In essence he found that the profile of the client seeking assistance from a pastoral counselor is one who has had a childhood religious background, who identifies with a religion, who attends church or synagogue regularly, who views the spiritual life as important and who wants a counselor to have a religious background even though the specific denomination of the counselor is not a critical variable.

The empirical data contributed by Henderson supports the pastoral experience of clergy who find that persons with religious values and an expressed religious commitment turn to the ministers of the Church when they experience the need for counseling. It also substantiates the expectation that people have of their churches in terms of the basic ministerial services which they need and are actively seeking.

There is no question about the need or the expectation. Preaching, teaching, and liturgical roles provide ministers with a visibility enjoyed by few other members of the helping professions. Through these activities they make contact with many people. If ministers project a sense of caring, coupled with competence, it is quite natural for people to seek them out. Relatively healthy, church-related people readily turn to the minister at times of special stress, looking for a supportive relationship with a person whom they already perceive to be understanding. Many people, when faced with important decisions, are eager for an opportunity to explore the short- and long-range implications of their choices. Some who seek out the minister are persons who are hurting deeply but who would not think in terms of going to a psychologist or psychiatrist because they do not perceive themselves to be mental patients. Frequently, for religiously sensitive people, intrapsychic and interpersonal struggles have spiritual implications.

In thinking about the place of counseling within ministry, I find it helpful to think in terms of the five basic functions of ministry as outlined by Henri Nouwen in *Creative Ministry* (1971). Nouwen suggests that the many activities of ministry can be ordered under the headings of preaching, teaching, organizing, celebrating, and individual pastoral care. Pastoral counseling, as I see it, is a specific form of individual pastoral care in which the minister leaves the ninety-nine to minister to the specific needs of individuals, couples, families, and small groups.

As the pastor, chaplain, or associate minister attempts to integrate a counseling ministry within the framework of the general ministry setting, which involves preaching, teaching, celebration, and an array of organizational activities, a number of important issues emerge as requests for help come from all directions. Chief among these questions is the basic issue of whether one should respond personally or whether one should be the vehicle for putting that person in touch with an appropriate agency or person from whom effective help can be received. The present chapter offers an overview of the role of the "counseling pastor" and attempts to clarify how I see counseling fitting into the overall role of one who serves a congregation in the role of pastor or chaplain with its multidimensional functions and relationships.

SHORTER-TERM COUNSELING

The pastor or associate with training in counseling is in a unique position to respond to a variety of short-term counseling needs of parishioners, particularly those who are relatively healthy and emotionally stable. Frequently, the request to "see the clergyperson" is a natural follow-up to preaching and teaching as individuals attempt to integrate and to internalize the Gospel message presented to them in the pulput and through the many forms of religious instruction. Preaching and teaching provide information and inspiration; pastoral counseling deals with clarification and integration.

Many healthy, well-functioning parishioners have a need, at a particular time of stress, to speak freely and from the heart with someone whom they know, respect, and trust. When individuals endure the loss of loved ones, are concerned about the illness and possible decision to place a parent in a nursing home, or are discouraged by the sudden loss of a job, they need someone they know and trust to turn to for support. Few professionals are in the unique position of the clergyperson to respond to such needs.

A few sessions in which a person can unburden himself or herself and receive the warmth and care of a person who represents God to them can be enormously freeing. Sometimes people move quickly from an unburdening of hurts to a focus on present and future goals. They may have had their wheels firmly stuck in the mud: the more they tried to get free on their own, the deeper they found themselves going. The critical need for some people is some temporary assistance to get moving again from a sensitive and mature adult on solid ground.

I believe that the observations of Leona Tyler (1961) on "minimal change therapy" makes a good model for the clergyperson. Tyler makes the point that sometimes an individual needs to make only a slight change in direction. The difficulties that a client experiences can be thought of as indications that the client is headed in a direction that is not working. Counseling creates a situation in which a person may become aware of the directional shifts that are possible, with the assurance that someone will be giving moral support through what might be a difficult rotation of the axis. In pursuing further the implications of this geometric analysis, Tyler comments that a directional shift of only 10 degrees makes a difference of 170 miles in one's destination on a journey of a thousand miles. Similarly, a relatively minor shift in the psychological direction in which a person is moving may change a client's life considerably over a long period of years.

The short-term counseling contract can often be made with the liturgical calendar in mind; one might propose, for example, to meet weekly during the remaining seven weeks before Christmas or Easter. A fixed time suggests that the concerns, though important, are well within normal range. It allows the minister the option to renegotiate the contract later, leaving the door open for referral if that is the judgment at the end of the stipulated period.

A unique feature of short-term counseling within the general ministry setting is the fact that the relationship between the minister and counselee continues and is reinforced even though the formal counseling sessions end. The pastor, chaplain, or associate continues to relate to the parishioner within the context of the general ministry. There is an intimate sense of community as the parishioner takes part in a worship ceremony led by a pastor-counselor who has shared in one's deepest feelings and aspirations. There is also a reassuring sense of security in knowing that an appointment could readily be made for a follow-up session or two as one experiences the need for feedback from a trusted consultant. During my decade of counseling within a college-level seminary, the experience of follow-up sessions with students was routine. Sometimes the need was for reassurance, support, and an affirmation of ongoing growth; at other times, subsequent developmental issues emerged and new directions needed to be taken. At times there was the need to acknowledge mistakes and to seek God's forgiveness within the sacrament of reconciliation through a minister who understood their struggles, frustrations, and hopes over a period of years.

A young Roman Catholic priest, enrolled in a degree program in pastoral counseling, reflected on his early "informal" counseling ministry:

> Upon ordination, I was sent to a large, rapidly growing parish in suburban Washington. I found that many people of various ages and backgrounds sought me out as a listener. I rarely had answers, but frequently I would be told that I had been very helpful. I also spent much time in those early days in ministry in visiting the sick in their homes. I found that I was not simply providing the sacraments (Eucharist, Penance, Anointing), but I was also being a "sacrament" to them by my listening attitude. Through me, these hurting and lonely people were experiencing the compassion of Jesus. These experiences together informed the nature of my preaching. As I survey my homily outlines even now, I note a continual progression from more heady and intellectual preaching to more feeling-oriented preaching.

The same young priest spoke of his ministry of pastoral counseling in terms of disciples on pilgrimage.

A pilgrim is one who is searching for the presence of God; he is like one who has tasted but hungers for more. There are, however, mountains to climb, rivers to ford, obstacles on the journey. Sometimes, like the pilgrim beaten by robbers on his journey down to Jericho (Luke 10:29–37) we need help to complete the trip. I see the process of pastoral counseling as one of empathic listening that helps a person see through the burdens that stand in his way to the real presence of Christ who is in him. The Christ who is in the counselor evokes and rekindles the Christ who is in the client. In a way, the pilgrim who is seeking help, the client, has returned to the shores of the Jordan and is asking again the question, "Rabbi, where do you live?" (John 1:38) The counselor responds as Christ, "Come and see!" (John 1:39)

A young Baptist minister, at the completion of the master's degree program in pastoral counseling, wrote with some eloquence of the impact of the counseling program on his ability to be an effective pastor. He comments:

The last three years of my life has helped prepare me for a ministry of helping others. The church I pastor had existed for twelve years before I first came. The congregation was made up of forty active members who were hurting. They had watched their church go down from about 150 members to forty. . . . The church today has a strong reputation within our Baptist Convention. The church is full on Sundays and we have moved to two services to accommodate a membership of over five hundred.

I have learned many things. First, people take their problems to someone they know and like. Second, people take their concerns to someone whom they respect. The pastor who leads an exemplary life, who is wise and discreet in his behavior, is one who is respected and held in high esteem. Third, people are most likely to seek help from a pastor who communicates that he is interested in being available for counseling and who is perceived to be competent.

Many of my members are heavily burdened. My primary joy comes from helping them to lift those burdens through Jesus Christ the Lord. I thoroughly believe, though I do not always understand the process, that Jesus gives rest to the conscience; he removes the sense of guilt; he gives peace to the heart; he offers support to the needy; he removes the thorn in the flesh; he enables many people to rise above their afflictions.

What I have, and am learning through time, is the reality of Jesus' statement: "Come unto me, all ye that labor and are heavy laden and I will give your rest." (Matt. 11:28) Before I could ever help anyone else, I first had to achieve rest from my own burdens of life. Having this rest and peace has helped me to achieve joy in my calling as a pastor and as a pastoral counselor.

REFERRAL FOR LONGER-TERM INSIGHT THERAPY

For a minister who serves a congregation or an institution as pastor or chaplain, it is important to think through the implication of engaging in longer-term counseling or therapy with members of the congregation. It is the consensus of most writers in the field of psychotherapy that the success of therapy is related to keeping its focus on "the therapeutic working alliance." This amounts to a contract between the therapist and the client to meet on a regularly scheduled basis to deal with the emotional life of the client. The focus is always on the interests, needs, and welfare of the client. Within the framework of this working alliance, the therapist does not introject personal needs and problems from without; rather the therapist's training helps to keep purely personal issues from interfering with dedication to the task of therapy.

In a ministerial setting, where there are multiple role relationships, the single-mindedly dedication to the task of long-term therapy is difficult. If a long-term client, for example, serves on the budget committee which deals with your salary and expense budget, feelings about the client are likely to be generated in you which are not derived from the ongoing therapy. Whether these feelings are anger because of curtailment of the budget, or gratitude because of a salary increase, they are feelings that are generated from experiences outside the therapy sessions. At the same time, positive or negative feelings on the part of the client, deriving from the work of the committee, may readily enter into the work of therapy. As roles multiply, confusion grows to the detriment of both therapist and client.

In shorter-term counseling for ongoing developmental concerns, the confusion can be kept to a minimum since the counseling relationship is relatively brief and typically does not involve the intensity of feelings which develop in longer-term therapy. Moreover, the conflicts and concerns dealt with in shorter-term counseling are, for the most part, conscious ones such as the person's need to cope with crises, the need to mobilize one's resources, the need for reflection and decision making. Frequently, short-term counseling involves normal developmental concerns as clients attempt to meet various levels of human needs. As one shifts to longer-term counseling, however, issues of transference and countertransference become more difficult to deal with, whether the longer-term counseling involves personal growth issues for relatively integrated clients or therapy for more disturbed clients.

At times in the parish setting it will be tempting to move from crisis intervention or from an initial request for shorter-term counseling into a longer-term therapy relationship, especially when resources in the area are lacking or when the client resists the referral. My experience leads me to recommend that you resist the temptation. If, however, you do elect to proceed despite the hazards cited above, it is especially important to seek out supervision to monitor the progress of the relationship.

Aside from the concerns intrinsic to the counseling relationship, both short-term and longer-term counseling with members of one's own congregation raise issues in terms of the allocation of one's time and energy and the charging of fees to members of the congregation. A solution which seems to work for some ministers is to work out with the board of the church the amount of time to be allotted to the counseling ministry. As for fees, there are dozens of variations depending on the unique characteristics of the congregation and the community at large. Some churches have a policy that shorter-term counseling up to a given number of sessions should be without fee, recommending that longer-term counselees pay a fee based on a sliding scale. In other cases, a counseling service is set up with the understanding that clients contribute in keeping with an approved fee scale. Typically, fees are expected of nonmembers. In all cases it is important to have an understanding of whether the fee is paid to the church or to the minister directly. As long as the arrangements are clear and appropriate to the given setting, many variations are possible.

ONGOING SUPPORTIVE COUNSELING

While I strongly recommend a policy of referral for longer-term therapy, I find the concept of *open-ended supportive counseling* well within the general ministry framework. I believe that pastoral support is one of the services that persons committed to the Church have a right to expect. Supportive pastoral counseling, as I see it, is a relationship in which the minister assists the client in dealing with the difficulties, frustrations, and tragedies of life. Frequently, people do not need further insight: They understand only too well the reality of their situations. What they do need is the strength to carry on.

A few years ago I entered into what turned out to be a five-year supportive counseling relationship with Lori, a woman whose five-year-old son had leukemia. Lori found herself in a heartbreaking situation. For five years she daily attended to the needs of her son, knowing full well that the probability of death was never more than a few weeks away. As each new drug had a temporary effect, Lori's hopes surfaced: Maybe God will cure my baby? Each surge of hope was followed by the depressing anticipation of loss as the temporary effects of each drug eventually wore off. I was able, through a weekly supportive counseling session, to help Lori call upon her religious values as she sought strength to carry on week after week. It was a relationship in which Lori found the faith to sustain what would be unendurable alone. I experienced Jesus saying to Lori through me: "Come to me, you who are burdened and I will refresh you." It was important for both Lori and me to remember that Jesus used the word *refresh*. He did not say: "I will *take away* your burden."

SPIRITUAL DIRECTION

Many people seek out a pastoral person when they wish to deal with their spiritual journey. They are not interested in counseling or therapy in relationship to emotional needs but are looking for someone who can help them to grow in the life of the spirit. Tilden Edwards, in the introduction to his book *Spiritual Friend* (1980), points to the need of many such people:

> A neighbor recently confided to me that she had been going through a "crisis of soul" for some time, but felt frustrated that there was no one she trusted to whom she could turn. She had been in therapy and knew that wouldn't suffice. She was a concerned social activist, but that did not alleviate the inner gnawing. She has a fine family, but they weren't prepared to be helpful here. She had been to Sunday liturgy, but that could not deal directly enough with her personal situation. She had considered seeing a priest or minister, but she was on the fringe of the Church, and anyway, she vaguely sensed that most clergy don't have the time or, if they do, don't have the special gift or training to deal with her situation. So where could she turn? (p. 1)

When individuals seek us out to speak about their spiritual lives, they expect us to be perceptive listeners who understand the journey of faith. Sometimes people come seeking information, with questions about prayer, meditation, and the Scriptures. At other times they come because of conflicts which they experience between what they perceive to be Gospel values and their own inner tendencies. Many times they come searching to be understood, accepted, and loved by a person who represents for them the God whom they experience as nebulous and elusive. In each of these situations the minister can be something of a guide and copilgrim as the story of the client's religious pilgrimage unfolds. Support, encouragement, direction, and challenge can be offered within the context of a pastoral counseling relationship.

It is my belief that ministers, with training in the listening skills of pastoral counseling along with their broad-based knowledge of human development, are well equipped to enter with clients into the journey of faith. In addition to calling upon one's theological background and therapeutic training, what is required is an understanding of one's own spiritual journey. This understanding can be significantly enriched through study of contemporary authors on the spiritual life as well as through an assimilation of the literature accumulated over the centuries under the rubric of spiritual direction.

EDUCATION FOR LIVING A FULLER LIFE

As I look forward to the future of pastoral counseling, I am struck by the possible significance of some of the movements within the field of psychology. In 1968 the counseling psychologist was defined as a professional who engaged in three primary roles: The first is the *remedial or rehabilitative* role, the second is the *preventive,* and the third is the *educative and developmental.* Eight years later, in 1976, while endorsing the three roles as constitutive of their profession, counseling psychologists called for a reordering of primary roles (Ivey 1980):

> It is believed that the educational/developmental role of the counseling psychologist must now be considered *primary* with the preventive role serving as the secondary function. The traditional remedial and rehabilitative role is not discarded, but becomes subsumed under a clarified and enlarged definition of counseling psychology. (p. 72)

Gilbert Wrenn, senior spokesman for the profession, projected the future activity of counseling psychologists in an article entitled, "Observations on What Counseling Psychologists Will Be Doing During the Next Twenty Years." He outlined nine areas of activity: (1) holistic health cooperation; (2) life stage specialization; (3) counseling for total life satisfaction; (4) career planning for those in midlife and older; (5) facilitating peer learning groups; (6) serving as counselors of men and women as persons, not as male or female; (7) counseling couples; (8) counseling with all ages in schools and colleges; (9) research. (1980, pp. 32–35)

As I reflect on the refocus of counseling psychologists from the dual vantage point of membership in that group and my experience of ministry, it seems to me that no professional group has the opportunities that ministers have for the educational/developmental function outlined above. There is almost no limit to the type of creative programming possible within the general ministry of the church to assist individuals, couples, families, and groups of people in their efforts to live full, satisfying, healthy, and meaningful lives. The list of activities cited above by Wrenn suggests the broad outline of a program for the parish-based pastoral counselor.

INCLUDING A PASTORAL COUNSELOR ON THE MINISTRY TEAM

The emergence of various forms of team ministry with a member trained in counseling is a phenomenon that is growing nationwide. For some denominations, this involves clergy with specialized training in counseling; for others, religiously involved lay persons with training in psychology, social work, or counseling are included as full-time or part-time members of parish staffs. A growing number of ordained clergy, religious brothers and sisters, laymen and laywomen are graduating from degree programs that focus specifically on pastoral counseling.

The counseling service in the parish setting is a powerful symbol of the Church's concern for the well-being of its members. It means that someone on the church staff is able and willing to hear the parishioner's personal story. When the Church, in the person of the pastoral counselor, can communicate acceptance, concern, respect, and love to a person at a time of deep personal struggle, that individual will experience something of God's abiding love. Conversely, when people find themselves abandoned by the Church's ministers in their time of need, it may well be experienced as abandonment by God.

A local pastoral counseling service can be immensely freeing for the minister whose gifts lie in other areas of ministry or whose responsibilities make it all but impossible to schedule regular counseling sessions with people needing more extended help. Referral to the parish-based center is beneficial to both the minister and the parishioner. The minister has the satisfaction that the Church is meeting the person's need; the client experiences the care of the local church.

A unique example of how a layperson from the congregation of the church can serve as a full-time staff person has been the experience of the mother of three children and a grandmother of six. Active in her church for many years, she has written of her counseling ministry as she has completed a master's degree program in pastoral counseling. She comments:

> I am living out my call to the pastoral ministry as a member of the staff of my local Presbyterian church. I do individual counseling, hospital and home visitation, and I am the staff liaison for our deacons, mission council, and congregation care council.
>
> Initially, I began as a volunteer in the area of pastoral care. In 1984 my position became a full-time paid professional one. Because of the way my position developed, I have been able to bring my own philosophy of pastoral ministry to the position. I feel that the congregation made a strong statement and commitment to each other when they affirmed the need for the position I now hold.
>
> Individual counseling is an important part of my ministry and it has become an important ministry of the Church. Jesus did not try to change the people he called to be disciples. He accepted them. He accepted who they were and how they were. He accepted them as already potentially unique and beautiful. He called forth the gifts that were already theirs. It is with this philosophy and commitment that I come to the pastoral counseling ministry.
>
> I lead two support/therapy groups; one dealing with divorce and separation and a second group which is focused on grief, especially designed for those persons dealing with the grief over the loss of a loved one by death. I am anticipating starting a third group composed of clients who would benefit in a relational way from the therapy group dynamics.
>
> I spend many hours visiting and being with individuals and families who are living through the traumas of illness and death; visiting the one who is ill and working with families whose dynamics are changing because of one member's illness or death.
>
> I believe in the priesthood of all believers and feel a part of my ministry is to equip members of my church to minister as they live in the midst of life in the

world. This thought is continually with me; whether it is a sermon I preach, a prayer I pray, or a course I teach. As part of this ministry last year I taught a five-week course dealing with loss; loss of childhood, loss of dreams and expectations, loss of relationships, and loss through the aging process. I also organized and participated in a four-week course on homosexuality and put together a community workshop on AIDS. I do ongoing training sessions for deacons and parish visitors in our church who call on church members who are homebound or going through personal crisis.

I am ministered to continually by those with whom I am on a copilgrimage through the pastoral counseling ministry. Over and over I feel that the Holy Spirit is in the midst of life on earth. I believe miracles still do happen when hate-filled relations are turned into loving ones, when victims are changed into leaders, and when depression is turned into hope.

EMPOWERING VOLUNTEERS

Every congregation has people who are ready to become involved in a caring ministry. What many need is training, guidance, and the call from the parish to become involved. Pastoral counselors have unique skills for training volunteers to share in the pastoral-care mission of the Church. With such training, lay volunteers can reach out to the bereaved, to new persons in the community, to the growing number of people in hospitals and nursing homes, to the housebound, and many more. In empowering lay volunteers, the pastor and the pastoral counseling staff not only multiply their ministry, but they invite volunteers to experience the "priesthood of all believers" as they share both in the burdens and joys of ministering to and with people. Through empowering the laity, churches can become more nurturing and caring communities in which the love of God is experienced by all, even those members isolated from the mainstream of the activities of the Church. The counseling minister is especially prepared by disposition and training to be a catalyst in fostering the ongoing personal and ministerial growth of lay ministers.

THE DECADES AHEAD

My proposal for the counseling pastor for the decades ahead is to take advantage of the unique strengths of the pastoral role for entering into the lives of members of their congregation through the counseling ministry. Short-term counseling, referral for longer-term counseling, open-ended supportive counseling, spiritual direction, and education for living a fuller life are specific ways in which the counseling pastor can personally utilize counseling skills within the ministry of individual pastoral care. The counseling pastor can extend this ministry through others by working toward the development of counseling staff and by empowering volunteers to take an active role in the caring ministry of the Church.

SOME CONCLUDING REFLECTIONS

In outlining potential roles for the minister with training in pastoral counseling, I am aware that the day of the typical pastor or chaplain runs a wide gamut of personal and ministerial contacts. Pressures arise from the sheer amount of commitments, but they also stem from a wide range of emotional investment, as the minister moves through a typical day: a morning funeral, administrative details, visiting the sick, making a series of committee-related phone calls, jotting down notes for the Sunday homily, a counseling session before and after dinner, followed by a wedding rehearsal in the evening and an unexpected crisis-related drop-in. My experience over the years has suggested to me that I am most effectively present in the counseling relationship when I am not running from one event to another, constantly shifting gears emotionally. What I have come to in my own schedule is a commitment to "block-counseling," setting aside given afternoons or evenings for seeing a series of ongoing clients.

I precede that block with a period of quiet in which I attempt to let go of personal concerns, moving to an accepting and understanding stance in which my own anxieties, concerns, and preoccupations are, for the time being, set aside. In addition to preparing myself for entering into the internal frame of reference of clients, I find an added dimension in my counseling when I take the time for prayer before beginning a counseling block. I find that the Peace Prayer attributed to Saint Francis speaks directly and with precision to the counseling session. The first section of the prayer addresses the goals of counseling: "Lord, make me an instrument of Your peace; where there is hatred, let me sow love; where there is injury, pardon; where there is doubt, faith; where there is despair, hope; where there is darkness, light; and where there is sadness, joy." The middle section of the prayer speaks to the process of therapy: "Grant that I may not so much seek to be consoled as to console; to be understood as to understand; to be loved as to love." The final section speaks to the rewards of the counseling ministry: "For it is in giving that we receive; it is in pardoning that we are pardoned; it is in dying that we are born to eternal life."

REFERENCES

Arnold, J., and C. Schick. "Counseling by Clergy: A Review of Empirical Research," *Journal of Pastoral Counseling,* 14, 2, 76–101.
Caplan, R. B. *Helping the Helpers to Help.* New York: Seabury, 1972.
Edwards, T. *Spiritual Friend.* New York: Paulist Press, 1980.
Gorin, G., J. Veroff, and S. Feld. *Americans View Their Mental Health.* New York: Basic Books, 1975.

Henderson, D. *Who Sees a Pastoral Counselor?* Unpublished dissertation, Loyola College, 1990.

Ivey, A. "Counseling 2000: Time to Take Charge!" *The Counseling Psychologist,* 8, no. 4, 1980.

Kim, K. H., and F. C. Van Tatehnove. "The Utilizability of the Pastoral Counseling Response Scale (PCRS)," *Journal of Pastoral Care,* 35, no. 2, 1981.

Nouwen, H. *Creative Ministry.* New York: Doubleday, 1971.

Schuller, D. S., M. L. Brekke, and M. P. Strommen. *Readiness for Ministry.* Vandalia, Ohio: Association of Theological Schools, 1975.

Tyler, L. *The Work of the Counselor.* New York: Appleton, 1961.

Veroff, J., E. Dovran, and R. Kulka. *The Inner American.* New York: Basic Books, 1981.

Wrenn, G. "Observations on What Counseling Psychologists Will Be Doing During the Next Twenty Years," *The Counseling Psychologist,* 8, no. 4, 1980.

RECOMMENDED READINGS

Bane, J., A. Kutscher, R. Neale, and R. Reeves Jr. *Death and Ministry.* New York: Seabury, 1975.

Bausch, W. J. *Traditions, Tensions, Transitions in Ministry.* Mystic, Conn.: Twenty-third Publications, 1982.

Brekke, M., M. Strommen, and D. William. *Ten Faces of Ministry.* Minneapolis: Augsburg, 1979.

Brister, C. W. *The Promise of Counseling.* New York: Harper, 1978.

Capps, D. *Biblical Approaches to Pastoral Counseling.* Philadelphia: Westminster Press, 1981.

Cobb, J. B., Jr. *Theology and Pastoral Care.* Philadelphia: Fortress, 1977.

Edwards, T. *Spiritual Friend.* New York: Paulist Press, 1980.

Farnsworth, D., and F. Braceland. *Psychiatry, the Clergy, and Pastoral Counseling.* Collegeville, Minn.: St. John's University Press, 1969.

Fenhagen, J. C. *Mutual Ministry.* New York: Seabury, 1977.

Kelsey, M. T. *Caring.* New York: Paulist Press, 1981.

LaPlace, J. *Preparing for Spiritual Direction.* Chicago: Franciscan Herald Press, 1975.

Nouwen, H. J. *Creative Ministry.* Garden City, N.Y.: Doubleday, 1971.

Oates, W. *The Religious Care of the Psychiatric Patient.* Philadelphia: Westminster Press, 1978.

Peck, M. S. *The Road Less Traveled.* New York: Simon & Schuster, 1978.

Switzer, D. K. *The Minister as Crisis Counselor.* Nashville: Abingdon, 1974.

Whitehead, E., and J. Whitehead. *Community of Faith.* New York: Seabury, 1982.

CHAPTER EIGHT

The Ministry
of Crisis Intervention

RACHEL CALLAHAN, PH.D.

A few years ago a friend of mine, Jane, called to say she was at the end of her rope. She was feeling anxious and depressed. Her husband was becoming quieter and less accessible emotionally. Her three older children were showing an unusual degree of irritable hyperactivity. Jane's upset about the way her family was behaving was only worsened by her own feelings of being unable to cope with it all.

As we talked about what had been going on in the life of her family, the following picture emerged. Although Jane thoroughly enjoyed her three older children (five to nine years old), she had been looking forward to going back to work when they were all in school. Just when this dream was going to be realized, she found herself pregnant again. During the time of her pregnancy her husband, Jim, received a promotion which demanded a great deal of travel, frequent business trips, in addition to a daily ninety-minute commute each way to work. Although Jim and Jane loved where they were living, it became clear that they would need to move closer to where he worked if they were to enjoy any kind of family life together. To move closer to Jim's job also meant moving closer to both sets of grandparents. Although both Jim and Jane had basically good relationships with their folks and the children were very fond of their grandparents, being an hour and a half away provided a good buffer and Jim and Jane had very mixed feelings about moving any closer to home. In addition to all this, the cost of living was higher in the area to which they needed to move. During almost her whole pregnancy Jane did a great deal of frustrating house hunting but the cost of housing remained a deterrent to buying. When their fourth child was born, Jim and Jane were still in the middle of an unsuccessful house hunt. A month after the baby was born Jim's mother died rather unexpectedly. Worry about his dad made Jim more determined to move closer to "home." Within a couple of months they settled on a house, large enough to house their expanded family but also carrying a mortgage payment that effectively wiped out any of Jim's financial gain from his promotion and had the family under a fairly serious financial strain.

As you read about the above family and its fairly typical saga of birth, death, relocation, and financial stress, you might wonder what this illustration is doing at the beginning of a chapter about crisis intervention. Certainly when Jane called she didn't complain about being "in crisis." She was in fact upset at herself for not being able to cope more effectively. As we talked in the course of several meetings, she was able to identify some of the stresses that her family was experiencing—a new baby, a new job, a new home, new demands from her parents—as well as some of the losses—Jim's mother's death, the loss of good friends and neighbors, the loss of some sense of financial security, the loss (or postponement) of a dream to return to work.

In our highly mobile American society this kind of masked crisis frequently occurs in families. An alert pastoral counselor needs to listen for the stressors which do not become less stressful even though they are frequently experienced by many families. Fortunately, Jim and Jane and their children were able to look at and work through some of these crisis events. In too many cases the "Jims" and "Janes" try to muddle through, assuming that they should be able to cope more effectively with these statistically "normal" crises. And too often the first time that a pastoral counselor sees Jim and Jane is when they come for marriage or divorce counseling because their marriage has broken down.

Crisis intervention. A new wineskin for some very old wine—responding to persons gripped by the pain of loss or upset which demands of them new adaptations, decisions, and choices. The word *crisis* derives from the Greek word meaning "decision" or "turning point." It is often used negatively, conjuring up catastrophe or acute stress. At one time or another it is a normal part of all our lives, calling us to stretch and grow, to be broken and heal. If I am involved in the ministry of pastoral care or counseling, crisis is not a stranger.

The purpose of this chapter is to review briefly the theory and technique of crisis intervention and to consider its implications for ministry.

CRISIS INTERVENTION THEORY

It is paradoxical that the issue that stimulated the first formal study in crisis intervention in the psychiatric community is one that has long been a touchstone of pastoral ministry—bereavement and grief. Following the tragic fire at the Coconut Grove night club in Boston in 1942, which claimed the lives of almost five hundred persons, the survivors of the fire were taken to the Massachusetts General Hospital. There Dr. Erich Lindemann observed that among the survivors there was acute emotional disorganization followed by patterns of either adaptive or maladaptive coping with the loss of a loved one. Expression of the emotions of grief were a better indicator of recovery than stoic nonexpression. Out of these observations in 1946 Lindemann wrote his now classic monograph, "Symptomatology and Management of Acute Grief." Shortly thereafter, Lindemann collaborated with Gerald Caplan in establishing a community mental health program which focused primarily on prevention of mental illness.

In his *Principles of Preventive Psychiatry,* Caplan presented his conceptual model of crisis intervention theory, which in turn stimulated more reflection on this area. Very briefly, he hypothesizes that a state of crisis occurs when a person's ordinary, unself-conscious state of equilibrium is disrupted. A person experiences a severe imbalance between the magnitude of the problem and the resources (internal and external) available to meet the painful situation. Habitual responses are no longer adequate. Relationships in which there is a balance of need demand and fulfillment are disrupted—for example, by absence or death—and the person is thrown temporarily into a state of disorganization.

Ordinarily, when a person is in crisis he or she will use old familiar means to restore equilibrium. If the old coping skills work, then the state of crisis is aborted and normalcy returns. If they do not work, then a person needs to redefine the problem and/or develop new skills for coping.

Crises are categorized under the broad labels of *developmental* and *situational* (or accidental). Developmental psychologists have identified fairly distinct stages of human development. The process of human development is one of progressive fragmentation and integration. As a person moves through the different stages, he or she is apt to experience pain and upset, normal but disorganizing, in the process of responding to new developmental challenges. Certain kinds of events that accompany our developmental journey are predictably stressful, such as leaving home, marriage, birth of a first child.

Developmental crises occur in every person's life. For many years the focus of study in developmental psychology was on children. But in the past decade more attention has been focused on identifiable periods of change and growth during the course of adult life. Since human development is a progressive and cumulative process, if a person has not successfully negotiated earlier developmental tasks they become more vulnerable in the face of adult developmental tasks. Levinson (1978) presents interesting hypotheses and data on the life structure of adult men, identifying phases of development and presenting case studies of persons who have moved through these phases of adult development with varying degrees of success or difficulty.

Levinson suggests that the life structure of adults can be considered in terms of three perspectives. The person's *sociocultural* world not only affects the meaning that one makes of life but also has definite consequences. A person's life is determined by a blend of choice and chance. The chance elements cannot be controlled but are part of the contingency of being alive. A person can and does make choices, however, choosing to live out certain aspects of life and to inhibit or neglect others.

A second perspective to be looked at, according to Levinson, is one's *participation* in work and family roles, both those aspects of the self that are lived out and those that are neglected.

Third, the developmental tasks involved in building a life structure include a series of alternating *stable* (structure-building) periods and *transitional* (structure-changing) periods. The transitional stages are particularly important, often times of crisis and decision making. When one is in a state of developmental transition, one needs to terminate the prior period of life, to accept the losses which that termination involves, to review and evaluate the past, to decide which aspects of the past to keep and which to reject, and to consider one's wishes and possibilities for the future.

The second broad category of crises, *situational* crises, include the wide gamut of hazardous events that can disrupt a life: illness, death, war, natural disaster, relocation, job loss, rape.

Probably the situational crisis most frequently encountered by the minister is the crisis of illness. Ministers by role definition are expected to visit the sick members of their parish. When there is serious illness in a family, both the patient and the other family members are going to be physically and emotionally depleted. Serious illness often demands a major realignment in family roles and in the provision of both material and emotional support. The patient has to cope with the pain, the loss of functional ability, weakness. Very often an illness makes a person feel dependent and passive, a condition that tests both the patient and family. The separation and aloneness that a hospitalized person sometimes experiences need to be recognized. The "sci fi" atmosphere of intensive-care facilities can sharpen this feeling and create a sense of disorganization with its frightening sights and sounds. This sense of disorganization and unrealness is often worsened by heavy dosage of narcotic or sedative.

While the patient endures that experience, the family is faced with its own fears, upset, and anxiety. They may find themselves expressing unusual feelings of anger, often targeted at the doctor or medical staff. In many hospitals today there is a pastoral care team who are attentive to working with these feelings both of patient and family. This presence does not diminish the need for the pastoral care of a person's own minister, and the minister needs to be aware of the fears and feelings that are present.

Reuben Hill (1958) presents a useful schema of external and internal stresses which may affect family equilibrium. He suggests that stressful events originating *outside* of the family—such as natural disaster, war, persecution—often solidify family effort to deal with the crisis, therefore enhancing crisis resolution. However, *internal* stressors—such as suicide, alcoholism, infidelity—tend to be more disintegrative. Hill also examines crises within families in terms of the generic *effects* of different kinds of events: *dismemberment* (death, hospitalization, war, separation); *accession* (unwanted pregnancy, aged parent moving in, new parent in a second marriage); *demoralization* (nonsupport, infidelity, alcohol or drug abuse, delinquency); *demoralization plus dismemberment or accession* (illegitimacy, runaways, desertion, imprisonment, divorce, homicide, suicide, institutionalization for mental illness).

The opening vignette in this chapter suggested just a few of the stressors upon the contemporary American nuclear family. Far more than in earlier days the isolated nuclear family is expected to supply the needs for all its members. As the role of woman continues to be redefined, there is further upheaval. Old expectations about who does what in the family can no longer be taken for granted.

Consequently, no chapter on the ministry of crisis intervention can fail to allude to the crisis of divorce, no less a crisis because of its frequent occurence. A minister needs to be very aware of personal feelings and beliefs about divorce. What kinds of feelings of resentment or anxiety get stirred up by the situation of divorce?

Anatomy of Crisis Development

Lydia Rapaport (1965) and, in even greater detail, her student Naomi Golan (1978) have conceptualized the anatomy of crisis development and resolution in a way that has practical utility for anyone working in this area. Because a correct understanding of the anatomy and dynamics of crisis is part of the successful resolution of crisis, this needs to be outlined in some detail.

In assessing a crisis situation, the pastoral counselor needs to be able to identify the precipitating event or *stressor*. As was indicated above, stressors can be categorized broadly as developmental or situational. We need to know the particulars of the event that the person experiences as stressful.

Why does one person experience something as overwhelming while another person appears to maintain a balance while living through the same situation? One of the personal factors that impact the outcome of a crisis is past experience: Does this situation evoke an unsuccessfully resolved crisis in a person's life? To the extent that a person is relying on defense mechanisms that are maladaptive, there is the likelihood that a stressor in such a case will evoke longer-lasting disorganization.

The other critical factor that enhances vulnerability is, not surprisingly, the person's perception of the event. The more that individuals perceive an event as serious and disruptive to their need supply, the more disorganized and regressed they are apt to appear. A clue to the person's perception of the event is the behavior and affect that the helper can observe. As a pastoral counselor working with someone in crisis, if I observe a great deal of *anxiety*, I can hypothesize that the person is experiencing the situation as *threat*. If I observe *depression*, I can surmise *loss*. If I observe *moderate anxiety* together with a *sense of excitement*, the person is probably perceiving the event as *challenge*. The same event—say, an elderly parent moving into the home—could be experienced differentially as threat, loss, or challenge with resultant differing levels of disequilibrium.

Another factor that determines how a person might experience a crisis is the degree to which this stress is cumulative. Holmes and Rahe have worked out a stress scale in which they assign stress weights to certain events. They hypothesize that the cumulative weight of stresses is literally bad for one's health. It is not unusual to see persons who have coped quite well under a prolonged situation of multiple stresses fall apart with the addition of one more apparently less significant stress.

A person in a state of *active* crisis often manifests disturbed and disorganized behavior that may appear pathological, but it is not. A person in active crisis may experience some kind of physiological upset—sleep disturbances, gastrointestinal problems, faintness, dizziness, and feelings of intense emotional pain, helplessness, confusion, paralysis, hopelessness, fits of weeping—all indicative of intense psychological upset. During this time of disequilibrium a person is quite defenseless. It is during this period of active crisis that a person is more accessible to receiving help. A small amount of help during this period can have a high return.

Crises are by nature time-limited. The relatively short period of disorganization and upset is one of the factors that enables us to differentiate between crisis states and more severe pathology. Recovery and reintegration are essential factors in the anatomy of a crisis. The minimal goals of crisis resolution include symptom relief and restoration to at least precrisis levels of functioning. In order for this to happen, a person needs an understanding of what has been experienced, must look correctly at the events that triggered the crisis as well as the remedial steps that need to be taken. If the person's vulnerability to the precipitating stress has been exacerbated because of prior experiences and/or conflicts, it is useful for the person to make that connection and if necessary consider the option of dealing with this in therapy in order to prevent a similar excessive vulnerability in the future.

The concepts that have been outlined above are useful not only for understanding the theory of crisis intervention but also for assessing crisis situations. Since crisis behavior can appear so similar to genuine pathology, it is important to be able to differentiate the two situations, which require different helping strategies. Too often the fledgling pastoral counselor, eager to sharpen therapeutic skills, will respond to a crisis situation by trying uncovering strategies or nondirective counseling skills instead of using a more directive and reality-oriented approach.

CRISIS INTERVENTION SKILLS AND TECHNIQUES

In addition to the basic helping skills which would be operative here, as in any helping situation, there are other skills that are particularly useful in dealing with a person in crisis. Comforting through support and reassurance is more important in crisis intervention than in other counseling situations. How do I as pastoral counselor comfort another? This is more easily experienced than described. Often touch is the only vehicle to express my own feeling of trying to touch a person's deep pain while acknowledging the awful untouchability of personal experiences of deep sorrow. Touching is ordinarily more permissible in informal helping situations than more formal ones. Each of us has to use personal discretion about using this most powerful of the supportive skills. However, at least with eye contact and an attending posture as crisis intervener I need to say to the person, "I am here."

Reassurance is another skill that I use more in crisis intervention than in other counseling situations—not the phony kind of nurturing noises that are more effective for reducing my own anxiety in the face of deep suffering, but the careful listening for my client's own expression of positive ways of dealing with the situation and the reinforcing of these. Sometimes I use a simple statement of factual assurance: that deep as the pain is at this moment, he or she will make it; that there are certain steps that can be taken. The use of reassurance is a two-edged operation. On the one hand I am trying to encourage my client to feel deeply and express emotions of pain or loss; on the other hand I am attempting to invite a person (not push!) into taking the necessary steps to resolve the crisis and get on with the business of living. In a time of crisis, reassurance is such a natural and easy skill to use that there is the temptation to overuse it and end up making the person feel at a distance and of not being understood. To suggest to a person in deep pain that "It's all right; don't worry" is only going to make the person feel misunderstood. Sometimes efforts to reassure come across as false sympathy and can jeopardize the helping relationship. There is always the danger of fostering dependency when one uses reassuring skills. If that happens, then I need to deal with it in the course of the helping relationship.

Since a person in crisis may experience overwhelming feelings of helplessness, I need to be able to facilitate feelings of hope in the person, while still acknowledging the awful legitimacy of feelings of despair. Despair often comes from the feeling of being hopelessly trapped in a corner. If I am able to open up alternatives, helping the person to see a way out of the corner where he or she feels so hopeless and helpless, the despair lightens.

Sometimes religious beliefs are a source of comfort and hope. How do I as a pastoral counselor strike the delicate balance of helping a person feel the comfort of a loving God when the individual may be experiencing an overwhelming sense of abandonment or punishment by a supposedly loving God? Sometimes I need to facilitate the expression of feelings of anger toward this God whose ways are incomprehensible. Many persons have been taught to view this expression of anger toward the Lord as somehow blasphemous and inappropriate. When I help a person to see that the God who created us does indeed understand and accept the expression of our deepest human feelings, I am doing a great service for the person. However, I need to be sensitive in reading whether explicit reference to God and/or faith fits in the particular situation or whether the Lord's presence in this event remains implicit in my own helping relationship.

If I am going to lighten a person's sense of hopelessness, I need to do more directive and interventive counseling than in other kinds of situations. A person in crisis needs to work through two broad kinds of tasks: *material-arrangemental* and *psychosocial*. After a crisis occurs, a person is often faced with having to make certain material arrangements or provisions for taking care of the needs of family members, such as children. When there is a death in the family, no matter how severe the emotion of pain, there are still certain things that need to be done: funeral and burial arrangements, caring for the children, and so on. If the crisis has deprived persons of their home, arrangements for shelter must be made. Sometimes persons are so distraught and paralyzed by emotional pain that they find it difficult to focus on what needs to be done. If the person's support network is adequate, other family members and friends will take over some of these tasks, but support network or no, the tasks still need to be addressed.

The psychosocial tasks are broader. They include coping with whatever threat to security or competence and whatever self-esteem the crisis precipitates in the person. A person needs to deal with feelings of loss and longing. As the person adjusts to a new role (such as widowhood) or reduced resources (such as financial or physical loss), one has to grapple with the anxiety and frustrations that attend making decisions and choosing new resources, new solutions, new roles. The person has to develop new standards of personal well-being and very often new ways of delaying gratification.

To walk with a person who is accomplishing these crucial tasks of crisis resolution, I fall back upon basic helping skills but often I need to use referring skills as well. Knowing the available community resources *before* being faced with a crisis situation is important. If it looks like the person is going to need the services of a mental health worker beyond the level of my own competence, I need to be sensitive to how that person is going to feel about being referred and to try to buffer whatever feelings of rejection that referral may elicit. More and more in crisis intervention the use of support networks are being used. Exploring the potential for support from other family members, friends, and Church or work associates is helpful. If I am feeling my own helplessness or hopelessness in dealing with a person, I should not attempt to compensate for this by implying that the referral source will be an automatic miracle worker. Raising unrealistic expectations is destructive.

Although I may not always have to use them in crisis intervention, I find it useful to have available some simple relaxation techniques. Breathing exercises are probably the easiest to learn and use. In our fast-paced society many of us tend to breathe shallowly from the upper chest instead of from deep in the diaphragm. Stress tends to accentuate this tendency and worsen physical components of anxiety. It is amazing how calming it is to do some very simple deep breathing exercises. A word of caution though: If a person is not used to deep breathing, it can make the blood become too oxygenated and result in feelings of faintness and dizziness. In addition to simple breathing exercises it is useful to have a simple verbal relaxation technique available to use.

A SPECIAL CASE: SUICIDE PREVENTION

In dealing with the crisis of suicide prevention, there are some specific *assessment* skills that are helpful. Before we look at these, however, a word about self-awareness. We all spend our lives at various points on a feeling continuum between the attractiveness of life and the attractiveness of death. When persons are actively suicidal, they are feeling very drawn to the death end of the continuum. Life holds neither hope nor any helpful alternative to their subjective pain. To the extent that a suicide threat touches my own feelings of pain or hopelessness, it can evoke a lot of anxiety. My own need for the suicidal person to feel better can screen out critical signals that he or she may be sending. There used to be a myth that the person who talked about suicide never would do it or that a person who unsuccessfully attempted suicide is unlikely to complete a suicide. In fact, 12 percent of those who fail in attempted suicide do attempt it again within a three-year period. The Los Angeles Suicide Prevention Center has developed a scale for assessing the suicidal potential of persons calling in to their hot lines. Some of the variables they include are:

Age and sex: Suicide potential is higher for men than for women and higher in the 50+ age bracket.

Symptoms: Suicide potential is higher if the person is severely depressed, is feeling hopeless or helpless, is suffering severe exhaustion, is alcoholic.

Stress: The greater the life stress, the greater the suicide potential.

Acute versus chronic: Suicide potential is higher if symptoms are chronic.

Suicidal plan: The more organized, detailed, and lethal a plan for suicide, the more likely that the person intends to implement it.

Resources: If the person has no source of support (family, friends, work), there is more danger of suicide than if he or she has available family, friends, clergy, financial resources.

Prior attempts: The likelihood of a suicide attempt is higher if there has been a prior attempt.

Medical status: Suicide potential is higher if a person suffers from a chronic debilitating illness.

Communications outlet: The more outlets that a person has for communicating feelings of guilt, worthlessness, shame, blame, the less likely the potential for suicide.

Reaction of significant others: Suicide potential is higher if the significant others will blame or reject the person.

These indicators are useful not only for assessing suicidal potential but also to help keep the person engaged in talking. The twin enemies in dealing with suicidal persons are overreaction and underreaction. Neither panic nor detached calm are helpful. As with any other form of crisis intervention, the supportive relationship itself is a part of the healing as well as the mobilization of an appropriate support network. The basic goal in working with a suicidal person is to enhance the individual's sense of alternatives, to help the person move away from the position where death appears to be the only viable alternative. If a person is using the suicidal gesture in a manipulative way, whether to get attention or to punish a significant other, this certainly becomes grist for the mill in post-suicidal counseling sessions. I would not use that confrontation at the height of a suicidal crisis. Sometimes a "no suicide" contract, open-ended and time-limited, buys time with a person and offers the chance to explore what is going on with the person without reinforcing the suicidal impulse.

If a person successfully completes a suicide attempt, I must deal not only with the bereaved family but also with my own feelings. In the final analysis I cannot prevent a person from taking his or her own life unless I place that person in a totally protective custody, such as a hospital. If the suicidal potential calls for that measure and family members cooperate, that is sometimes the best action to take, but unless the person attains a greater sense of hope, he or she may eventually complete the suicide, leaving the family and the help to deal with their own feelings of guilt, anger, and loss.

A MODEL FOR CRISIS INTERVENTION

The work with a person in crisis is ordinarily time-limited (five to six weeks). Like other forms of counseling/therapy, it has identifiable beginning, middle, and ending phases. Naomi Golan in her excellent *Treatment in Crisis Situations* presents the following model:

A. Initial Phase

In the initial meeting with a person in crisis, focusing immediately upon the crisis itself is important. What brings this person to you "here and now"? Even if you think you already know the answer by reason of your pastoral role, it is good to check out the individual's perceptions. The person needs to tell the story, to ventilate feelings. As you listen, try to tune in to the person's subjective, affective experience and try to get some sense of the objective nature of the crisis. Does the person experience it as threat or loss or challenge? What is the vulnerable state of the person? Is the person experiencing changes in coping ability? If so, how so? During this initial meeting you are making your initial assessment of the person's state of crisis while facilitating client expression. It is important that you share your evaluation of the person's current predicament and what he or she regards as the most pressing problem area needing attention. In sharing this perception of the problem and some beginnings of a solution, you are starting to assist the person in feeling he or she can get a handle on what is happening.

B. Middle Phase (Sessions 1 to 4)

During this period of crisis work your main goal is to help the person see and use his or her own resources of self, community, family, and know the ways in which each of these resources can be used to cope with the present state of crisis. If you hear central themes, such as loss or threat to self-esteem, it is useful to check out where these have been vulnerabilities in the past. At this point a cognitive understanding of, rather than a therapeutic working through of these themes is useful for crisis resolution. During this phase the working out of some specific tasks should be discussed and agreed upon. Initially you may have to be very directive but as the person starts to feel better there is less need for being so directive.

C. Ending Phase (Last 1 or 2)

Since some crisis situations are passing, they sometimes take care of themselves. As the necessary recovery tasks are undertaken, the client may simply want to get on with things himself or herself. Golan identifies three kinds of termination reactions: (1) the client who realistically wants to terminate when the work is done, (2) the client who resists termination by asking for more therapy or counseling, (3) and the client for whom therapy is appropriate. There can be resistance on your part also, an unwillingness to let go after traveling briefly but intensely with another person in pain.

If there has not been a clear contract made at the beginning, there needs to be a review of where the person has been. Looking at where the person was in terms of affective issues and where the person has come in terms of tasks done, goals reached, necessary changes in direction initiated—all these are part of the ending process. Planning for future activity needs to be done. Termination in crisis intervention is the delicate balance of saying good-bye but not closing the door. The person needs to feel independent and yet free to return.

CRISIS INTERVENTION AND MINISTRY

Crisis intervention, like any ministry of pastoral care and counseling, draws upon therapeutic discipline, the discipline that has been very briefly outlined in the pages above. But presumably ministry also offers a different breadth and perspective. Crisis intervention theory and technique apply a pragmatic, problem-solving approach to the mystery of human suffering as it occurs in the multiple experiences of human crises. Can ministry offer the breadth of mystery while drawing upon the effective model of dealing with human pain that crisis interventionists present?

If the ministry of crisis intervention is true to itself as pastoral, it has to address the mystery of human suffering as well as attempt to alleviate the problem of human suffering. Charles Gerkin in his *Crisis Experience of Modern Life: Theory and Theology of Pastoral Care* (1979) addresses this pastoral dimension. The following reflections represent my own reactions to his thought.

The basic theological issue at stake in the human experience of crisis is the question of the Lord's providential participation in what is happening to the persons so affected. Older religious forms proclaimed a powerful sense of the Lord's participation in human crisis and an assurance of the ultimate meaningful outcome of such an event. The ministry of crisis intervention in a more faith-dominated time was in fact this proclamation. However, today crises of faith are more the rule than the exception. The vision of God's power and control over events has dimmed. Life crises assume the potential for geometric progression as chaotic experiences collide with muddled faith. Persons in ministry struggle with their own questions and doubts.

None of these issues needs to be considered by a person who is concerned only with the behavioral science of crisis intervention but they cannot be ignored by someone who is professing pastoral ministry. It can be assumed that if a person in crisis is turning to someone in ministry for help, the person has at least an implicit concern about these things.

Gerkin points out the close relationship that crisis, either developmental or situational, has with our own personal experience of limits and vulnerability. Paradoxically, we are living at a moment in history when technology and the advertising media foster a sense of unlimited aspiration, while the global reality is one of fragile vulnerability. The media feed the myth that we can (and should) achieve unlimited beauty, wealth, happiness, and other good things. But this same technology which lends an aura of credibility to unlimited aspiration and achievement has also rendered us exquisitely vulnerable. Production and distribution of limited resources in a progressively more interdependent "global village" have made obsolete the old ways in which nations used to relate to each other. The global problems of hunger, the arms race, the oil situation with its Lilliputian hold that OPEC nations have on the superpowers are but a few examples of the paradox. The myriad ecological issues in the wake of technological progress bring their own radical vulnerability. Nevertheless, expectations about the possibility of the good life remain very high. Studies about stress show that expectation is an important factor in how a person will experience stress. Stress is often the disappointment ratio of the difference between the expectation and the reality.

What does all this philosophizing have to do with the ministry of crisis intervention? Simply this: The normal developmental and situational crises, upsetting as they can be in and of themselves, today carry the additional weight of being an existential affront to our sense of unlimited aspiration, and when they occur it is natural that a person gets engaged in questions about the meaning of life.

Gerkin (1979) poses a question that is central to the ministry of crisis intervention.

Can modern persons be helped towards a renewed faith in God's providence as participant in the crisis of finite life while at the same time (and the second is dependent on the first) they are enabled to open themselves to the changes and possibilities thrust upon them by the radical experience of human vulnerability in times of crisis and transition? (p. 32)

There is no easy answer to that question. Each person in ministry has to find a personal response.

An easier question to grapple with is how the role of the person in ministry is unique from the role of persons in other helping professions in the area of crisis intervention. By nature of the role, a person in pastoral ministry often has more direct involvement with a greater number of persons than the psychiatrist, psychologist, or social worker. By reason of a long tradition of pastoral care, a person in ministry can exercise an initiative that is denied to persons in the other helping professions. The minister is expected to go where people are. The person in ministry has accessibility to persons at home or in the hospital and has the opportunity to know the people to whom he or she ministers in a much broader way than the psychiatrist or psychologist, for whom the expectation is that the people wishing help will present themselves in a setting where the limits of time and structure are made quite clear. The person in ministry has access to persons in their wellness as in their pain, in their ordinariness as in their crises. Mental health workers readily recognize the value of persons in ministry in the important work of preventive mental health.

There is also a social expectation about pastoral initiative in the time of crisis. It is expected, say, that at the time of bereavement a member of the pastoral team will take the initiative in offering support and comfort. The minister is thus allowed to do some very helpful facilitation of the grief work that needs to occur after a person has suffered loss. Furthermore, because those in pastoral ministry have the advantage of ongoing relationships with persons in their community, they can be in a better position to evaluate the level of disorganization that accompanies crisis and therefore be able to distinguish between crisis behavior and deeper levels of disturbed functioning.

The ministerial role carries its own symbolic value. No matter where the person in ministry is in a personal faith struggle, the ministerial role ordinarily signifies a belief in the transcendental, providential action of God in human history. Depending upon the personal religious experience of the person in crisis, this symbolic reality can be a help or a hindrance and the helper needs to be aware of the transference potential sparked by this role. The helper needs to be aware that the role has been often used in the past as a way to evade the experience of vulnerability and the sense of helplessness engendered by crisis situations. Inappropriate "God talk" which in effect denies the pain of the crisis has often been used by persons in ministry. Attempts to comfort by inappropriate proclamations of a loving, provident God impede rather than facilitate the human work of crisis resolution.

Another (and often advantageous) way that the role of the person in ministry facilitates the work of crisis intervention is the possibility it allows for building support networks within the parish as well as the opportunities it provides for broad educational programs which can help people learn to deal with various kinds of crises. The pastoral care potential that could be developed through lay crisis ministry has probably not yet been tapped. Both the organizational and the teaching components of pastoral ministry are elaborated on by David Luecke in Chapter 10 of this book, but each of these components has powerful possibilities in the ministry of crisis intervention.

Crisis intervention is not magic. It is a helping technique which is effective in touching persons who are in the kind of pain that anyone in ministry knows well. Like any other of the behavioral disciplines, it is better learned by doing than by reading.

The appended readings have enhanced my own work in crisis intervention. It is hoped they can be helpful to the reader as well.

REFERENCES

Gerkin, Charles. *Crisis Experience in Modern Life: Theory and Theology of Pastoral Care.* Nashville: Abingdon, 1979.
Golan, Naomi. *Treatment in Crisis Situations.* © 1978 by the Free Press, a Division of Macmillan Publishing Co., Inc. Quoted passage reprinted by permission of Macmillan Publishing Co.
Hill, Reuben. "Generic Features of Families Under Stress." In Howard Parad (Ed.), *Crisis Intervention,* pp. 32–52.
Levinson, Daniel. *Seasons of a Man's Life.* New York: Knopf, 1978.
Lindemann, Erich. "Symptomatology and Management of Acute Grief." In Parad (Ed.), *Crisis Intervention,* pp. 7–21.
Parad, Howard (Ed.). *Crisis Intervention: Selected Readings.* New York: Family Services Association of America, 1965.
Rapaport, Lydia. "The State of Crisis: Some Theoretical Considerations." In Parad (Ed.), *Crisis Intervention,* pp. 22–31.

RECOMMENDED READINGS

Brammer, Lawrence M. *The Helping Relationship: Process and Skills.* Englewood Cliffs, N.J.: Prentice Hall, 1973.
Caplan, Gerald. *Principles of Preventive Psychiatry.* New York: Basic Books, 1964.
Darbonne, Allen. "Crisis: A Review of Theory, Practice, and Research," *International Journal of Psychiatry,* 6 (November 1968), 371–79.
Farberow, Norman L., and Edwin L. Schneidman. *The Cry for Help.* New York: McGraw-Hill, 1961.

Fisher, Sheila A. *Suicide and Crisis Intervention: Survey and Guide to Services.* New York: Springer, 1973.
Gerkin, Charles V. *Crisis Experience in Modern Life: Theory and Theology of Pastoral Care.* Nashville: Abingdon, 1979.
Getz, William, Allen E. Wessen, Stan Sue, and Amy Agnes. *Fundamentals of Crisis Counseling.* Lexington, Mass.: Heath, 1974.
Glick, Ira O., Robert S. Weiss, and C. Murray Parkes. *The First Year of Bereavement.* New York: Wiley, 1974.
Golan, Naomi. *Passing Through Transitions.* New York: Macmillan, 1981.
———. *Treatment in Crisis Situations.* New York: Free Press, 1978.
Hill, Reuben. "Generic Features of Families under Stress," *Social Casework,* 39 (February–March 1958), 139–50; Reprinted in Parad, *Crisis Intervention,* pp. 32–52.
Holmes, T. H., and R. H. Rahe. "The Social Readjustment Scale," *Journal of Psychosomatic Research,* 11, 1967, 213–218.
Jacobson, Gerald F. "Programs and Techniques of Crisis Intervention." In Silvano Arieti (Ed.), *American Handbook of Psychiatry,* 2nd ed. New York: Basic Books, 1974, pp. 810–25.
Johnson, Paul E. *Psychology of Pastoral Care.* Nashville: Abingdon, 1953.
Levinson, Daniel J. *The Seasons of a Man's Life.* New York: Knopf, 1978.
Lindemann, Erich. "Symptomatology and Management of Acute Grief," *American Journal of Psychiatry,* 101, no. 2 (September 1944). Reprinted in Parad, *Crisis Intervention,* pp. 7–21.
Lukton, Rosemary C. "Crisis Theory: Review and Critique," *Social Service Review,* 48 (September 1974), 384–402.
Morley, Wilbur E. "Theory of Crisis Intervention," *Pastoral Psychology,* April 1970, pp. 1–6.
Parad, Howard J. (Ed.). *Crisis Intervention: Selected Readings.* New York: Family Service Association, 1965.
Parkes, Colin Murray. *Bereavement: Studies of Grief in Adult Life.* New York: International University Press, 1972.
Pretzel, Paul W. *Understanding and Counseling the Suicidal Person.* Nashville: Abingdon, 1972.
Puryear, Douglas A. *Helping People in Crisis.* San Francisco: Jossy-Bass, 1979.
Rapaport, Lydia. "The State of Crisis: Some Theoretical Considerations," *Social Service Review,* 6 (June 1962), 211–17. Reprinted in Parad, *Crisis Intervention,* pp. 22–31.
Schneidman, Edwin S, Norman L. Farberow, and Robert E. Litman. *The Psychology of Suicide.* New York: Science House, 1970.
Sheehy, Gail. *Passages: Predictable Crises of Adult Life.* New York: Dutton, 1974.
Switzer, David K. *The Dynamics of Grief.* Nashville: Abingdon, 1970.
———. *The Minister as Crisis Counselor.* Nashville: Abingdon, 1974.
Whitehead, Evelyn E., and James D. Whitehead. *Christian Life Patterns: The Psychological Challenges and Religious Invitations of Adult Life.* New York: Doubleday, 1979.

CHAPTER NINE

Premarital Preparation and Counseling

REV. JOHN R. COMPTON, D. MIN.

The warm afternoon sun streamed through the windows of my church study, but the rays seemed unable to penetrate the emotional chill that filled the room. Jennifer, a young woman of twenty-seven, the mother of two preschool children and a member of my parish, sat stiffly in the chair beside me. She rubbed her tear-filled eyes as she poured out the tragic events of her ten-year marriage to Larry. Estranged from her parents, she had eloped at age seventeen. Larry was only a year older. Verbal abuse, alcoholism, and infidelity were all parts of the painful story—and now physical abuse. Then in a moment of pathos, torment, and regret she slowly spoke these words: "If I had only talked with someone before getting married, maybe things would have been different."

The pain of Jennifer can be multiplied many times over as we look at the devastating statistics of our decade: there is one divorce for every two new marriages. "Why doesn't someone do something?" is being asked with increasing urgency. It is the question asked by the educator, sociologist, anthropologist, psychologist, as well as concerned people from all helping professions. The question is posed also by the Church, and appropriately so, for it needs to be addressed as an issue by people in ministry today.

Western society does not demand nor does it even seem to expect preparation for marriage. Anyone may marry provided he or she fulfills the meager requirements of state law. This is usually less than what is expected to obtain an automobile driver's permit. The prospective bride or groom may know practically nothing about marriage or its responsibilities, but that does not prove to be an impediment to getting married. The bride-to-be may be making an obviously poor choice of a mate. The groom-to-be may have preparation so slight that with an equivalent amount of vocational training he would be unable to hold down even the lowliest of jobs.

Unfortunately, the Church has for the most part abdicated its strategic and crucial role in providing adequate premarital preparation. There are clergy today who commit themselves over the telephone to performing wedding ceremonies without even meeting the couple. During a recent discussion with a fellow clergyman regarding premarital preparation and counseling I was surprised to hear him comment: "Quite frankly, I don't do any premarital preparation. What good does it do anyway?" I responded that it is just such an attitude that is one of the factors contributing to the chaotic and discouraging rate of marital failures in our day.

I'm not sure what will be effective in stemming the alarming increase in broken marriages in this decade. Studies on the effects of premarital counseling on marital success are difficult, if not impossible, to obtain. The issues involved are terribly complex, and the many variables plus the factors of control present a dilemma for serious research in this area. However, I do believe that the Church can make a serious contribution through preparation and counseling.

In this chapter I share some of the thoughts and ideas that have come to me during my thirty-three year commitment to ministry. I hope these thoughts will give impetus to a renewed interest in, and commitment to, responsible premarital preparation and counseling.

I have divided this chapter into six sections: the nature of premarital preparation and counseling, the purpose and goals of premarital preparation and counseling, circumstances that warrant special caution, exploring the four main areas of marriage, structuring premarital sessions, and resources available. These sections are followed by a bibliography.

THE NATURE OF PREMARITAL PREPARATION AND COUNSELING

Ideally, premarital preparation is simply another step in an ongoing process designed to educate and meet the needs of the people in a congregation or parish. Early attitudes toward family life and marriage are first learned by a child in the home—from mother, father, and other family members. A child's concept of marriage and the roles of husband and wife are learned from seeing and observing family before a more formalized process of religious education such as Sunday school, vacation Bible school, or confraternity of christian doctrine has begun.

Parishes striving to meet the needs of their members will provide special classes and discussion groups for parents, helping them to be teachers and living examples for their children. Successive stages of instruction will gear curricula to the special needs and readiness levels of children as they progress from grade school, through junior high and high school, and into the young adult and adult years. There is a special opportunity for teaching and learning when persons are preparing themselves for adult church membership. This is a time when youth can get to know their clergy more personally. In this experience, the dimension of faith and life, especially as related to dating and marriage, can be discussed and explored. Youth groups are ideal settings for discussing what it means to be a Christian and how this influences dating patterns and the selection of a lifelong mate. Young adult, college, and adult groups also provide fertile ground for premarital dialogue and informal preparation.

When a man and woman have moved through such an attitudinal, moral, ethical, and educational process, the task of premarital preparation is more easily accomplished. If one or both have not had this advantage, then more time is needed for this purpose.

Is premarital preparation the same as premarital counseling? Is there one without the other? I have used the two terms *premarital preparation* and *premarital counseling* because I view the two as being different. Counseling is usually sought when there is a crisis or problem. This is not the situation when couples come to the church to be married. They are not usually asking the question, "Should we marry?" or "Are we compatible for marriage?" Generally their attitude is: "We have decided to marry— now what is the next step?" Because this is the case, we begin with premarital preparation, which is more of an exploratory, facilitative, and educational process than a counseling process.

It is not unusual, however, if the preparation goes beyond touching superficialities, for problems to emerge in premarital preparation. Perhaps the process brings out the fact that one or both sets of parents are opposed to the marriage. Or it may emerge that the bride-to-be is deeply concerned about her fiancé's drinking habits. Another problem might surface as they prepare the budget: perhaps a struggle for control and dominance through money. On occasion the premarital preparation uncovers problems that have been long denied or avoided, and the blame for the problems is then projected onto the counselor.

This is not to say that every couple must have deep and severe problems; however, as most couples look more realistically at their situation and the realities of life, areas of tension and disagreement are uncovered. When this happens, premarital preparations move into premarital counseling.

At the point where premarital problems emerge, ministers or priests can call on their counseling skills and help the couple to: (1) articulate and define their problems and their feelings about these problems, (2) look at the viable alternatives, (3) explore the pros and cons of each alternative, and (4) finally come to a decision that will be constructive and one with which they will be able to live.

In summary, I would see premarital preparation and counseling as a natural part of an ongoing family-life educational program in the parish. It is a time when a couple contemplating marriage becomes involved in a more personalized process of awareness and education. When problems emerge from these dynamics, premarital preparation moves into premarital counseling. Because counseling is involved with a majority of couples, I will refer from this point on to the minister, priest, or lay counselor, male or female, as *the counselor.*

THE PURPOSE AND GOALS OF PREMARITAL PREPARATION AND COUNSELING

There are basically five goals that must be kept in mind as one prepares couples for marriage. They are: (1) to encourage interpersonal dialogue between the man and woman, (2) to provide information through a variety of resources, (3) to help the couple relate marriage to the faith experience, (4) to make an evaluation, and (5) to complete administrative details.

Encourage Interpersonal Dialogue

The first task of the counselor in premarital preparation is to serve as a catalyst or facilitator to help the couple enter into dialogue. The counselor motivates the woman and man to talk about themselves, their relationship, expectations, problems, hopes, dreams, plans, and their future together. As the couple respond to the questions and interventions, the counselor can observe how they relate to one another. Does one take an active role while the other takes a passive role? Does one express feelings while the other talks mainly on a cognitive level? Is one able to show affection while the other has great difficulty? Do the personalities seem compatible? Divergent? Does one respond spontaneously while the other remains hidden and guarded? Are both able to identify their strengths and discuss their limitations and areas for growth? Is one an introvert and the other an extravert? The observations regarding these questions, as well as their answers, help the counselor to learn about this couple firsthand.

What form does this interaction take? Much depends on the personality, skills, and inclination of the counselor. Approaches vary from a natural unfolding of a nonstructured dialogue to a series of predetermined questions, or even the use of audiovisuals. Some of these tools are explained later in this chapter. Examples of good introductory questions might be:

1. How did you first meet?
2. What were some of the things that first attracted you to one another?

3. What attributes have you come to appreciate in the other person since then?
4. How long have you known each other? Dated steadily? Been engaged?
5. How do you feel about the length of your engagement?
6. Do you like, versus love, each other?
7. What habits does your fiancé(e) have that irritate or annoy you?
8. How have you handled disagreements in your courtship?
9. When was your last disagreement and how was it resolved?
10. What do you expect to get out of marriage?
11. What do you expect to put into your marriage?
12. What reservations do you have about getting married?
13. What hopes, dreams, and aspirations do you have for the future?
14. What would you like your marriage to be like in five years?
15. What would you like your marriage to be like in fifteen years?

This list of questions is by no means exhaustive, but it is offered as a basic list which counselors can modify, adding or subtracting as experience suggests.

Provide Information

In exploring the nature of the couple's relationship, the counselor should try to determine what gaps of information are evident. One would not want to make assumptions about what a couple knows or doesn't know.

I once counseled with a banker's son and assumed he would be well versed in setting up a budget and handling the financial aspects of marriage. I was wrong. Another time I assumed that a nurse would be well informed about family planning. I almost didn't explore this area because of her vocation. I'm glad I did, because there was basic information that needed to be discussed. The moral of these stories is that it is best that the counselor not assume anything. We need to establish for ourselves the level of knowledge in the essential areas.

When it is determined that there is a knowledge gap, the counselor has a number of options. If the gaps are not extensive, the counselor might choose to do some teaching, sharing of facts, providing information based on the experiences of other couples and one's own experience, drawing from one's nuclear family or one's own marriage experience. Material can also be drawn from the knowledge of working with other couples. If the knowledge gap is quite wide, more extensive remedial steps may be required. Books and pamphlets can be recommended, or even seminars and courses. Other resources include study manuals, audio tapes, filmstrips and movies, premarital discussion groups, Pre-Cana Conferences, and Engaged Encounter. Dialogue with one's own family and friends can also be enlightening.

Help the Couple Relate Marriage to the Faith Experience

A third goal, as one prepares couples for marriage, is to help the prospective bride and groom look at their past faith experience, determine where they are now, and enable them to move toward a richer and stronger faith experience.

It is not unusual for older teenagers to question or even fall away from their faith and their involvement with the Church. This is a natural part of teenage rebellion and the search for personal identity. As the teenager refuses to accept a secondhand faith from his or her family, there is a struggle which is at times disruptive and violent. If the family is understanding and supportive without being oppressive and autocratic, the sprout of a new faith begins to emerge—a faith that is increasingly owned by the young person.

As couples move toward marriage, they are frequently open to renewing a closer relationship with the Church. Premarital preparation and counseling present an ideal opportunity for the counselor to help the prospective bride and groom think about and assess their faith. The attitude of the counselor can go a long way to either encourage or discourage growth. If the prospective bride and groom feel judgment, anger, and resentment from the counselor for what has been missing or lacking in the past, it will in all probability "turn them off," discouraging them from taking the forward step of faith. On the other hand, if the counselor is open, noncondemnatory, faithful in witness, yet not judgmental, this could be the very relationship that fans the embers of faith and awakens new fervor and commitment. The stance of a loving and committed counselor conveys the message of concern, care, and challenge to the couple. Good counselors always remember the cardinal rule: *Begin where the people are, not where we want them to be,* for then and only then can we assist growth and forward movement toward a new or greater experience of faith.

Make an Evaluation

The counselor makes two distinct evaluations in meeting with a couple for marriage preparation: (1) Are both parties mature? (2) Are they sufficiently suited for each other to make a lifelong commitment?

No marriage will survive the pressures of life and the stresses of our age unless the prospective bride and groom are both truly mature. Signs of maturity would include: (1) an ability to forego an immediate gratification in order to receive a greater benefit in the future, (2) an ability and willingness to share and compromise, (3) a concern for the well-being of others, (4) an ability to look at life realistically, and (5) a willingness to face problems and seek solutions.

I once met with a couple who sought me out through the yellow pages of the phone book. As I sat down to talk with them, it became evident that neither of them was ready to undertake the commitment of marriage. Both were still teenagers, the boy nineteen and the girl only seventeen. As we talked further, the boy told me that he had been out of work for six months with no prospect of another job in sight. He also stated that he had no money saved. Thinking they could make it financially by living with his family and supporting themselves through her small salary seemed totally unrealistic, since she didn't make enough to support herself, much less support a husband.

As I began to share with them my feeling that marriage was premature, the girl blurted out the fact that she had to get married because she could no longer stand living with an alcoholic mother and father. It was obvious that she was going into marriage because she was desperate and saw no other alternative. Chronologically, financially, and emotionally this couple was not ready for marriage. I had to tell them so.

After maturity, compatibility is the next area for evaluation. There are numerous testing materials available to help determine the level of a couple's compatibility. Some of the materials I have found helpful are:

1. The Taylor-Johnson Temperament Analysis Test
2. The Mooney Problem Check List
3. The Marriage Expectation Inventory (Form 1)
4. The Marriage Role Expectations Inventories
5. A Marriage Prediction Schedule
6. The Love Attitudes Inventory
7. Dating Problems Check List
8. The Premarital Counseling Kit
9. A Courtship Analysis
10. The Crane and Coffer Religious Attitudes Inventory

An expanded description of these materials can be found in the section on resources available.

According to a comprehensive study conducted by Stanford psychologist L. M. Terman of factors in marital happiness, it was found that the most important predictor of a happy marriage was the happiness of the parents in their marriage. Happiness during childhood and firm and consistent discipline during childhood were also found to be important factors.

Other studies, such as the one mentioned by Kirkpatrick in his book *The Family as Process and Institution,* indicate that additional premarital factors that are favorable to marital success include: (1) lack of conflict with parents, (2) ease of premarital contact with the opposite sex, (3) acquaintance for more than a year, (4) approval of the relationship by both sets of parents, (5) similarity of age, (6) satisfaction with the amount and intensity of affection, and (7) sharing of common interests. Unfavorable premarital factors include: (1) divorced parents, (2) parent or parents deceased, and (3) marrying because of loneliness or to escape from one's family.

From the same study, postmarital factors that have a positive impact on the success of marriage are: (1) equalitarian attitudes, (2) good relationships with in-laws, (3) not living with in-laws, and (4) a mutual desire for children. Negative postmarital factors include: (1) dominance by either the husband or the wife, (2) jealousy, and (3) one spouse feeling superior to or more intelligent than the other spouse.

Predictors of marital happiness found by the W. A. Barry study in 1970 were:

1. Possession of positive personality traits
2. Similarity of cultural backgrounds
3. A socially responsive personality
4. A harmonious family environment
5. Compatible religious orientation
6. Satisfying occupation and working conditions
7. A love relationship growing out of companionship rather than infatuation
8. A wholesome growth of attitudes toward the sexual relationship.

Complete Administrative Details

Every wedding involves administrative details. At one time it was the Church, and not the county or state, that kept the records of all weddings. Even though the civil authorities have assumed this record keeping, it is important that the Church be responsible in this matter also.

Denominations vary widely in their regulations, forms, and procedures. It is critical that serious attention be given to these ecclesiastical procedures. Other administrative details that need to be discussed are the scheduling of rehearsals and arrangements with people involved, such as musicians, acolytes, custodians, florists, photographers, and caterers. If there are any fees involved, these can also be clarified. The choice of appropriate music can also be discussed.

CIRCUMSTANCES THAT WARRANT SPECIAL CAUTION

Over the years I have come to realize that there are certain situations that wave red flags and make me think, "Go easy—this is an area that needs special scrutiny and evaluation." Additional counseling is almost always warranted when one or more of the following risk areas are present: (1) chronological immaturity, (2) pregnant bride, (3) grieving or rebounding, (4) serious drug involvement, (5) emotional problems, (6) wide chronological age difference, (7) wide gap in education, (8) no financial security, (9) recent mental illness, (10) serious mental or physical handicaps, (11) divergent religious traditions, (12) dated no other person, and (13) divergent racial or cultural backgrounds.

Chronological Immaturity

Statistics show that the divorce rate of teenagers is much higher than that of the general population. There is probably no other single factor that affects the success or failure of a marriage more than the chronological ages and maturity of the prospective bride and groom.

One reason for the high failure ratio in teenage marriages is obvious when we reflect on the fact that the personality of the teenager is very fluid. There are many changes that take place as one moves from adolescence to young adulthood. What often happens is that seven to ten years into the marriage, after two or more children have entered the picture, the husband and wife come to realize their basic incompatibility.

Pregnant Bride

If a prospective bride and groom have a mature, loving relationship, were truly contemplating marriage prior to the pregnancy, and want to make a lifelong commitment, then by all means they should move forward with their plans for marriage. However, if these three factors are not present, then the counselor needs to help the man and woman discuss their feelings and thoughts about the marriage decision so that they can explore the difficulties they may encounter if they decide to marry. Recent doctoral research shows that teenage marriages where a pregnancy is present will have a 60 percent chance of failure within the first year and 80 percent within five years.

An unwanted pregnancy is a poor reason for marriage, yet often this is the major motivation. I remember one couple in this situation. The young man said, "I want to marry her because I want to give the baby my name." There was no mention of love or a desire to build a lifelong relationship, only to "make the baby legal," as he phrased it. Although the young man's intentions were honest, marriage was the least desirable option for this couple.

Grieving or Rebounding

Before most people can establish a mature and healthy relationship, a certain disengagement is needed from other unresolved relationships. A broken engagement to another person, a rebound from divorce, an annulled marriage, or the recent death of a spouse—all these involve the grieving process, which requires time. Shock, denial, anger, and the other stages usually need to be experienced before real healing can take place. Moving too soon into another deep and serious relationship can prove disastrous for both the grieving person and the new spouse. A healing period of at least twelve to eighteen months is needed before one enters into a serious commitment like marriage. This is especially true following the death of a spouse, a divorce, or an annulment.

Because there are so many remarriages in our day, we as counselors will want to offer special help to the couple in this situation. I found Darlene McRoberts's book *Second Marriage* a very helpful resource in this regard.

Serious Drug Involvement

We are living in a drug culture in the 1990s, and the effects of this milieu on the couples who come for premarital counseling can be dire. Persons suffering from addiction may be found at every level of society—the rich and the poor, the uneducated and the educated, people who live in both rural and urban areas. Addiction touches every family in our land in one way or another. It is one of the most serious illnesses affecting our culture today and the prospects for the future are not encouraging, despite the money and programs available.

If the counselor realizes that a person is seriously addicted to alcohol or other drugs, the counseling needs to move to an exploration of the possible implications of this illness on the marriage relationship. This would probably need to take priority in the counseling at this point in the process.

Emotional Problems

The old saying "love is blind" is so often true. Occasionally, some very serious emotional problems are revealed during premarital counseling: a repeated pattern of lying emerges, wide mood swings become evident, possessive jealousy comes to the fore, or strong suspicious tendencies bordering on paranoia are revealed. I once counseled with a couple who seemed quite compatible on the surface, but as we moved deeper into the premarital process the young woman spoke of giving up her friends because of her fiancé's demand for exclusivity. The more we talked, the more it became evident to me that the young man's jealousy and possessiveness were destructive and out of control. A referral was made for psychological evaluation and therapy.

Wide Chronological Age Difference

Maturity is much more important than chronological age. However, when a wide age gap (ten years or more) is present, it needs to be explored and the various ramifications discussed and weighed. Wide age differences can affect the number and timing of children. If one spouse is much older, he (or she) may prefer not to have any children at all. Age differences can affect the sexual relationship drastically as well as the social adjustment, especially in later years. I recently counseled with a couple where the husband was considerably older than the wife. The husband had retired to relax, while the wife was pursuing a fulfilling vocation and was looking for opportunities to grow and enlarge her world. He longed for her to retire and travel with him, but he was ten years ahead of her in his dream. She hoped he would find renewed interest in life. He hoped she would see it his way. The conflict was deep and painful.

Wide Gap in Education

Usually, couples with a wide educational gap do not marry, but often there are plans for the bride-to-be to work and put the groom-to-be through college or graduate school. This can cause serious problems later on. Often when the husband completes college and graduate school, the wife who has put him through seems dull, uninteresting, and not intellectually stimulating to him. At the very least, she feels inadequate associating with his friends and professional acquaintances. Couples can be helped to plan their professional development together. A couple that has explored future plans prior to marriage will probably not have to look back in regret.

No Financial Security

Some couples feel that they can live on love, and perhaps that is true for a while, but such prospective brides and grooms need to be helped to face the economic facts of life more realistically. Most brides and grooms today find it necessary that both work in order to establish the marriage on a strong financial foundation. This is especially true if they are saving for a down payment on a home. Couples will feel more secure in their financial situation when they are able to show in black and white how they are going to make it economically.

Recent Mental Illness

The key word here is *recent*. There is no reason why a recovered mental patient should not marry after a sufficient period of time which allows the person to become independent and self-sufficient. I served two years as a chaplain in a mental hospital and ministered to men and women who found a loving relationship in that setting. It was my practice to encourage them to set their wedding dates far enough in the future to allow time to become independent and self-sufficient after their release from the hospital.

Serious Mental or Physical Handicaps

It takes a very special kind and quality of love when one or both marital partners are handicapped, either mentally or physically. Both the person who is handicapped and the future partner need to look carefully at the implications of the handicap involved. Will there be vocational limitations? How will they affect the financial direction of the marriage? Will there be physical limitations—perhaps no children? What will this mean for the quality of life? Handicapped persons have every right to lead lives that are rich and rewarding, but they have the added responsibility to determine in what ways their handicap will affect their future mate and the marriage relationship.

Divergent Religious Traditions

What a tragedy it is when two people who are deeply devoted to very different religious traditions become married and one or both feel impelled to sacrifice their faith in order to make the marriage work. In such instances it is possible that they will later resent, either consciously or unconsciously, the sacrifices which must be made, thus affecting the relationship negatively.

The birth of a child frequently heaps coals on the fires of resentment in such a dilemma. How will the child be raised? What happens to the tradition of the other parent? What will be the effect on both families?

When the bride and groom share the same or similar faiths, this is usually a positive factor. When the faith is radically different, however, it can become a divisive and destructive element, detracting from rather than enhancing the marriage. Deep religious conflict can destroy an otherwise positive relationship.

Dated No Other Person

Many social environments condone and even encourage steady dating from a very early age. Because this is true, many young people become committed to a one-on-one relationship in high school, or even in junior high, and find themselves tied to that person, never experiencing a variety of dating partners. It is an arrangement that gives a lot of security at the time, but it limits the boy and girl and deprives them of the opportunity of getting to know a variety of people in a dating setting.

When young people have broad dating experience, they can make a choice of a lifelong partner on the basis of comparison. For the young person who dates and then marries only one person, there is no such basis for comparison. Questions that might arise include: I wonder what it would have been like to date others? I wonder if I might have found someone more compatible than my mate? I wonder if I would be happier married to someone else? The last question could be asked in any case, but it becomes more painful and perplexing when there is no basis for comparison.

Divergent Racial or Cultural Backgrounds

A mobile, shifting society brings people of many cultures, races, and traditions together. Sometimes people of drastically different races or cultures fall in love and want to marry. What will the ramifications be if a girl from a liberated, egalitarian background marries a boy from a macho-dominated background? Even when the young man and woman are able to work out their differences, there is also the influence of the families to be considered. Family role expectations do impinge and cast their shadows. These are factors to be explored and weighed seriously before the step of marriage is taken.

What does a counselor do when one of the above areas of concern emerges in the premarital counseling process? Good judgment indicates that a more searching and probing exploration is needed. Exploration takes time, of course, so delay in setting a wedding date may need to be discussed. The additional time can be put to best advantage through a more extensive counseling process helping the couple to explore the various conflict areas. Individual and joint sessions could be held with both the groom- and bride-to-be.

Time can also be used advantageously for the couple to do reading in the area of concern. They might also have dialogue with others who have faced similar situations, couples who have made their marriage work, as well as those whose marriages didn't work under similar circumstances.

EXPLORING THE FOUR MAIN AREAS OF MARRIAGE

There are four main aspects of marriage that deserve to be explored carefully in premarital counseling sessions. These are (1) the psychological and sociological, (2) the financial and economic, (3) the physiological and sexual, and (4) spiritual and church relationships. Each area is an integral and important part of the total marriage relationship.

Psychological and Sociological

How do the couple fit each other emotionally and socially? Ideally, the prospective bride and groom are "alike" enough for compatibility and "individual" enough to add zest and interest to the relationship. Here are some questions which I have found helpful in exploring this first area with the couple:

1. What interests do you share?
2. What interests do you have that are different?
3. Do these differences ever cause tensions?
4. How would you describe your time clocks—are they similar or different? Are you both "doves" (best in the morning) or "owls" (most alert in the evening)?
5. Are you both extraverts? Introverts? Or one of each?
6. What is your basic attitude toward life? Optimistic or pessimistic? Carefree or worrier? Conservative or liberal?
7. Is your attitude toward having fun similar? Is one a butterfly and one a workaholic?

8. What is your attitude toward your fiancé(e)'s family? Are you compatible?
9. What is your family's attitude toward your marriage?
10. Will there be emotional support from both families for the marriage?
11. How do you want your marriage to be different from your parents' marriage?
12. Do you enjoy the same friends?
13. Does your fiancé(e) have friends that you do not respect or appreciate?
14. Do you have friends or relatives who have good marriages? What makes them good?
15. Do you have friends or relatives who do not have good marriages? What makes them poor?
16. Is your attitude toward children similar? Toward discipline similar?
17. What will you do differently from your parents in raising your children?
18. How do you define the role of husband? Wife?
19. How will the housework responsibilities be shared?
20. Will both the wife and husband help with the yard work?

Financial and Economic

Because love often casts an illusion on the couple's world, it is usually necessary to help them look with the eyes of reality and do some financial planning. Above and beyond the structuring of a budget (some couples prefer to call it a guide to spending), the counselor will want to help them assess their financial attitudes and priorities. The counselor can explore with the prospective bride and groom:

1. What is your basic attitude toward money at this point in life?
2. Will your goal be to skimp and save for a home of your own, or will this be a time for fun and travel before you start your family?
3. What are your financial backgrounds?
4. How do your backgrounds differ?
5. How does this affect your marriage?
6. What are your financial goals for the future?
7. Where do you hope to be financially in five years? Ten years? Twenty-five years?
8. How closely do you want to account to each other for your spending?
9. How much money do you plan to set aside for a "rainy day"?
10. What are your vocational and career plans?
11. Are your marriage plans based on both persons working?
12. If so, how long will both partners work?

13. How was your budget decided? Together? (At this point you can review the couple's budget. Is it realistic?)
14. Who will see that the budget is carried out?
15. Who will write the monthly checks? Will this rotate?
16. How did you determine your personal allowances?
17. What are your attitudes toward insurance?
18. Have you made your fiancé(e) your beneficiary?
19. Have you written a will?
20. When and how will you revise your budget?
21. Will you use charge cards or pay cash only?
22. Are there debts that you bring into the marriage?
23. Is there anything financial that you have not discussed or resolved?
24. Does one partner tend to spend lavishly?
25. If so, how does the other partner feel about that?
26. How does the lavish spender feel about the other partner?

The use of money can be a source of satisfaction for a couple or the source of great contention. Wise planning can go a long way to help the management of resources become a positive force in the new marriage.

Physiological and Sexual

Even when there is an openness to discussing the physical and sexual aspects of life in the nuclear family setting, it is important to include a discussion of these in the premarital counseling dialogue. Many colleges offer courses on marriage and the family, and even on the high school level similar instructions are a part of the curriculum.

Needless to say, this is not a time for the counselor's curiosity to intrude, but rather an opportunity for the couple to discuss in an open way questions that touch on these vital aspects of life. Some important questions to explore are:

1. How is your health?
2. What health problems have you experienced?
3. Have you discussed the implications of these health problems?
4. Will you plan a complete physical examination prior to marriage?
5. What books have you read on marriage, sex, and the family? What courses have you taken?
6. Are you on the same level when it comes to expressing affection?
7. Does one need more verbal affection?

8. Does one need more physical attention?
9. When do you plan to start your family?
10. How many children do you plan to have?
11. Which method of family planning will you follow?
12. Have you examined the percentage of safety this method offers?
13. Which partner, or will both be responsible for family planning?

This is an opportune time to talk about sexuality as being a gift of God and a beautiful part of his divine plan of creation. Although most young couples are no longer sexually naive, sometimes they fail to capture the joy and insight of being a part of God's creative plan. It is an ideal time to refute the triple myth, "Sex is a sin, sex is dirty, sex is only for men." Another myth to be buried is, "Only men should initiate sex." In an age of human liberation (not just women's liberation or men's liberation) it is important for couples to discuss how they can meet their mutual needs for affection, love, touching, and sexual fulfillment.

Spiritual and Church Relationships

For the most part, couples are open to discussing the spiritual aspects of their marriage. For some this becomes a time of reviewing and renewing their commitment of faith. Premarriage preparation can provide an excellent opportunity for the working of the Holy Spirit.
Some questions you will want to pose are:

1. What place will faith have in your life together?
2. Will you join a church together?
3. If not, will you worship together?
4. If so, with what frequency will you worship together?
5. Do you plan to participate in any church groups or organizations? Either individually or together?
6. Will you pray before meals?
7. Will you pray at other times of the day?
8. Do you plan to have home devotions?
9. What leads you to wish to be married in a religious ceremony?
10. Do you have any religious differences?
11. How will you work these differences out?
12. Are you in agreement about the religious heritage you will give to your children?
13. Will you both be responsible for the religious instruction of your children?

If the persons are members of different religious traditions, this is an ideal time for each to become educated as to the teachings, customs, and traditions of the other. What religious customs will they bring to their new life together? What effects will these have on their lives? For instance, if one partner is used to giving a tithe to the Church and the other is not, how will this be worked out?

STRUCTURING PREMARITAL SESSIONS

For the average couple, where there are no special complications or warning signs, a four-meeting series is generally adequate. Ideally, the sessions would begin five or six months prior to the date of the wedding, to allow time for additional sessions if they are needed. The parish needs to educate couples to this six-month schedule. These sessions are usually about an hour and a half each. If couples come only eight to twelve weeks prior to the proposed wedding date, the schedule needs to be accelerated. A structure for the four sessions might follow this pattern:

The First Session

An introductory meeting can serve a number of purposes. A beginning goal would be to help put the couple at ease regarding the sessions together and to get acquainted with them as persons. Second, this is a time to share something about oneself and to express gladness to have this opportunity to get to know the couple and assist them in their preparations for marriage. Third, if the couple has completed information forms ahead of time, this a good time to review and clarify the information received. If there are forms that cannot be completed ahead of time, these can be completed at the first session. The fourth purpose is to explore the story of the couple's relationship. The general questions found in the section "Encourage Interpersonal Dialogue" can assist in this step. The counselor's involvement in the dialogue will depend upon how verbal the man and woman are. If they tend to be shy, the counselor will want to encourage and draw them out. If one partner tends to monopolize the conversation, the counselor will want to gently direct some questions to the more silent partner. If one or both tend to get carried away with verbiage, the counselor can gently move them along.

Depending on the time remaining in the first session, there might begin an exploration of the psychological and sociological implications of marriage as discussed in the section on that subject (p. 157).

At the end of the first session the counselor can offer to lend a book or two of a general nature to the couple to read and discuss together. Recommended books are *Getting Ready for Marriage* by David Mace and *Your First Year of Marriage* by Tom McGinnis (see References).

The counselor can also ask the couple to prepare a budget together to bring to the second meeting. It is helpful to give them a printed guide to assist in this preparation. A suggested guide follows on page 164.

Each session can begin or end with prayer if the counselor feels it appropriate for the couple's needs. This should not be done mechanically, but as a response to the guiding of the Holy Spirit.

The Second Session

The second meeting with the couple, which would normally follow the first session in three or four weeks, would begin with an updating of events since the first session. It is important to communicate to the couple an interest in their lives, relationships, and wedding plans. After this the counselor would continue exploring the remainder of the psychological and sociological aspects of marriage.

Note should be made of any questions where problems or differences emerge, or where it is evident that the couple has not had sufficient dialogue. They can be encouraged to discuss these as a part of their homework assignment. The counselor should always refer back to these areas in the next session to see what progress has been made or to determine whether further dialogue is needed.

Next should be a consideration of financial and economic matters. Questions from that section of this chapter (p. 158) can serve as a basis for this discussion. The couple's budget should also be discussed and reviewed. Did the couple prepare it together? If not, the counselor will want to explore what this means. Is their budget realistic? Are they allowing for adequate funds for rent, food, gasoline, church and charity, birthdays, Christmas and other holiday gifts? An important item, often overlooked, is the personal allowance of both. What are these to cover?

As conflicts arise, it is helpful for the couple to clarify these trouble areas. Each needs to have an opportunity to share both throughts and feelings in regard to the issues involved. Often the conflict cannot be settled during the session. When this is the case, reading materials can be suggested and the couple can be directed to discuss the area of conflict further before the next session.

Books relating to the areas of sexuality and spirituality can be suggested or loaned to the couple at the end of the second session. Some possible suggestions might be: *Sexual Harmony in Marriage* by Butterfield, *Sex without Fear* by Lewin and Gilmore, *The Spirit of Your Marriage* by Ludwig, and *Beginnings* by Mattison (see References).

The Third Session

The third session, about three weeks after the second, should focus on the physiological, sexual, and spiritual aspects of marriage. Exploratory questions like those found in the two appropriate sections can be posed to open up these discussion areas. While people often feel free to offer advice and instruction regarding the other areas of marriage, the primary responsibility for the spiritual dialogue often falls upon the pastoral counselor. He or she should avoid using this opportunity for preaching but instead see it as a time to share the joy of one's own faith experience.

Toward the end of the third session, after completing the interpersonal dialogue questions and discussing further developments and decisions on trouble areas, the counselor will want to meet individually with the young man and woman. Are there questions that need to be raised? Is there anything troubling the man or woman that can't be discussed with the fiancé(e)? Usually, these individual meetings are not extended, but this time alone with each is an important and necessary component of the process.

At the close of the third session reading materials focusing on unresolved problems or areas that need further clarification and illumination can be suggested. At this point the couple can be asked to think about the kind of wedding ceremony they desire. This would include selecting Scripture and music and deciding upon any personal touches they want included as a part of the ceremony. Books like *Together for Life* by Champlin and *The Wedding Handbook* by Fuelling and Quesnel might be suggested to help plan their ceremony. The former is for use with Roman Catholic couples, the latter with Protestant couples.

Ideally, by the end of the third session the counselor will feel comfortable with agreeing to perform the ceremony. Adequate time still remains for the printing and mailing of wedding invitations. If there are still serious problems that are not resolved at this point, the counselor needs to share these reservations and doubts and would want to explore the various options available.

If serious problem areas emerge early in the counseling process, the interval of three weeks between sessions can be reduced to one or two weeks, thus providing the extra time for the added counseling that might be needed.

The Fourth Session

The last session gives the counselor an opportunity to review any problem areas that have emerged to see if they have been resolved adequately before moving on to the final phase of the preparations. If the trouble areas have been worked through, then the counselor can proceed to discuss the form and meaning of the actual wedding liturgy. When trouble areas are still present, additional sessions may be needed to explore these conflicts.

If the couple decides to follow the traditional marriage ceremony, the counselor will want to take each sentence or phrase of the liturgy and explain its meaning for the couple. Both the joys and responsibilities need to be emphasized. When the couple decides against the traditional service and wants to frame its own service, the counselor will want to give special attention to their individual needs. Often the couple desires to add a personal touch to the wedding liturgy, such as special music, the lighting of a wedding candle, the presentation of a flower to the mothers, or some other symbol.

A GUIDE FOR SPENDING FOR NEWLYWEDS

Make all entries based on anticipated *monthly* income and expenditures.

I. ANTICIPATED INCOME:
    GROSS INCOME
        Groom's Salary $_____
        Bride's Salary   _____
        Investment Income   _____
        Other _____   _____
        TOTAL GROSS INCOME $_____
        Deduct: Taxes & Social Security −_____
    NET MONTHLY INCOME $_____

II. ANTICIPATED COST OF LIVING:
    A. FIXED EXPENSES
        House Payment (or Rent) $_____
        Property/Household
            Insurance   _____
        Taxes (not Income Tax)   _____
        Utilities:
            Telephone   _____
            Gas/Electric/Oil   _____
            Heat   _____
            Water/Sewer   _____
        Total Utilities $_____
    TOTAL FIXED EXPENSES $_____

    B. HOUSEHOLD EXPENSES
        Food $_____
        Laundry/Dry Cleaning   _____
        Furniture   _____
        House Furnishings   _____
            (Curtains, dishes, etc.)
        Other _____   _____
              _____   _____
    TOTAL HOUSEHOLD EXPENSES $ _____

    C. PERSONAL EXPENSES
        Church and Charity $_____
        Medical: _____
            Physician $_____
            Medicine   _____
            Medical Ins.   _____
        Total Medical Expense   _____

Life Insurance _____
Recreation / Vacation _____
Entertainment _____
Clothing _____
Personal Allowances _____
Savings _____
Other _____ _____

TOTAL PERSONAL EXPENSES $ _____
TOTAL EXPENSES $_____
BALANCE CARRIED FORWARD (Subtract
Total Expenses from Net Monthly Income) $_____

These personal touches combine to make the wedding liturgy a truly personal, memorable, and unique experience. A date and time for the wedding rehearsal can then be set. The counselor will want to celebrate with each couple as they move step by step through the premarital experience.

In some parishes the premarital preparation and counseling are done solely by the minister. In other congregations this is shared by a team, other members of the staff, and specially qualified members of the parish. A well-adjusted married couple willing to serve in this capacity can become a most valuable adjunct resource.

Conclusion

Premarital preparation/counseling is a vital part of the ministry of the Church. The pastoral counselor serves as a catalyst and an enabler to the necessary sharing and dialogue that help to prepare for a marriage built upon a solid foundation.

Premarital preparation/counseling is not a panacea for preventing divorce. Even couples with the best preparation will experience adjustments and difficulties. However, this can be a process that strengthens faith, gives support and direction, and presents an opportunity to have dialogue about pertinent issues. Certainly, this is a ministry that takes a positive step toward marital success.

RESOURCES AVAILABLE

Testing Materials

1. *The Taylor-Johnson Temperament Analysis.* The T-JTA, designed for diagnostic and counseling purposes, serves as a quick and convenient method of measuring certain personality traits which influence personal and social functioning and

adjustment. It is uniquely appropriate for use in premarital and marital counseling. The Regular Edition is for high school students, college students, and adults. Scoring sheets and stencils may be ordered. The T-JTA materials are available from Psychological Publications, Inc., 5300 Hollywood Boulevard, Los Angeles, Calif. 90027.

2. *The Mooney Problem Check List.* This test helps persons to identify problems relating to health, work, family, temperament, and so on. It comes in three forms, high school, college, and adult, and is available from the Psychological Corporation, 757 Third Ave., New York, N.Y. 10017.

3. *The Marriage Expectation Inventory* by P. J. McDonald. The MEI investigates expectations in nine vital areas of marriage: love, communication, freedom, sex, money, selfishness, religion, relatives, and children. Form I is for engaged couples and Form II is for married couples. Respondents provide written answers to 58 questions. The MEI is available from Family Life Publications, P.O. Box 427, Saluda, N.C. 28773.

4. *The Marriage Role Expectations Inventories* by Dr. Marie Dunn and J. N. DeBonis. The REI capitalizes on research indications that the marriage role interpretations and marriage expectations directly relate to success in marriage. Expectations in seven areas are explored: authority, homemaking, care of children, personal characteristics, social participation, education, and employment support. Available from Family Life Publications (see item 3 above).

5. *A Marriage Prediction Schedule* by Dr. Ernest Burges. The AMPS is basically a compatibility quiz covering expectations about a future marriage and courtship adjustment. The couple completes it together and their answers and score provide important discussion topics. Available from Family Life Publications (see item 3 above).

6. *The Love Attitudes Inventory* by David Knox. The LAI is a unique instrument that helps the counselor teach the difference between romantic and realistic love without labeling either concept as good or bad. This inventory helps individuals discover and question their own attitudes about love. Available from Family Life Publications (see item 3 above).

7. *Dating Problems Check List* by Gelolo McHugh. The DPCL is a 125-item questionnaire which allows individuals to report on the dating atmosphere in which they socialize. They respond by (1) indicating whether or not a particular attitude or situation exists, and (2) whether or not it is a problem for them. This inventory can be used with groups as well as individuals. Available from Family Life Publications (see item 3 above).

8. *The Premarital Counseling Kit* by Millard J. Bienvenu, Sr. The PCK is designed to help the prospective bride and groom realize the complexities of setting up life together. It consists of six separate forms designed to provide a thorough introduction to marriage and to encourage participation by the couple in the

counseling sessions. Available from Family Life Publications (see item 3 above).

9. *A Courtship Analysis* by Gelolo McHugh. This instrument is a 150-item questionnaire designed to allow partners in courtship, or individuals, report the dynamics of their relationship by indicating the presence or absence of positive and negative character traits and behaviors of the courtship partner. Available from Family Life Publications (see item 3 above).

10. *The Crane and Coffer Religious Attitudes Inventory.* The CCRA provides a quick and thorough assessment of religious beliefs and promotes productive discussion toward resolving conflicts in this area. It consists of a 107-item inventory responded to by degree of agreement/disagreement in areas of responsibility, belief, child rearing, and so on. Available from Family Life Publications (see item 3 above).

11. *Sex Knowledge Inventories* (Form X and Form Y) by Gelolo McHugh. The SKI are objective information-gathering questionnaires for the assessment of individual levels of sex knowledge. Form X contains eighty multiple choice questions and is self-administered. It can be scored in ten seconds using a prepunched key. Form Y structures the teaching of basic sex vocabulary, anatomy, and the function of anatomy and helps the counselor to teach beneficial facts about human sexuality. These inventories are available in English and five foreign languages. Available from Family Life Publications (see item 3 above).

12. *Pre-Marriage Awareness Inventory Kit.* The basis of this counseling system is a multiple choice questionnaire which is completed by the couple individually. The completed questionnaires are then compared in order for the couple to discover their attitudes and expectations in marriage, to discuss in a positive way the possible adjustment challenges offered by any differences in attitudes and expectations, and to discuss how those challenges might be handled in a constructive manner. The PAI is available from the Shepherd's Staff Publications, Box 371, Cannon Falls, Minn. 55009.

Specialized Materials

1. *Mosaic* by Julien Mercure and Frank Dolphin. This is a unique kit composed of seven folders each containing beautiful illustrations, narrations, and questions for discussion for the prospective bride and groom. The titles are: To Be Alive, Make Contact, Explore Your Differences, A Sign of Love, A Place to Live, Sexual Intimacy, and Parenthood. The publisher is NOVALIS, St. Paul University, 1 Stewart Street, Ottawa, Canada.

2. *Growing Together in Marriage* by Rev. J. Murray Elwood. In this two-cassette series Fr. Elwood talks about the stresses facing married couples today and the factors that make for marital success and happiness. Available from The Modern Cassette Library, Ave Maria Press, Notre Dame, Ind. 46556.

3. *Preparing for Marriage.* This series of filmstrips analyzes the factors that contribute to lasting Christian marriages in today's complex world. They are suitable for junior high, high school, and adults. The four filmstrips are titled: (1) "Getting Yourself Ready for Marriage," (2) "What to Look for in a Life Partner," (3) "What to Expect from Marriage," and (4) "Christian Marriage is Different." Available from Family Films, 14622 Lanark Street, Panorama City, Calif. 91402.

4. *Making the Best Choice.* This is a two-part filmstrip series dealing with mate selection: Part One is "Predicting Success" and Part Two is "Beyond Engagement." These filmstrips encourage thoughtfulness in choosing a companion for life by examining the factors in mate selection that often influence marital success or failure. They are produced by Human Relations Media, 175 Tomkins Avenue, Pleasantville, N.Y. 10570.

5. *Values for Dating.* This is a four-part filmstrip series, which contrasts current dating values with those of the past. Part One is "Pressures," Part Two is "Traditional Values," Part Three is "Love and Friendship," and Part Four is "Two Couples in Love." Produced by Human Relations Media (see item 4 above).

6. *What About Marriage.* A three-part filmstrip series which fosters realistic expectations and gives a deeper understanding of the personal commitments that accompany marriage. The three parts are entitled "Till Death Do Us Part," "Romantic Love and Dirty Dishes," and "Two Case Studies." Produced by Human Relations Media (see item 4 above).

7. *Marriage Counseling Kit* by James R. Hine. A useful and unique card set which helps to put a young couple at ease during the premarital conferences. The card-sorting sequence creates a setting in which the young couple can freely reveal important factors about themselves in terms of their coming marriage. Use of the kit makes discussions of differences of opinion necessary and helps the couple evaluate strong and weak points in their ability to discuss problems and reach satisfactory agreements. Available from the Interstate Printers and Publishers, Inc., Danville, Ill. 61832.

8. *Talking It Over Before Marriage* by Millard J. Bienvenu, Sr. This twenty-four-page pamphlet (No. 512) focuses on exercises for building communication skills. The skills seek to explore (1) trust, (2) safety of expression, (3) listening for understanding, (4) empathy, (5) expectations, and (6) stroking. Available from Public Affairs Pamphlets, 381 Park Avenue South, New York, N.Y. 10016.

Pre-Cana Conferences

Pre-Cana Conferences are a part of the educational program of the Roman Catholic Church and are usually sponsored by the various dioceses. These conferences are designed for group preparation of couples contemplating marriage. They usually run five or six sessions and draw upon local speakers, such as priests, doctors, lawyers, and other resource persons. In some areas attendance at the Pre-Cana Conferences is expected for Roman Catholic couples prior to the individual preparations in the parish. In other dioceses attendance is optional.

Engaged Encounter

Engaged Encounter is a spinoff patterned after the very successful Marriage Encounter Program. The format is the same: an intensive Friday evening through Sunday afternoon experience which incorporates the instructional approach along with dialogue. Whereas Pre-Cana Conferences are primarily instructional, the EE Weekend has its primary focus on an experiential dimension. The Pre-Cana Conferences stress the need for communication in married life, whereas EE not only teaches the Marriage Encounter technique of dialogue, it also gives an opportunity to practice dialogue for an entire weekend. In most dioceses EE is seen as a supplement rather than a substitute for Pre-Cana.

REFERENCES

GENERAL

Barry, W. A. "Marriage Research and Conflict: An Integrative Review," *Psychological Bulletin,* 73(1), 1970, 41–45.
Fryling, Robert, and Alice Fryling. *A Handbook for Engaged Couples.* Downers Grove, Ill.: Intervarsity Press, 1977.
Geiseman, O. A. *Make Yours a Happy Marriage.* St. Louis: Concordia, 1971.
Kaluger, George, and Meriem Kaluger. *Human Development: The Span of Life.* St. Louis: Mosby, 1974, pp. 243–63.
Kirkpatrick, C. *The Family as Process and Institution.* New York: Ronald, 1955.
Mace, David R. *Getting Ready for Marriage.* Nashville: Abingdon, 1972.
Mattison, Judith. *Beginnings.* Minneapolis: Augsburg, 1980.
McGinnis, Tom. *Your First Year of Marriage.* Garden City, N.Y.: Doubleday, 1967.
McRoberts, Darlene. *Second Marriage.* Minneapolis: Augsburg, 1978.
Powell, John. *The Secret of Staying in Love.* Niles, Ill.: Argus Communications, 1974.
Rolfe, David J. *Marriage Preparation Manual.* New York: Paulist Press, 1975.
Stewart, Charles William. *The Minister as Marriage Counselor.* Nashville: Abingdon, 1970, pp. 50–78.
Tate-O'Brien, Judith. *Love in Deed.* St. Paul: National Marriage Encounter, 1980.
Thomas, John L. *Beginning Your Marriage.* Chicago: Buckley Publications, 1975.

FINANCIAL

Howver, Carl F. *Basic Principles in Family Money and Credit Management.* Washington, D.C.: National Consumer Finance Association, 1972.
Howver, Carl, and Roy Burkhart. *Money and Your Marriage.* Washington, D.C.: National Consumer Finance Association, 1972.

SEXUAL

Butterfield, Oliver M. *Sexual Harmony in Marriage*. New York: Emerson Books, 1974.

Greenblat, Bernard R. *A Doctor's Marital Sex Guide for Patients*. Chicago: Budlong Press, 1970.

Lewin, S. A., and John Gilmore. *Sex Without Fear*. Scotch Plains, N.J.: Medical Research Press, 1974.

Short, Ray E. *Sex, Love, or Infatuation: How Can I Really Know?* Minneapolis: Augsburg, 1978.

Wood, Leland Foster. *Harmony in Marriage*. Old Tappan, N.J.: Revell, 1979.

SPIRITUAL

Ludwig, David J. *The Spirit of Your Marriage*. Minneapolis: Augsburg, 1979.

Trobisch, Walter. *I Married You*. New York: Harper, 1971.

WEDDING CEREMONY/LITURGY

Champlin, Joseph M. *Together for Life*. Notre Dame, Ind.: Ave Maria Press, 1973. (An edition is also available for marriage outside the Mass.)

Fuelling, Daniel, and Jean Quesnel. *The Wedding Handbook*. Minneapolis: Augsburg, 1976.

CHAPTER TEN

Counseling with Couples

REV. DAVID L. LUECKE

Troubled couples have come to me for help since the beginning of my thirty years of ministry. Their choice seemed appropriate. They knew a pastor would put value on healthy family life and stable marriages. Some couples knew of no other available resource. Some couples came from other churches or religious groups, being reluctant to reveal inner weaknesses, inadequacies, or unfaithfulness to their own pastors. Some whom I had counseled in preparation for their wedding were returning to a familiar resource. Whatever the reason, troubled couples sought me out as a pastoral counselor.

Their assumptions were mostly correct. I did want to help. I was ready to give marriage counseling a high priority in my ministry. I had solid biblical, ecclesiastical, organizational, and personal values supporting the importance of strong, stable marriages. The cost of broken relationships seemed high in spiritual and human terms. I responded eagerly to the call for help. I soon discovered, however, that good intentions were not enough even when richly laced with Scripture, exhortation, encouragement, and prayer. Other skills were needed.

THEOLOGICAL AND PERSONAL REFLECTIONS

Pursuing relationship-counseling skills was motivated both by theological considerations and priorities in ministry. Successful relationships seem to me essential for wholeness and successful living. Most emotional difficulties, whatever problems an individual presents, have relational issues at the roots. *Salvation* and *shalom* describe a total kind of healing of body, mind, and spirit that includes a restoration of relationships. A healing of relationships whether with God, the world, oneself, or significant others is essential to the "abundant life."

Healing of relationships is a work and gift of the Spirit who calls people into community and enables them to overcome barriers to giving and receiving love, emotional support, and caring confrontation. A caring and accepting climate frees people to be themselves, open and self-revealing before God and one another and thus receptive to the possibility of growth and healing.

The Scriptures portray the marriage relationship as one to which God gives particular attention. This special relationship is described as mystical, profound, full of potential, paralleling God's own relationship with His people. For many Christians, the marriage relationship is built upon a sacrament. Other Christians understand marriage as an "office" to which partners are "called." Almost all Christians affirm marriage as "ordained by God" in some sense.

Sometimes I think people undervalue the spiritual dimension of a relationship, failing to see God's own investment in unifying relationships. At other times it seems to me that people overmystify the practical and natural dimensions of relating, leaving too much to intuition or blind luck. Every relationship that works, it seems to me, is a gift of God's love and a reflection of His Spirit. At the same time every relationship can be analyzed and understood in terms of its component parts, strengthened and enriched in practical ways.

As a pastoral counselor, I put a high value on marital stability. I want to see marriages succeed not only for children, security needs, emotional and material well-being, or the sanctity of vows, but for the sake of the relationship itself. As a gift of God and a reflection of His Spirit, every working relationship enriches all human life.

Yet, as a pastoral counselor, *especially* as a pastoral counselor, I do not play God. I do not take more responsibility to control the decisions of a couple than God does. It is not my responsibility and far beyond my capacity to "save" marriages. Couples make their own relationships succeed or fail. I can be helpful, even critically important, to couples deciding about their relationship and implementing their decision, but the decision and the relationship belong to the couple.

SEARCH FOR RESOURCES

From the beginning I was confronted with both theoretical and practical problems in my efforts to help couples. Counseling procedures I had learned for working with individuals did not seem to apply to working with couples, yet most of the recommended procedures and techniques, though often controversial, suggested doing just that. Some respected authorities, especially psychoanalytically oriented ones, questioned the very possibility of doing therapy with couples. I had my own questions. What is marriage counseling? Is marriage counseling doing therapy with two people simultaneously? Is the relationship itself the client? If so, what heals a relationship? Does a counselor need to separate relational issues from personal ones? How does one draw the line when the issues are fused? Is marriage counseling unique from individual counseling with an art and skill of its own?

Although I did not find definitive answers, I did find help. Efforts were being made to translate a variety of therapeutic modalities to marriage counseling. Each of them was helpful, none was conclusive. Here, in brief, is how I saw the strengths and weaknesses of applying psychoanalysis, behavior modification, family systems, and transactional analysis to working with couples.

Psychoanalysis

Psychoanalysis developed as a treatment for individuals. Gradually, not without controversy, innovative analysts applied its theory and practice to working with couples. Analysts understood their task as treating three subjects simultaneously: two partners and the marriage relationship.

Using a developmental approach, analysts explore the influence of previous experience on current behavior, for example, the impact of the family of origin on the choice of a marriage partner. Thus a couple in treatment builds insight into how past relationships are transferred into the interaction in disruptive and deceptive ways. An important goal is to complete the individuation process both from the family of origin and from the partner so that genuine intimacy becomes possible.

A strength of the psychoanalytic approach in working with couples is that it uncovers unresolved developmental issues each partner brings to the relationship so that the couple can gain perspective and cognitive insight into dysfunctional behavior. A potential weakness of such an approach can be its failure to deal effectively with immediate disruptive behavior patterns. In addition, some couples may not be willing or able to make the long-term commitment such an approach often requires.

Behavior Modification

Social learning theory, like psychoanalysis, was developed for the treatment of individuals. Nevertheless, its methods have proven readily applicable to working with couples. Unlike analysis, behaviorists have little concern for past developmental issues; history taking may be limited to the life of the relationship. The basic assumption of this approach is that marital dysfunction results from too little reciprocity and too many coercive behaviors. A healthy marriage is self-reinforcing as cooperative behaviors are rewarded with relational satisfactions. An unhealthy marriage reinforces its dysfunction as coercion leads to aversive behaviors, which result in increased relational dissatisfaction, which leads to coercion, which results in aversive behaviors, and so on in a spiraling circle. Behavioral therapists tend to emphasize the value of explicit marriage contracts and the development of problem-solving skills and *quid pro quo* negotiations. The goal is generally to enable a couple to cooperate like "adults" in their efforts to keep their marriage working.

Strengths of the behaviorist approach include its capacity to provide emotional distance from issues in conflict and to keep conflict manageable by teaching communication and conflict-resolution skills. Its educational language and tone together with its focus on immediate practical issues may elicit less anxiety and greater cooperation than a more psychological language and stance. Potential weaknesses of this approach might include its inability to deal with underlying problems of perception which may fuel dysfunctional behavior. This approach may be unrealistically optimistic in assuming the capacity and willingness of both partners to take responsibility for cooperative problem solving early in the treatment. Finally, an "adult" problem-solving approach may be too dull and unrewarding, failing to allow couples alternately to satisfy each other's dependency needs, to play, to engender romance, and to enter into the less rational dimension that can make a relationship special.

Family Systems

Family systems approaches applied to working with couples have gained prominence in recent years. (This method needs to be distinguished from the *relational systems* discussed later in this chapter.) A basic assumption of this approach is that marital dysfunction results from and is sustained by pathology in the family system with roots deeply embedded in the families of origin. Therapeutic change is accomplished by skillful alterations in the family systems that support the problematic behavior. Such an approach aims at rapid change with little attention to specific issues or intrapersonal dynamics. What counts is the process, not the content.

A family systems approach may have an advantage for working with couples with minimal investment in the counseling process or where brief therapy is required for whatever reason. An additional strength of this approach is that it keeps a focus on the contextual sources of dysfunctional behavior. A possible weakness, however, is the failure of this approach to equip a couple with either self-understanding or relational skills for taking charge of the relationship; nor does it provide a role model for relational skills in the counselor.

Transactional Analysis

My interest in understanding relationships and in working with couples motivated me to take a second look at Transactional Analysis, which defines the subject matter of psychology in terms of stimuli and responses between an organism and its environment. Transactional Analysis as a treatment method focuses on human interaction and is therefore readily applicable to working with couples. Its tools provide for exploring intrapersonal and interpersonal dynamics as well as the developmental roots to larger patterns of relational interaction.

A strength in the use of Transactional Analysis for marriage counseling is that it provides both counselor and couple with relatively easily understood cognitive tools both for the counseling process and as an ongoing resource for the couple after termination. Among the weaknesses of Transactional Analysis may be the reluctance of the infinite variety of human behavior to fit into its analytic categories and the appropriate resistance of couples to counselors who might try to force a fit. Also, cognitive description is not necessarily healing. The use of Transactional Analysis "fad language" can reduce the authenticity of the counseling relationship and process.

MY OWN EVOLVING APPROACH

Each of the theories and methods discussed provided, and still provides, useful insight and tools for working with couples. Although sharp differences and contradictions exist among them, much is also held in common. All of them include the following short- and long-term goals in the counseling process: (1) defining the problem from each partner's perspective; (2) clarifying what each partner needs and desires from the relationship; (3) overcoming blame and coercion by each partner's ownership of appropriate responsibility for difficulties; (4) building effective and satisfying communication; (5) increasing flexibility in role expectations and increased reciprocity for cooperative problem solving.

Gradually, my own theoretic perspective began to emerge, shaped partly by my taking what seemed most useful from the resources briefly described above, partly from my own clinical experience, and partly by the type of couples I was seeing— mostly middle-class, above average in education and intelligence, with strong verbal skills. Yet, with all these assets, the couples were anxious and defensive dealing with personal issues. In short, these are the sort of couples one typically finds in many parishes.

A more objective, manageable understanding of what makes relationships work seemed needed. Even exceptionally successful people in other areas of achievement frequently become mystified and insecure, unable to apply their competence to personal issues. Personal relational problems raise threatening questions: "Am I loveable?" "Will I be rejected?" "Will I be taken advantage of?" "Can I be married and still be me?" Such people seemed to me to need a relatively nonthreatening and practical perspective on their relationship, a way to apply logic and skills to personal relational issues.

A RELATIONAL SYSTEMS APPROACH

Over my thirty years of working with couples such an approach began to emerge as I identified four systems essential to every complete relationship. An understanding of these four systems offers a practical framework for diagnosing any relationship and provides directions for building or enriching it. Just as physical symptoms can be traced to a malfunctioning system in the body—circulatory, respiratory, digestive, muscular—so relational difficulties can be diagnosed and treated in terms of systems essential to every complete relationship. At least four relational systems can be identified: compatibility, cooperation, intimacy, and emotional support. Although not exhaustive of relational possibilities, these four systems provide a structure for marriage counseling. A brief overview of each system follows here; a more thorough description comes later in the chapter.

Compatibility

People move into marriage carrying a load of "baggage"—often more than is realized. Such baggage includes attitudes, opinions, and values on such issues as the use of money, importance of status, social causes, politics, sociability, choice of friends, sex roles, parenting methods, work, play, use of leisure time, religion, and much more. As we grow up, we make decisions about the kind of lifestyle we prefer, although we are not always aware of our real priorities.

Such accumulated attitudes, opinions, and values need to blend with those of the partner. At times the combined baggage may fit easily together; at other times adjustments are needed and sometimes the conflicts may seem irreconcilable.

Differences in values and lifestyle are inevitable and need not be devisive. Deeper and more fundamental shared values often lie beneath the surface of conflicting ones. For example, people with conflicting political perspectives may share an underlying patriotic commitment. People with differing religious beliefs or affiliations may share a common underlying heritage and moral values out of which they can build a common lifestyle.

Couples with compatibility problems can explore their values in depth, probing for the positive side of their partner's values with which they disagree. In this way compatibility can be constructed in spite of variations in values or lifestyle preference.

Cooperation

Cooperation difficulties include frequent hassling, blaming, competitiveness, difficulties solving problems or making mutually satisfying decisions, inability to work together on a project or even sustain a conversation without bad feelings.

Cooperation often breaks down when a couple becomes competitive. Such competition may be a contest for control (who gets to say how it is, that is, "You don't earn enough" versus "No, you overspend") or a contest for dependence (who has to take care of whom). Such competition may have roots in childhood, may be a reenactment of sibling rivalry, or can result from conflicting sex role expectations, fears of exploitation, or fear of losing one's individuality in marriage.

Cooperation can also break down for more practical reasons such as the lack of relational skills: communication, listening, problem solving, conflict resolution, and so forth. Some people grow up without adequate models for learning these skills and have never had the opportunity or felt the need to develop them.

Couples with cooperation difficulties can learn to identify and modify competitive responses. They can learn communication and listening skills so that issues are faced, defined, and resolved. Couples can learn to accept conflict and disagreement as normal and inevitable. They can learn to respond creatively so that both feel respected, affirmed, and satisfied. They can learn to make decisions in ways that take the feelings, desires, and thinking of both fully into account, allowing both to get as much as possible of what is wanted.

Intimacy

Intimacy difficulties are signaled by a lack of self-disclosure, a withholding of feelings, desires, inner thoughts, and fantasies. Such couples lack the closeness that makes a relationship special. They experience little romance or excitement.

Most people yearn for a close, open, and intimate relationship. Yet many fear it almost as much as they yearn for it. Being intimate means being vulnerable. Fearful of criticism or rejection, mates keep too well hidden to allow real intimacy. Some protect themselves by withdrawing. Others protect themselves by pushing their partners away with humor, anger, or controlling behavior. Still others allow themselves to be physically close but remain emotionally distant.

Intimacy occurs—or fails to occur—on a variety of levels. *Conversational intimacy* has to do with self-revelation and openness, especially about each other. *Emotional intimacy* has to do with spontaneous expression of feelings, especially toward one another. *Physical intimacy* has to do with the kind and frequency of physical closeness apart from explicit sexual activity. *Sexual intimacy* has to do with sharing fantasies, feelings, and desires openly and spontaneously when engaged in sexual relations.

Couples can identify areas in their relationship in which they experience intimacy difficulties and explore methods or exercises to overcome them. Emotionally blocked partners can learn to be in touch with feelings, identify them, and act on them. Couples can learn to say more directly what feels good and what does not, what is wanted and what is not wanted. Couples can restore fun or romance to their relationship if they have forgotten or never learned to play.

Emotional Support

A fourth system has to do with nurturing. Couples naturally turn to each other to satisfy dependency needs, that is, for understanding and emotional support, especially when they are hurting. The need for emotional support is an important motive for marriage, although some people lose touch with their need to be taken care of at times and they deal with such dependency needs indirectly and unsatisfactorily.

If either partner fails to receive emotional support when disappointed, anxious, or hurting, dissatisfaction with the relationship is likely to occur. Marital infidelity is more likely to occur in search of emotional support than for sexual gratification. The explanations are familiar: "She really understands me." "He takes time to listen to me and is sensitive to my needs."

Sexual relations and nurturing are often confused especially by men who ask for sex when wanting emotional support. Women sometimes think that they can receive nurturing from men only by having sex. In the confusion of nurturing and sex, neither works well.

Couples can learn to listen to each other with empathy and understanding. Each can learn to ask for the emotional support each wants and needs. Couples can learn to understand and accept each other's needs and to respond effectively. When nurturing needs are satisfied, couples are more likely to be responsive sexually.

COUNSELING PROCEDURES

An understanding of the four systems enables a counselor to identify problem areas and sources of dissatisfaction rapidly, often within a few minutes. However other preliminary work may need to be done to enable a couple to participate in such an analysis and benefit by the results. The process begins with the expectations and goals of the couple and the readiness of each partner to respond to key interventions. Appropriate timing is important as the process moves from step to step through the stages: (1) assessment, (2) working through, and (3) termination.

Assessment

The ultimate results of counseling couples depends largely on their underlying motivations and readiness for the procedures employed by the counselor. A careful assessment of motives and readiness early on sets the stage for an effective process and prevents later disappointment.

The fundamental questions in my mind at this early stage are: Why is this couple here? What does each really want? Sometimes couples are not aware of their real goals or motives, and clarification is needed to focus their work. Others, for their own reasons, keep their motives concealed.

With these questions in mind, I listen to the *presenting problem* that brings the couple to seek help. For clarification and specificity, I may enquire into the *precipitating problem* motivating the couple to seek help at this particular time. As I listen, I am aware of who does the talking, interrupting, defining, contradicting, controlling, complying, asserting, retreating, and other patterns in their relating to each other and to me. I also begin to assess the *underlying problem,* of which the couple may not be aware but which prevents them from dealing successfully with their issue themselves. Here is an example:

> *Presenting problem:* Betty and George describe their relationship as drifting, cold, distant. George says Betty is always angry, nagging, frigid, and rejecting. Betty says George is uncaring, is insensitive to her feelings and needs, and is controlling.
>
> *Precipitating problem:* A few days ago Betty discovered a temporary affair of George's when he worked on a project in another city. She has threatened to leave him if he doesn't seek counseling with her.
>
> *Underlying problem:* While it is uncertain at this stage, an early hunch is that both live secretive lives, hiding their wants, feelings, and needs from each other, unwilling to risk criticism or rejection. Lacking emotional support and intimacy, they substitute competitive hassling.

Assessing Motivation. The questions remain: Why is this couple here? What does each really want? Does Betty want to punish George? To prove she has a right to a guilt-free separation? To enlist the counselor to get George to behave differently in the future? To get sympathy for being an abused and betrayed wife? What does George want? To mollify Betty by attending a few counseling sessions, trying only to survive them as painlessly as possible? To alleviate his guilt by pointing to Betty's coldness and "frigidity"? To set the stage for a guilt-free separation? The naive counselor who zealously sets to work to "save" the relationship without assessing inner goals may be well intentioned but will be ineffective and ultimately defeated.

A well-motivated couple is ready to explore cooperatively their relationship, identify unresolved issues, and seek resources for dealing with them. Such a couple responds well to relationship counseling and the counselor can proceed with confidence. For example:

> Betty expresses the expectation that counseling will help them both to understand each other's needs and feelings. She wants to discover what she can do to help this happen. George is aware that he lacks some basic communication skills and is ready to learn.

Most couples are not so well motivated in this early stage as Betty and George described here. Most couples, before they can work effectively together, need to disentangle from well-established, self-defeating behavior patterns that tend to keep their problems unsolvable. Here are a few such behavior patterns frequently encountered.

"You Be the Judge."   Many couples enter the counseling room as they would a courtroom. Each makes a case for the partner's guilt and their own personal innocence. Each contradicts the other's testimony, produces evidence or "proofs" for his or her own case, and tries to win the counselor's sympathy and support. Such a couple seems to believe that a verdict from the counselor will solve their problems. It never does. The naive counselor who plays "judge" and rules in favor of one or the other only reinforces the defeating competitive behavior pattern that prevents them from solving problems. One partner may have a moment of triumph at the verdict, but ultimately nobody wins—least of all the counselor.

(Frank and Trudy enter the room, sit sullenly. Finally . . .)

FRANK: Well, she did it again. I came home tired and hungry and she was gone. Who knows where! She didn't get home until after 11:00. . . . (*to me*) Don't I have a right to know where my wife is?

TRUDY: I was home before 10:00. And besides I told you I was going to see Mom. Anyway, you're no cripple, you can get yourself something to eat. (*to me*) Is that too much to ask of a full-grown man?

Frank and Trudy are likely to continue arguing their case in this way until one feels an advantageous moment and turns to the counselor and says, "Well?" If I render a verdict, someone loses. Result: Everybody loses. The "winner" has the right to say "See!" but has no better relationship. The "loser" is likely to sulk or fight back and ultimately appeal to another court. Nothing really changes. If I render a verdict in which nobody wins and nobody loses, both Trudy and Frank will be dissatisfied and frustrated. They will likely seek another "judge." The challenge for the counselor is to interrupt the competitive pattern itself, to enable the couple to begin to work cooperatively in defining the problem and discovering solutions in which they both can win.

"Fix 'im"; "Fix 'er."   Some come with the hope that I will solve the problem by changing the partner. Underlying the explanation of the problem is the unmistakable request: "Fix 'im" or "Fix 'er." Each describes the problem in terms of the other's behavior. One or both are likely to phone between sessions to provide more "helpful" information so that I can work more effectively *on the spouse*. I am seen as having professional competence for bringing about change in people upon request, whether they want it or not. Sometimes a desperate partner exerts considerable pressure to accomplish this impossible task almost instantly. If I allow myself to be seduced into

trying to "save" the relationship by changing the partner, I am likely to end up disappointed and frustrated, resented by one partner, rated as a failure by the other.

> BETTY: George never listens to me. He doesn't seem to care about my needs. He's so insensitive! After ignoring me and putting me down all day, he expects me to be all lovey and sexy at night. I just can't stand it any longer.
>
> GEORGE: How can I be sensitive when all she does is nag all the time. She's never warm or affectionate toward me like she used to be. She's bitchy all day and frigid at night. What kind of wife is that?

Betty and George each define the problem in terms of the other's behavior. The only solution they see is for the partner to change. Unable to change each other, they look to me to change their partner. If I pick up on Betty's veiled threat and try to get some concessions from George or if I respond to George's lament and urge Betty to be more affectionate, I get involved in the competition. Again, nobody wins. The counselor's task is to help Betty and George redefine the problem in terms of their own behavior so that each takes appropriate responsibility for causing and perpetuating it. Redefined in this way, the problem becomes solvable and the couple is ready to work productively.

"At Least I Tried."   Occasionally, one or both partners seek counseling with little or no intention to build or improve or even sustain the relationship. They come for counseling only to set the stage for a guilt-free separation or divorce. Such a person appears to make a sincere effort to cooperate with the counseling process but in fact undermines it. If I am naive enough to play the game, I will put forth my best effort only to wonder why nothing seems to help. I can avoid this trap by keeping clearly in mind the two basic assessment questions: Why is this couple here? What does each really want?

> BARBARA: No matter how hard I try, it's never enough for him.
>
> BILL: I've tried, too. We're both trying. It just won't work. Nobody's fault. I guess it's just not meant to be.

Bill seems to be trying, yet he does not allow the counseling process to succeed. When separation or divorce occurs, it is easy to imagine him telling anyone who will listen, "Well, at least I tried." The counselor needs to deal openly with Bill's goals. His desire for a guilt-free separation can be understood and accepted. If his decision is ambiguous, he may want to continue counseling with a more workable goal such as "to decide about the relationship." If either or both have withdrawn commitment to the relationship, individual or separation counseling might be appropriate.

Other Blocking Attitudes. The marriage counseling process is sometimes blocked at the outset by mindsets that hinder or prevent cooperative problem solving. Here are a few that are frequently encountered.

"You'll have to accept me the way I am." If a spouse is unhappy, that is simply not his or her problem. No room is allowed for negotiation, compromise, or even discussion. Such a stance seems most frequently taken by those who feel threatened and defensive in the relationship.

"If you really loved me you would know how I feel and what I want." Such expectations demand the "magic of love" to cure all ills without an effort to work out problems together. The counselor has the unpopular task of dispelling the notion that being in love endows a couple with mind-reading powers.

A third blocking mindset comes from an overdependence on romantic mysticism. "If we have problems or issues to deal with, something must be wrong with our relationship." Such an attitude motivates some people to deny problems or negative feelings in an effort to preserve the happily-ever-after illusion. For others it leads to rapid withdrawal of investment in the relationship at the dispelling of romance. Such couples need to accept problems and conflicts as normal and inevitable even in happily-ever-after romances.

The self-defeating behavior patterns and blocking mindsets discussed in this section signal a breakdown in the cooperation system in a relationship and need to be altered before a couple can deal with problem areas effectively. Couples with such behaviors and attitudes need to come to accept the reality that a relationship can be romantic, fun, loving, intimate, spiritual, and still have problems to solve, conflicts to work through, and differences to reconcile in practical and cooperative ways.

Working through such defeating attitudes, behavior, and thinking patterns may achieve the counseling goals of some couples. Learning to cooperate may be all some couples need in order to take charge of their relationship and move on to the change and growth they desire. In any case, a couple is not ready to solve relational issues by themselves or with the help of a counselor until they can work cooperatively. They need to be able to cooperate in identifying the role each plays in perpetuating their problems, cooperate in exploring alternative solutions, cooperate in setting goals for growth or change, and cooperate in determining what each is willing to do to achieve these goals. Unless the cooperation system is working, it will be difficult or impossible to work effectively on other systems.

Working Through

When a couple is appropriately motivated, reasonably free of defeating behavior patterns and blocking attitudes, and ready to work cooperatively, the counselor can invite them to diagnose their own relationship in terms of the four relationship systems: compatibility, cooperation, intimacy, and emotional support. The counselor helps the couple become sufficiently familiar with these systems to enable them to identify and affirm their strengths and their needs for growth or change.

When a troubling or unsatisfying area in a relationship is identified, the counselor helps the couple explore the problem and set goals for growth or change. Four questions in the back of the counselor's mind provide a structure for this process: (1) How does each experience the relationship? (2) What does each yearn for? (3) What can be done? (4) What is each willing to do now?

1. *How does each experience the relationship?* This question probes underlying feelings, fantasies, dreams, ideas, fears, hurts, sadness, and disappointments, the nonrational side of each partner that contributes to the problem. Exploring this question in depth seems to me the primary function of a counselor. Inexperienced counselors frequently make assumptions and projections, failing to enter the couple's unique frame of reference, to be with the couple from within, to understand and convey accurate empathy.

2. *What does each yearn for?* The counselor helps the couple sift through each partner's emotions and fantasies, needs and desires, to clarify what is wanted. The couple needs to decide what, if anything, each wants to be different in their relationship. Each partner is likely to have conflicting desires and yearnings which need to be resolved. ("I want a closer, more intimate relationship, but I don't want to be vulnerable.") Clarifying questions for a counselor to keep in mind at this stage include the following: What is each partner *yearning* for at the deepest level? What would the relationship be like if each partner had it exactly as he or she wanted?

These first two questions are critical to the counseling process. To move on to problem solving before they are adequately explored is usually a serious tactical error. An awareness of underlying dynamics and the establishment of clear goals as opposed to confused and conflicting desires is all some couples need from a counselor.

3. *What can be done?* After couples have clarified what each wants and established goals for growth or change, they are ready for problem solving. The counselor restates the problem, checking to see that both partners agree and are equally invested. Additional resources are brainstormed. Past experiences dealing with the same issues are explored to discover how the couple may try to undermine efforts in the future.

4. *What is each willing to do now?* From the alternative solutions identified, the couple decides what seems most helpful to do at the present time. Each is invited to state what he or she is willing to do to implement the decision. If couples desire significant growth or change in their relationship, they will need to be

specific about what they will do and when they will do it. Appropriate homework can be chosen, suggested, or assigned.

We are now ready to return to the four relational systems briefly described earlier in the chapter: compatibility, cooperation, intimacy, and emotional support. A counselor with a variety of suggestions and resources for dealing with each relationship system can be particularly helpful to a couple dealing with questions 3 and 4 above. Here, briefly, are some suggestions for working on each of the systems.

Building Compatibility.   Partners who initially attracted each other by their diversity of family, cultural, social, and other background differences are most likely to experience compatibility difficulties. Each partner, however, brings unique values, attitudes, and ideals to the relationship.

Couples seeking counseling are not always aware of compatibility problems. Such difficulties are often discovered as an underlying source of conflict. For example, conflict over spending, saving, or giving away money may be perpetuated by underlying values about the use of money. Conflict at special holidays may be fueled by conflicting early family traditions. Hassles about household chores may disguise a conflict in attitudes toward sex roles. Dissatisfaction or disappointment in marriage may result from a vague and generalized failure of a relationship to measure up to a childhood ideal of love and romance.

Clarifying actual values can be a helpful first step in dealing with compatibility problems. Partners are often unaware of their real values, what matters most to them. One partner, for example, contending that marriage was a top priority, in fact gave more time, energy, effort, and money to building a beautiful lawn than to building a relationship. Couples can be invited to list what is important to them and to arrange their values in priority based on the thought, energy, and time given to each. Lists can be compared and discussed; differences can be clarified.

The couple can then explore how they deal with the differences in values they have identified. Does one control and the other conform? If so, how does this work out? Are differences denied or hidden to preserve an uneasy uniformity? If so, how does this work out? Are differences accepted and affirmed so that a common lifestyle can emerge from both? If so, how does this work out?

Difference in values can often be resolved by discovering fundamental shared values underlying the difference. For example, a couple with different religious traditions and values may discover common basic beliefs, moral standards, or social commitments upon which to build a common lifestyle.

Conflicts over such differences can also be resolved by acceptance and affirmation of diversity. Differences become most disabling when a marriage allows little room for each partner to be a separate, whole person with individual values, attitudes, and ideals. Typical models of marriage leaving little room for differences include: the marriage and the woman conform to the husband's traditions; the man and the marriage conform to the woman's traditions; the man and the woman both conform to an image of an ideal marriage. These models require the values of either the wife or the husband or both to be sacrificed to the marriage relationship. A couple can be invited to explore other alternatives such as one in which both husband and wife preserve individual traditions while remaining committed to their marriage.

Building Cooperation. Couples need to accept disagreement and conflict as normal and inevitable. Cooperation difficulties result when a couple is unable to accept problems as normal and solvable, to disagree agreeably, and to resolve conflict so that both partners are satisfied with the process and the resolution. Couples with severe cooperation difficulties may be unable to sustain a casual noncontroversial conversation, play a game, work together on a project, or share in any activity without a hassle. Conflict is not the problem; the breakdown occurs when a couple fails to deal with issues cooperatively.

Many people grow up with no training and few adequate models from which to learn basic communication and relationship skills. A counselor can provide training in such skills for couples who need to learn or review them. Ten skills or behaviors basic to helping professions but also helpful to any relationship are: attending, listening, empathizing, communicating understanding, showing respect, accepting, assertiveness without aggression, self-revelation, straight talk, and immediacy. Each partner can be asked to identify from such a list his or her own strengths and weaknesses. They can be invited to set goals for growth in the skills they want to develop. Partners can give each other feedback to help identify needs. Developing such skills can be a secondary goal throughout the counseling process.

Some couples compete over "symbiotic issues"; they tend to define relationships as one stronger, more responsible partner taking care of a weaker, more dependent one. Such couples may compete for control: "I'll take charge of you." "No, I'll take charge of you." Or they may compete over dependency needs: "You take care of me." "No, you take care of me."

Some couples caught in the "competition trap" may be competing for control, most commonly over who gets to define a situation or problem. Whatever the issues, the struggle for control to define goes something like this: "This is how it is. . . ." "No, this is how it is. . . ." Some couples think that a conflict inevitably leads to a winner and a loser and thus compete to win or at least avoid losing whenever disagreements occur. Of course, whenever one wins, the other loses; the result is resentment, resistance, and further cooperation difficulties. If anyone wins, nobody wins. If anybody loses, both lose.

Couples caught in the "fairness trap" feel cheated by each other. In their single-minded need for fairness, they fail to find practical and satisfying solutions to problems. For example, if one wants to vacation in the mountains and the other at the beach, they are likely to settle for the "fair" solution, deciding to go nowhere. Such a solution is unsatisfying and miserable for both but at least it is fair. Such couples need to learn that their life together does not need to be fair, it only needs to be workable and satisfying.

Couples caught in the "guilt-fixing trap" fail to deal directly and effectively with differences by focusing on whose fault it is. Determining blame perpetuates hassling while never solving the problem to their mutual satisfaction.

Couples can become aware of these traps and identify which is most likely to catch each of them. Couples wanting to free themselves can agree to stop the action and identify the trap whenever either becomes aware of a breakdown in cooperation. The counselor can offer to intervene whenever a trap is triggered, enabling a couple to understand how to prevent such hassling from starting.

A couple equipped with basic communication skills and relatively free from such traps is ready to learn problem-solving and conflict-resolution skills. Some couples can profitably be taught specific step-by-step problem-solving or negotiating skills in the counseling interview. The goal of effective problem solving or conflict resolution needs to be clear: *to find a way for both to win, for both to get as much as possible of what is wanted in the situation.*

The process of negotiation provides a simple step-by-step method for couples to solve problems so that both partners can win. A counselor can teach a couple to negotiate and coach them as they practice. The negotiation process consists of the following four steps:

1. Clarify what each wants most, what each may not want but is willing to accept, and what each is not willing to accept.
2. Offer a proposal that seems to give as much as possible of what each wants.
3. Modify or make counterproposals until agreement is achieved.
4. Celebrate a solution in which both win.

Some couples resist the formality of such a problem-solving structure. Nevertheless, with practice and experience, negotiating can flow naturally without attention to the structure. Such resistance may disguise an unwillingness to give up competing, controlling, blaming, or other behaviors that prevent cooperation.

As a couple practices negotiating methods, they are likely to continue to experience difficulty with communication or spring one of the traps. The counselor continually calls attention to the *process* when the couple is not dealing effectively with *content*. In this way, a couple becomes increasingly aware of both content and process in their interaction with each other.

Building Emotional Support. Couples need to understand and accept their own and their partner's need for personal and emotional support and to respond appropriately and helpfully. Some people have difficulty accepting fearfulness, sadness, disappointment, frustration, or other kinds of hurting in themselves or in their partner, perhaps defining such feelings as "negative" or "weak." Such people are not likely to accept support for themselves or respond nurturingly to the partner. They are likely to block awareness of such feelings in themselves and react with criticism, rejection, or resentfulness to such feelings in the partner. It is critically important that they learn to accept the need for emotional support as being normal and healthy even in strong, competent people and to learn how to respond to these needs appropriately.

Couples can increase their awareness of each other's feelings and needs by a simple role reversal exercise. Each can be invited to get into the role of the partner, to experience his or her feelings, attitudes, and desires from the inside, and to talk about what he or she wants and needs from the other. Many people are surprised to discover in this exercise that they understand the partner more deeply and thoroughly than they had thought possible, realizing that they allow competitiveness or defensiveness or some other feelings to get in the way of awareness and sensitivity. Such a discovery allows them to empathize more readily when they decide to give emotional support.

The role reversal exercise can be enhanced through the addition of guided reflection on the experience. Helpful questions include: How does it feel to become your partner? Do you think you express your partner's thoughts and feelings accurately? What difficulties do you encounter when you put yourself into the role of your partner? What is it like for you to experience your partner in your role? Do you think your partner understands you? How would you have wanted your partner to act out your role differently? Such reflections help couples express their inner feelings and needs more directly and to check out assumptions about each other.

Empathy is not enough; a couple needs to understand how to respond to each other in genuinely helpful ways. Partners often want to be helpful but respond inappropriately; the result is disappointment and frustration. Partners need to be aware of the kind of support that is most satisfying to each other. Couples may find it helpful to explore nurturing patterns from childhood, recalling what they did when they were scared, disappointed, sick, or hurting in some way and what sort of nurturing responses they wanted and received. People often discover that they want to receive the kind of nurturing they received or wanted as children. Furthermore, they tend to give the kind of nurturing they themselves were given, but they don't tell their partner what they want or ask what is appropriate and helpful to their partner.

To identify the specific responses each needs from the other, each partner can be invited to remember a recent time when he or she was frightened, lonely, or hurting and someone responded in a way genuinely helpful and satisfying. As they add other responses each has found helpful, they can make a list of responses they want from each other. A typical list might include:

1. Taking time to give me your full attention.
2. Showing that you really understand me.
3. Touching me in a nurturing way, such as putting your arm around me, holding my hand, holding me.

4. Showing me that you understand my feelings as well as my situation.
5. Letting me know it is okay for me to feel the way I do and for me to want the support I need.

Each partner can then be invited to recall a fearful, lonely, or hurting situation in which someone responded in an *unhelpful* way. These responses can also be listed with the others that have been experienced. Typical unsatisfying responses include:

1. Asking me how I got myself into the situation.
2. Joking about my problem as a way to cheer me up.
3. Telling me what to do or how to solve my problem.
4. Trying to get me to feel better by saying things like: "Cheer up," "Don't worry," or "You'll feel better tomorrow" when I want you to hear and understand me.
5. Analyzing or interpreting what I feel, saying something like, "Let me tell you what your *real* problem is. . . ."

Such responses, though often well intentioned, fail to show understanding and acceptance of the partner's feelings and discount his or her competence to deal with the situation adequately. Such responses tend to increase dependency feelings without satisfying them.

In summary, these steps help couples to get in touch with how each experiences and expresses dependency needs, how each gives and receives emotional support, and what responses are most helpful and which are inappropriate and unsatisfactory.

Building Intimacy. Intimacy makes a relationship special. A couple can maintain a workable relationship and solve problems reasonably well without intimacy, but their relationship is likely to lack energy or excitement and not satisfy the most basic and essential relational needs. Counselors are likely to find difficulty with intimacy underlying other relational problems.

Intimacy is sought and experienced on a variety of levels and in a variety of expressions, including conversational intimacy, emotional intimacy, physical intimacy, and sexual intimacy. Intimacy also plays a part when a couple is romantic or playful with each other. Couples can explore the kinds and levels of intimacy most satisfying to each and set goals to achieve what they want in their relationship.

Couples that want to build conversational intimacy can explore the level of openness and self-revelation when talking to each other and can set goals for growth or change. The continuum below helps a couple to identify the level of conversational intimacy in the discussion on any subject. A couple can learn that a conversation becomes more intimate as it becomes more personal, more self-revealing, more focused on each other and on what is going on "here and now."

1	2	3	4	5
Facts about the subject	Ideas of others about the subject	Your own ideas or opinions about the subject	Your likes or dislikes and feelings about the subject	Feelings and desires about each other related to the subject

With such a continuum in mind, a couple can at any time build awareness of the level of intimacy in a conversation and of how to increase intimacy if they want to do so. A couple might want the counselor to interrupt conversations during counseling sessions to ask about the level of intimacy and what each could do to increase or decrease it.

A first step in building emotional intimacy is to explore current patterns of emotional expression in the relationship. How freely does each partner express feelings? How well does each accept and affirm the feelings expressed by the other? What feelings are most easily accepted and which are suppressed; for example, some people feel free to express "positive" feelings such as joy, pleasure, appreciation, and perhaps grieving but not "negative" ones like anger, disappointment, or fear. Couples can then set goals for each accepting and expressing his or her own and the partner's feelings. Counselors can help couples work toward their goals by focusing attention on feelings during counseling interviews, whatever issue or problem is discussed. Couples can be given exercises or assignments to help them experience and share their feelings. For example, they might be asked to talk to each other about their relationship by completing the following sentences using all of the listed feelings.

As I think about our life together, I get: (1. sad   2. scared   3. frustrated   4. angry   5. hurt   6. irritated   7. happy) about. . . .

Some couples need to reflect on such feelings alone and write them down separately before sharing them. Couples need to learn that no authentic feelings are bad in themselves, that all kinds of feelings are natural and inevitable in a close relationship, and that the level of closeness is related to how freely all kinds of feelings are shared.

Couples that want to build more nonsexual physical intimacy can begin by exploring their present patterns of touching, holding each other, or engaging in other kinds of physical closeness. Each can identify initial resistant reactions and behaviors when feeling uncomfortably close—for example, finding an excuse to withdraw, pushing away physically or verbally, or tuning out mentally. Couples can also explore who usually does the touching, who gets touched, where and when each likes or does not like to be touched, and what kind of touching feels good and what does not. The couple can then set goals for growth or change to better satisfy their desires and needs for physical intimacy. The counselor works with the couple to determine specific behavioral homework between sessions to achieve these goals.

Couples build sexual intimacy as they grow in their ability to talk freely about their sexual relating, to tell each other what feels good and what does not, and to ask more directly for what is wanted while being sensitive to the partner's needs. Such sexual intimacy requires a free and unrestrained enjoyment of each other without demands or expectations of self or the partner. Of course not all sex is intimate. Sexual relating can be detached, ritualized, mechanical, casual, or manipulative. Most couples want to experience sex in a variety of ways. Yet almost everyone at times yearns for intimacy in sexual relating. When exploring difficulties with intimacy in sexual relations, couples need to distinguish between *relational* blocks (resentment and other negative feelings taken to bed with them) and *sexual* blocks (mental or physical difficulties not present until found in bed). Most "sexual" difficulties are actually relational problems expressed sexually. After couples have explored their present level of sexual intimacy and the difficulties preventing them from giving themselves more openly and freely to enjoying each other, they can set goals for growth or change to build the level of sexual intimacy they desire. They can practice talking more openly in the counseling sessions about their sexual feelings, desires, and frustrations and follow up with appropriate homework.

Sharing romantic experiences and playing together can contribute to a couple's intimacy and, conversely, building intimacy can also contribute to playfulness and romance. Both require an accepting, affirming, nonthreatening climate, each focusing attention on what is attractive and delightful in the partner. Both romance and playfulness help a couple to experience each other in the "here and now."

In summary, couples can identify their patterns of intimacy, deal with blocks and resistance, decide on the level of intimacy desired, and set goals for developing and practicing what they want to achieve.

Working on their relationship in terms of systems provides clarity so couples can diagnose their own needs, set their own goals, and explore methods and resources for achieving their goals and for knowing when they have accomplished what they set out to do. When goals are achieved, couples may decide to move on to other systems they want to build or enrich. Or they may feel ready to take charge of their own relationship issues and to terminate counseling.

Termination

Termination may occur at the decision of the counselor, of the couple, or, ideally, as a cooperative decision by all involved. Whatever the timing or the cause, termination can provide an opportunity to solidify learnings, affirm new relationship skills, and reinforce new behaviors.

Termination is natural and easy to celebrate after the successful completion of counseling goals has been established and stabilized. The couples can use one or more terminating sessions to review their issues, restate their learnings, and describe new behaviors and skills. They may also want to make a new commitment or contract as part of termination to maintain their gains and keep growing.

Even an apparently premature decision by a couple to terminate before issues are adequately resolved or goals achieved can sometimes provide an opportunity for affirmation and celebration. Some couples feel competent to deal with their problems after becoming aware of defeating behavior patterns or attitudes. They may decide to finish whatever else needs doing by themselves. Such couples can be affirmed in the decision to take charge of their relationship and to use their own resources to deal with their issues. Termination can include a clarification of the behavior patterns and attitudes that have hindered effective problem solving and what they have done to overcome them. Termination might also explore the growth or change still wanted or needed and what they plan to do for their relationship in the future.

Some terminations occur when couples decide not to deal with their issues or make changes. They may have hoped for some sort of counseling magic that could make things better without change. They many decide that their familiar behavior patterns, though unpleasant much of the time, provide some security and continuity with the past; change would bring uncertainty, discomfort, even existential anxiety. Termination for them is a retreat from frightening possibilities back to familiar ways. Yet all is not lost. The counselor has not "failed." Such couples have gained awareness of their issues and made a decision about their relationship. Awareness and decision free them to take responsibility for the quality of their life together and open doors to future alternatives. At termination, the counselor can affirm the couple's decision about their relationship, help them identify what they have learned about how their relationship works, and affirm its strengths. They may also be invited to discuss alternative resources if they decide to deal with their issues in the future.

Occasionally, a couple terminates when one partner, perhaps rather suddenly, decides to end the relationship. Both may have been sincere initially in their effort to make the relationship work. Further exploration or insight has led to the conclusion that maintaining the relationship requires too much investment for too few rewards. Building the relationship is no longer a viable counseling goal. A decision by one of the partners to withdraw investment from the relationship does not mean the counselor has failed. All is not lost. Each partner is likely to have grown in self-understanding, insight into relational needs, and relationship skills. Alternatives have been clarified. Awareness of self-defeating behavior patterns allows for wider future possibilities. Such couples may want to continue with the counselor as they work through separation issues. Individual counseling may be recommended for either or both partners. In any case, termination sessions can be used to summarize learnings, identify new relational skills, and deal with feelings associated with separation decisions.

In summary, whatever the timing or cause of termination, even when the counselor sees termination as evasive or irresponsible, the termination process can reinforce what has been learned, identify and affirm specific new skills and behaviors, and set the stage for keeping the relationship alive in the future. A "celebration" at termination might include the sharing of feelings about closure, images of the future, exchanging "verbal gifts," and a barrage of personal affirmation and stroking.

SUMMARY

Pastoral counselors are an appropriate resource for troubled couples and might well see relationship counseling as close to the center of pastoral ministry on theological grounds. Specific skills are needed for effective marriage counseling in addition to more general pastoral and counseling abilities. While responding pastorally to the less rational and spiritual dimension in a marriage relationship, the pastoral counselor needs a practical, systematic understanding of how relationships work and what can be done to build or enrich them. A *systems approach* to relationships provides an objective, relatively nonthreatening perspective from which couples can take charge of their own relationship, diagnose their own strengths and weaknesses, and set realistic goals for growth or change. Most couples, however, need help from a counselor to work through a variety of kinds of resistance, self-defeating behavior patterns, and inner emotional blocks before they can work productively toward such systematic goals. Well-motivated couples intent on building or enriching their relationship can work together to identify and strengthen unsatisfactory systems. Whether couples achieve their chosen goals or not, termination provides an opportunity for the counselor and couples to summarize new awareness and learnings and to affirm the right, responsibility, and capacity of couples to take charge of their relationship and to keep the door open to further growth.

REFERENCES

A more detailed description and explicit resources for working with couples using the systems approach can be found in two books by the author listed below, published by the Relationship Institute, 10751 Evening Wind Court, Columbia, Md. 21044.

Luecke, David L. *The Relationship Manual: How to Diagnose, Build, or Enrich a Relationship*, 1981.
————. *A Guide to Relationship Counseling and Leading Couples' Workshops*, 1981.

RECOMMENDED READINGS

Bach, George R. *Pairing*. New York: Avon, 1970.
Clinebell, Howard J., Jr. *Growth Counseling for Marriage Enrichment*. Philadelphia: Fortress, 1972.

————. *Growth Counseling for Mid-Years Couples*. Philadelphia: Fortress, 1977.

Clinebell, Howard, and Charlotte Clinebell. *The Intimate Marriage*. New York: Harper, 1970.

Fitzgerald, R. V. *Conjoint Marital Therapy*. New York: Jason Aronson, 1973.

Kennedy, Eugene. *Sexual Counseling*. New York: Seabury, 1977.

Lederer, William J. *The Mirages of Marriage*. New York: Norton, 1968.

Ludwig, David J. *The Spirit of Your Marriage*. Minneapolis: Augsburg, 1979.

Mace, David. *Sexual Difficulties in Marriage*. Philadelphia: Fortress, 1972.

Mace, David, and Vera Mace. *How to Have a Happy Marriage*. Nashville: Abingdon, 1977.

Miller, Sherod (Ed.). *Marriages and Families: Enrichment Through Communication*. Beverly Hills: Sage Publications, 1975.

Otto, Herbert A. *Marriage and Family Enrichment*. Nashville: Abingdon, 1976.

Paolino, Thomas J., Jr., and Barbara S. McCrady. *Marriage and Marital Therapy*. New York: Brunner/Mazel, 1978.

Smith, Gerald W. *Couple Therapy*. New York: Collier Books, 1971.

Stewart, Charles. *The Minister as Marriage Counselor*. Nashville: Abingdon, 1970.

CHAPTER ELEVEN

Counseling with Families

B. JOHN HAGEDORN JR., PH.D.

PASTORAL COUNSELING AND THE FAMILY

In the beginning God created Adam. God saw that Adam needed a companion and created Eve. Adam knew Eve, and she conceived Cain, then Abel. Cain knew his wife, and she bore him Enoch; to Enoch was born Irad. So the Bible begins. Our Judeo-Christian faith begins with the story of a family. Our faith grows with each successive generation and with each successive family spreading out like branches on an eternal tree. Our faith is developed and shared in and through people, in the story of their lives and in the story of their relationships to each other and to their God.

How natural, then, for the pastor to be sensitive to the people who make up the current chapter of the story of faith. The contemporary pastor knows the individuals, the couples, the families, and the extended family systems to whom the story of faith is told and through whom the story of faith is continued. It is hard to think of our faith outside the context of a peopled event. Adam and Eve ate of the tree of knowledge, and we understood original sin. Cain killed his brother Abel, and we understood the pain of death and of broken relationships. Abraham led Isaac to the altar, and we understood faithfulness. Even the Incarnation came through the birth of a babe to a mother and a father.

Ministry is being with people: One person shares the story of faith with another. Parents bring a child to the font of baptism to receive from the hands of another the waters of salvation. One person breaks the bread and gives it to the outstretched hands of others. Ministry is a man and a woman joined before God and in the company of others. It is a hug of closeness in the moment of grief. We who minister are with people.

The ministry of pastoral counseling is therefore grounded in the continuing ministry to people. As a pastoral counselor, I cannot see a counselee without seeing in that individual the many facets that define him or her as a person and the many connections and relationships with others that have helped to form that identity. My counselee is not an isolated person; he or she is a person from a family and from a family tradition and lineage. He or she has a faith or belief system taught by persons and experienced through persons. He or she has a concern or problem which has brought him or her for counseling: a concern or problem defined and detailed through relationships to others. I cannot see a counselee without seeing a multitude of others who have shaped and formed the very moment of our meeting.

If I am to be true to my own heritage as one who comes to counseling from a position of ministry and from a community of faith, there is no way I can be with a counselee without an awareness of his or her immediate and extended family. Let me give some examples from my own practice.

A couple concerned about problems within the relationship of their marriage came to me. The wife announced at the beginning of one session that the marriage was finished: that she now knew conclusively that her husband did not love her, and that she did not want to be with him. I asked what event had taken place during the week, and the wife reported that she had been ill. Asking the husband to be a silent observer, I had her explain in detail what it was like to be a child in her family of origin: especially a child who was ill.

She explained that when she was ill her mother would stay home from work in order to be with her. During the day she moved from her own bedroom into the big bed in her parents' room, where she was entertained with television and stories and conversation. She was fed all her favorite foods—anything she wanted—and remembered especially the Danish pastries she would request every day. When her father returned from work every day, he would bring little gifts to cheer her up and spend special time with her. Being sick was physically no fun, perhaps, but it was a time of closeness with her family and being special to them that she held fondly in her heart.

While she was talking, her husband began to turn a little pale. I reversed their roles and asked her to become a silent observer while he described in detail what it was like being an ill child in his family of origin. He explained that his mother was a nurse and she kept him in his own room and insisted that he remain there undisturbed because she thought he needed all the rest and quiet he could get in order to recover. He was left alone and fed hot tea and unbuttered dark toast, the standard diet of illness in his household. Being sick was never a time for games or fun or entertainment, nor was it a time for his favorite foods.

When the husband finished talking, the wife began to smile and then to laugh. During her illness the past week her husband had given her the most loving thing he knew how to give when someone was ill. He had left her alone and brought her hot tea and toast. He was not unloving, as she had thought. He was not insensitive and cold, as she had believed. He was just loving her out of his past experience: an experience that up until then she had not known. As they continued to talk, they developed their own compromises and their own style and expectations for handling illness.

Had I not been able to perceive each of them as a product of their individual family systems, this problem might not have been solved and the future of the relationship might have been in jeopardy. There is an important sequence to be noted here. The wife's internal feeling of loving and being loved was dependent upon the external actions of her husband and upon the context in which those actions were performed. Her husband's actions were dependent upon an internalized feeling and memory system created by the actions of his family of origin. The wife's feelings then were connected through present action to internalized memories of the past.

Another example of how family systems affect relationships is evident in the story of another couple who came to me for marriage counseling. In the routine family history I take at the beginning of therapy, I found that both the husband and wife were the same age and that both of them were from families of seven children. However, he was the oldest of seven in his family whereas she was the youngest in hers. Immediately, I became curious about a number of things. Since they were the same age, their place in their family systems dictated that their two sets of parents had to be almost a generation apart in age. It turned out that her parents were seventy-six and seventy-three and his parents were fifty-three and fifty-one. I surmised that they had been reared with rather different styles of parenting, hers being much more protective and his being much more permissive. This was true.

As I grew to know this couple, I found that the husband, as the oldest child, had been given a lot of early freedom and responsibility. In fact, he had become a parental child for a number of his younger brothers and sisters. He had gained a lot within his family system by being the oldest. He could order the rest of the children around. He had his own room, where he could seek privacy and keep the others away. He did things first and led in social development. He never wore hand-me-down clothes. Also he enjoyed the freedom to get out of the house and escape from the confusion of a large family whenever he chose.

The wife, on the other hand, being the youngest, had developed her own set of gains and losses. She had eight parents—her natural parents and her six older brothers and sisters—all of whom had responsibility for her at some time during her growing years. As the baby of the family, she had been taken care of and had things done for her all her life. She knew little about freedom and self-responsibility. She almost always wore hand-me-downs. She always shared a room with someone and rarely had any privacy at all. She loved being around her big happy family and, in fact, often had no choice but to be around all of them.

This couple's presenting problem was the strain on their marriage caused by these different lifestyles learned from their families of origin. The husband complained that the house was never free of guests. His wife was always inviting her brothers and sisters and their families for visits. The house was beginning to feel like Grand Central Station to him. He resented the intrusions into his privacy. He also had problems with his wife's confessed inability to do anything without the help of another to guide and praise her. As a result, he spent more and more time away from home, living in a quieter, more private world with a mistress.

The personal characteristics and the styles of interpersonal coping learned by each of these individuals as children in their own families affected their marriage so much that it almost ended. As we explored together the past and the present situations confronting them, they were able to recognize and even enjoy the differences as well as the similarities that made them who they were.

Every counselee who enters the office of a pastoral counselor provides for that counselor an entry point into a family system and a family history that will need to be explored if wholeness and growth are to occur in the counseling process. This is the basis of the family systems approach to pastoral counseling. It is the approach I use in my own ministry of counseling, and by sharing some of my insights with you, I hope to encourage further exploration by other pastoral counselors into this way of dealing with families in a counseling setting.

DEVELOPING A FAMILY ROOT SYSTEM

How does a pastoral counselor gain access to a family system and tradition that have shaped the life of a counselee? How does the counselor begin to "join" the counselee's family so that the one hour of therapy is not sabotaged by the other 167 hours of the week the counselee spends with his or her family? One approach I have found helpful is the development by counselor and counselee of a family root system or family map.

A family root system is far more than a collection of statistical data. Made with care, it becomes a creative tool for self-discovery and growth. In the beginning stages of therapy, when it is often perceived by the counselee as an intellectual process, it is usually less threatening to talk about family history than to proceed with more confrontive, uncovering therapy. Gradually, the counselee develops a sense of curiosity about himself or herself that is useful in the later stages of therapy. A family root system also helps the counselee begin to think beyond the presenting problem and into the forces that have shaped his or her coping mechanisms.

Developing a family root system is a good way to begin to think about the questions: What is a family? When does a family begin? How does a family develop and form itself? As an educational exercise, it helps the counselee understand the total context of his or her life, and it helps the counselor understand what it is like to live in the counselee's unique family system.

I find it helps to look at the cultural background of the family to discover its folkways, mores, and values. I look at the ethnic roots and at the psychological characteristics associated with each subsystem. I want to know about the religious heritage of the family, especially its folk faith. The folk faith is the God concept that the family believes, as defined by their own words and fantasies. I have discovered that such a folk faith often defines the interactional characteristics of the family members.

The significant events within the history of the family are also useful to me as a counselor. How often were geographical moves made and how did they affect the family and its members? What deaths or crisis events happened to the family and what coping styles were produced during those periods of stress? What myths surrounding particular family members were developed by the family and what function do those myths serve? What family secrets can be discovered and what would happen if they were revealed? What has been the vocational development of the males and females within the family system? How has the vocational expectation that developed in the family system affected the growth of the members of the system?

I find it interesting to look at the constellation of each family subunit and to see what duplications and differences appear. Has an oldest son married a youngest daughter and duplicated the constellation of his parents? Has a middle child married a middle child and produced an identity crisis? I also look for the significance of names within the family structure. Have the characteristics of the last family member with a particular name been projected upon the present one who bears it? Or, as I have discovered in some cases, has a later child in a family constellation been given the name of an earlier child who died in infancy? What expectations has this placed upon the later child?

I ask the counselee to give me personal adjectives to describe each important member of the family system. These adjectives are personal opinions and may differ from the impressions of other family members. Frequently, I find that the same family member is given opposing adjectives by different individuals in the same family system. Although this is usually revealing, it is hardly surprising. Each person's mental images and memories of the significant others in his or her family system are based not so much in factual reality or in mutual agreement as in his or her own unique experiences and interpretations of those experiences.

In some family systems I find that the characteristics and personal adjectives of an individual in one generational level are embraced by someone in another generational level as a guide for identity formation. One example from my own practice was a woman who turned to the image and characteristics of one of her grandmothers as a guide for her own adult identity. For this reason, I often ask my counselees to concentrate on three generational levels in their family maps.

I believe that developing a family root system is as important for the counselor as it is for the counselee. If, as a counselor, I am unaware of the family forces that have shaped me, I will be less sensitive to the biases, differences, and possible countertransference issues affecting the relationship between the counselee and myself. The process of developing my own family root system was a crucial part of my own personal and professional growth and I would like to share it with you.

A PERSONAL EXAMPLE

My paternal grandfather's family came from the northwestern part of West Germany, called Ostfriesland, a region reclaimed from the marshes and subdivided by canals. The people were hard-working and their interest in clean, somewhat compulsive living is still very much in evidence. The reclaimed land, cleared of peat moss, was used for gardening and grazing. The houses, many of them identical in style, were built from locally produced brick. Most houses held two families, and often three generations of a family lived under the same roof. At the rear of each house was a barn and stable directly connected to the house, and behind them was an outhouse. As the area matured, the men of the region turned more and more to the sea and to the production of materials that could be shipped down the canals to the sea. Even today, the area is filled with large manufacturing plants that ship goods all over the world.

These are not just interesting facts about a geographic area; they are also part of the shaping of the psychological characteristics of the people who lived there. They are also the precursors of a cultural and family style that lives on in me today. I am very much concerned about neatness and orderliness, and much of my thinking is practical and production oriented. I enjoy projects and am always thinking about how they could be more developed and more useful. This style also affects the way I relate to other people and has been one of the biggest issues of my personal growth. It affects the way I do counseling, and I have discovered in myself a great desire to solve the problems of my counselees efficiently. As a result of this self-discovery, I pay greater attention to being curious about my counselees. Increasingly, I am able to support them in their struggles to make sense out of their own lives rather than attempting to do it for them.

The names in my own family system—discovered as I prepared my own family map—fascinate me. My great-great-grandfather's name was Berend Ulpt Berends. In the tradition of the area, he named his son Uplt Berend Ulpts. Ulpt altered the tradition and named his son Berend Ulpt Hagedorn. Family tradition holds that he chose the name Hagedorn from the name of the hedge that surrounded the family's house. How much of the tradition is real and how much myth will never be known, but its effect on the family is very real. The Hagedorn hedge has become a symbol for me in a comical as well as in a serious sense. It is a hedge of attractive, bright green leaves. Under each leaf is a very sharp thorn. How often people tell me I have a pleasant, inviting appearance. Later, as they get to know me, they discover that I am capable of making some very sharp, pointed comments.

Berend Ulpt Hagedorn had five children. My three great aunts all remained in the small German town, where they married and produced large families. My great-uncle married and followed the canals to the sea, where he established a resort hotel on one of the North Sea Islands. The Haus Hagedorn exists even today. My grandfather also followed the canals to the sea: He became a sea captain for one of the German freighter lines. Bernhard Anton Hagedorn, my grandfather, was a handsome, assertive, hard-working young man. He soon became the youngest captain in the company. His ship traveled between Bremerhaven and New York City.

Anton made friends with an older captain of the line, Johannes Erbo, and often visited Erbo during shore leave in Bremen. Soon he married Erbo's daughter Gesine and they set up housekeeping in a small apartment. Ten months later, in 1908, my father, Bernhard Johannes Hagedorn was born, and the young family moved to a house two doors away from Erbo. As was the custom, Gesine often traveled with Anton on the freighter, acting as hostess for the small group of paying passengers on their way to New York. During these trips she left her baby with her parents in Bremen.

Anton and Gesine were in New York City harbor when World War I broke out in 1914. Anton's German ship was impounded in the harbor for three and a half years, during which time Anton and Gesine lived aboard ship. In 1915 a second son, Herbert Anton Hagedorn, was born aboard ship.

In 1918 the U.S. government took Anton's ship and sent him to an internment camp in Georgia. Left to fend for themselves, Gesine and the baby were eventually taken in by a widower, Mr. Schmidt, and his young daughter. Gesine became severely ill, so ill that Anton was released from camp to join his dying wife. Upon his return to New York, Gesine amazingly recovered.

Finally the war ended, and Anton returned to a position as a sea captain, but when he discovered that his ship was carrying contraband, he resigned his commission and never went to sea again. Instead, he and Mr. Schmidt set up a house-painting business and moved into a joint home on Staten Island.

All this time, my father was with his Grandmother Erbo in Germany. He had lived as if he were the youngest member of her family, and his Aunt Louise and Uncle Hans had played the roles of older brother and sister rather than aunt and uncle to him. In 1920, almost six years after his separation from his parents, he came to New York to join an already established joint family system that included his parents, his five-year-old brother whom he had never met before, Mr. Schmidt, and Schmidt's daughter.

Psychologically, these early events in the history of my family system created new characteristics for the members of my family. Grandfather Hagedorn lost some of his pride and assertiveness and began to make the best out of the remnants of his life. He never returned to Germany or to the style of living that he had had there. Grandmother Hagedorn, on the other hand, began to be more assertive. She was also passively aggressive in her anger toward her husband, whom she held responsible for her new, less prestigious lot in life.

I think, however, that my father was most affected by the changes in his family system during his growing-up years. He went from being the only child of a proud sea captain and his beautiful young wife to being the youngest child reared by a doting grandmother and two adoring quasi-siblings. When he returned to the family system of his birth, it was much altered and included members that he did not know in a country that he did not know. The effect was that he never really felt he belonged and he never gained a sense of self-affirmation. He has retained the productiveness of his family tradition and a sense of pride in his work, but he has often retreated into silence and, at times, powerlessness. To me, these traits seem to duplicate the changed styles of his parents.

I have shared this small segment of my own family root system to demonstrate how the factual data collected can become a point of entry into the psychological makeup of the person doing the family root system. I am the product of my father before as well as after his marriage to my mother. Even though Grandfather Hagedorn died before I was born and Grandmother Hagedorn died before I was two, they have affected me greatly through their son, my father. Not only have I struggled with my German compulsiveness, I have had to struggle with a sense of entry, of belonging, of fitting. I have also struggled with a sense of rootlessness, developed primarily from my family tradition but enhanced by my own family's frequent moves because of my father's occupation as a Boy Scout executive.

I have also found in my midlife years that I have been drawn to the image and characteristics of my Grandfather Anton before the life-altering events of World War I. I have regained a sense of pride, not only in my work but also in my personhood. In wrestling with myself, I have developed a sense of self-affirmation and have gained a feeling of control and direction and purpose in my life. I find myself mellowing as I get more in touch with an understanding of and a caring for the persons who constitute my family root system.

In this personal example I have concentrated on my paternal grandparents and on my father's childhood. In the complete family root system that I have been developing I have also explored my maternal grandparents and the childhood of my mother. I have also gone back three additional generations. The discovered material gives me a sense of the family tradition from which I come. Of course I have continued my family root system from the childhood of my parents, through their courtship and marriage, through the rearing of my sister and myself, to the very present. I have now added my own marriage and my own children, and thus another generation to the family root system.

When one is doing a family root system, a vehicle is useful. I suggest a family genogram, diagramming the members of each generation and including significant dates and personal adjectives. The genogram is a starting point for a person's living history, to be fleshed out in dialogue with that person. A beginning genogram for my father is shown on the next page.

A number of things happen as a result of preparing a genogram. Often people begin to be much more curious about themselves; they start to make discoveries that help them pull together the events and psychological results that shape their lives. I

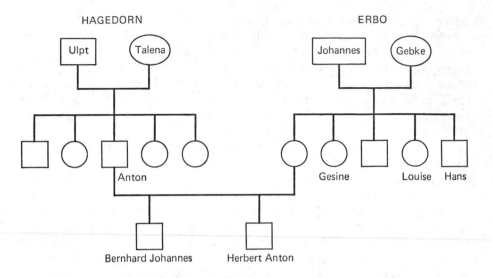

HAGEDORN   ERBO

Ulpt   Talena   Johannes   Gebke

                        Anton   Gesine   Louise   Hans

Bernhard Johannes   Herbert Anton

HAGEDORN
      Berend Ulpt Hagedorn 1836–1896 – never known by Bernhard
      Talena Hagedorn 1845–1916 – kind, quiet, little known by Bernhard
      Bernhard Anton Hagedorn 1876–1939 – hard working, proud, assertive,
                              sea captain, conscientious, resigned, right,
                              later house painter
      Bernhard Johannes Hagedorn 1908 –   – hard working, proud of his
                              productions, not assertive nor aggressive

ERBO
      Johannes Erbo 1862–1933 – stern, world traveling sea captain, not
                              around much
      Gebke Erbo 1865–1948 – kind, loving, liked children
      Gesine Margarethe Erbo Hagedorn 1888–1941 – beautiful, proud, then
                              angry, passive, aggressive

find that the more I share my own genogram and the living history surrounding it with others, the more I gain from their insights and from the connections they see. Often, the process of gathering the data leads a counselee into actions that begin to heal and correct some of the issues within the family system.

In my own case, I began to research the European roots of both my mother and my father and found myself planning a trip to Denmark and Germany to visit the persons and places in my life. I actually made the trip. Uncle Hans and Aunt Louise were both alive and we talked for hours. Since three of my grandparents died when I was very young, I have always felt disconnected from a third generational level. Regaining that connection with Hans and Louise produced a new sense of rootedness and wholeness in my personhood. The excitement I felt at the idea of the trip led to my sister's joining me on the journey, to a new level of communication between my parents and their family systems in Europe, and to visits to this country by some of our European relatives.

In summary, a family root system is a method to help both you and your counselee get in touch with the context, traditions, events, and persons that have shaped the psychological fiber of the counselee. The process is educational and therapeutic as it unfolds in the telling and relating—the living dialogue—between counselor and counselee. The process of developing a family root system can take weeks. For some counselees it will be especially useful to visit the family of origin and gather the needed information in person. I have been working on my own root system for over four years and still am finding new and exciting material—and therefore new and exciting additions to my psychological understanding of myself. I will probably never finish learning all that I can from my roots, for my family history is not finished: it is not a history so much as a process that is continuously emerging, growing, and evolving.

Developing a family root system is only one form of family ministry available to the pastoral counselor. I find it a wonderful tool for general growth. Sometimes, however, an immediate problem requires more immediate intervention. In that case, instead of constructing a family root system, the pastoral counselor must assist the counselee in restructuring interactions within the immediate family system. This requires family systems therapy. In the next section, I will discuss some of the underlying assumptions as well as some of the methods I use in family systems therapy.

SYSTEMIC FAMILY THERAPY

The parish pastor and the pastoral counselor are often contacted by families experiencing stress and pain. Often the point of entry has to do with a member of the family system, usually a child, who is acting out in a way that has become troublesome for another member of the family system or for the family system as a whole. At these times it is necessary to do a more immediate and active form of family intervention than that described above. The family is in some kind of pain and is looking for some quick relief of that pain. It is useful in such situations to use a systemic family therapy approach.

The history of the family therapy movement has its own roots in the study of schizophrenic patients. For many such patients the growth gained as an inpatient was often totally eradicated by a home visit or by an institutional visit by the family. Early investigators in the field developed the concept that one component of schizophrenia was a dysfunctional alliance between the patient and his or her mother. In this alliance the parent would often give two messages, one through words and one through actions, which contradicted each other. As the patient attempted to cope with such a double message, the characteristics of schizophrenia developed. Clearly, the family system context of the patient had an important effect upon the internal world of the patient.

The same theory is the basis for systemic family therapy. The identified patient is often acting out in relation to his or her family system and developing external symptoms that are manifested by internal tensions produced by the family system. Simply stated, an individual's context affects the inner processes of that individual. The goal of therapy for the family therapist, then, is to assist the family in restructuring itself so that the identified patient need no longer act out. Changes in the context will produce changes in the individual. The therapist's behavior in relation to the context is significant to the change of that context. Therefore, the therapist needs to join the context and assist in its modification to transform the context and in turn the individual. The altered family context is self-perpetuating and will be maintained in the absence of the therapist once the change has been produced. Two very significant assumptions underlie these theories. The one is that "health" is the "preordained" developmental path of the individual and the family and therefore therapy is the removal of blockages in this path toward health. Second, the family therapist is an enabler who assists the family in its quest to remove the blockages. "Health" resides within the family, not within the expertise of the therapist. The therapist's job is to join, help to restructure the context as a new member of the family, and then to leave.

The major purpose of a family is to support its members in their continuous movement toward identification and selfhood. In the past, family purpose has included economic survival, cultural socialization, reproduction, and sexual companionship. All these purposes still remain, but in many instances they can be attained outside the family structure. The development of self-concept and identity often rests within the early nurturing relationships between a child and the parents, thus within the family system.

I see the family system as a matrix of identity formation. A "healthy" model of a family is one in which the system is structured yet is always in transformation. Just as a person passes through a number of developmental stages as he or she grows, so does the family undergo continuous developmental changes. As a family grows, with new members joining and older members leaving, it needs to restructure itself in relation to its current needs and expectations. The model family structure needs to be able to adapt to its changing circumstances so as to maintain continuity and to enhance the psychosocial growth of each of its members. Flexibility and consistency need to be held in tension within the family system.

This tension is best described by the stress between belonging to a family system and being separate from that system. Each of us lives with that tension symbolized within our name. I am John Hagedorn: as John I am separate, and as Hagedorn I am a belonging member. In family system language, this tension is conceptualized as a continuum between total disengagement (separateness) and total enmeshment (belongingness). In order to understand the continuum, let us look at both extremes.

The extreme of too much disengagement is that of a family whose separateness boundaries are too tightly and clearly drawn. In such a family system, identity and selfhood have a large component of independence related to them. In fact, independence is warped to such a degree that the members of such a family system show a marked lack of loyalty to each other, a lack of belonging, a lack of interdependence, and a lack of ability to support others. An example from my own practice is a woman from a very wealthy family in which there were very clear and inflexible rules and expectations. As a child she lived in a private space different from that of her parents. She was reared by a succession of "Nanas," each of whom was dismissed when the relationship became too caring and personal. When she was allowed to join her parents for meals, she was to sit silently and listen. She was an only child and was taught that appearance and materialism were the most important things in life, much more important than relationships. She grew up learning not to trust, not to show her emotions, especially outwardly, and not to expect much from others. Her motto was, "I'll do it myself."

On the other end of the continuum is enmeshment. In a family system that is too enmeshed, belongingness is carried to an extreme. The boundaries within such a family system are so loose and diffuse that separateness and uniqueness are hard to maintain. Dependence becomes the byword and members develop a lack of autonomy, a lack of the ability to solve a problem by themselves; their affective skills are inhibited, and their competitive skills are reduced. A sense of togetherness is often achieved by the process of self-negation. What is important is not how I feel, but how the family feels. Such families have developed a lack of the need for privacy and have as a motto, "Don't rock the boat." A classic example is the family shown by Salvador Minuchin in the videotape "Open Door." In this family's house all the doors had to be left open so everyone could be accessible to everyone else in the family. Things were done as family events, and individuality was not enhanced. In such families, children often have to develop radical symptoms to differentiate themselves from the all-encompassing enmeshment of the family.

The healthy family model falls between these two extremes. It is a family in which the boundaries between separateness and belonging are permeable, yet in place. Members are seen as unique and there is a sense of joy about each other's differentness. Rules and tasks encourage self-control as well as demonstrating the effectiveness of teamwork and cooperation. A shared family session becomes the governing body of this family, which respects both the individuality and the commonality of each member.

When a family comes to me, it is useful for me to envision them somewhere upon the disengagement-enmeshment continuum and to look at the presented symptoms of the identified patient in light of the tension between separateness and belongingness. It also helps me to get a clear picture of the important boundary subsystems within the family. In a healthy family there are clear subsystem boundaries around each individual that enhance both separateness and belongingness. There should be clear, yet permeable boundaries between the various generational groupings within the family structure. Each family has at least two generational subsystems: the parental generational level and the child generational level. Many families add a third generational level by having a grandparent living either within the home or in such geographic proximity that the grandparents are included. Within each generational strata there are also many subsystems. The most important subsystems for family therapy are within the parental generation, where there is both a subsystem of the parents (mother and father) and of the spouses (husband and wife). Often families fail to realize that good parenting, and therefore good family functioning, begins with good spouses, and that spousing functions are within the adult generational level while parenting functions cross over the generational boundary into the child generational level. Some families who come for counseling have lost the care and maintenance of the spousal subsystem. Such families need to differentiate and reclaim the spousing functions. (Minuchin 1974, pp. 46–60)

THE INITIAL SESSION

Writers in the field of family therapy such as Salvador Minuchin and Jay Haley suggest that the initial session is vitally important for getting a clear understanding of the family coming to see the counselor. (Haley 1976, pp. 9–47)

I use a four-stage initial session: the social stage, a problem-definition stage, an interactional stage, and a task or directive stage.

In the social stage I meet the family presenting itself and begin to get a flavor of the dynamics of its particular system organization. By greeting each member at the door with a personal word or contact, I begin the process of individually joining with each member of the family. I try at the very beginning to convey the attitude that the family itself is the expert on the family, and that I, as the therapist, am a student learning about the family from the family. I pay close attention to nonverbal clues. Thinking about the following questions gives me more information: Who made the initial contact? What does that say about that person's position within the family? How do the members of the family enter the counseling room? In which order? Who gives directions, if any, as to seating? How do they seat themselves? It is especially interesting to note the initial seating arrangement of the family members. A room in which all the chairs are simple, movable, and identical helps me because there is no hierarchy predetermined by the chairs themselves. Often the distance between members defined by their seating selection is also descriptive of the psychological distance between those members. All the while, I am painting structural pictures in my head about how the family functions so that future tasks can be defined to alter the structure where it proves dysfunctional.

In the second, or problem-defining stage, it is vital to get a clear statement of the presenting problem from each member of the family system. How the question is asked and of whom is often significant. I word the question as neutrally as possible. To ask, "What's the problem with Johnny?" automatically joins you with the assumption of the family that the problem resides in one of its members and not within the family system as a whole. I prefer, "Why are you here today?" and I address the question to the less involved parent first. If such a distinction between less and greater involved parent cannot be made, I direct the question to the floor or to the ceiling, again gaining another bit of structural information when someone responds. It is also useful to ask all members of the family the same question and to receive answers directly to me as the therapist. Discussion between members and interaction between them at this stage often does not allow for clear, personal statements about the presenting issues of the family as seen by each individual member. The above suggestions have proven helpful to me and to others in the field; each therapist must develop his or her own personal style. It is important to get a full understanding of the reason for the family's request for counseling. Thus the problem-definition stage cannot be complete unless all members of the family who live together are present at the initial session. If one member cannot come, I often reschedule the initial appointment. Again, the resistance of any member to attending this vital session teaches me something about the family.

Two concepts are helpful at this point in the therapy. The more the family is in crisis and the more unstable it feels, the more ability there will be to change. Just as in individual therapy, the more the client is in pain, the more amenable he or she is to change. Second, the counselor should often listen to the statements being made in the problem stage on a two-level approach. The words tell about the tensions between the person speaking and the identified patient, but they are also metaphors for the tensions between the person speaking and some other significant person within the system. For example, a mother who complains about her son's lack of affection and respect for her is often reflecting the same attitudes about her husband. The therapist soon begins to conceptualize the "problems" of the family as symptoms chosen to serve some greater unspoken systemic problems of the family structure. Johnny's running away, for example, serves the family system by detracting from the greater problem that the husband has emotionally run away from his wife. It is often much easier for a family to concentrate on an acting-out child than on an intimacy issue between the parents.

The third stage of the initial session is the interactional stage. In this stage I get the family members to talk to each other while I observe and listen. I prefer having a family act out its tensions directly in the counseling room to filling the hour with the family telling me what it is like at home. Some therapists even assign tasks within the hour to watch family organization and functioning. In this way, they get an even clearer picture of the way the family system operates and identify the dysfunctional aspects of the family system that will need to be restructured later on.

The final stage of the initial session is to define a task, or homework, for the family that will help them experience a new way of functioning that will have a direct bearing upon the presented family tensions. A family came to me with the complaint that one of the teenaged daughters was acting out in school, being disobedient, and lying. Upon further questioning, I discovered that the parents had arranged their lives in such a way that they rarely saw each other at all. The husband worked from 7 A.M.

to 6 P.M. and the wife left the home around 4 P.M. to do volunteer work and to attend church meetings and did not arrive home until after her husband was already in bed. As a result of this arrangement, messages between husband and wife were sent through the daughter. The daughter's acting out was a direct reaction to the confusing and often double messages she received from each of her parents and to their lack of unity. I chose to exaggerate the systemic dysfunction of the family as the assigned task. The husband and wife were directed *not* to communicate directly with each other during the week but were to send all messages through the daughter. Upon arrival at the next appointment, the couple stated their belief that the task was stupid and said that they had made special efforts all week to be in direct contact with each other through phone calls and personal meetings. The daughter's acting out began to diminish when she was removed from the position of message transmitter.

JOINING AND RESTRUCTURING

The most important initial therapeutic move by the counselor is to "join" the family system as it exists. All too often the family therapist remains on the outside as the observer of the family, and from that position begins to assign tasks to change the family structure. Much to his or her surprise the therapist finds the family resisting and even sabotaging the suggested directives. If the therapist has not been accepted by the family, the family will unite against him or her and change will be aborted.

There are a number of ways to join a family. The first method is to maintain the family structure already present until joining has been accomplished. By maintaining, the therapist supports the rules and organization expected by the family. This can be done by acknowledging the existing household head, by following the interactional rules and patterns of the family, and by supporting the strengths present in the family system. If a mother expects others to seek her permission before they assign a task to her children, the therapist must obey this family rule. Only after the therapist has been accepted and not perceived as a threat can restructuring begin.

Another method of joining a family is to follow the content of the communications and the behaviors of the family. It is a good idea for the therapist to approach the family from the point of view of the learner who knows very little about the family. Even being stupid and having the family repeat or clarify adds to the therapist's growing knowledge of how the family perceives itself. It is useful to help the family expand the content being presented, especially around the concern of the presenting problem. Often such material can be used as the basis for the development of tasks later to restructure the system. For example, a family came with the presenting problem of a seventeen-year-old son who was currently wetting his bed. As I helped the family expand on the topic of bed wetting, a number of interesting connections were revealed. The son was from a previous marriage and had only recently joined his father's new family, which was constituted around a second marriage. The son felt like a new child fighting to claim space and mark out territory. He also felt like a new young adult and was especially interested in claiming an adult relationship with his father. As I tracked the topic even further, the father revealed that he himself had been an adolescent bed wetter and could empathize with his son's ambivalent feelings. The father was also a salesman of medical supplies, including adult diapers. A task was arranged in which the father and the son handled the bed wetting as an adult concern between two adults. In such a way the father and son were connected with each other and the son could control the symptom. The bed wetting stopped within the week.

A third, generally accepted way to join a family is to duplicate the family's conversational tone and style by choosing words that fit the family's speaking patterns. I try to speak with similar inflections and spacing. Such twinning can often be the root for subtle hypnotic suggestion. By duplicating body movements and body postures, I blend initially with the family rather than standing out in my differentness. Only after one has been accepted can differentness be tolerated.

During the process of joining the family, the therapist will be gaining all kinds of useful information, and on the basis of it he develops a working diagnosis as to the structural changes needed for the family to unblock its growth flow. The working diagnosis will be aimed at removing the symptoms and the source of the presented problem. If the systemic source can be isolated and restructured, the symptoms will often handle themselves. (Minuchin 1974, pp. 123–29)

The restructuring phase of family therapy develops naturally out of the joining phase. It is often helpful to begin the restructuring within the therapy hour by requesting experiential changes while the family is interacting in your presence. Changes in communication styles can sometimes shift the structure of the family. To encourage a child to finish a thought before being interrupted by another member clarifies the need for accepting each member's uniqueness and independence while paying attention to each member's position as part of the total family system. Helping a family to hear each other and to listen gives greater emphasis to each member's wants and desires from the family system.

One good restructuring method uses the space within the counseling room to help visualize and create a boundary system that appears to be lacking within a family. The spousal subsystem can be defined by moving the husband and wife into side-by-side chairs in another section of the room from the sibling subsystem. Sometimes the therapist will become the generational boundary by sitting between the parents and the children. Particular dyads chosen for relational emphasis can be asked to remain or leave the room depending upon the task chosen. (Minuchin 1974, pp. 138–57)

At times tasks given for the family as a whole can be started within the therapy session and continued while at home. Excellent material on task design can be found in Jay Haley's book, *Problem Solving Therapy*. Again, the point of the restructuring task is to get the family to experience a new way of functioning aimed at removing the blockages to healthy family growth.

SOME CONCLUDING THOUGHTS

Family therapy is an art that will develop with each therapist in his or her own unique style. Many parish pastors have been taught few pastoral counseling skills during seminary training. These skills are picked up and developed through a variety of educational opportunities. The art of counseling must be practiced under direct supervision of a more accomplished pastoral counselor. Family therapy too must be learned and practiced under supervision to become effective. Perhaps this chapter will arouse an interest in the reader to learn more about family therapy. Many excellent programs are available around the country for the parish pastor or pastoral counselor to learn family therapy. Trained family therapists have found that constant supervision and sharing of family cases are extremely valuable and creative for their own continued growth in the field. Each family is unique, and each therapeutic experience with a family is a new opportunity for learning. The family is a vital part of the religious system and the arena for much ministry. The pastor interested in counseling has an entry to the family unique among the helping professions. Families often call their minister at the first sign of tension. The minister, in turn, can see the presented problem as residing within the total family and not just the identified patient. The minister's care and concern for the family and for the individuals who make up the family give him or her added opportunity to bring health to a number of persons.

A major asset for the pastor or pastoral counselor is a sense of curiosity. First, he or she needs curiosity about himself or herself as a product of a family system. I hope the brief look into my own family system has aroused your desire to look into your own family root system and to explore your own unique development. Second, the pastor and pastoral counselor needs a sense of curiosity about those who come for counseling. Continually learning from the family seeking help gives the counselor an excellent opportunity to join the family and to do effective therapy. Out of this sense of curiosity, the restructuring of the family will occur and the experiential tasks will emerge. Once the family has gained its own sense of curiosity about itself, growth will continue.

I am indebted for the content of this chapter to my own sense of curiosity and for my personal experience as a student, especially as a student of those families that have come to me for help, and as a student of Salvador Minuchin and Jay Haley.

In addition to the Recommended Readings at the end of the chapter, I recommend the following to the reader's curiosity:

Haley, Jay (Ed.). *Changing Families: A Family Therapy Reader.* New York: Grune and Stratton, 1971.
———. *Strategies of Psychotherapy.* New York: Grune and Stratton, 1963.
———. *Uncommon Therapy: The Psychiatric Techniques of Milton H. Erikson, M.D.* New York: Norton, 1973.
———. *Problem Solving Therapy.* San Francisco: Jossey-Bass, 1976.

————. *Leaving Home: The Therapy of Disturbed Young People.* New York: McGraw-Hill, 1980.

Haley, Jay, and Lynn Hoffman. *Techniques of Family Therapy.* New York: Basic Books, 1967.

Minuchin, Salvador, et al. *Families of the Slums: An Exploration of Their Structure and Treatment.* New York: Basic Books, 1967.

————. *Families and Family Therapy.* Cambridge, Mass.: Harvard University Press, 1974.

Minuchin, Salvador, and H. Charles Fishman. *Family Therapy Techniques.* Cambridge, Mass.: Harvard University Press, 1981.

REFERENCES

Haley, Jay. *Problem Solving Therapy.* San Francisco: Jossey-Bass, 1976.

Minuchin, Salvador. *Families and Family Therapy.* Cambridge, Mass.: Harvard University Press, 1974.

RECOMMENDED READINGS

Blander, Richard, John Grinder, and Virginia Satir. *Changing with Families.* Palo Alto, Calif.: Science and Behavior, 1976.

Carter, Elizabeth, and Monica McGoldrick. *The Family Life Cycle: A Framework For Family Therapy.* New York: Gardner Press, 1980.

Ferber, Andrew, Marilyn Mendelsohn, and Augustus Napier. *The Book of Family Therapy.* Boston: Houghton, 1972.

Guerin, Phillip, Jr. (Ed.). *Family Therapy: Theory and Practice.* New York: Gardner Press, 1976.

Gurman, Alan, and David Kniskern (Eds.). *Handbook of Family Therapy.* New York: Brunner/Mazel, 1981.

Jones, Susan. *Family Therapy: A Comparison of Approaches.* Bowie, Md.: Brady, 1980.

Madanes, Cloe. *Strategic Family Therapy.* San Francisco: Jossey-Bass, 1981.

Neill, John R., and David Kniskern (Eds.). *From Psyche to System: The Evolving Therapy of Carl Whitaker.* New York: Guilford Press, 1982.

Papp, Peggy (Ed). *Family Therapy: Full Length Case Studies.* New York: Gardner Press, 1977.

Reiss, Ira (Ed). *Readings on the Family System.* New York: Holt, 1972.

Satir, Virginia. *Conjoint Family Therapy.* Palo Alto, Calif.: Science and Behavior, 1964.

————. *Peoplemaking.* Palo Alto, Calif.: Science and Behavior, 1972.

Satir, Virginia, James Stachowiak, and Harvery Taschman. *Helping Families to Change.* New York: Jason Aronson, 1975.

Stewart, Charles William. *The Minister as Family Counselor.* Nashville: Abingdon, 1979.

Visher, Emily, and John Visher. *Step-Families: A Guide to Working with Stepparents and Stepchildren.* New York: Brunner/Mazel, 1979.

Whitaker, Carl, and Augustus Napier. *The Family Crucible.* New York: Harper, 1978.

CHAPTER TWELVE

Adult Developmental Counseling

ROBERT F. DAVENPORT, D. MIN.

When we look at paintings of children from seventeenth and eighteenth century America, we get a clue to how novel the notion of humans as developing persons really is. Our forebears thought of children as miniature adults. That notion was so thoroughly set in consciousness that artists, who were perfectly capable of painting what they saw, painted children as though they were shrunken grown-ups.

In 1847, over fifty years before William James began to publish early psychological works, Horace Bushnell, a Connecticut congregational pastor, published *Christian Nurture*. Bushnell had the revolutionary idea that children are intellectually and psychologically developing persons who are able to comprehend and assimilate both the data and the emotional message of faith in graduated stages. Children were described as children, not little grown-ups. Bushnell's work made him father of the religious education movement.

In the twentieth century Erik Erikson and other psychological theorists have taught us to see that we continuously develop not only in childhood but from conception until death. As pastoral counselors, we need to understand that about *ourselves,* so that we may wrestle with our own griefs and grievances respectfully. We also need to understand that persons who seek our counsel are often struggling with perfectly normal issues. The issues may seem so normal that *they* tend to dismiss them as having little importance. If so, they will miss clues to how they can make use of normal and expected losses to promote human growth.

212

The aim of this chapter is to review important insights on human development and to alert the reader to *developmental diagnosis* which can inform us as pastoral counselors. The emphasis will be on developmental issues in midlife.

The pastoral counselor who is sensitive to psychological development in adults is in a particularly effective position to be useful to persons seeking to comprehend and work through developmental issues. Meeting clients nonjudgmentally, with a predisposition to empathize with their pain, the pastoral counselor can enable them to accept inevitable circumstances of human change while at the same time respecting their feelings of grief, anger, and helplessness which accompany change. Life's crises are, as the root of that word suggests, turning points, and thus potentially occasions for growth. When I take a detailed history from a client in our early sessions, prior to making decisions on either the nature of the client's difficulty or forming a recommendation for a therapeutic strategy, I listen for and ask about experiences that tell me how that person has or has not moved through the stages of development. I want to know about memories of everyday life and traumatic experiences in preschool, elementary school, junior and senior high school, and early adulthood. The "map" which guides my particular listening and questioning of a client was drawn by Erik Erikson, whose works I have studied carefully. Erikson's writings have taught me to be sensitive to the impact of a client's recall of important events. Our lives are influenced deeply by varied experiences: the loss of significant adults in childhood, geographic moves, important beginnings and endings, first menstrual period for women, the changing relationships with both parents and peers which accompany puberty, early sexual or dating experiences, school successes or failures, and changes in the quality of our parents' marriage.

Erikson's widely known epigenetic chart (1959) identifies eight stages of human development from birth to death. At each stage, Erikson posits polar potentialities which inform the psychosocial task of that stage. In the first years of life an infant is met by either caring or noncaring adults and gains a sense of *trust* or *mistrust*. By the second year, struggling to gain control of bladder and bowels without being over-controlled, a child teeters between *autonomy* and *shame and doubt*. In the next several years, before formal schooling, as a child experiences a wider environment of things to try, the polarities are *initiative* versus *guilt*. The early school years, when work is related to acceptance, lead the child to face *industry* versus *inferiority*. The onset of puberty, the growing importance of peers, and the need for self-acceptance as male or female face adolescents with *identity* versus *identity confusion*. In early adulthood, where choices in love and work call for commitments, we work through *intimacy* versus *isolation*. Midlife with its demands to produce and nurture what we produce faces us with *generativity* versus *stagnation*. Finally, the end of life, when we look back either to say yes or no to who we have been, offers us *integrity* versus *despair*.

Recent writings, for example Gilligan et al., have alerted us to the potential for a male bias in Erikson's work. These theorists note that while young boys are apparently inclined and clearly encouraged to *compete,* young girls are apparently inclined and encouraged to *cooperate*. Thus, it is suggested that intimacy precedes and informs identity in female development.

Erikson's chart is misread if it is viewed as an achievement schedule with the emphasis on one-sided positive adjustment. Erikson notes: "What a [person] acquires at a given stage is a certain *ratio* between the positive and negative which, if the balance is toward the positive, will help him to meet later crises with a predisposition toward the sources of vitality." (1968)

Erikson (1959) expanded Freud's views by treating development as social as well as psychological. He writes: "Each society meets each phase of the development of its members by institutions . . .specific to it, to ensure that the developing individual will be viable in it." *Institutions* in this context is a more inclusive term than its usual connotation; it suggests traditions, folkways, mores, and socially sanctioned patterns of behavior. Erikson has had most to say about childhood and adolescence, but his seminal contribution to our thinking has been his insistence that *we are developing persons throughout our lives*. In fact, by implication, at least, his emphasis on childhood serves not only to alert us to the importance of our pasts as influencers in our adult present, but to call our attention to what children need from us as adults. He is very aware that history is influenced by how we raise our children. Imagine the implications of this statement for our social order, for the stability of our institutions, and for world peace:

> It is human to have a long childhood: it is civilized to have an even longer childhood. Long childhood makes a technical and mental virtuoso out of man, but it leaves a lifelong residue of emotional immaturity in him. (1963, p. 16)

A winsome aspect of Erikson's work is his unapologetic willingness to address values: personal and societal. Compared to much psychological theorizing, which seldom ventures beyond descriptions of phenomena based on observations from quantification of data, Erikson's works are, variously, treatises, biography, and psychological philosophy. In the best and broadest sense of that word, Erikson is a moralist. He writes:

> [M]an's psychological survival is safeguarded only by vital virtues which develop in the interplay of successive and overlapping generations, living together in organized settings. Here, living together means more than incidental proximity. It means that the individual's life stages are "inter-living," cogwheeling with the stages of others which move him along as he moves them. (1964, p. 114)

The word *virtue* in Erikson's work does not mean goodness; it is not the opposite of *vice*. *Virtue* is used as in the Latin word *vertus,* meaning "potency" or "strength." Thus, Erikson notes that each of the life crises or turning points, well resolved, yields a virtue peculiar to that stage Erikson's (1964) definitions of these virtues are well worth our careful attention. Readers who are interested in either faith development or moral development, as subtopics of psychological development, would benefit from study of the works of James Fowler and Lawrence Kohlberg, respectively.

One use to which the knowledge of development through the life cycle enlightens my work is the subject of the bulk of this chapter. Many who seek pastoral counseling are suffering more from problems in living than from any demonstrable clinical conditions even though the "style" (Shapiro 1965) of their suffering and of their dealing with it reflect neuroticlike characteristics. Storr (1980) describes and gives therapeutic clues for these typical "styles." These people are undergoing stresses in living which, while phase-specific to their development, are causing them or others close to them enough pain and confusion for them to seek professional help.

Years ago Erikson coined the phrase, "the psychopathology of everyday adolescence" to describe just how bizarre the experiences of normal development can be for both the adolescents themselves and adults who deal with them. Increasingly, we are recognizing that adult development has its own peculiar "everyday psychopathology." Growth is seldom painless.

Briefly, this is Erikson's important contribution to our understanding of human development. When we look at the issues of midlife and the compelling way in which three generations interplay in our middle years, we will see that a careful look at midlife is a look at all of life.

MIDLIFE TASKS OF SEPARATION AND INDIVIDUATION

Midlife in general, and the midlife of married persons with children in particular, is a time filled with compelling developmental issues which have major implications for both individuals and society. Among the complicating factors of midlife is the reality that we bear the major responsibility for the various institutions that give society its cohesion. Erikson's polarity for midlife is generativity versus stagnation. If generativity suggests "making," then the virtue Erikson identifies for this period suggests sustenance, care, and a widening concern for what has been generated by love, necessity, or accident. My intention here is to briefly outline a thesis that will enable us to think about the major developmental issues for adults and ourselves and will help us to comprehend internal and relational issues that threaten to undermine effectiveness and a sense of satisfaction with life in the middle years. This is hardly to be viewed as a definitive treatment of the issues in midlife development, and the reader is referred to the references for further study.

The thesis is that the middle of our lives presents us with a *three-generational task of separation and individuation*. That is, at midlife we are faced with a need to define ourselves as individuals in certain important ways, to separate from our parents, our spouses, and our children. That defining task is critically important to us and presents us with a variety of difficult issues.

SEPARATION AND INDIVIDUATION FROM OUR PARENTS

By the middle of our lives our parents, or people who raised us in the place of parents, are at the end of their lives. The change in our relationships with them occasioned by their aging presents both them and us with new relational demands. In this mobile society we will often live at some distance from our families of origin, perhaps because commitments to love and work have taken us to new places or because our folks have moved in their retirement. However, we know that geographical distance does not guarantee psychological distance, or individuation, as Carl Jung has taught us to call adult maturing. In fact, the illusion of psychological distance which geographical removal provides may be shattered when we find ourselves having to respond to a crisis in our parents' lives and learn that old patterns of authority and deference have not been worked through but only postponed. When we are called upon to deal with such issues as a parent's terminal illness, hospitalization, or alternative living arrangements, we discover that those adult strengths which we are used to exercising in our daily work and family lives are sacrificed to strange feelings of guilt, helplessness, and fear. Thus, at the very time our parents need our strength as our roles are reversed, we may surprisingly find that, not unlike our kids, our parents resist us even when what we are attempting to do for them is clearly (to us) in their best interest. This crisis of midlife suggests to us that we need to attend early to issues of our own autonomy *vis-à-vis* our parents, not only for the sake of our own maturation but for their sakes as they need our mature strength.

If these issues of aging in our parents present us with hard choices which assume our maturation, their deaths present us with even more compelling issues. The deaths of our parents remind us of our own mortality. Whatever mechanisms of denial have been operating to give us a sense of endless time to live give way to a sense of having become the older generation, the next ones to go. Not the least of the griefs we experience at the death of a parent is the loss of the illusion of our own immortality.

When we have not established our individuality from our parents, their deaths can raise other problems for us. To the extent that we felt dependent on them for approval or for financial support, we will experience a loss of esteem in the reminder of our dependency. To the extent that we have been counterdependent rather than independent and have acted out a feigned autonomy to cover our unwillingness to establish our maturity with them, we will likely experience guilt that it is now too late to let them know of our feelings for them.

In any case, in the middle of our lives the changes we experience in relation to our parents remind us that we need to know ourselves as separate from them with all the griefs and grievances which accrue to even those inevitable separations in life.

Clients who present themselves to us as suffering confusion of identity and direction in midlife can often profitably give time and attention to how they feel about their parents and just how freely they experience themselves in relation to their parents, living or dead.

The issues that adults have with their parents are often so far in the past that they seem to have little to do with their here-and-now, elderly parents. Unless there is some reason for me to see them all in a multigenerational family therapy, my strategy is to work with the client and the memory, not to have the client confront the parent. The offending parent is that long-ago parent in the client's head, not the old person down the street or across the country. I deal with this issue as an intrapsychic rather than an interpersonal phenomenon. Sometimes that is as simple as asking the client to tell the story of the aggrieved relationship. In hearing the story and letting the client feel and give free expression to those memories, I get a clue to possible points of developmental fixation as well as allowing the client to vent old grievances and feel some relief. Working through poignant or painful memories can often clear the client's way to deal with the real needs of the real old folk which parents have become, rather than acting out in either codependent or hostile postures the unresolved issues of childhood.

Well-resolved, the freedoms and obligations which accrue to individuating from our parents can give us a sense of being in charge as well as being the generation on the line as mere mortals. There are losses, to be sure, for we are never quite so "special" to anyone as we were to our parents, but there are gains as well, as we take on our mature autonomy.

SEPARATION AND INDIVIDUATION FROM OUR SPOUSES

In doing marriage counseling with middle-aged clients, we may see couples who are struggling among either finding means of individuating from one another, drifting into stagnant, interminably incompatible marriages, or leaving one another. The current middle-aged generation married under the influence of a "togetherness" mythology. Listening to the songs we danced to as teenagers and young adults, we hear the plaintive call to merge, to find ourselves by joining ourselves to one another. Twenty or so years later our mergers are often suffering from each party's feeling over-determined by the union. By that time the marriage has usually defined itself around the needs of children who have the temerity to begin to act as though they no longer need us. Our new song is likely to be, "Is that all there is?" reflecting not only our fear at the loss of the children, who supply a reason for the marriage to continue, but a growing sense of reality that our early dreams will not be realized in either love or work.

In the middle of our marriages that early fascination with one another which we call "being in love" yields either to boredom or to a less exciting but more realistic and willful appreciation of one another which we could call "loving." Peck (1979, pp.

81–105) provides a compelling description of the differences between "being in love" and "loving." In either case, that early preoccupation with one another in which our personal boundaries became diffuse is gradually replaced by a renewed attention to our individual identities, with larger and larger amounts of our energy being directed outside rather than into the marital relationship.

This change of focus from inside to outside the home is often more apparent for the woman in the marital relationship than for the man. The man's efforts have already typically been invested in work outside. In fact, not the least of the marital conflicts of midlife can be a man's new interest in home and kids at the very point his wife is looking outside. At midlife, in response to children's maturation, increased economic pressure on the family, or boredom, women will often return to education or enter a career. A wife's understandable enthusiasm for these new possibilities is often in sharp contrast to her husband's sense of being on a vocational treadmill, serving what seems like interminable time toward a retirement which he begins to invest unrealistically with the romantic expectations that no longer fit at work. The husband's responses to his wife's new possibilities are ambivalent at best: he is glad for her help or ashamed of the family's need for a financial boost; he is proud of his wife's ability and envious of her enthusiasm; he wants to encourage her autonomy and is fearful of losing her to a world from which she has long been hidden.

Not the least of a middle-aged man's attraction to a younger woman is her emotional and biological predisposition to "nesting" in contrast to his wife's newly possible and quite attractive inclination to try her vocational or professional wings. Such attraction is considerably more significant than mere appearance, and serves, as well, to express a man's need to deny the reality of his own impending death by a new beginning which seems to promise endless years.

Thus, individuation in marriage refers to that redefined "I" which must replace the intense "we" of earlier married life. While those "I's" continue to participate in varied "we's" in family, job, or volunteer work, husbands and wives face a need not to be subsumed or overdetermined by their union. Simply stated, spouses have the opportunity to become companions respectful of one another's individuality. One of the forces at work in marital individuation is the already noted new sense, in the face of parental aging or death, that we are on the front line, the next generation to die, an experience we all must do as "I's."

With individuation failing in the marriage, stagnation is likely—a "selling out" or resignation to definition solely by role, job, income, social class, neighborhood, habit. In denial of that stagnation, either or both spouses may make a radical break; they may "drop out," rupturing remaining ties, often denying inevitable aging by associating with younger people, their habits, speech, dress, or causes. In search of an illusive "we" in midlife we seek to deny the final reality of being alone in the world with a compulsive, relentless, and repeatedly frustrated effort to find other spouses, other children, other jobs.

The middle-aged person struggles to replace an earlier sense of unlimited satisfaction with the acceptance of a considerably more realistic, if somewhat pedes-trian, competence. That struggle informs our work, our vocational dreams, our marriages, and our lives with our children.

There is a sense in which our recently burgeoning divorce rate is a testament to the failure of midlife couples to individuate successfully. Refusing to resign ourselves to overdetermination in loveless relationships, tempted to start over in new relation-ships and defer the inevitable rigors of institutionalization on love, expecting too much from our lives, being unwilling or unable to redefine and move on to individuated unions, we often see a radical break as the only source of personal survival.

A major issue in individuation is a couple's willingness to allow one another and themselves to cultivate previously disowned parts of themselves. If we hide our parts from ourselves, we clearly have not let a spouse see them. We disown parts of ourselves because we fear that something about ourselves will be unacceptable to us or to others. Ironically, however, it is often some disowned part of ourselves that we see in a potential mate and which attracts us to them. For example, if I am emotionally expressive, I will likely be attracted to a person who is organized, predictable, controlled. If we mate, she leans on my effervescence and I depend on her controls. That protects me from having to claim my controlled side and her from finding her spontaneity. The plot thickens when we discover that what attracts us in the other (our disowned half) can also be a source of alienation. After all, we learned to disown because the people who raised us rewarded what became our dominant side. In fact, when we first come home with a potential mate, saying, in effect, "Look who I found! Can I keep him/her?" we may be met with a horrified look from the people who raised us not to be "one of those"; this is one way to view the perennial conflicts we have with in-laws. So we have the interesting and confusing situation of being both attracted to and alienated from someone for the same characteristics.

If we allow ourselves and our spouses the time and energy to individuate—that is, to discover and claim our disowned parts, making peace with our *internal* alien-ation—we can come to one another with a new sense of wholeness. Then a spouse is *chosen* rather than *needed*—as a whole person by a whole person. Clearly, if a spouse can be chosen, then as a result of individuation he or she can be unchosen as well. However, two individuated adults who decided to give one another up would be doing so from a position of strength rather than weakness. One of the problems a pastoral counselor may face is a client's precipitous inclination to reject a mate as a result of insights gained in counseling. Such a person can be urged to look beyond first inclinations, or, if the client acts capriciously, can be led to use even a marital separation as a further occasion for self-discovery and rediscovery of the more compelling attractions that brought the mates together. When I am working with separated persons, I urge them to spend at least a year without seeking important relationships with others. That year provides the time and space needed to work through the grief of the separation, noting and enduring all the feelings that accrue to important anniversaries and holidays. At the end of that year, much of the individuation work will have been done, serving either reconciliation on a more realistic basis, or the maturity needed to begin life anew without a spouse. Without such a regimen, new alliances will likely dull the edge of a person's pain and serve as a means to avoid grief, delay individuation, and risk repeating the same patterns with a new partner.

Couples willing to work at their unions and on themselves can discover and celebrate those common ties of sex, affection, respect, friendship, and comfortable habits of mature marriage. That process involves each spouse in a sometimes scary investment in personal satisfaction which surrenders earlier mutual dependency and overdetermined coupleness in the service of a more comfortable, mutually affirming interdependency. Only then can spouses truly say they *choose* to be married rather than *needing* to be married to claim some disowned part of themselves.

SEPARATION AND INDIVIDUATION OF AND FROM CHILDREN

In their adolescence, our offspring face the inevitability of surrendering the dependencies and securities of childhood along with the necessity of resolving issues of identity which differentiate them from us; thus they go through a more or less prolonged period of counterdependence marked by alternating needs to be close to adults and seemingly to reject adults and their values. Part of that process is to revisit the crises of earlier stages, this time with the intention of resolving unfinished childhood issues in order to move on. The most important, and at times most dramatic, of these issues is the move from identification or primary affiliation with the parent of the opposite sex to the parent of the same sex, since the sexual identity crisis is a large part of the more inclusive identity resolution. The kid who wins the Oedipal battle, loses the developmental war. The young man or woman who is unable to separate from being mother's or father's special kid in order to identify with the same-sex parent will be stuck in a no-win union which obviates growth and allows for no success.

Why would an adolescent do that? The answers are complex and tied up in parents' relationships to one another and to each parent's own clarity of sexual identity *vis-à-vis* the adolescents. When parents are comfortable with their sexual relation they will respond positively to the normal loss of specialness that accrued to the "mother's boy" or "daddy's girl." Then the adolescents begin to define the physical and emotional distance from opposite-sex parents with which they are comfortable in light of their newly experienced and ambivalently accepted sense of sexuality. When parents are not clear in their sexual relation, they may find the new sexual identity of their adolescent children a source of awkward attraction or threat. Under those conditions the off-again-on-again closeness/distance maneuvers of the adolescents will be a problem to the parents. Nor is this situation helped by the common experience these days of marital breakups in which kids can become the prizes over whom couples fight in order both to beat one another and to salvage something from the union. The young adolescent girl who is subtly invited to "take care of Daddy" or the boy who is now the "man of the house" for Mama experiences a surge of nonspecific grandiosity which is seductive in its false presumption of power—false because those are powers which will never be exercised, or if they are will lead to devastating results developmentally. In marital separations, an adolescent's development is complicated by the grief over the lost family solidarity and the common response of an opposite-sex parent to seek to perpetuate the past by wanting a special relation with a child.

It is one of the ironies of our personal histories that we are faced with our own life redefinition issues at the very chronological point that our kids are asking their identity questions and want us to be most sure of who we are. That is not to suggest that they would want to identify with us—far from it, for in the service of their individuation through distancing themselves from us, they respond to us by offering either clear and open or thinly camouflaged contempt for our values, our ideas, our religion, our politics. Peppered with shock language, their condemnation is often delivered in words and phrases which are reductionistic in the extreme. We err if we assume that they want or need us to fold before this onslaught, for the name of the game is getting away, and what they need most is for us to be sure of what they are sure they wish to disavow. From Salem's "witches" trial until recent American history, adults in our refusal to maintain our values in the face of adolescent testing have not only failed the adolescents but have risked serious harm to social institutions for which adults are responsible. This is not to suggest that youthful criticism of our institutions is not a necessary ingredient in social reform, but only to warn against the social danger of we adults' doubting ourselves and our values so much that we surrender our responsibilities.

In midlife we feel in an otherwise natural process a sense of loss, grief, and guilt as the family battle rages to give us and our adolescent children pseudo-issues over which to split from one another. Needless to say, most of this operates below awareness, would be denied by both parents and adolescents, and takes place over a considerable period of time in alternating approach/avoidance modalities. The whole process is complicated for parents and their kids by the fact that the youngsters' financial needs are notable at this period of their lives, leaving parents in the unenviable position of being strapped financially by a process that causes great familial stress.

Helm Stierlin (1974) identifies three ways parents or parents and kids can subvert this natural process of separation and individuation.

First, for our comfort or to provide needed glue for homes that might otherwise fall apart, to create the illusion that we are not aging, to occupy our time and energy and provide couple conversation, to serve as in-house consciences to keep us from following impulses that might bring them and us shame, or to create family crises the acting out and resolution of which can give us the illusion of marital cohesion, we can *bind* our adolescents to us. We say, in effect, "Don't grow up and leave us," and we reinforce the plea with various restrictive, infantilizing efforts aimed at keeping them with us.

Second, often in response to the disillusionment we are experiencing in our own lives at midpoint, to fulfill our unfulfilled ambitions, to experience vicariously the thrill of our kids acting out sexually or with drugs while officially condemning them, or to serve a family script we have failed to live out, we can *delegate* our adolescents. We say, in effect, "Go do it for us and make sure we know about it." In our popular literature, Willie Loman's need for Biff and Happy to do successfully what he had failed to do illustrates well the delegating phenomenon.

Third, as parents who need to deny the pain we feel at losing our kids by actively taking the initiative in getting rid of them dramatically, or who want them out of the way so we will be free to end uncomfortable marriages, we can *expel* our adolescents. In recent years that expelling of youngsters before they are ready to leave has created a subculture which numbers in the high thousands of runaways or barely grown-up young adults marginally related to the larger society with very tenuous connections to love and work.

As pastoral counselors we are often asked to help families in stress over issues with adolescents. We often erroneously assume that the problem is with the adolescent, who is however unwittingly, serving as an identified patient for a troubled marriage or family. Stierlin's typology can alert us to some hidden issues relating to the middle-aged parents and their needs for which the troubled adolescent may be only a symptom.

Binding, delegating, and expelling are clearly unsatisfying ways to let our adolescents separate and individuate from us and us from them. These approaches arise from our failure to work through our own issues of separation and individuation in our marriages or reflect our own unfinished separation tasks from our parents, neither of which our adolescents have any power to affect. When we deal with these issues, we take an important step toward enabling our offspring to distance themselves from us at paces specific to their needs. The alert pastoral counselor will not naively treat acting-out adolescents whose real role is to call attention to parental issues that are clouded by the adolescents' dramatic behavior.

CONCLUSION

The natural, predictable, and expected family processes of midlife involve us in experiences of three-generational loss and grief. When we do that grieving and find satisfaction, we can resolve those issues. However, grief unresolved tends to come out in unexpected, camouflaged ways to debilitate us without any sense of what the cause is. The commonly reported depressive malaise of midlife may in no small part be a function of unacknowledged grief which surfaces in various symptoms seemingly unrelated to specific stimuli. As pastoral counselors informed by the insights of both psychopathology and human development, we can offer clients the occasion to work through the psychopathology of everyday "middlessence." We can do that if we alert them to the need to grieve the losses we have been identifying and to move on to the redefinition which issues of separation and individuation necessitate in midlife.

Ignored or poorly resolved, our failure to define an "I" we can live with yields what Erikson has taught us to call "stagnation," that polar possibility with "generativity" in midlife, and leads predictably and inevitably to "despair" at the end of life rather than to the "integrity" which old age can offer to those who are "yea sayers" to the only lives we can now have lived.

REFERENCES

Bushnell, Horace. *Christian Nurture*. New York: Harper, 1880.
Erikson, E. H. "Identity and the Life Cycle." *Psychological Issues,* I, no. 1. New York: International Universities Press, 1959.
————. *Childhood and Society,* 2nd ed. New York: Norton, 1963.
————. *Insight and Responsibility*. New York: Norton, 1964.
————. *Identity: Youth and Crisis*. New York: Norton, 1968.
James, William. *The Varieties of Religious Experience*. New York: New American Library, 1958.
Peck, M. Scott. *The Road Less Traveled*. New York: Simon & Schuster, 1979.
Shapiro, D. *Neurotic Styles*. New York: Basic Books, 1965.
Stierlin, H. *Separating Parents and Adolescents*. New York: Quadrangle, 1974.
Storr, Anthony. *The Art of Psychotherapy*. New York: Methuen, 1980.

RECOMMENDED READINGS

Caine, L. *Widow*. New York: Morrow, 1974.
Capps, Donald E. "Pastoral Counseling for Middle Adults," in *Clinical Handbook of Pastoral Counseling*. Mahwah, NJ: Paulist Press, 1985.
Dittes, James. *The Male Predicament*. San Francisco: Harper, 1985.
Gilligan, Carol. *In a Different Voice*. Cambridge: Harvard University Press, 1982.
Fowler, James. *Becoming Adult, Becoming Christian*. New York: Harper, 1984.
Kohlberg, Lawrence. *Collected Papers on Moral Development*. Cambridge: Center for Moral Education, 1976.
Levinson, D. J. *The Seasons of a Man's Life*. New York: Knopf, 1978.
Lidz, T. *The Person: His and Her Development Throughout the Life Cycle,* rev. ed. New York: Basic Books, 1978.
Miller, J. B. *Toward a New Psychology of Women*. Boston: Beacon Press, 1976.
Norman, W. H., and T. J. Scaramella. *Midlife: Developmental and Clinical Issues*. New York: Brunner/Mazel, 1980.
Sheehy, G. *Passages*. New York: Dutton, 1974.

CHAPTER THIRTEEN

Counseling the Grieving Person

ANN KAISER STEARNS, M. DIV., PH.D.

Bereavement comes from the word *reave,* meaning "to be dispossessed," to be robbed of something belonging to oneself (*Oxford English Dictionary,* 1933). When a woman has a mastectomy, something is forcibly taken away, a possession rightfully hers. When a fifty-five-year-old man has a heart attack and has to change his way of living and working, something is taken away, choices and decisions that previously belonged to him. When parents lose a child, they are dispossessed of something very precious. In words that have been attributed to Camus: "The order of nature is reversed. Children are supposed to bury their parents." When persons of any age undergo the ordeal of a divorce or suffer the loss of a loved one by death, they are often left with a sense of having been robbed, dispossessed. Having an abortion or miscarriage or finding oneself unable to have children—one can see how these losses also could be experienced as losing something rightfully one's own.

Many other situations can carry a sense of irrevocable injury: rape, chronic illness, the birth of a handicapped child, the breakup of a love affair, the loss of a job, the loss of a dream or goal, the loss of personal belongings in a fire or flood, a major geographical move which involves leaving behind one's roots and friends. And, of course, perhaps the ultimate dispossession: facing the loss of one's own life.

There is another kind of grief that counselors and therapists often encounter. Usually, it happens in the client's twenties or thirties, sometimes later. The person in counseling may begin to realize that his or her childhood is as it will always be: a broken family, an alcoholic or mentally ill parent, a loved one who died prematurely, a parent who could never provide the love that was always yearned for. Even in the happiest of families there are sorrows of various kinds. The client realizes that his or her parents and siblings can't be changed. They can't be made happier, or less unhealthy, or more careful of themselves, or less misunderstanding. Grief sets in, for the events of the past are unalterable, and the sense of loss may be experienced as a death that has occurred.

Life involves almost all of us in losses of significant magnitude. When I was twenty, I thought that all of my dreams were capable of being realized. If an older person said I couldn't have it all or control it all, I felt insulted. What is clearer now is that there are choices we make; and there is the reality that in pursuing some of our dreams we leave others behind. Through events of our own making and events beyond our control we come to realize our human vulnerability. As I've seen in the people with whom I've worked in counseling, it's a realization that none of us likes to face, but it's something we can come to understand.

Sometimes I think I've managed to come through my own losses because I've been so caught up in trying to understand grief in others. But it works both ways. I've had to grow more accepting of the craziness, pain, and pride of grief in myself in order to become an effective helping professional.

Understanding and making peace with personal losses, in my opinion, is the *sine qua non* of becoming a good grief counselor. We can hardly help those who are ashamed to weep if we are ashamed of our own tears. We can scarcely provide the reassurance of a calm response to people in sorrow if we ourselves are alarmed by intense emotion. We would lack the patience to see the client through the long process of hopeful progressions and painful regressions if we did not have the knowledge that our own wounds have required months and years for healing.

Nobody wants a therapist who presents himself or herself as being without vulnerability to suffering. People learn best from human beings. Not that we tell our clients about the losses in our lives; I don't believe this is usually an effective approach to grief counseling. Yet it is necessary to take our own losses seriously and not cling to the idea that we are not entitled to mourn because others have greater sorrows. Grief, when ignored or denied, can take its toll on counselors as well as clients. Facing one's own losses is part of how a person becomes comfortable enough to help others face loss.

THE GRIEVING PERSON'S FEAR

Grief is not a mental illness. It just feels that way sometimes. If a person had all the symptoms of grief but no loss experience which triggered the multitude of troublesome feelings and behaviors, that would be a different story. In that case, the person would probably need a full psychological and medical examination.

Sleeplessness, anxiety, fear, intense anger, a loss of interest in activity, a preoccupation with self and with sad feelings—the grieving person may think these all add up to "going crazy." Actually, each of these things can be a part of a normal grieving process. The client doesn't need to be told that "this is all very normal," which is something the inexperienced counselor is apt to say. What the client does need is a counselor who is knowledgeable about grief and therefore able comfortably to be empathic. To the one who is mourning, the material that he or she presents frequently is disturbing. A counselor who can listen calmly and reflectively while acknowledging powerful feelings is a counselor who will rarely find it necessary to reassure the client directly about the normalcy of the process.

A young woman, soft-spoken and poised, was talking with me. It had not yet been forty-eight hours since her brother's death by suicide. Theresa seemed older than her eighteen years. She was not crying, although an occasional wetness came across her eyes. With extraordinary rationality, Theresa outlined why she wanted to begin counseling. She spoke in a monotone, as if reporting an unnewsworthy item on a news program. She had wanted, she said, to overcome her self-destructiveness for a long time. She wanted to learn to take better care of herself as her brother's suicide was a reminder of her own suicidal thoughts in the past. Continuing in a calm voice, Theresa, who had just come from the funeral home, began to speak about her brother.

In the first several days the emotions are blunted and the impact of the loss is not fully experienced. Theresa's strange sense of presence is typical of very early grief. She was in a state of shock.

At first the grieving person is apt to move back and forth between a calm frame of mind and tearfulness. He or she feels bewildered and stunned, although often quite capable in manner. There is disbelief toward what has happened. On awakening in the middle of the night or in the morning, the person may wonder for a moment whether the loss really happened.

Gradually, usually within the first six to eight days, increased sadness begins. A depressed mood sets in, a mood that for many months will affect all that the person is, thinks, and does. (Parkes 1964) Everything is a reminder of the loss. It's as if a great cosmic conspiracy were in operation, inflicting pain. Other people's conversations, some of them wholly unrelated to the individual's circumstances, intensify the preoccupation with the loss. Songs on the radio play memories across hidden screens behind the eyes. Particular foods, strangers on the street, certain models of automobiles, items of clothing, a hospital or a restaurant or a school which the bereaved tries to avoid—all of these call out as tragic reminders.

If the person has lost a marriage partner or lover, he or she will notice every couple there is to see, hand in hand. Happy people will seem to be everywhere, intensifying the sense of isolation. If the person has had a miscarriage or an abortion, every pregnant woman pushing a grocery cart may be a reminder of what might have been. Every little child or tricycle along the street may speak to her. Preoccupation with the loss is especially intense in the earlier months. There is a tendency to avoid people, certain places and experiences. There is the fear that the once precious but now painful memories will be engulfing. There is a fear of being overwhelmed. At the same time, the grieving person may sort through objects associated with the loss—old photos, letters, or other keepsakes—over and over and over. That which once brought joy now brings sadness and sometimes comfort.

Preoccupation is not a sickness. It is part of the normal process of separation. The grieving person needn't put away any cherished thing until feeling ready to do so. Often, people give or throw away reminders of the loss much too soon and deeply regret it later on.

A widower may come home from work at night and open the door to the aroma of his wife's dinner cooking. Dinner is not on the stove, yet it was for many years. What is real is perceived as an unreality. More vivid to the widower's experience than the absence of his wife are all the years that went before. He is not mentally ill. He is going through what one-fourth to one-third of all bereaved persons experience, especially in the early weeks and months. He is having a hallucinatory experience. If you ask him, he will tell you that he knows his wife is dead. But he may also tell you that he hears her in the kitchen at night, having gotten out of bed for a midnight snack as she so often did. She is gone, but her memory in his mind is vividly present.

Although more all-encompassing in the early months, some remnants of preoccupation with a loss continue to emerge much later. A student of mine was convinced that he saw his father at a baseball game at Baltimore's Memorial Stadium more than a year after his father's death. He was greatly relieved to learn that such experiences are quite common to grief. Had this young man been a client in therapy, I would not have reassured him directly about the normalcy of his experience. Reassurance can close down feelings which are better explored in depth and released. Instead, I would have listened calmly to his story and then responded emphatically: "You miss so much those precious times that you shared with your dad." Also: "What things do you especially miss?" Responses along these lines will encourage the client to speak in detail of sad and sweet memories as well as feelings of longing.

A greatly distraught woman in her fifties came to her family physician complaining of having frightening hallucinations. She was afraid she was losing her mind. The woman's thirty-year-old daughter had taken her own life with sleeping pills six days before. Twice since the suicide the woman had seen her daughter come into the house, real as life. The first time she brought a phonograph record and played it for her mother before departing, as she had come, through the front door. The second time the daughter came as though she wished to speak to her mother, but she was unable to. Because this woman was highly upset by her hallucinatory experiences, her family wisely decided to take her to the family physician. Fortunately, he understood her grief. The woman was not mentally ill. She was suffering two of the most traumatic losses a person can endure: the loss of a child and the loss of a loved one by suicide.

Although profound loss does not usually precipitate mental illness, it can. (Parkes, 1964) A person with a previous history of mental illness or a history of mental illness in the family is especially vulnerable. Mental illness can produce hallucinations, as can a severe grief reaction. For this reason, if the hallucinations persist or are accompanied by a massive denial system or are found in a person with a personal or family history of mental illness, a psychological consultation is needed. Such a consultation is also recommended if the grieving person has a specific suicidal plan and the means within reach to complete that plan, or if the person presents symptoms of affective disorder, schizophrenia, or an organic mental disorder.

The vast and overwhelming majority of grieving persons, it must be emphasized, are not precipitated into mental illness. The widower hearing his wife in the kitchen and smelling her good suppers cooking is simply struggling with separation. He misses her terribly, that is all. For some years after my divorce I occasionally waved vigorously at strange men in automobiles on the freeways and streets of Baltimore. At first glance I had believed each of these men to be my former husband and I yearned to talk with him once more. Those whom we have loved or with whom we have unfinished business often remain with us in vivid ways.

When a significant loss has a person in its grip, a minimum of six months to one year is usually required for healing. Some intense aspects of the grieving process can be expected to continue into the second year. Resolution may not come until an even later time.

Grief is profoundly misunderstood in American society. A visitor in one of my college classes came because he heard we were talking about grief. He said he was worried about an uncle who was "not taking his marital separation well at all." The visitor was obviously troubled that his uncle talked almost constantly about his estranged wife and was "still tearful." When asked how long it had been, the well-meaning nephew replied, "Well, it has already been four months!" He had not yet learned that people aren't having emotional breakdowns just because mourning takes a long time. Unfortunately, a large gap exists between what the grieving person feels and what others seem to expect. The unrealistic expectations of others often lead the one who is mourning to feel anxious, self-doubtful, and afraid.

Well-intentioned friends, and even some professionals who ought to know better, will behave as if the grieving person has become overly self-centered. Too self-preoccupied and inward, they will say. Usually, this is an indication of the speaker's own uncomfortableness with loss and with troublesome but human emotions. Self-centeredness is almost always an essential aspect of separating from someone or something precious that has been lost. I'm not saying that returning to work as soon as possible is not a good idea. It is helpful for the grieving person to continue the activities of living, even if continued activity is difficult and painful in the beginning. However, the ability to concentrate is apt to be impaired for a period of many months.

Therapists should take care not to burden their clients with recommendations or expectations for recovery. The grieving person doesn't need to be made well, doesn't need suggestions or advice. As time goes on, it is all right for the counselor to ask the client such questions as, "What do you think would help you to feel better? To go to work? To spend more time with friends? Not to expect so much of yourself so soon?" What needs to be remembered, however, is that it is not the counselor's job to think of the right questions to ask or to suggest alternatives or make interpretations. Such counselor efforts to produce insight on the part of the client are usually counterproductive. The counselor's central task is simply to understand that a long process is required for healing and that empathic and reflective listening facilitates the process. As Carl Rogers has written, "To recognize that insight is an experience which is achieved, not an experience which can be imposed, is an important step in progress for the counselor." (Kirschenbaum 1979)

THINGS WILL NEVER BE THE SAME

Loss changes people and changes the course of their lives. It is not that one can never again be happy following an experience of loss. The reality is simply that one can never again be the same.

Once a family member has been lost, that loved person is no longer available to share joys and hurts, accomplishments and milestones. The milestones can be shared with others, but things are never the same. Someone always will be missing.

One of the most difficult realities of grief involves the loss of potential. A psychologist friend was talking with me about the death of his father. "My father was a truck driver and able to do very little for me financially," Sheldon said. "But when he died that possibility was never there again, the possibility that he could help me if I needed him."

When a person loses a part of his or her physical body, gives up a child for adoption, has an abortion, ends a marriage, or suffers the loss of a career, a whole world of potential comes to a halt. What must now be developed is an entirely new life, with new self-definitions. This is true as well of many other loss situations.

Human emotions cannot be ordered away from the arena like misbehaving fans at an athletic event. Although our grieving clients will not *always* believe that their lives have been permanently ruined, they do need the freedom to feel their feelings of ruin fully. After weeks or months they can go on.

In my own counseling work I have found that speaking the truth of the moment is a powerful therapeutic means of facilitating emotional release. By this I mean that the counselor speaks in a straight-talking way to the client, accurately reflecting the client's feelings, without being hesitant to use bold words. An example of speaking the truth would be a counselor response such as, "He's gone now and you know that you can never have the relationship with him that you so desperately wanted." This response uses the strong language of "gone," "never," and "desperately." When these words echo the client's own strong feelings, which are apt to have been minimized, often the client is enabled to experience emotional release. In addition, harsh realities straightforwardly spoken by the counselor often bring relief to the grieving person because someone has finally said the truth. As Rollo May (1969) has written, it is in the "naming of the demons" that the demons lose their power.

In attempting to restore the part of themselves that has come to ruin, people tend to glorify the past and to render the good and happy times larger than life. They remember the best qualities of a lost person, career, or experience. Counselors need to understand that people idealize in this way because it is a great comfort to them. Usually, the idealization phase of mourning will be resolved by the client in a gradual way as the counselor simply acknowledges the client's strong feelings as being genuine and real. A counselor response such as, "You feel that you had a very special relationship with your husband," goes much further in the therapeutic process than does trying to argue with the client that her perceptions are exaggerated. When her pain is less intense and she is less in need of justification, she will begin to remember (quite on her own) the human-sized dimensions of her husband and their marriage.

FEELINGS OF GUILT AND SELF-BLAME

Seven-year-old Matthew, whose five-year-old brother had died six months earlier, brought home a sentence completion schoolwork assignment. The first five words were the teacher's and the last five words were his. "The worst thing about me," Matthew wrote, in the awkward script of a second grader, "is that I make mistakes." It was strange to see a little guy, whose head didn't yet quite reach my waist, thinking thoughts an adult of any age might have.

"If only I had been wiser, chosen differently, acted differently, had better judgment," people say to themselves, the grown-up version of Matthew's words. "If only . . ." sentences are part of the vocabulary of mourning.

When a loved one dies, people seldom feel that they've done enough. Even when they've loved well and offered extraordinary sacrifices, still there is the feeling that what was given was not enough. Guilty feelings are almost inevitable in the presence of loss. Whatever the situation, people are apt to blame themselves.

While there is a genuine feeling of being blameworthy, usually the grieving person's thoughts are unrealistic. Men and women, almost as often as children, stretch their imaginations to believe that they are responsible for anticipating or preventing events which ordinary mortals could not possibly have prevented. Human mistakes are twisted into near criminal proportions; guilt is felt as if the person had intentionally brought harm to him or herself or to another, something that is rarely the case.

My doctor was like a priest to me during times when I felt guilty in a period of mourning. "If you had been able to act differently then, you would have acted differently," she would say. It took me a long time to realize, in my own experience of bereavement therapy, that it is simply not in our human power to play out our lives in perfect ways.

Usually, the client's guilt feelings need to be answered by the counselor. Yet if the counselor tries to comfort the client by reassuring too soon, the client will shut down his or her expression of guilty feelings. The client will then retain these thoughts and go away from the counselor thinking, "If you only knew the whole story, you'd know why I'm to blame." For this reason it is important for the counselor to hear a complete account of the client's guilt, to listen, acknowledge feelings, ask questions, and assure that the full story is told. By listening attentively for signals of unrealism in the events described, later on the counselor will know how to reply.

One of the resident physicians at the community hospital where I teach sought my advice concerning a recently widowed woman with profound feelings of guilt. The woman's husband had died of a heart attack within minutes after they had had sexual intercourse. She blamed herself for her husband's death. Remembering a supervisor in my training who had once explained to me how to help people separate realistic from unrealistic guilt, I gave the widow's physician a list of questions he should ask her: What makes her feel that she is to blame? How is it that she feels the decision for having intercourse was her decision rather than theirs together? Did the husband's heart specialist tell them that their normal sexual relations should cease entirely? If they were not medically cautioned, how could she have known what the consequences would be?

Once the full story has been heard, it is helpful for the counselor to ask, "How could you have known that? Are you expecting yourself to have known things that couldn't have been known? Are you tormenting yourself with thoughts of self-blame, as if the other person had no choice or responsibility at all for the events that happened?" These questions appropriately asked, one at a time and without prematurity, usually will enable the client increasingly to view events with more self-compassion.

The widow might say to her physician or counselor, "We shouldn't have been having sexual intercourse. The autopsy report showed that he had only a 40 percent blood supply to the heart." The helping professional can then reply, "But how could you have known that? Even the medical people didn't know it until after the autopsy."

Most of the time the grieving person's guilt is unrealistic. Only in situations of genuine negligence, involving direct responsibility, can guilt and self-blame be seen as realistic. If the person was driving an automobile that crashed, bringing death or permanent injury to another person, the driver's guilt could be realistic or unrealistic, depending on the circumstances. In the event of recklessness—driving far over the speed limit or driving under the influence of alcohol or other drugs—the driver's guilt would be realistic. Realistic guilt would also be produced by a person's accidentally killing or maiming a loved one or an innocent stranger with a firearm, or by leaving a child unattended as a result of which the child was victimized by a catastrophic fire, accident, or rape. At any time when the client's clearly negligent behavior has brought suffering or death to another person, feelings of remorse are almost unbearably bitter. The client may for a time massively deny that the event occurred as a way of surviving the assault of guilt which he or she would otherwise feel.

When either type of guilt is present, people sometimes become self-destructive in a host of ways in order to punish themselves for the event for which they feel responsible. Self-sabotage in love, work, or school, accident proneness, and drug or alcohol abuse are the most common means of self-punishment which I have observed. I have also seen profound weight gain or weight loss, spending sprees and reckless business deals. Suicidal behavior can also signal a problem with guilt.

With the presence of genuine culpability, regretful feelings are not transitory; they are fierce and abiding. Realistic guilt cries out for a counselor who believes in a loving God, a God who accepts human frailty and forgives the tragedies human beings bring upon themselves. While the entire counseling process is made richer by the counselor's having started from this faith position, a spiritually based counselor can be particularly helpful to the client who is struggling with realistic guilt. As was called for earlier, the counselor hears the whole story, responding empathically and clarifying the circumstances of self-blame. As the client shares excruciatingly painful feelings of remorse, the counselor listens respectfully, acknowledging these feelings, but most of all communicating a silent, caring presence.

In working with realistic guilt, it is good to establish whether the person believes in a forgiving God. If the client professes a belief in God, even a belief in a God who would judge and condemn but not forgive, the counselor can then ask why the client feels unworthy of forgiveness. Other appropriate questions are: Who is doing the punishing? Is it really God who would not forgive or is it that self-forgiveness is being withheld as a punishment? At some point the counselor might say, "It seems very hard for you to feel that God loves you and forgives you while you are not forgiving yourself."

PHYSICAL EXPRESSIONS OF LOSS

A wide range of marked physical changes can accompany an experience of loss. Not only through tears do we cry out pangs of grief. Under the stress of what has been unrecoverably lost, our bodies have more than a dozen ways of weeping with us.

Headaches, digestive disturbances, and aching limbs are the most common disturbances that people have expressed to me. Insomnia, irritability, restlessness, moodiness, and loss of appetite or increased appetite are also frequent complaints. Some people engage in frenzied activity. Others lose interest in activity. Muscle tension, fatigue, poor memory, and difficulty concentrating are also discomforts that can accompany grief. Some people have allergic reactions. Some have acute anxiety attacks, characterized by trembling hands, heart palpitations, dizziness, and shortness of breath. Some have physical symptoms resembling the illness of a loved one who has died. Many people experience tearfulness. Studies show that people in their thirties and younger show more physical symptoms in a process of mourning than do older people. (Clayton 1975; Maddison and Viola 1968)

Usually, the physical symptoms will diminish after the first three months of bereavement. If the symptoms persist or are particularly troubling to the client, the counselor can ask whether the client has considered seeing a physician. A medical examination can be valuable, especially for the person who has had a high number of intense life changes. As the 1979 *Surgeon General's Report* has stated, "The greater the number and intensity of changes in a subject's life over a certain period, the higher is his risk of undergoing a subsequent decrease in health status." (Levi 1979)

What I have found is that the therapeutic process itself is the best medicine for physical expressions of loss. The client rehearses the loss event, expressing troublesome feelings and receiving acknowledgement. Slowly, the physical symptoms show improvement.

ANGER AND BITTERNESS

While still in graduate school, I was working as a chaplain intern at a college in North Carolina, counseling young people in crisis situations. Eighteen-year-old Brian walked through my door for his first counseling session with his arm curled around a motorcycle helmet. He looked something like an overly thin high school football player coming into the locker room after taking a beating on the field. We talked for nearly two hours, but I was unable to get out of him whatever was the story of his battered spirits. The next day I was called to the hospital emergency room by Brian's parents. In an apparent period of depression, Brian had shot himself in the abdomen with a shotgun. His action could have been a genuine accident, but it probably wasn't.

By the time I drove across town, he was in surgery. I met the parents in a waiting area outside the operating room. We sat in a row on a bench with soft padding, Brian's father and I on either side of his mother. I thought I had come to console them, but their parental reaction was not what I expected. While it was still uncertain whether the young man would survive, his mother repeated several times an angry statement that at the time was startling to me. "He has always caused us trouble, and now he has done it again! How can he do this to us?" She began angrily to recite virtually every worry Brian had given them in eighteen years. Meanwhile, Brian's father brought forth no argument to his wife's anger. He simply sat with his eyes blankly fixed on the sterile white wall in front of us.

I remember feeling rather judgmental and superior to these bewildered parents. "I can't believe it," I thought to myself. "Their only son may be dying on the operating table and they're angry at him!" I was unaware, then, of the normalcy of such feelings of fury.

Whenever life puts human beings against a wall for whatever reason, I now understand, great anger is usually generated. Some people, like Brian's parents, are immediately angry in the face of loss or impending loss. Their feelings focus quickly on the most obvious cause of their anger. Other persons are more apt to express a generalized fury, the buckshot effect of a wide array of angry feelings expressed toward medical people, relatives, clergy, funeral directors, and the like. Still others are preoccupied with other worrisome emotions in the early months of grief or are unaware of the angry feelings held tightly within themselves.

No matter how much we may wish it not to be so, anger is unavoidable in life, particularly in bereavement. One of the few times that anger isn't an important aspect of the mourning process is when an elderly loved one dies, having lived a full and happy life and died a dignified death. Sometimes grief on such an occasion is free of regret and emotional turmoil. One may be very sad and miss the loved person; yet unless the person was a marriage partner or someone on whom there was great dependency, it's the kind of loss that seems just and fair.

People feel angry when an untimely crisis interrupts their living and dreaming. I remember a young doctor who became pregnant with an IUD in place. "With a ninety-seven percent chance of not getting pregnant," she protested, "why should I be one of the women for whom the contraceptive didn't work?" As commonly happens, Dr. Carr's anger at having to choose between her residency and her pregnancy spun off in other directions. "If more women were doctors and scientists," she raged, "we'd have reliable contraceptives for men! Why do women have to take all the risks?"

Dr. Carr was in love with the man by whom she was pregnant but neither of them wanted to be married. Her religious beliefs made it very difficult for her to decide whether to seek an abortion. She felt she could not continue her medical training, without ridicule, were she to continue the pregnancy and not to marry. Even should she marry, the completion of her residency would have to be postponed. In this multiple-bind situation, it is understandable that Dr. Carr was engulfed in a sea of anger and sought the help of a professional counselor.

Had I been in the role of Dr. Carr's counselor, I would have listened to her fury and helped her to ventilate it by reflecting back her feelings. It would be important to show no alarm or judgment over the intensity of her emotion; this would be accomplished by matching my words, as counselor, to the intensity of her verbal and nonverbal expressions. I would use the strong words of "fury," "rage," and "unfairness" that I was hearing from her. It would concern me not to minimize her experience by understating either her anger or the gravity of her situation. I would keep my own value system out of Dr. Carr's decision-making process or refer her elsewhere, if I found that I needed her to behave in accordance with my own moral values. It is of critical importance, in working with the client who is already apt to be fantasizing others' condemnation, for the counselor not to contribute to the sense of condemnation.

In working with any client who is struggling with anger, one need not be surprised if the client's anger at times turns toward the counselor. Anger expressions directed toward counselors are best handled by the counselor's listening, asking questions of clarification, and reflecting back the client's angry feelings. Counselor defensiveness only causes the client to feel that his or her feelings are not being heard or that the counselor isn't capable of receiving anger. Apologies by the counselor, particularly those spoken before the anger is fully expressed, rob the client of ventilating the anger and examining it. Both defensive responses and apologies obstruct the transference material which can emerge when anger is directed toward the therapist.

Sometimes the anger of the grieving person so predominates the mourning process that outlets are needed other than talking about the anger to the counselor. People who exhibit homicidal ideations, who show suicidal or other self-destructive behavior, or who report being consumed by anger have demonstrated to me the therapeutic value of tears, physical activity, and vivid fantasy.

Many clients will express in therapy a deep yearning to be able to weep. Well-meaning counselors will often reply, "Go ahead and let yourself cry," which is the second least helpful of all things to say, the least helpful being telling the client that such a thing would be foolish. Nothing dries up tear ducts faster than a client's trying to produce them on command or request. It is better that the counselor reflect the client's own sentiments: "You wish so much that you could weep all of this sorrow and anger out of your system," or "You're crying and hurting inside and you yearn to have the release of crying outwardly, too." Another possible response would be the reply that Carl Rogers in one of his films (American Personnel and Guidance Association 1977) gave to a man struggling with leukemia: "If you were to cry, what would be some of the themes of that crying?" In general, the most effective counselor behavior toward the liberation of tears is empathic responsiveness, genuineness, patience, and the straightforward speaking that was earlier described.

A significant number of persons working through anger and other phases of a grieving process have described to me the value of physical activity. Lawn and garden work, individual and group athletic activity, carpentry or house cleaning, pillow beating, even yelling and screaming have been recounted as helpful. I will not usually directly recommend that a client pursue a physical activity. When the client says, "I wish I could do something to get this rage out of my being," I will ask what the person has done in the past in order to work out feelings of fury. I might inquire whether any particular physical activity has been a help in the past. Does the client think it might now be a help to try again the activity that previously brought release? Later on, when the person returns to tell of the physical activity, it is useful to listen attentively, ask questions, and acknowledge the feelings of release or continued frustration.

Vivid fantasy is also a potentially effective means of dissipating powerful emotion. A woman with whom I worked on only one occasion provides an example of the use of vivid fantasy in working through feelings of protest and anger. Louise was an attractive woman in her middle forties whose marriage of twenty-five years was falling apart and who had just learned that their teenage daughter was taking narcotics. "All my life I've been a good Catholic," she cried. "No birth control. Five children lined up in a row. I never complained, I just kept having children. And I never missed church or confession." She was weeping bitterly. "I've always been good; I've worked at being good. Now look what's happening! Everything is falling apart!"

Louise's crisis was a spiritual one, the kind of assault on one's inner sense of fairness that yanks away all illusions. Louise was asking from the core of her inner self whether it matters at all how hard a person tries to live a good and decent life. She felt betrayed, she said, not merely by the Church's teachings. Somehow she felt betrayed by God as well.

Most people will ask, "Why me?" when suffering through a crisis, but for Louise there was also a direct contest with God. She was angry at God that all her efforts to be a good person did not protect her from suffering serious marriage and family problems.

Initially, it was necessary for me to hear the full account of the problems at home which Louise was experiencing and to respond with accurate empathy. Later on, I asked Louise if she thought that she could tell God, speaking aloud in my presence, her feelings of anger.

"It just isn't fair," she said. "I've been loyal to You for forty-seven years!" Her voice grew louder and louder. "We've raised every child in the Church and I gave everything I had to those children and my husband. How can we be having all these problems now? I tried everything I knew to keep our family together!"

When she seemed to have finished her protest, I asked Louise if she thought that she could pretend that she was God, answering Louise. Cooperating with the fantasy, I began, "God, Louise is very upset. She has been weeping for thirty minutes now, and she's furious at You. What do You have to say to her?"

God, not having the problem with words that mortals do, even in this fantasy exercise had the ability to sum up everything in a single, powerful sentence. "Louise," God said, as spoken by Louise, "I want you to seize your freedom!"

I was deeply touched by these words. I had hoped that somewhere in this woman's experience she had learned of an accepting God who would not condemn her now. I asked Louise if she could answer what God had just spoken.

"I know, God," she said. "I've never been able to speak my real feelings before, especially feelings that I thought weren't nice. I know You're telling me that You can accept my anger. That You want me to be free from all these guilty feelings I have, that You never expected me not to complain in twenty-five years of marriage, that maybe I'd have been better off if years ago I had complained."

The experience with Louise was a powerful one for me. Whatever else the reality of God is about, I remember thinking, it certainly is all about receiving acceptance and seizing our freedom.

Anger and bitterness can be a good sign. These strong emotions often signal that the healing process is well underway. The phases of mourning previously discussed—shock, fear, preoccupation, feelings of ruin, a long period of depression, idealization, guilt, and physical symptoms—all represent highly inward emotional experiences. Once the person is openly angry, many feelings are projected outwardly. Whether the anger is displaced or directed at the one who died or directed toward God, still there is the sense that the bereaved person is mobilizing his or her energy once again. The grieving person is fighting for life and that's a good sign.

WHAT ONE GETS IS WHAT ONE RESISTS

That people put up a resistance to feelings and thoughts associated with a loss is understandable. Grief is a very painful process.

Generally, the more fully a person mourns in the early months, the more relief the person will feel as time goes on. It still isn't easy. Almost without exception, whenever I've given a public lecture on this subject, someone in the audience has asked, "Isn't there any way to make the process less painful?" Or, "Why can't there be a quicker way to recover than having to grieve like this?" I always reply that I wish there were another way.

A few people are able massively and successfully to deny their loss experiences. They give little or no apparent evidence of mourning. The counselor respects the highly developed defensive systems of these persons. Upon hearing a clear and consistent message that the person cannot handle an exploration of the loss event and does not want to explore it, the counselor neither intrudes nor confronts nor challenges the denial system.

For most people, mourning remains a process that must be gone through. Most do not have denial mechanisms so thoroughgoing as to be able to escape themselves. It simply isn't possible for these men and women to go around their grief without jeopardizing themselves in love and work, which are the cornerstones of functionality and of a satisfying life. Hurtful, angry, or guilty feelings which these persons try to deny stay with them for years and years. If they resist what they feel, they continue to have the troublesome feelings for their entire lives. For these persons it is better to learn how to *be* their feelings, to surrender to them at times with trusted significant others.

Water, as it freezes and the molecules expand, has the power to burst steel pipes wide open. Likewise, frozen emotions—feelings that are resisted or denied—assume a power out of proportion to their original nature.

The counselor works with resistance in grief counseling just as he or she works with resistance in any other form of counseling. It must be remembered that resistance is not a conscious behavior, for the most part; hence, confrontation and interpretation from the therapist are neither appropriate nor effective. In fact, confrontation and interpretation can serve to intensify the client's resistance.

What is appropriate and effective is patience and compassion, combined with skillful and empathic listening and responding.

CUE POINTS FOR EVALUATING THE HEALING PROCESS

The healing process does not follow an even course. There are progressions and regressions and there is never a definite date when the grief work is finished. The grieving person will have good days, even weeks or months, only to experience again periods of great difficulty. The person will wonder at times if he or she will ever get better. For example, anniversary reactions and holiday unhappiness, particularly keen in the first year, may go on for years.

Yet there are sure clear signs that a person is healing. Usually, grief and healing are one and the same process. Periodic bouts with depression, yearning, loneliness, guilt, fear, anxiety, or anger are part of what is necessary to healing. We know that healing is taking place because the person is passing from one phase of grief to another.

The stages of grief are seldom distinct and sequential. Features of one phase often persist into the next. (Parkes 1970) Still, the fact that one's grieving process is fluid and multidimensional signals healing. Unless the person lingers many months in a single phase, the healing process is probably underway. The counselor will become aware, as will the client, that the disquietude of grief is interspersed with increasingly longer periods of calm.

The ability to continue one's work, the ability to sustain good friendships and working relations with others, the ability to maintain self-care habits, the ability to safeguard oneself from harm—all of these are positive indicators of personal functioning and of the healing process. They are cue points for evaluating the client's grieving process.

Everybody has some difficulty with personal functioning following a significant loss. Not until considerable time passes do most find their "thinking sharper, judgment more reliable, concentration improved, view of the world less self-preoccupied." (Colgrove, Bloomfield, and McWilliams 1976)

Dorothy, a nurse at one of the hospitals where I trained, was having a difficult time accepting her divorce. Dorothy and Paul had tried everything, it seemed, in attempting to resolve the personality conflicts between them. They had pleaded, argued, tried temporary separations, and gone for marriage counseling. Each partner continued to blame the other. Each behaved as if someday the other partner would change and a resolution would come about. Since neither Dorothy nor Paul was prepared to give up the anger that was felt, many poisonous verbal exchanges continued to pass between them.

One day in the nursing station I noticed that Dorothy wasn't wearing her wedding band. Paul and Dorothy were planning a final separation within a few months. I wondered aloud what the missing wedding band was saying.

"I've decided not to wear the ring anymore," she said, comfortable with talking about it. "My wedding band is at the jewelry store. I decided to have the diamonds taken out and made into a necklace as a remembrance of the good times. I don't want to be married to Paul, but I also don't want five years of my life to be thrown away."

An important transition had taken place. Dorothy's and Paul's anger had finally run its course. Keeping the anger alive, she said, was a way of denying the inevitability of their separation. They had agreed now, Dorothy proudly announced, to work together on selling the house and accepting the end of their marital relationship. The whole thing would still be painful, she said, but she wanted to be able to separate from Paul without denying that anything good had ever existed between them.

When people are able to take along reminders of the good times while facing the full reality of a loss, another cue point of healing can be said to be present. The progress is slow, but symbols of the transition begin to emerge.

"It used to be," said one woman grieving the death of her middle son, "that whenever I'd catch myself in repose, I'd be aware that I wasn't happy. Every time I sat still, was alone with myself, or wasn't thinking about anything in particular, sorrow is what I would feel. Somewhere along the way there has been a change. I'm no longer feeling that ever-present sorrow. I feel comfortable again in moments of repose. Sometimes I feel very happy."

Enjoying laughter, choosing more colorful clothes, paying more attention to events in the news, talking about the loss in a normal conversational tone, making plans for the future, noticing and attending to things that need repair, enjoying things of beauty, experiencing one's moods as less fluctuating and more predictable—each of these things, too, can symbolize healing and an increasing attachment to life.

As people heal, a reevaluation process begins. Learning and growing take place around one's beliefs and attitudes, personal goals, feelings toward self, relationships with family and friends. When people are learning from the struggle, every new learning signifies healing.

Lindemann studied grief and grieving people for more than twenty years, beginning with the 1942 Coconut Grove fire, in which 499 people perished. What "grief work" entails, according to Lindemann (1976, p. 199), is finding a way to replace "that which seems at first irreplaceable." People look within themselves and look to others—reviewing, scrutinizing, and rearranging their lives—in an effort to replace the irreplaceable.

At the same time that the irreplaceable can never be replaced, people find that it can be replaced. As Lindemann (1976, p. 198) found, in the case of a lost loved one, the lost person is not completely absent because what he or she had to give remains an ongoing part of the survivor's life experience. The loved person assumes a new life even though physically dead.

FROM OUT OF THE ASHES

When a part of one's self has been lost—through surgery, an illness, an accident, an act of assault, the loss of a dream, or the loss of a loved one through death or divorce—the person one is, and is capable of becoming must be resurrected in new form. Even if an individual wished to remain the person he or she previously was, it simply is not possible. A life may be permanently damaged by the dispossession that bereavement entails. No one stays the same.

Many people find that the spiritual dimension in their lives enables them to construct a meaning from the suffering they endure. It does not come easily. Grieving people are reluctant to gain from their losses a life that is spiritually and emotionally richer than the life before. Especially early in grief, one of the common ways we humans protest the sorrow that catches us in its web is to resist growing and learning from it. Following a period of resistance that may last for weeks, months, or years, however, the person with the spiritual value that compels him or her to find meaning in sorrow is the one who will prevail. As the grieving person learns from the loss something of value that benefits self and others, the loss is transformed. An event that takes away something precious becomes an event that provides something new.

A bereaved mother, Mary Phelps Seidel (1981), illustrates the tremendous power of the will to impart meaning in her poem which she dedicated to her lost son. The poem is entitled "For Andrew":

> *Near and far away son*
> *Your coming and leaving*
> *Has made much of life*
> *Happen to me—*
> *Pitched me headlong*
> *Out of a complacent spirit*
> *Into a tortuous journey*
> *To my center.*
> *I know now*
> *What I am about; and*
> *I name my colors*
> *By their own names.*
> *While I sorrow*
> *In your absence*
> *There is gratefulness*
> *For your once presence*
> *With me.*
> *But for you,*
> *I might not have struggled*
> *And birthed*
> *Myself.*

What is necessary for the completion of the healing process is something no person can do for another, no counselor can do for a client. Only the grieving person can search out, for himself or herself, the answers concerning the changed life and self that will emerge. To be sure, the counselor can be an invaluable partner in the search—but not by advising or recommending or teaching or providing insight or interpretations. The counselor becomes a partner in the search simply by valuing the client as a person, trusting the client's own inner processes and timing, and being compassionately present.

REFERENCES

American Personnel and Guidance Association. Two films: *Carl Rogers Counsels an Individual on Hurt and Anger* and *Carl Rogers Counsels an Individual: The Right to Be Desperate,* 1977.

Clayton, P. J. "The Effect of Living Alone on Bereavement Symptoms," *American Journal of Psychiatry,* 132, February 1975, 133–137.

Clayton, P. J., L. Desmarias, and G. Winokur, "A Study of Normal Bereavement." *American Journal of Psychiatry,* August 1968, 168–78.

Colgrove, M., H. Bloomfield, and P. McWilliams. *How to Survive the Loss of a Love.* New York: Leo Press, 1976.

Kirschenbaum, H. *On Becoming Carl Rogers.* New York: Delacorte Press, 1979.

Levi, L. "Psychosocial Factors in Preventive Medicine." In *The Surgeon General's Report on Health Promotion and Disease Prevention.* Washington, D.C.: U.S. Government Printing Office, DHEW Publication No. PHS 79-55071A, 1979.

Lindemann, E. "Grief and Grief Management: Some Reflections," *The Journal of Pastoral Care,* September 1976.

Maddison, P., and A. Viola. "The Health of Widows in the Year Following Bereavement," *Journal of Psychosomatic Research,* 1968, pp. 297–306.

May, R. *Love and Will.* New York: Norton, 1969

Oxford English Dictionary. Oxford: Clarendon Press, 1933, I, 810–11, and VIII, 217–18.

Parkes, C. M. "Recent Bereavement as a Cause of Mental Illness," *British Journal of Psychiatry,* March 1964, 198–204.

———. "The First Year of Bereavement," *Psychiatry,* November 1970, 444–67.

Seidel, M. P. "For Andrew," *The Compassionate Friends Newsletter,* Baltimore Chapter, February 1981.

RECOMMENDED READINGS

Barker, Rodney. *Hiroshima Maidens.* New York: Viking Penguin, 1985.

Brownstein, Karen. *Brainstorm.* New York: Macmillan, 1980.

Caine, Lynn. *Widow.* New York: Morrow, 1974.

Goldberg, Jane. *Psychotherapeutic Treatment of Cancer Patients.* New York: Free Press, 1981.

Guest, Judith. *Ordinary People.* New York: Viking, 1976.

Jackson, Edgar. *Telling a Child About Death.* New York: Channel Press, 1965.

Kübler-Ross, Elisabeth. *On Death and Dying.* New York: Macmillan, 1969.

———. *Death: The Final Stage of Growth.* Englewood Cliffs, N.J.: Prentice Hall, 1975.

Kushner, Harold S. *When Bad Things Happen to Good People.* New York: Schocken Books, 1981.

Lindemann, Erich. *Beyond Grief.* New York: Jason Aronson, 1979.

Pincus, Lily. *Death and the Family*. New York: Pantheon Books, 1974.

Rubin, Theodore Isaac. *The Angry Book*. New York: Macmillan, 1969.

Saldana, Theresa. *Beyond Survival*. New York: Bantam, 1986.

Schiff, Harriet S. *The Bereaved Parent*. New York: Crown, 1977.

Schneidman, Edwin. *Death: Current Perspectives*. Palo Alto, California: Mayfield Publishing Company, 1980.

Stearns, Ann Kaiser. *Coming Back—Rebuilding Life After Crisis and Loss*. New York: Random House, 1988.

CHAPTER FOURTEEN

Counseling with the Recovering Alcoholic

JOSEPH W. CIARROCHHI, PH.D.

Pastoral counselors frequently show an enthusiasm for helping alcoholics which is often lacking in medical and mental health professionals. Professionals are perhaps discouraged by the generally low recovery rates among alcoholics, while pastoral counselors are perhaps attracted to suffering individuals who openly admit their illness is partly spiritual. In any event, a rich tradition of pastoral counselors helping alcoholics has evolved. The early discussions of the Jesuit theologian John Ford with Bill W., cofounder of Alcoholics Anonymous (AA), and the acclaimed work of Father Joseph Martin and Rev. Vernon Johnson attest to that ongoing involvement.

The field of alcohol studies, however, is experiencing a new climate, especially with regard to understanding treatment of alcoholism. The advent of controlled research, the experience of self-help groups such as AA, and the commitment of more carefully prepared clinicians have all contributed to this new climate. Just as the suffering alcoholic is harmed by unenlightened professionals, it would be equally harmful for pastoral counselors to ignore modern developments in this field. Ironically, the pastoral minister by virtue of his or her holistic training, is probably best prepared to assimilate this new information and to keep in perspective all aspects of this complicated illness.

In this spirit, therefore, the present chapter presents a developmental overview of the recovery process. This brief presentation can only highlight the more common issues relating to alcoholism recovery. Readers requiring further information are encouraged to consult the list of recommended readings at the end of this chapter. A developmental approach is a most helpful model to understand the recovery process, an approach which is gaining increasing popularity in alcoholism treatment as well as in other counseling fields (see Chapters 8 and 12). In this approach three separate, but not always distinguishable, phases occur. The first stage involves "de-compulsifying" the impulse to drink and focuses primarily on physical recovery. The second stage deals primarily with many of the psychological and life problems which make the effects of alcohol so seductive. The third stage integrates the person's identity as an alcoholic with an acceptable vision of the meaning of life, with an emphasis on the spiritual meaning. As with all developmental models, considerable overlap occurs. The movement from one phase to another does not preclude the resurrection of issues dealt with in an earlier stage, nor does it preclude major issues from advanced stages protruding into an earlier one. Nevertheless, a developmental model conveniently fits the traditional AA understanding of alcoholism as a threefold illness—physical, psychological and spiritual—without doing too much violence to the scientific data.

The scope of this chapter includes only recovery and will not dwell on intervention, the important but complicated process of leading the alcoholic to seek treatment. Intervention requires technical expertise and should be carried out only after careful preparation with alcoholism professionals. (Ciarrochhi and Burns 1982; Johnson 1973) Since so much is at stake, it is best not to risk a poorly planned intervention, which only serves to make the alcoholic more resistant to treatment.

PRELIMINARY OBSERVATIONS

Perhaps the major insight that is provided by treatment outcome studies is downplaying sobriety as the sole criterion for alcoholic recovery. These studies confirm that sober, recovering alcoholics may continue to function quite poorly in their jobs, as members of families, and in overall psychological well-being. For example, the suicide expectancy of the recovering alcoholic as late as one year in sobriety is quite high. *Of all alcoholics who die in the first year of sobriety, nearly 20 percent are from suicide*. Certainly, this illness has an impact which extends far beyond mere not-drinking. As is its custom, AA has understood at the experiential level what scientists later unveil. The fellowship has traditionally used phrases such as "dry drunk" syndrome and "white knuckle" sobriety to describe sober alcoholics who do not have "quality" sobriety.

Given the complexity of recovery, what role then is the pastoral counselor best suited for? In my opinion two situations may present themselves. The first is the alcoholic who is bonded to AA yet still is experiencing difficulty and desires help. The role here is a supportive one which reinforces and elaborates upon the essential insights of AA. Although this role may be subsidiary, it is not subservient. AA, after all, emphasizes that it is a fellowship and not a treatment program. The psychological and spiritual expertise of the counselor is capable of providing alternative coping skills not necessarily found in the fellowship.

A second condition occurs for alcoholics in recovery who are not bonded to AA. Despite my own bias that AA is the most helpful single resource available to the alcoholic, many are unable to bond to AA. What little research is available suggests that dropout rates are high. (Miller 1980) My own strategy during the course of treatment is periodically to invite the alcoholic to attempt AA again, usually relating some current struggle in his life to the potential support AA would provide. When this fails, the pastoral counselor emerges as the primary support, a situation which creates special demands on the counselor, as well as the need for discernment as to his or her ability to provide such support.

Finally, counselor attitudes are critical in the helping relationship. Foremost is an understanding of the disease model of alcoholism. The alcoholic will respond, generally negatively, to even the most subtle judgmental inferences from the counselor. These moralistic inferences will weigh heavily, especially since they emanate from a person vested with spiritual authority. The communication of such attitudes is countertherapeutic—reinforcing guilt and shame, which in turn make denial even more attractive to the alcoholic. Proper counselor attitude also entails a willingness to remind the alcoholic continually, throughout the process, of the disease nature of the condition. Negatively, it means reining in one's propensity to draw moral lessons. Positively, it means continually reminding the alcoholic that the disastrous behavioral and spiritual impairment he or she suffers is the consequence of an illness and not a moral choice. There will be plenty of time in the advanced stages of recovery to reflect leisurely upon the issue of ethical responsibility.

THE STAGES OF RECOVERY

Early Stage

The two central issues here are "de-compulsifying" drinking behavior and the body's physical restoration.

Physical Recovery. Since few therapists have medical backgrounds, we need to educate ourselves continually in this area in order to understand the phenomena of the early stages. Suffice it to say that alcohol can harm virtually every major organ system in the body. As the counseling relationship begins, referral to a physician knowledgeable about alcoholism is essential for many reasons. First, the withdrawal process itself often presents a medical emergency. Client and counselor may be ignorant of medical conditions that would be exacerbated by abrupt withdrawal from alcohol. Certain devastating neurological conditions common to alcoholics may be averted by prompt treatment, for example, thiamine injections to prevent Wernicke's encephalopathy. Heavy drinkers may experience seizures in withdrawal, and those who experience delirium tremens (DT's) present the most serious risk, in that 15 percent will die despite the most advanced medical treatment.

Beyond the necessity of primary health care, however, a knowledgeable physician can be extremely helpful in the therapeutic process. The physician can correlate a variety of vague physical ailments with excessive alcohol intake. This provides the counselor with valuable information which can be used to point out the disease aspects of alcoholism, and, if necessary, to confront the alcoholic during periods of complacency or denial. Optimally, with the client's permission, the pastoral counselor would consult with the physician to learn the extent of the particular client's physical involvement. The counselor's input is also important medically because alcoholics typically minimize the amounts of alcohol consumed when speaking with their physicians. If physicians are not alerted they frequently prescribe drugs that permit cross-addiction and impede recovery.

The natural bodily restoration is a lengthy process lasting up to two years. You will be reminded of the slow recovery from illnesses such as hepatitis, mononucleosis, or pneumonia. In early recovery the alcoholic is rather easily fatigued, and sleep patterns will fluctuate dramatically for at least a year. Alcohol dramatically alters sleep physiology since brain restoration is slow, and occasionally this sleeplessness tempts the alcoholic to drink or take a sedative.

Extended alcohol use also severely impairs cognitive functioning. It may actually alter the structure of the brain, but more commonly it results in measurable intellectual deficits. This impairment is not limited to periods of intoxication but constitutes chronic brain damage. Neuropsychological methods of assessing brain damage have become so sophisticated that they can now document significant damage related to even nonalcoholic social drinking. The alcoholic's brain takes about thirty to sixty days to regain some measure of prealcoholic functioning. Recovery of cognitive functions may not be total but does continue for several years. From a practical standpoint, therefore, the pastoral counselor should attempt little in the nature of insight-oriented therapy for the first couple of months. The alcoholic's short-term memory is often poor, so elaborate interpretations are lost. The ability to deal with abstractions is typically impaired, rendering new learning programs difficult. The best counseling strategy at this point is to concentrate on the day-to-day struggle of staying sober, focusing on situations to avoid and resources that are supportive.

Psychological Recovery. The primary work of the alcoholic here is to learn the "triggers" to the alcoholic behavior. To use the language of social learning theory, it means discovering the antecedents of drinking. The early months of sobriety are a natural laboratory wherein client and counselor together can map out automatic psychological responses to stress. The pastoral counselor's major task here is to assess the client's vulnerable situations. During these early months the obsessive nature of the illness is usually strongest, generating a continual flow of thoughts centering around drinking. However, some alcoholics report never experiencing this, and many claim that the obsessions decay considerably as sobriety continues. Further encouragement may be found from empirical studies which suggest that only about 11 percent of alcoholics who relapse do so as a result of craving for alcohol. (Marlatt 1978)

The model that I have found to be most useful is the relapse prevention model for addictions developed by Professor Alan Marlatt and his co-workers at the University of Washington. (Cummings, Gordon, and Marlatt 1980) It provides a useful framework for understanding why alcoholics relapse, and at the same time it provides a framework for assessing the client's high-risk situations. According to their research two major categories account for most relapses. The first includes intrapersonal/environmental determinants. Within this category the following situations account for most relapses: (1) negative emotional states, such as anger, depression, anxiety, not related to interpersonal situations (38 percent); (2) urges and temptations (11 percent); and, (3) testing personal control, that is, experimenting with whether or not one can "handle" alcohol (9 percent). The second category accounting for relapse involves interpersonal determinants. Within this category two situations account for most relapses: (1) interpersonal conflict, such as disagreements and negative confrontation (18 percent); and (2) social pressure, that is, pressure from others to take a drink (18 percent). The rank order, therefore, of situations most problematic to recovering alcoholics is (1) negative emotional states, (2) interpersonal conflict, and (3) social pressure.

For this information to be useful the pastoral counselor must first assess high-risk situations for the alcoholic and, second, devise alternative strategies for helping the alcoholic cope with the high-risk situations. To assess such situations, it is my practice with outpatients for the first few weeks to give homework assignments such as daily monitoring of negative emotional states and the situations that trigger them. A practice of our inpatient program is to have clients turn in to their therapist a daily significant event. Another standard practice among alcoholism counselors is to assign the client to write an autobiography detailing important psychological events beginning with earliest childhood memories. The most important assignment involves the client's writing a comprehensive drinking history, starting from the earliest recollections until the present. The client is instructed to recall the emotional correlates of his or her drinking as well as times, places, and amounts of alcohol consumed. This latter request may seem implausible but alcohol memories are central to the alcoholic, and their capacity for recall of this material is truly phenomenal. At first the drinking history may be quite sparse and this merely indicates denial is still operating. The usual custom is to return it to the client and ask him or her to try harder. All these data, taken together, will allow the counselor to determine high-risk situations empirically rather than on the basis of intuition alone.

Once deficiencies and high-risk situations have been assessed, a number of techniques are excellent resources at this point. For example, role-playing or assertiveness training provides methods for dealing with such issues as interpersonal conflict or social skill in refusing a drink, both issues that are strongly related to relapse. Relaxation techniques as well as meditation are useful tools for dealing with anxiety and sleep disturbance.

Dealing with negative emotional states is tricky because of the confusing clinical picture alcoholism presents. For example, in the state of alcoholic drinking and during the period immediately following detoxification and withdrawal, the alcoholic presents a behavioral pattern identical to clinical depression. Indeed, because the syndromes are so similar, psychiatrists often prescribe antidepressants to drinking alcoholics who are not forthright about their alcohol use. Depression, then, is most common for a month or two after withdrawal. In most cases gradual mood improvement occurs so further intervention is not warranted. Some notable exceptions exist, however. As the case history below will indicate, mood disorders such as major depression and bipolar affective disorders (manic-depression) are commonly hidden in alcoholism. These individuals have self-medicated their mental disorder through alcohol. The estimates for alcoholism developing from manic-depression go as high as 20 percent while as many as 10 percent of all alcoholics may suffer from a major mood disorder. Excellent sources for identifying mood disorders are the most recent *Diagnostic and Statistical Manual of Mental Disorders* (DSM-III) as well as Nathan Kline's *From Sad to Glad* (Kline, 1981).

A good rule of thumb for dealing with negative emotional states is to refer for evaluation any alcoholic who continues to present a picture of clinical depression after four or five months of sobriety. To help your assessment of this condition, it is a good idea to administer the Beck Depression Inventory (Burns 1980) on a weekly basis until the client consistently scores in the nondepressed range. The same rule applies for severe anxiety, phobias, or unusual thought processes which do not show gradual improvement. Suicidal clients, of course, should be referred immediately.

Spiritual Recovery. Alcoholics with spiritual values, in my experience, tend to react in one of two ways during early recovery. One response entails small tentative steps toward reconciliation with formal religious practice. The very fact that they have approached a pastoral counselor may be part of that process. For these individuals sobriety encompasses reconciliation with church or synagogue. It may include a return to sacramental life and/or liturgical services. They seem to have a spirit of wanting to start over, to wipe the slate clean. You may hear such statements as, "I have started to pray again." Such persons are best helped by quiet encouragement and by minimizing moral judgments. Coming to terms with one's behavior during the active alcoholic phase is a lifetime struggle, but probably most acute during early sobriety. The religious alcoholic needs to hear two messages simultaneously: (1) God has a healing, loving, forgiving nature, and (2) although alcoholism as an illness has spiritual consequences, as an illness it has no spiritual origins.

A second response style is for the alcoholic to experience extreme alienation from God and religion. Some will claim they have lost their faith. Although a genuine crisis of faith is possible here, generally this reaction is a temporary defense against dealing with the issues of shame and guilt from drinking periods. Since these clients find it necessary to put questions of faith on hold, the counselor should reciprocate by not forcing the issue until sobriety has taken hold.

Middle Stage

In this stage physical recovery recedes in importance, psychological recovery is crucial, and spiritual recovery unfolds in new ways. The central feature of this stage is the sense of the honeymoon being over. Without the comfort of alcohol the exhilaration of sobriety fades and the alcoholic faces his or her primary life struggles.

Physical Recovery. Assuming no drinking has occurred, the recovery period is marked by continual physical recovery. From time to time fatigue and sleep disturbance will occur, but significantly less so than during the early stage. For those whose physical damage from alcohol is chronic, the very condition may be brought up periodically by the counselor to keep the disease aspect of the condition in focus. The client should be encouraged to have more frequent medical evaluations, even if he feels well, to deal with residual effects. He must identify himself to physicians and medical personnel as an alcoholic. His chemical dependency, for instance, often results in his having greater tolerance for anesthetics and thus requiring larger than normal dosages. This tolerance may complicate even simple procedures such as dental work. Any reluctance to share his alcoholic identity may be used therapeutically by the counselor to discuss issues relating to denial of the illness.

Psychological Recovery. This stage frequently generates crisis in the sense in which developmental psychology uses the term, that is, as a critical decision period for life goals. Now that the brain is detoxified and insight has returned, the alcoholic focuses more clearly on fundamental realities such as family relationships, marriage, career choice, and friendships. Often the person does not like the reality he or she sees. What was tolerable or easily ignored when drinking suddenly becomes painful. The tendency at this point is to escape, if not via alcohol, at least from the environment. Again, as a practical guideline, many professionals recommend that no major life decisions be made minimally for eighteen months after sobriety, and optimally for two years. By forcing himself or herself to deal with fundamental psychological issues, the recovering alcoholic can learn new skills for coping with stress other than the bottle or withdrawal.

In this stage the individual embarks on the painful process of picking up the pieces of a life alcoholism has shattered. Within the family his or her expectation is reestablishment of the role as parent and/or spouse. Family systems therapists, however, have pointed out the delicate equilibrium existing in the family structure. Though individually pleased to have a member well again, the system members have adapted to the dysfunction of the identified patient—in this case the alcoholic. Spouses and children have picked up the slack, so to speak, and will naturally resist letting go of roles and responsibilities, painful as they may have been. An analogy could be made to the difficulty Vietnam War prisoners had in readjusting to their family structures. As roles become reestablished, it is not uncommon for resentment and territorial arguments to ensue. Another common experience is for a family member—frequently a child—who has been holding it all in psychologically during the acute phase of the alcoholic's drinking, to suddenly let go and develop problems. For these reasons marital counseling or family therapy may be appropriate at this point (see Chapters 10 and 11).

A second feature to undergo scrutiny is past relationships. Often the alcoholic's friends were simply drinking partners, and a terrible sense of isolation develops with sobriety. AA can be especially helpful now, for it includes healthy social outlets while at the same time providing a context for understanding the illness.

A corollary to understanding relationships is seriously examining the role sexuality has played in the alcoholic's life. The importance of this area cannot be overemphasized. As noted above, negative emotional states account for many relapses, and guilt over unresolved sexual issues is intensely aversive. It should be stated frankly at the outset that the concern is not immediately one of morality. The pastoral counselor, of course, is sensitive to the client's ethical and moral concerns. The pressing problem, however, is that conflict over sexual issues will lead to drinking. I once interviewed an alcoholic serviceman who had engaged in homosexual activity during alcoholic blackouts but who was otherwise heterosexual. Because of his sensitive job, he was now preoccupied, as were his superiors, with the issue of his sexual identity. My advice to him was to deal with his alcoholism first since homosexuality would not kill him but drinking would. Morality issues may be rightfully addressed once the basic sexual issues are uncovered and placed in perspective psychologically.

Sexual issues require special emphasis because few alcoholics have no problems in this area. It should be recalled that alcohol depresses central nervous system functions, thereby disinhibiting brain processes involving social judgment. Alcoholics frequently behave in a manner at odds with their own value system, and remorse over these activities may be powerful. At the same time it is misleading to suggest that having sexual issues is synonymous with profligate behavior. Sexual issues are a continuum ranging from drinking to repress unacceptable sexual feelings to behavior leading to incarceration. The prudent approach is for the counselor to take a sexual history in a matter-of-fact manner. (Masters and Johnson 1970) Most pastoral formation now includes courses in human sexuality which familiarize the pastoral counselor with such an approach. Once an adequate history has been taken, the counseling process can explore the triad of loneliness, alcohol, and sex. The interrelationship of this triad is one of the most important pieces of therapeutic work for the alcoholic, and it is essential that innovative coping skills be developed.

When inappropriate sexual behavior is noted, two patterns, broadly speaking, may be distinguished. The first pattern involves sexual behavior that is so closely intertwined with drinking as to be functionally inseparable. In this pattern sexual acting out begins and nearly ends in drinking. The counselor may be amazed to see the once fervent office affair or cruising for prostitutes cease with sobriety. The second pattern involves sexual behavior which, although facilitated by alcohol, has an inner dynamic apart from it. The problems may range from inappropriate sexual object choices to sexual dysfunctions in performance. This pattern requires major work and possibly referral to a specialist in sex therapy. A thorough drinking history and sex history are necessary to distinguish these patterns.

Spiritual Recovery. Some alcoholics during the middle stage of recovery discover the distinction between spirituality and religion. For those who begin seriously "working the steps" of AA, fundamental insights regarding the transcendence of God and human powerlessness emerge, being more or less forced upon them as a means of coming to terms with their alcoholism. Recovery for the alcoholic in AA involves a surrender to the power alcohol has upon him or her and a "turning over" of that powerlessness to the Higher Power. This spirit of surrender permeates the twelve steps of AA:

1. We admitted we were powerless over alcohol, that our lives had become unmanageable.

2. Came to believe that a Power greater than ourselves could restore us to sanity.

3. Make a decision to turn our will and our lives over to the care of God *as we understood him.*

4. Make a searching and fearless moral inventory of ourselves.

5. Admitted to God, to ourselves, and to another human being the exact nature of our wrongs.

6. Were entirely ready to have God remove all these defects of character.

7. Humbly asked Him to remove our shortcomings.

8. Make a list of all persons we have harmed, and became willing to make amends to them all.

9. Make direct amends to such people wherever possible, except when to do so would injure them or others.

10. Continued to take personal inventory and when we were wrong promptly admitted it.

11. Sought through prayer and meditation to improve our conscious contact with God *as we understood him,* praying only for knowledge of His will for us and the power to carry that out.

12. Having had a spiritual awakening as the result of these steps, we tried to carry this message to alcoholics, and practice these principles in all our affairs.

In those simple statements are embedded the seeds of mysticism from many of the world's great religions. The AA member who is a spiritual enthusiast will even find specialized AA meetings which are hard to distinguish from prayer groups. At the same time the program leaves the less fervent members respectful distance in these matters. It is quite common to hear that the AA member finds greater fellowship at AA than in his or her church or synagogue.

One aspect of turning over one's life to God at this stage is resolving guilt from the alcoholic period. The terrible toll alcoholism extracts societally is well known. Marriages may have failed, jobs have been lost, paychecks targeted for child care have been diverted, sexual indiscretions have been committed. The AA program has built in a most powerful tool for dealing with these issues: the fourth and fifth steps of the twelve steps. They require the alcoholic to take a moral inventory of his life, concentrating particularly on the moral consequences of alcoholic behavior, and then to tell this to another human being. The purpose of these steps is not to wallow in guilt but to release the alcoholic from it and to put the moral deficiencies in the context of the illness. The AA tradition permits the alcoholic to share this inventory with any person of his or her choosing. My own practice, however, is not to take my own client's fifth step. Since I have a professional relationship with the client, the client does not face the leveling aspects of his alcoholism with me nearly as much as when he takes the step with a nonprofessional, particularly a fellow alcoholic. In this same vein I feel that fourth and fifth steps should not be assimilated into the liturgical practices of confession, giving testimony, or reconciliation.

The case of Brian M. illustrates a situation requiring further evaluation due to incomplete recovery during the middle stage.

THE CASE OF BRIAN M.

Brian M. was a forty-seven-year-old single man employed by a large corporation as a midlevel management specialist. Recently retired from the Air Force, where he was a supply officer, he was having great difficulty adjusting to civilian life. Although an excellent worker, he was in constant conflict with a variety of immediate supervisors and had been transferred frequently. Socially, his life was in chaos, characterized by one self-defeating sexual experience after another. The women he selected as partners were often involved in highly problematic situations such as being already married or suffering severe emotional problems themselves.

He entered outpatient treatment voluntarily, already convinced that he had a serious drinking problem, and motivated by a former girlfriend's decision to enter residential treatment for her alcoholism. The initial stages of recovery were relatively uneventful. He maintained sobriety with no relapses through the support of frequent AA meetings. His drinking history was a rather typical one, starting early in college and gaining steam during military service. He developed alcoholic hepatitis and abstained from alcohol for an entire year under doctor's orders. Incidentally, contrary to popular belief, this demonstrates even the most advanced alcoholic's ability to control drinking, at least temporarily. After he left the Air Force, his drinking increased until its recent heavy daily pattern.

His sexual history revealed a pattern of either casual sex with prostitutes, or torrid relationships in no-win situations as noted above. The impulsive quality of his relationships coupled with a high need for excitement provided important clues for a final diagnosis. Gradually, despite his continued sobriety, occasional crises erupted. Periodically, he would have major confrontations with his immediate supervisors over minor matters, usually resulting in his firing off an angry letter to the corporate director. Once this resulted in a transfer. This pattern was characterized by a two- to five-day period of intense excitement and anger, followed by remorse. Also, periodically, there would be a single episodic return to his former sexual patterns, characterized by two to five days of activity followed by regret.

At first he was seen weekly, then gradually at intervals ranging from two to four weeks. After twelve months of therapy I noted a cyclic pattern to the impulsive behavior and certain associated features such as sleep disturbance and post-episode depression. Brian was asked to chart his moods over the past ten years, noting in particular high and low periods. As markers to aid his memory I suggested he recall job transfers, sexual encounters, and binge drinking episodes. The resultant data clearly demonstrated cyclic mood swings relating to two periods annually, one in July and one in December. A recurring pattern is common for individuals suffering from a major affective disorder. A psychiatrist confirmed the diagnosis of bipolar affective disorder, and lithium treatment commenced.

His recovery became less troubled by his periodic mood swings. He learned to deal assertively rather than aggressively with his superiors and remained in his current position. His sexual conduct became more measured, less impulsive. In his own words his attendance at AA became "less compulsive," that is, less frenetic in searching out new and stimulating meetings but more settled with a few comfortable ones weekly.

Later Stage and Beyond

This stage is characterized by having potential for the greatest growth, yet the saddest failure. Although statistically speaking the chances of maintaining sobriety after the second anniversary are quite good, the very length of success magnifies guilt should relapse occur. It is also characterized by more complete integration and acceptance of one's identity as an alcoholic. Physical and psychological recovery tends to stabilize and the spiritual dimension opens to unlimited possibilities.

Physical Recovery.   At this point only chronic conditions should remain. Brain recovery is nearly as complete as it will be. The alcoholic must accept the physical or intellectual impairment that remains. Awareness of these aftereffects is an important antidote to denial.

Psychological Recovery.   This period often involves major decisions with regard to occupational and marital choices. Despite marital counseling or family therapy, a couple may decide that there has been too much water over the dam to save the relationship. More often the nonalcoholic spouse initiated separation proceedings prior to recovery and the alcoholic must come to terms with the accomplished fact. New evidence indicates nonalcoholic wives are just as likely as nonalcoholic husbands to divorce their spouses. Or, if the couple is still physically together, reexamining and renewing earlier commitments to each other are in order. At this point, too, the alcoholic may reasonably change career goals whether by necessity or choice. Perhaps his drinking past has ruined advancement in his current position, or, upon reflection, he sees other career possibilities.

Relapse at this stage should be treated the same as at any earlier one, that is, by minimizing its catastrophic features and using them as a learning device. It may require more effort to deal with the abstinence violation effect, that is, the guilt over transgressing an absolute norm. (Marlatt 1978) Indeed, the astute counselor will use such a slip positively to explore further the client's denial system.

Spiritual Recovery.   I strongly recommend during this stage that all alcoholics with spiritual values read E. Kurtz's excellent volume on the spiritual history of AA entitled *Not-God.* (1981) The title itself reflects what the author feels is the core spiritual insight of the recovering alcoholic that "first of all we had to come to realize that we were not God." From this central insight, the alcoholic could then accept his or her own powerlessness over alcohol along with the entire range of ego-deflating statements about the illness. The founders of AA, influenced as they were by the spiritual movements of their era, saw that only through a radical self-surrender analogous to the prayer of quiet could an alcoholic develop the attitude necessary for quality sobriety. Viewing sobriety in this manner has endless spiritual applications, and the counselor is limited only by interest and initiative in this dimension.

The case of Albert J. illustrates problems arising in the later stage of recovery requiring appropriate referral.

THE CASE OF ALBERT J.

Albert J. was a thirty-six-year-old married engineering salesman, who had been in recovery five years. He sought out our clinic upon the referral of an attending physician on the psychiatric ward of a private hospital where he was a patient. Albert was experiencing little difficulty with regard to his alcoholism since he was active in AA, although he had had numerous slips prior to his renewed commitment to AA five years before.

His immediate problems centered around a "nervous breakdown" which he experienced nine months before and for which he was hospitalized. His diagnosis was anxiety reaction and he had been placed on antidepressants plus low-level dosages of antipsychotics. He had been placed on temporary disability by his company and was about to be released from the hospital to return to his family and resume light duties at work. He sought out a therapist for support during the transition.

His drinking history revealed an alcoholic pattern, including seven years of heavy drinking. Sexual behavior during his alcoholic years consisted of numerous affairs of the one-night-stand variety. Even after sobriety it took a few years to wind down the frequency of his adulterous contacts. He reported that his family life now was good, with a supportive spouse who ran a successful business, and with two young children.

Although one would expect that nine months of inpatient treatment would ensure an appropriate diagnosis, such was not the case. Albert revealed some behavior patterns typical of depression such as frequent crying spells in the morning followed by gradual improvement during the day. Obviously, this behavior motivated the hospital psychiatrists to prescribe antidepressants, which, no doubt, were appropriate. However, as I listened to Albert's history of his breakdown, his symptoms implicated other problems as well.

The precipitating event leading to his breakdown was a severe anxiety reaction to a host of ego-alien and frightening thoughts. These thoughts centered around homicidal and incestuous ideas toward his wife and children, and the resultant panic led to his seeking hospitalization. Further questioning revealed that these intrusive thoughts were chronic and led to a full assessment of his obsessive-compulsive disorder. His past behavior included compulsive rituals associated with fears of contamination and bodily injury. Although it was important to keep his depression in perspective, it was equally important that his obsessive-compulsive disorder be evaluated and treated. For example, despite nine months' hospitalization, no one had talked openly to him about his unusual thoughts. One psychiatrist went so far as to instruct him not to share them with anyone but her. In our sessions we talked quite frankly about his thoughts being a product of his disorder, probably the result of some biochemical abnormality which affects thought processes. He identified quite readily with my description of this relatively rare disorder and found considerable relief in the notion that his own symptoms were typical. Only with a complete assessment could we begin to address his myriad difficulties, and, not incidentally, maintain his sobriety.

SPECIAL POPULATIONS

The pastoral counselor on occasion may feel inadequate to meet the needs of certain groups. Two groups that sometimes have special needs with reference to alcoholism are women and homosexuals. The pastoral counselor can at least be alert to some common concerns of these groups and direct them to other resources when appropriate.

Women alcoholics have largely remained an unknown entity until recently. Most research has been conducted on men and illustrates the problems of male alcoholics. Even the estimates of the occurrence of alcoholism in women fluctuate widely. (Gomberg 1979) Researchers concluded that women alcoholics show greater physical damage, possibly because fear of stigma keeps their drinking under wraps much longer than men. (Greenblat and Schuckit 1976) Some researchers have also felt that the very pattern of brain damage is unique for women but these assumptions are being challenged now as better controlled studies are produced. It appears that only certain subgroups of women drink differently than men, such as suburban housewives, and that the physical damage is not as dissimilar as was once thought. Whatever conclusions are warranted by further research, the overwhelming clinical experience of alcoholism treatment professionals suggests that women are especially sensitized to the guilt and shame associated with the social labeling of alcoholism. This does not necessarily mean that their recovery rates are poorer in comparison to men's, but it indicates the level of suffering is intense. As a result of society's expectations, they are more vulnerable to guilt associated with deficient parenting practices or sexual misconduct. Women often express discomfort in sharing such weaknesses in mixed groups, and for this reason women's groups in AA and other specialized groups of alcoholic women such as Women for Sobriety are becoming increasingly popular. These groups can be a most useful adjunct to individual counseling.

Since most alcoholics encountered will be men unless the counselor is in a specialized ministry, it is important that the counselor not project male alcoholic patterns onto female clients. Many alcoholic women consume far smaller amounts of alcohol relative to men, and have shorter drinking histories. The effects of their drinking are equally devastating, however. At the same time women alcoholics are more likely to be poly-addicted, that is, abusing other addictive substances in addition to alcohol. Dealing with one chemical dependency (alcohol) while ignoring the others is futile. The cross-addiction of women is especially frustrating to the counselor, since there is no simple means to monitor a client's intake. The effects of alcohol tend to be noticeable, whereas the effects of pills tend to go unnoticed. Such cases may only be amenable to residential treatment.

Homosexual alcoholics have also formed specialized AA meetings which can be found in larger metropolitan areas. Pastoral counselors, no matter what moral position they or their churches take on homosexual behavior, need to be alert to the pastoral concerns of the homosexual alcoholic. Gay AA meetings are conducted in the serious manner typical of AA meetings with the clear focus on the disease of alcoholism. Nonetheless, the very composition of the group communicates to the homosexual instant acceptance and the freedom to discuss a wide range of topics. As one member told me, "At gay AA I get to discuss the three things that are most important to my life right now: alcohol, sex, and religion." The benefit of gay AA is that alcoholics with different values regarding homosexual behavior can coexist. Whether the religious tradition advocates celibacy for the homosexual or responsible sexual relationships, the individual can feel at home. Gay AA has proven most beneficial for my clients whose alcoholic drinking is intertwined with sexual identity conflict. By providing an alcoholic with an accepting atmosphere, gay AA ensures that the illness of alcoholism will receive proper attention.

REFLECTIONS

Recovery from alcoholism, as conceptualized in the model outlined here, is a process out of step with many of the assumptions of modern secularism. The personal journey of the recovering alcoholic includes a conversion experience through which he or she surrenders to a Higher Power. Implicit in this surrender is the paradox of admitting one's own limitations as a path to the most complete self-fulfillment. None of these concepts easily fits into a society that glorifies the individual and accentuates materialism. The pastoral counselor, whose own stance toward the counseling process includes belief in transcendence and the limitations imposed by human sinfulness, is predisposed, I believe, to assist the recovering alcoholic to explore these realities.

Somewhat less emphasized, however, is the role such a stance can have in the spiritual development of the counselor. Unless the counselor experiences a personal surrender to the disease analogous to the alcoholic's own surrender, continued counseling with alcoholics soon becomes unbearable. The frustrations inherent in working with this population become so aversive that many will avoid it altogether. The counselor who accepts his or her own powerlessness over the disease and accepts reliance on a Higher Power as the path to recovery will be able to accept the inevitable setbacks.

Counseling alcoholics reveals to me the spiritual dimension of human existence. When I experience relapse with my clients, I become aware of my own limitations as a person and therapist. In a sickness unto death my healing skills are for nought, and often I am reduced to silent observation of human deterioration. At those moments when I forget this fact of my powerlessness, many self-defeating notions arise. I may blame myself or the alcoholic, perceive his or her first drink as a personal insult to me, and even resort to moralizing about the client's behavior, thereby falling into the same trap that blocks the alcoholic's own surrender. Only a personal surrender to the power of the disease affords me a measure of serenity in these circumstances.

Conversely, when the recovery process works, there is no more awe-inspiring experience, in my opinion, than to have participated in the alcoholic's resurrection. It is a process only a poet could adequately describe. Yet the humbling aspect is to know that the individual counselor's contribution is but one part of a larger environmental system. Indeed, some research suggests that the environmental supports for the alcoholic are much more significant in recovery than any system of treatment. If true spirituality entails being conscious of one's right order in the universe, such an experience cannot help but deepen that consciousness. The recovery process invites both veneration of the miracle of change in the alcoholic and humility in recognition of the important but small role the counselor plays.

CONCLUSION

In summary, four concepts emerge in the process of counseling the recovering alcoholic. First, although this issue was not treated directly in this chapter, many alcoholics, because of their denial system, do not seek treatment voluntarily. Frequently, they are "motivated" by the intervention of spouses, family members, employers, or the legal system. Alcoholics retain this propensity to deny their illness throughout recovery, and frequent reference to this mechanism by the pastoral counselor is necessary.

Second, to a greater extent in this population, recovery is influenced by a host of biological-medical conditions which, if not attended to, directly hamper the therapeutic relationship. Factors such as compulsion to drink, sleep disturbances, attentional deficits, and poor abstraction skills may create roadblocks for counselors who do not modify their helping style to compensate for their clients' deficiencies, especially in the early stages of recovery.

Third, the developmental aspects of recovery suggest certain alterations in the counseling strategy. Early stages of recovery generally require more frequent contact to support the alcoholic who is disengaging himself or herself slowly from the compulsion to drink. Later stages do not always necessitate the traditional once-a-week session. Since drinking is a genuine illness in its own right, the counseling process ought not entail endless analysis of the "underlying causes" of the drinking. Analytic approaches to addictions have a half-century failure record, and there is no reason for pastoral counselors to resurrect them. Further, the counselor's goal is to become "less and less" and to encourage the social network of AA to become "more and more." The pastoral counselor is a temporary resource, whereas AA will become the permanent program for supporting sobriety.

Finally, the centrality of the surrender experience permeates recovery, generating an experience of transcendence which is uncommon to other client populations. The surrender experience, whereby the chemically dependent person acknowledges powerlessness over the addiction, is the point of departure for recovery. To date no satisfactory empirical analysis of this surrender experience exists. Clinically, however, alcoholics repeat terms such as "letting go" and "turning it over" to signify that experience. Recovery, therefore, stands at the intersection of biology, psychology, and the spiritual life. Pastoral counselors who are open to the physical and psychological dimensions of alcoholism as well as to the spiritual will see their roles develop into a necessary and vital resource in the treatment of this fatal illness.

REFERENCES

Alcoholics Anonymous, 3rd ed. New York: Alcoholics Anonymous World Services, Inc., 1976.

Burns, D. *Feeling Good.* New York: New American Library, 1980.

Ciarrochhi, J. W., and C. M. Burns. "Intervention with the Religious Alcoholic." Unpublished manuscript, 1982.

Cummings, C., J. R. Gordon, and G. A. Marlatt. "Relapse: Prevention and Prediction." In W. Miller (Ed.). *The Addictive Behaviors: Treatment of Alcoholism, Drug Abuse, Smoking, and Obesity.* Oxford: Pergamon Press, 1980.

Diagnostic and Statistical Manual of Mental Disorders. 3rd ed. revised. Washington, D.C.: American Psychiatric Association, 1987.

Gomberg, E. S. "Problems with Alcohol and Other Drugs." In E. S. Gomberg and V. Franks (Eds.). *Gender and Disordered Behavior: Sex Differences in Psychopathology.* New York: Brunner/Mazel, 1979.

Greenblat, M., and M. Schuckit. (Eds.). *Alcoholism Problems in Women and Children.* New York: Grune & Stratton, 1976.

Johnson, V. *I'll Quit Tomorrow.* New York: Harper, 1973.

Kline, N. *From Sad to Glad.* New York: Ballantine Books, 1981.

Kurtz, E. *Not-God: A History of Alcoholics Anonymous.* Center City, Minn.: Hazelden Educational Services, 1981.

Marlatt, G. A. "Craving for Alcohol, Loss of Control, and Relapse: A Cognitive Behavioral Analysis." In Nathan, P. E., G. A. Marlatt, and T. Loberg (Eds.). *Alcoholism: New Directions in Behavioral Research and Treatment.* New York: Plenum, 1978.

Masters, W. H., and V. E. Johnson. *Human Sexual Inadequacy.* Boston: Little, Brown, 1970.

Miller, W. R. *The Addictive Behaviors: Treatment of Alcoholism, Drug Abuse, Smoking, and Obesity.* Oxford: Pergamon Press, 1980.

Twelve Steps and Twelve Traditions. New York: Alcoholics Anonymous World Services, Inc., 1953.

RECOMMENDED READINGS

Clinebell, H. J. *Understanding and Counseling the Alcoholic.* Nashville: Abingdon, 1978.

Cohen, S. *The Substance Abuse Problems.* New York: Haworth Press, 1981.

Ewing, J. A., and B. A. Rouse (Eds.). *Drinking: Alcohol in American Society—Issues and Current Research.* Chicago: Nelson-Hall, 1978.

Fann, W. E., I. Karacan, A. D. Pokorny, and R. L. Williams (Eds.). *Phenomenology and Treatment of Alcoholism.* New York: Spectrum, 1980.

Hoff, E. C. *Alcoholism: The Hidden Addiction.* New York: Seabury, 1974.

Mendelson, J. H., and N. K. Mello (Eds.). *The Diagnosis and Treatment of Alcoholism.* New York: McGraw-Hill, 1979.

Miller, P. M., and M. A. Mastria. *Alternatives to Alcohol Abuse: A Social Learning Model.* Champaign, Ill.: Research Press, 1977.

Paolino, T. J., and B. S. McGrady. *The Alcoholic Marriage: Alternative Perspectives.* New York: Grune & Stratton, 1977.

Poley, W., G. Lea, and G. Vibe. *Alcoholism: A Treatment Manual.* New York: Gardner, 1979.

Sorensen, A. *Alcoholic Priests: A Sociological Study.* New York: Seabury, 1976.

Zimberg, J., John Wallace, and Sheila Blume. (Eds.). *Practical Approaches to Alcoholism Psychotherapy.* New York: Plenum, 1978.

CHAPTER FIFTEEN

Pastoral Group Counseling

ROBERT F. DAVENPORT, D. MIN.

A THEOLOGICAL PREFACE

In an anxious conversation with H. Richard Niebuhr eighteen years ago I was confessing my fear of writing a paper in a seminar he was leading. In response to my discomfort Mr. Niebuhr said that he read everything through the first time with a predisposition to be convinced by the author, a second time to converse with the author, and a third time to judge, confront, or argue with the author. I wrote the assigned paper. Unwittingly, Mr. Niebuhr in his remark has since given me a typology for my work, which is, I believe, consistent with the Judeo-Christian tradition. I identify a typology of three essential modes or postures for my work in counseling clients: the *priestly,* the *pastoral,* and the *prophetic.*

As a pastoral counselor, I understand myself to stand in an ancient theological tradition. Yahweh is portrayed as a deity who hears—attends to—the needs of people. They may come before Yahweh as they are, full of need, fear, doubt, and be assured a hearing by a God for whom grace antecedes and succeeds law. My posture of receptivity to a client is a response to the hearing, attending God. I meet a client to hear a story which is painful enough to have led the client to share it with a professional. First, I want to hear the story uncritically, to believe that while it may not be accurate, at a more compelling level than accuracy I am hearing truth as the client perceives and experiences it. It is in response to that subjective truth that the client has formed a style of thinking, feeling, and relating which is causing problems in living. My office, then, offers a "sanctuary," a place of protection in which a person may unapologetically be him or herself. In early meetings, that very nonjudgmental receptivity may be in sharp contrast to the client's attitude of self-contempt, and my acceptance may initiate a relation that is healing. Modeled on the hearing-attending God, that careful, nonjudgmental, accepting, respectful listening to a client is a *priestly* expression of my pastoral identity. Over time, being so received may begin to influence the client to a gentler style of receptivity to himself or herself.

If my priestly posture is reflective of the hearing-attending God, then my *pastoral* mode is a response to the God who cares for people by actively engaging in our well-being. As pastor, I am not limited to the essentially passive receptivity of the priest. I enjoy a calling to express actively my concern for my clients, giving clear statement in word and action of my interest in their discovering satisfying lives as they relate to themselves, to important persons in their lives, and to their larger worlds. Here, as I insist on respect for myself in defining the parameters of our work, I model a quality of self-respect which enfleshes my common benediction, "Take care of yourself." When I fail so to model self-respect by allowing a client to take advantage of me, I peddle "cheap grace" which does nothing helpful to anyone.

Practically, being pastoral means that I freely exercise a breadth of responses which includes not merely verbal interaction in our sessions, but visitation when a client is sick, a willingness to minister to family members in times of need or crisis, including responsiveness to requests for larger pastoral ministry such as weddings or funerals, especially when our work has prepared the way for such ministry or when religious isolation has kept a client unrelated to a faith group. When our contacts include such diverse and extended interaction, I pay close attention to what that means to the more narrowly conceived counseling relation, carefully processing the meaning of the more inclusive or extensive contacts. This pastoral stance gives me an opportunity, in therapy, to offer sustenance as I become an advocate of my clients' well-being. Anticipating growth, I seek to be a guarantor that their investments in themselves will yield a return to them and in their relations to others.

Our theological tradition takes human history very seriously as the setting in which we are to discover evidences of God's love and judgment. A person's history makes a statement of the client's relative sense of responsibility for life. The Hebrew-Christian tradition clearly understands that we are the makers of our own history, not pawns manipulated by capricious gods. Thus, if the priestly ministry is an attending-hearing service, and my pastoral ministry is an interactive, advocating relation, then my *prophetic* ministry is one in which I may stand over against either my client's self- and other-diminishing styles or a social order which dehumanizes and demeans persons. In this modality I am called to confront what is destructive and bear witness to options in the interest of healing broken relationships. I judge those personal and social patterns which either underrate the value of persons or overrate the potentialities of persons who feel grandiose expectations of unlikely or impossible goals imposed upon themselves or others. Since we are part of a tradition which begins with an assumption of human vulnerability, pastoral counselors are in a unique position to stand over against philosophies or therapies that overpromise and inevitably lead to new frustrations for those who believe in utopian potentialities and assume that their failure to achieve the promised ends lies in their weaknesses.

In this prophetic stance, I am more likely than in the others to reveal myself, reveal my values, share my own pilgrimage, when I believe that will be of use to a client. Here I acknowledge my essential parity with a client, disowning any claim to being superior or invulnerable. Timing and the careful generation of a therapeutic bond capable of sustaining my realistic self-disclosure are carefully assessed.

Any typology oversimplifies in the service of clarity. At a given point in the therapeutic relation any of these three modes might be emphasized as I seek to respond to my sense of a client's needs and to the quality of our therapeutic bond. In the main, however, they are sequential modes, following Mr. Niebuhr's order. Early in the relationship, the attending-listening stance will be predominant; as we continue and issues of transference and countertransference are being worked through, the interactive posture will be more central; as we move to termination and the transferences are giving way to reality-based perceptions of one another, the confrontive, self-disclosing, parity-affirming mode will be more common.

This typology informs my work as an internal frame of reference though it is not something which I would likely make explicit to a client. In fact, since the client sets the content agenda of our meetings, such explicit theological language is rare in my work. When a client is theologically informed, I might use theological language, illustrations, or metaphors, just as I would use the language of business, sports, or any others with a client for whom that language provides a clarifying point of contact.

When I make the shift from my own internal frame of reference for work with individual clients to the underlying assumptions for group work, I struggle to see if the essence of this typology can inform the work of *clients* in a group. I assume that in a group *each member* has an opportunity to give or receive therapeutic responses. In that sense, theologically, a group is an experience of the priesthood of believers. In order for the members to respond to one another therapeutically, the same sequence or insequential mixing of nonjudgmental attending, advocative interaction, and critical confrontation will be necessary skills for the members to develop. Again, I do not present them theologically, nor would I even outline them as therapeutic skills. What I do is model them, suggest alternative postures for a stuck interaction, comment on the process of a series of interactions, over and over again, until members learn these skills in much the same unwitting ways a child learns language. The process is slow, but it has built in the reinforcing influence of constant repetition in a setting of mutual trust and expectation. For many of my clients who are alienated from their religious roots, such a setting begins to have about it many of the relational aspects of a church fellowship.

MY PERSONAL EXPERIENCE IN GROUPS

I suspect that it is far from coincidental that when I began to reflect here on my own group experiences, the first thing I thought of was my junior and senior high school church groups. I grew up as a physically sickly, mother-dependent child who came to believe that I was not and could not be socially, academically, or athletically proficient. Thus any sort of leadership in the world was beyond my wildest expectations, though the importance my mother assigned me in her life of estrangement from my father subtly suggested an expectation which touched my young male grandiosity. It was in church youth groups that I first began to experience a quality of responsiveness from peers and adult leaders which gave me any encouragement to build self-esteem and, eventually, to develop leadership capacity. I now know that the Church's message was a corrective to my paradoxical family identity: powerful/sickly. The Church said: we are all sinners equally needy of the grace of God; and, we are all saved, equally recipients of the grace of God. That message has cut many a neurotic bond in the last several millennia and it freed me to claim my real strengths without exaggerating them. I didn't *hear* that message so much as *experience* it. I experienced it in the relationships with peers and adults in church groups—experiences specific to the resolution of the conflicts that had informed my earliest group experience: my family. In this sense, my youthful church experience gave me what Erik H. Erikson calls the "virtue [strength] of fidelity": "the ability to sustain loyalties freely pledged in spite of the inevitable contradictions of value systems. It [fidelity] is the cornerstone of identity and receives inspiration from confirming ideologies and affirming companions." (Erikson 1964, p. 125)

Significant participation in various groups in one way or another related to Christian belief and practice (college groups, national Church leadership positions, seminary, team teaching at a church-related college) continued to inform my development before I became interested in either having or doing group counseling. In addition, with marriage and family, I began a second effort at making *that* all-important "group" healthful for myself, my wife, and my daughters. Since neither my wife nor I had models of family life in our own pasts which we would choose to replicate, we have gone about the tricky business of making our own models (and our own mistakes). In that sense, our children have provided the impetus for us to do better than we were done to and we have benefited as individuals in the process.

My training in group therapy was chosen following my doctoral work, my thesis having presented a model for a college chaplain's short-term counseling of students. That work had grown out of my sense that students in difficulty casting about to answer the phase-specific, "Who am I?" question could choose "psychiatric patient" as an option if it were made available and attractive to them. That seemed to me a less than satisfactory situation. On returning to work as director of counseling in the college where I had taught and been pastor for six years, I sought a way to begin to tap the well-known influence of peers for late adolescents in our counseling program. We began to work with student groups and found that they were most effective and that the students would take confrontation, support, and comfort from one another which they resisted from designated adult counselors. I believe their resistance was a healthy mark of their own individuation and that the adult-dependent relations we had earlier offered reflected our needs to be needed more than the real needs of students to grow up.

When I left the college to become a professional pastoral counselor, I immediately began developing groups among my clients. At the same time, as part of our continuing education and network of sustenance, other staff members and I participated in a group with a well-known group therapist. In all my training in group work, the learning has occurred through a mix of being a participant in a group, leading a group, learning the theory from reading, and discussions of the groups' processes. We have carried over this design in our training of pastoral counselors in group counseling at Loyola. In that training I was introduced to the interactional, here-and-now group model which Yalom (1975) has so effectively described. The rest of this chapter focuses on interactional groups in which the therapist's major responsibility is to facilitate the work of members with one another.

This interactional style is one of two essential modalities of group counseling. The other style was practiced and promoted principally by Perls (1969) and Berne (1966). In that style the therapists work sequentially, one-on-one with individual group members. The rest of the group may be utilized at the therapists' initiative but will more often observe the work in progress. Members are invited to work and the work continues dyadically to some point of closure, after which the invitation, "Who wants to work?" is repeated. My early training was in this method and I learned a great deal from it, but I have adopted the interactional mode because I believe it is more respectful of the capacities of members to interact therapeutically and because it takes the focus off the therapist and puts it on the group processes.

THE EXPERIENCES OF SOME CLIENTS IN GROUPS

As I thought about what would make this chapter useful to readers, it occurred to me that much of what we read professionally is written by professionals to professionals against a background of shared assumptions which in our writing and reading we wish to have reinforced. So, preachers tell preachers of the efficacy of preaching, and therapists tell therapists that therapy is useful, and we all feel good. What might parishioners say about preaching? What might group counseling clients say about group therapy?

At this writing I have three active groups. One is a men's group which has been meeting for nine months, with a constant membership of six men in their thirties and forties. This is a somewhat specialized group, reminiscent of women's consciousness-raising groups in the 1970s, although all the men came out of my individual practice. A second group has been meeting for only four months at this writing and is very new at its cohesion-building tasks. It is a group of eight adults of both sexes who range in age from late twenties to mid-forties. That group is a successor in my schedule to an eight-year group which recently terminated. The third group is eight years old in my experience of it, but the members—seven adults of both sexes in midlife—range in longevity from two years to three months. I work with a female cotherapist in that group.

I asked members who were willing to do so to write a brief statement about their group experience. I told them that I wanted the statements for this chapter and that I was not interested in testimonials. Having asked once, I did not repeat the request and returns were sparse. Only one in the men's group responded. In the two mixed groups, response was better, with six of fifteen members giving me written responses—three from each group, three from men and three from women.

Some of the comments are quite personal, others more analytical, and others a mix. Not all the responses were doxologies to the efficacy of group counseling. One forty-year-old man, twice married with a severely handicapped child, who had been in the longest running group for about eighteen months, praised the process with faint damnation. However, the group is clearly a corrective to an otherwise often unsatisfying life.

> In spite of an attitude of disdain for the pleasantries and cliches which abound in the group, I find it basically useful to have a group, a ninety-minute space in which I may, if I wish, cry or express feeling in some way. There are situations about which I need to cry, and group offers me an opportunity to do this, more or less legitimately. The members of the group are strangers who happen to be thrown together, and their concern for me or one another usually strikes me as slightly ungenuine, or rather unvalid because it is so arbitrary and haphazard. But I am probably too arrogant.

Rereading this quotation in preparation for revising this chapter, I am struck with the fact that, despite his cynical attitude toward relations among members, this man is very well and warmly remembered by two men who are presently in the group and who knew him briefly as they began the group near the end of his tenure.

In the same group a young woman with a history of psychiatric hospitalizations, recently separated after a ten-year marriage to an alcoholic fifteen years her senior, is struggling to establish herself independently. She reflects both her fear and her hope as well as the beginnings of new-found esteem related to her work in the group. Her identification with others and her "use" of them outside the room is an example of the group's providing those resources which families can provide and which her life as a foster child did not provide.

Sharing the Hurt and Pain

I want to touch everyone and take it away from them even if it's just for a few seconds.

It's so heavy. I feel crushed! When my pain overwhelms me, I think of my friends in group and how hard they are fighting. When I'm ready to give up it helps me change my mind. The pain is less difficult to bear and even seems to ease when I share it at group. *It's scary when I let go of it* [italics hers], but when I do it's not so crushing anymore.

I think it must be like that for all of us, and that makes me feel good, because I *can* help ease their pain too!

Some months after that was written, this young client made a suicide attempt and was hospitalized again, briefly. Later, a no-suicide contract with the group became the protection from her own internal "terrorist" which she needed to begin to turn her life around.

If those two comments are the extremes of responses from that group, the third is more of a mix, its style and content reflective of the character of the over fifty-year-old, recently divorced, technically oriented professional man attempting to reorient himself to single life after more than twenty-five years of marriage. He has been in the group for about one year after three years of individual and marital therapy. This client compared and contrasted individual and group work, clearly identifying the intrapsychic character of the former and the interpersonal impact of the latter. He concluded his remarks on his individual work: "metaphor—washing away dross and surprisingly finding joyfully some bedrock which has existed all along." Of his group experience:

1. Opportunity to express (not always safely!) thoughts and feelings in a lab situation. [When asked what his parenthetical "not always safely" meant, he replied that he sometimes cried in the group. A former military officer with substantial combat experience, tears had been an unacceptable means of expression prior to therapy.]

2. Interchange in group—develop curiosity and insight about people which relate to self and people outside.

3. Reaction and criticism of group—sometimes difficult to take—clue to same from people outside.

4. Develop deep personal attachment to group leaders and sometimes to members. Varying attachments to other members.

5. After group time get high on imaginary conversations with group.

6. Receive many surprises about real character and problems of people in group. Frequently will identify with people with whom I thought I had nothing in common.

7. Somewhat of a problem—deferring to others who have an immediate and overwhelming problem.

As I worked with these responses from this long-term group with a stable population of persons who stay an average of one to two years, I was struck that each referred to the experience as "group," not "the group," as all the members in the newer group speak of it. Since I also hear the members use the word without either adjective, article, or possessive pronoun, I have had the impression that "group" is used as regular church members refer to "church" without particularizing or identifying modifiers. This suggests to me the institutionalization of the group therapy experience for the clients in an established group. That is to say, this group has established its cohesiveness by its longevity and by the establishment of norms for its life which old members teach new members.

In the newer mixed group of eight adults, two of the responses were of multi-page length and I will select from them rather than reporting them whole. The third is brief and pointed. A recently separated father of two young children, in his thirties, came for therapy after being left by his wife. He has a high school education and a highly skilled blue-collar job. He manifests great curiosity about himself and his situation and thus a willingness to learn and change which has overcome a fairly rigid character structure which had damaged his marital relationship. For him, the group experience has, among other things, been an exercise in socialization and increased esteem.

> It seems that my whole life I've strived to become an individual. When I reached my goal it seemed if I wanted to talk to people I didn't feel easy or know how to convey personal problems to others. As a grown male I didn't think I should need others except my wife. Through this group I'm conveying honest feelings to other adults for the first time without feeling hindered, stupid, or restricted.

A single woman in her late twenties struggling with resolving issues of maturation to adulthood in both love and work was in the previous long-term group and speaks comparatively of the two experiences, seeing both as:

> places for me to express thoughts and fears; receive and react to feedback about characteristics in my personality, lifestyle, and mannerisms (to the extent that I have been willing to share).

In her former group, where she spent nearly a year:

> I often had a sense that many of the issues I am battling with were issues others in the group had dealt with before [in the group], therefore were able to give constructive and sometimes not so constructive help.

> [W]hen a cotherapist was present, I felt as though there was more of a balance in the group interaction. I miss having a cotherapist present.

Summarizing:

> [M]uch of the healing which has gone on inside of me has been a direct reflection of the experiences I have gained by participating in the two groups.

Another single woman with similar developmental struggles has come into the group after about a year's individual therapy. She has wrestled particularly with separation and individuation from her parents, complicated by family business connections to them. She expresses irritation at the slowness of the pace, the varied abilities of members to work together, and then identifies my relative transparency in the group (as compared to individual therapy) as one of the gains in the experience. Since this is a new group, and since its success as a healing medium is contingent on members' willingness to disclose themselves to one another, I will often model for them with transparency about my experience with them in the room, and, less often, in general comments about my history when I believe those will enable others to risk self-disclosure.

> One of my favorite things about the group is getting to know—on a basis of equality within the group —you. While I can't help but perceive your participation as more educated, more studied, more aware, I find myself particularly delighted by your self-revelations.

In these statements, and in countless other ways, my clients have taught me the impact and limits of group counseling. I am grateful for their candor here as I am for their self-disclosures which make our group work possible.

CRITERIA FOR INVITING CLIENTS TO A GROUP

How is a decision made to refer a client to a group? All of the members of my ongoing therapy groups have come to them out of my individual practice. Those clients have typically come to me on referral from former clients, physicians who know my work, other therapists, and, less frequently, clergy, teachers, or attorneys. They came as individuals or as couples with a wide range of presenting complaints. When I first see a client, I initiate an intake process of from three to five meetings during which time I wish to hear the person's presenting problem in as much detail as the client desires and then to spend one or two appointments taking a comprehensive history of the client's psychosocial development—from whence and whom and under what mix of experiences did the client come to this point in life. In the case of an individual who is married or living in a sexual relation, I ask to see the partner one time. My reason for that is to avoid the unnecessary divisiveness of established relationships which can result from a family member's being in individual therapy. In one meeting with a client's partner I seek to gain some sense of who that person is, the person's feelings about a partner being in therapy, the person's sense of the partner's needs, and the relative health of their relationship, and, in general, I present myself in such a way that I am perceived as an ally to the family, not an enemy. Granted, there are some relationships that need dividing and therapy can serve that need, but others which need strengthening may be spared a new trauma from a sense of an unknown alien influence as a shadow figure in the relationship. This process also gives a partner a chance to signal his or her own therapeutic needs or the needs of the relationship.

When the "client" is a relationship, as when a couple comes for marriage counseling, I see them once together, each separately once or twice for individual history taking, and again as a couple. There, my intention is to evaluate the strengths and weaknesses of the relationship as well as to respect the individuality of the partners and their peculiar histories.

Following that sequence of meetings with an individual or a couple, I have a consultation with a psychiatrist in which I present the major issues discovered in these meetings with the intention of arriving at a two-part statement for the client: first, a *descriptive* statement which says as clearly and succinctly as possible what is crucial in the client's current situation; second, a *prescriptive* statement which recommends a program of therapy intended to address the client's needs. In a subsequent meeting with the client I present these, discuss them, and we agree either to pursue the recommendations or not. When a client has a reservation about me and the recommendation entails working with me, we seek to resolve the issue or I offer a referral. If I am recommending someone other than myself, I tell the client why.

Among the recommendations that can be made at the end of that intake process are: individual counseling, a group, a sequence of more individual sessions followed by a group at some future point, individual and group concurrently, or, in the case of a couple, marital work or a combination of marital and individual or group work for one or both parties. Unless it is manifestly clear that a couple intends to separate maritally, I would hesitate to separate them in therapy but would work out a combination of marital and individual and/or group work or a sequence that respects the needs and the viability of the marriage. In all cases, fees are negotiated and I ask clients to work out with me a fee for the family's work which respects their financial limits while still providing an incentive for purposeful work and protecting my needs. While a fee appropriately "pinches," it should not "choke."

I think of a group experience as the therapy of choice for an individual when certain developmental or psychopathological indications suggest to me that a group is specific to a person's needs and that the person will be in the group's interest as well.

For example, for persons in technical fields (engineering, computers) or other fields where things are more important than persons and where criteria for evaluation are more often quantitative than qualitative, experiences in satisfying conversation and the development of social skills can be correctives to unsatisfying relationships with intimates or colleagues. A group can best serve those socialization needs. Since such persons often carry over their patterns of rigidity and "one best way" thinking from vocation to intimacy, the very influence that multiple responses from group members can bring may break through resistance which individual therapy could not. In addition, the fact that six or seven other adults are there for such a person provides multiple models for thinking, feeling, and responding. Invariably, group members provide one another with people similar to those in their lives with whom they experience difficulties; thus they provide opportunities to express warmth or hostility where the relational stakes are not as high as they are with persons with whom they live or work.

Further, persons who are separating or divorcing and dealing with the issues of loneliness, loss of esteem, grief, guilt, and needed reconstruction of lives can make excellent use of the supportive, instructive, hope-instilling processes which a therapeutic community offers them. Especially in urban settings where intentional communities are rare, therapy groups can be a vital experience for a person in a developmental crisis such as a marital breakup or the death of an intimate. Group members at various stages of resolving similar issues provide understanding, promise of success, and corrective confrontation.

Still another use of a group in my work is to provide an experiential learning situation where a long-term individual client can test the intrapsychic gains made in therapy in the sort of "halfway" setting a group provides. In such cases, that client also has an opportunity to wind down from the sense of specialness which one-to-one therapy provides and to begin to surrender the illusions of transference responses to the reality of knowing a therapist in a more nearly typical situation. The group provides a two-part graduation of the client's therapy: a gradual reduction in the frequency of our individual contacts as the person affiliates with the group, and the use of the group itself as a graduation from therapy, though the latter may be an extended process of a year or more.

With respect to a group's needs, when I am considering a person for membership, I don't refer deeply disturbed people like schizophrenics or sociopaths, but I do not hesitate to refer a borderline client whom I am also seeing individually for the socialization/modeling/support functions a group can serve. I also protect an age and sex mix in my groups, with men and women in nearly even numbers and age span of early twenties to early sixties, so the group members offer a variety of family transference potentialities to one another. That latter criterion provides the occasion for members to work through issues with people who remind them of problem parents or offspring as well as providing some new objects for parenting or being parented (or "kidded," as the case may be) which enrich members' lives and offer corrective familial experiences. In my experience, persons who are recovering from an addiction and are in twelve-step programs find the relatively unstructured setting of group therapy anxiety-producing. They often respond to that anxiety by rigid allegience to the twelve-step belief system, often stated in aphorisms defensively delivered. Since the twelve-step program is crucial for their new-found sobriety, I am loath to question its tenets even when employed defensively. Thus, I seldom refer such a person to an ongoing, interactional, open-ended group.

THE PARADOX OF LIMITS AS PERMISSION

When a potential or active member of a group is resisting the group's usefulness, one of the principal arguments is the group's artificiality. In fact, a therapy group *is* a highly stylized social creation and paradoxically that accounts for a significant part of its effectiveness. Precisely because the group meets for a limited amount of time but with predictability and consistency, it becomes an arena in which members can try out new ways to present themselves without fear of being stuck if they aren't comfortable with themselves or the response of the group. In a group, for example, a member who expresses anger does not risk what the same expression could yield at home, school, or work: no one will walk away, turn on a TV, report the behavior to someone else, or withdraw for an extended period. The presence of a therapist whose task is, among others, to enable members to find satisfaction in their relating to one another can make even a potentially explosive situation into "grist for the therapeutic mill." The promise of absolute confidentiality (excepting the therapist's use of a consultant if necessary) protects members from exposure beyond the walls of the room.

I ask my group members not to contact one another outside the room and time of the group and to honor the group's confidentiality should they meet in other situations. Members usually respect that; if they do test it, they quickly see the destructive influence of subgrouping on the larger group's life and they sanction one another.

The time limit (ninety minutes) also seems artificial, and is, but it puts pressure on the members' ambivalence in seeking satisfaction in ways that more typical relationships do not, feeding the illusion in our larger lives that we can put something off indefinitely. The time limit also protects against the opposite feeling, that we are timelessly caught in difficult situations.

The controlled access to and exit from a group is artificial, but it protects members from abrupt losses and unannounced arrivals and teaches members how to respect their feelings when surrendering a member or accepting one, teaching them to count rather than discount the griefs and grievances of everyday life. Members promise to stay in a group at least three months and, whenever they leave, to give at least two weeks' notice of their intention. In combination these two norms enable the group to include a new member and also try to influence another member not to go. Each member is given time to enter with respect for individual style and to receive the benefit of others' and his or her own expression of grief or joy at leaving. When a new person arrives, I leave introductions up to the members. Since one of the common experiences of persons seeking therapy is a refusal to honor life's griefs and grievances, this careful attention to group members' comings and goings is a purposeful, ritualized correction to the denial of anxiety and loss which living in a world of constant changes imposes on us.

In my groups I expect a client to "buy a seat in the room," that is, to pay for a session whether present or not. Since other norms obviate substitution which is possible in individual counseling hours, this requirement protects me financially. Its other effect is to make absence rare and a consistent gathering predictable, with important implications for the group's cohesion. I allow two weeks off from payment in a year's time for sickness, vacation, business, in addition to the two or three times a group does not meet because of holidays. When I work with a cotherapist, our usual pattern is for both of us to be present, though working as cotherapists allows each of us to have occasional time off and the group to meet regularly. If neither of us is able to be present, which is quite rare, I encourage the group to meet without us but to work under the usual time limits. Of course there is no charge for those meetings. Meetings following those often center on work with members' transference responses to the therapists without whose assumed magical powers the group was able to function quite well.

THE CASE FOR COTHERAPY

I find my group work most effective and personally more satisfying when I work with a cotherapist. I will not work with a male cotherapist in a mixed group because I find that combination altogether too reinforcing of sexist patterns which have skewed the emotional development of both men and women in this society.

In choosing a woman to work with, I look for someone with whom I share basic assumptions about people and their needs, whose therapeutic orientation is compatible with but not necessarily the same as my own, and whose personal style is complementary to mine. In the service of our own satisfaction and our working effectiveness, I want to meet with my cotherapist regularly, preferably weekly, to attend to our sense of the group's needs and to work through any problems we are having with one another. When a new member out of my individual practice is considering entering a group, I require one meeting of that person with my cotherapist. In that meeting my cotherapist can assess the individual's potentiality for group therapy, learn something of the person, and present herself in such a way as to establish her authority and potential usefulness to a new member. If she feels a person would either not benefit from the group or would not be beneficial for the group, she may exercise a veto. This meeting with my cotherapist is a means of making her therapeutically important to a new member and a means to obviate a member's inclination to view her as the "wicked stepmother."

Cotherapists provide a powerful "mother-father" in charge of a "sibling" familylike setting for the group. That familial setting encourages transference responses, acting out, and gradual establishment of parity which successful growing up and successful completion of therapy both require. This replication of a family setting can be a specific corrective experience for clients whose families of origin created problems in development. In addition, by modeling complementarity within a relationship of equal authority, the cotherapists provide clients with important models of mature conflict resolution and cooperation. This function signals the need of the cotherapists to maintain the quality of their relationship in such a way as to make clear to the group members that they are indivisible in the group—the one dyad that cannot be violated by any member's "divide and conquer" efforts or Oedipal maneuvers. A group needs that solidarity in its leaders just as a family does in the parents' insistence that they are the continuing dyad in a mix of people where the others (children) are clearly, albeit slowly and complexly, passing through.

The presence of a cotherapist in the room gives each therapist a sense of freedom in several important respects. First, simply having another professional's company in the therapeutic effort is a welcome change from the "loneliness of the long-distance therapist." Second, when my countertransference issues with a given client skew my perception and my work with that person, a cotherapist can offer a corrective to me both in the group and in our meetings with one another. That is, the cotherapist relationship between respectful equals has an unwitting ongoing supervision potentiality for each person. Third, when either of us is working intensely with a particular person in the group, the other is available to be a facilitator of that work, freeing the more active therapist to put himself or herself more fully into the interaction, or the less active therapist can pay attention to the responses of other group members to note their reactions and to follow up on them or to invite them to enter the work in progress if that is appropriate.

DEVELOPING THE GROUP-THERAPEUTIC MEDIUM

In an interactional therapy group the most important work for members' growth is that which is oriented to the here and now in their struggles to find satisfaction with one another in the room. Members will revert to the familiar, opt for easy answers, and avoid success, but those maneuvers are part of the sequence through which a new group, or new members of an established group, will go in arriving at more effective work.

It is predictable that group members, like their counterparts in individual therapy, will likely begin their efforts by talking about situations in their current work and love lives. That is an implicit and tempting invitation to group members to give advice. An experienced therapist knows that advice is mostly for not taking, but also knows that deftly handled, the presentation of frustrations in a client's life can be the occasion for addressing and working through issues of personal style which are implicit in the situation. That same shift from advising (and being told the advice is too late, too shallow, already attempted unsuccessfully) to inviting curiosity about the self and style of the client is the shift the group needs to make. The move that will make such a beginning into something most useful to the presenter and to the other group members is to bring the issue into the room, to see how it corresponds to or is in contrast to the client's life in the group. A question such as "Who among us would you most likely have such a problem with?" can enable that shift. In an experienced group the shift would as likely come from a member with something like, "If I were your (wife, boss, lover, child), I would. . . ." In some such sequence the work can move from advising to more compelling corrective interaction with curative implications not only for the presenting client but for other group members.

Another means to shift from the temptation to advise to more fruitful interventions is to focus on the person to whom the problem appears to be addressed, that is, to view the content as less relevant than the process. This can be done by noting that the presenter seems to be talking to a particular person and by asking the presenter to be curious about what he or she may want from or want to offer the other person. The person addressed can also be invited to respond with his or her feelings about being addressed and may begin with advice but can be encouraged to explore the relational process rather than the content.

In an experienced interactional group, however, initiatives are more likely to originate within the room, often picking up on some unfinished issue from a previous session, and addressed to the difficulties or successes the members are having with one another or with one or both of the therapists. Here the deft use of the various transference relations in the room and the working through of those to reality-based satisfaction-for-now in the room will be important cues to clients for their larger relationships in their worlds. Here the learning will be experiential as well as intellectual, and so that learning will have a particularly powerful impact. Often, at the end of some in-the-room sequence between members or between a member and a therapist, a therapeutic comment on the relation of the work to the client's life in the world can help the client and others who have witnessed the experience assimilate the experience. That satisfaction in immediate issues of conflict or caring between members, skillfully interpreted to closure by being related to the client's larger life and history, is the essence of effective group psychotherapy.

It is a further peculiarity of group counseling that no matter what a member brings up, the issue or topic will have personal implications for other group members. For example, a member who talks about the illness or death of a parent will have tapped deep feelings in all the members about their parents, living or dead, or about other important griefs. The observant therapist will see evidences of various members' discomfort and may choose to invite them to disclose their feelings. Often, a particular session may turn out to have had a "topic" though there had been no intended agenda. Again, without the stimulus of others in the group, members may not likely have addressed those issues in therapy.

The sensitive leader will often make a comment on the processes a group seems to be going through as it works out issues of control, affiliation, and expressions of affection or conflict. When a group's process seems to have a "topic," that is, when a whole or a significant part of a meeting seems to come down to a particular issue such as affiliation, though the content was quite varied, a therapist might observe: "We seem to be testing our relations with one another to see if we can trust one another with important issues." Such an observation may not be responded to, whether it was accurate or not; it may be challenged, whether accurate or not. In any case it will serve to sensitize members to self-consciousness about their processes and make them curious about issues that may be more revealing of intentions than the manifest content is.

In the service of immediacy and ever-increasing personal interaction, I always speak directly and personally and attempt to teach members to do the same. For example, I would not say, "How did *it* feel to do that?" but rather, "How do *you* feel, doing that?" Again, I avoid the general in favor of the particular. I would avoid saying, "We often feel angry when someone dies," in favor of "You seem to be feeling angry." In my experience, in a similar vein, the jargon of the various therapeutic schools or of the human potential movement in general, often developed to encourage more direct communication, in time becomes a new source of confusion and mystification. Thus, I avoid the use of jargon and use the simplest of all possible speech in the conviction that the most important things we have to say to one another may be stated quite simply and are more likely to be understood. When members are addressing one another, I encourage the most direct and immediate speech. For example, a member will be tempted to talk *about* another member who is in the room by using the member's name and the third person pronoun. I ask the speaker to talk to the member by name with the pronoun *you*. In all of this, my intention is to facilitate direct, clear, and intimate interaction among the members.

A group can become a corporate benign introjection for its members. Sometimes that simply seems to happen, as in the case of the young woman quoted earlier who thought of other group members and how hard they were struggling when she was tempted to give up. A therapist can also make self-conscious use of this phenomenon. For example, when a member seems potentially self-destructive, I will work for a promise from that person to the group that he or she will neither by omission nor commission risk personal harm. A client will often respond by denying the value of such a promise. I then ask if that means the client is not someone who keeps promises. Gradually, the person can usually be persuaded to make the promise. If I cannot get a blanket promise, I go for a time-limited one, in which case I ask for its renewal when the time is up. In an experienced group, members will work together with a therapist on such an effort. I recall a woman saying to another, "When you are tempted to cut yourself, think of me asking you not to do that." The group or particular members then become an auxiliary ego or superego for the client, whose efforts are diverted from self-destruction to keeping the promise. That buys time and insurance for the client to work through the life issues which seem so overwhelming. Without such a promise, the very process of working through the issues in therapy may unwittingly reinforce the impulse to self-destruction. If I cannot get such a promise—and I will not accept an "I'll try" sort of response—I tell the person in front of the group that I am notifying a family member, close friend, or physician of his or her intentions and then I do that if that statement does not bring cooperation. Often, my insistence will lead to a diversion of the self-directed anger to me with a resulting relief of mood which will then make the promise possible.

Certainly, a group takes time to get to a level of effectiveness, and a group, like any other human enterprise, will falter, regress, require redirection, and threaten to destroy itself with aberrant behavior. At such times, the influence of firm but patient and graceful leadership will be a needed corrective and the threats will become more "grist for the therapeutic mill" as the members experience the possibility of finding new effectiveness coming out of the group's ills. The impatient, rigid, threatened leader will be antitherapeutic here as in so many other critical times in working with people. That argues for the inexperienced group counselor to seek continual supervision, for the tired therapist to seek supervision or continuing education to regain energy and enthusiasm, and for any of us to go back to our own therapy for seeing where our old issues have reappeared in disguise to trip us up and be harmful to our clients.

CONCLUSION

In brief scope I have attempted to share my experience in and enthusiasm for doing counseling in heterogeneous interactional groups of adults. I have not dealt with more homogeneous groups—couples groups, single-sex groups, adolescent groups, and the like. These have their peculiar potentialities and specialized problems too complex to pursue here. However, the interactional model which I have introduced can be used in homogeneous groups as well.

At best, counseling groups offer members the experience of finding that they are not alone in their struggles to make sense of life in these trying times. As they work together striving to find satisfaction in their relationships with one another, members learn those empathetic skills which will enrich their lives at home, at work, and in their voluntary associations. In being respected by others they will come to respect themselves—the only secure base from which to extend respect to others. In trusting others with self-disclosure in a group, members will learn that the exposure of their deepest feelings will not yield contempt as they might have feared, but a deepened acceptance from others. In risking the expression of anger at members and therapists, clients will see that their rage does not destroy others and that its expression may lead the way to deepening relationships. While group therapy is not the approach of choice for all our clients, it is a particularly clear way to enable people to learn experientially. Most of us live in families and work among others: we are called to function in groups of all sorts. That peculiar social construct, the therapy group, can make us more effective and more sensitive participants in the common life.

As pastoral counselors we know better than to expect perfection of ourselves or our clients. We are part of a tradition that comprehends and is not surprised at our own or our clients' proclivity to foul our nests. We understand that grace informed Creation and succeeded Fall and endures to renew us when we acknowledge our needs and avoid expecting too much of ourselves, our lives, our peers, our clients. My work in groups continually reminds me that, as a former colleague noted, "God works in mischievous ways," and that good things come out of Nazareth as well as other unlikely places. For myself, work in groups is a source of renewal of my energies and of my belief in the healing impact of knowing we are not alone. In my groups I not only function myself as priest, pastor, and prophet, I also have the opportunity to teach others a sort of ministry of hearing, conversing, and confronting which, I would hope, they take out to their larger worlds. One client said it well: "Here I have learned to be a better friend."

REFERENCES

Berne, Eric. *Principles of Group Treatment.* New York: Oxford University Press, 1966.
Erikson, Erik H. *Insight and Responsibility.* New York: Norton, 1964.
Mullen, Hugh, and Max Rosenbaum. *Group Psychotherapy: Theory and Practice,* 2nd ed. New York: Free Press, 1978.
Perls, F. S. *Gestalt Therapy Verbatim.* LaFayette, Penn.: Real People Press, 1969.
Yalom, Irvin. *The Theory and Practice of Group Psychotherapy,* 2nd ed. New York: Basic Books, 1975.

RECOMMENDED READINGS

GENERAL

Berne, Eric. *Principles of Group Treatment.* New York: Oxford University Press, 1966.
Clinebell, Howard J., Jr. *The People Dynamic.* New York: Harper, 1972.

Johnson, D., and F. P. Johnson. *Joining Together: Group Theory and Group Skills.* Englewood Cliffs, N.J.: Prentice Hall, 1975.

Lieberman, M., I. Yalom, and M. Miles. *Encounter Groups: First Facts.* New York: Basic Books, 1973.

Mullen, H., and M. Rosenbaum. *Group Psychotherapy: Theory and Practice,* 2nd ed. New York: Free Press, 1978.

Yalom, Irvin D. *The Theory and Practice of Group Psychotherapy,* 2nd ed. New York: Basic Books, 1975.

SPECIALIZED

Berkowitz, Irving H. *Adolescents Grow in Groups.* New York: Brunner/Mazel, 1972.

CHAPTER SIXTEEN

Professional and Ethical Issues in Pastoral Counseling

MELVIN C. BLANCHETTE, PH.D.

"Theoretical and practical psychology, the one as much as the other, should bear in mind that they cannot lose sight of the truths established by reason and by faith, nor of the obligatory precepts of ethics. . . . This fundamental attitude can be summed up in the following formula: Psychotherapy and clinical psychology must always consider a human being (1) as a psychic unit and totality, (2) as a structured unit in itself, (3) as a social unit, and (4) as a transcendent unit, that is to say, tending towards God." (Pius XII, 1953)

We live in an ever-changing world. For the pastoral counselor, the possibilities inherent in the process of change are grounded in the compassion of Christ for all of God's people. This work, *Pastoral Counseling*, is an example of how change is always with us. Since its first edition in 1983, this exposition of pastoral counseling has changed in design but not in purpose. The first edition endeavored to address the challenges of pastoral counseling in our day. In a scholarly manner, the authors composed a comprehensive presentation of pastoral counseling. It lacked, however, a specific chapter on professional ethics as a valid concern for pastoral counselors. Perhaps this was an oversight. But it is more likely that this omission stemmed from a mindset that took ethics as a foregone inclusion in all professional relationships. It was assumed that since pastoral counseling is a ministry practiced in faith by religiously oriented people, they would be totally ethical and incapable of any ethical violation.

Even in the Bible (2 Sam. 11), we are reminded of how King David, while remaining at home in Jerusalem as other determined Israelites were waging war, seduced the wife of one of his most dedicated soldiers. Only the prophet Nathan, through a small but effective case scenario, was able to get the king to reflect on his moral and ethical behavior.

Our world and endeavors are continuously changing and developing as we gain new insight and realize new visions. Often, we have an opportunity to improve upon our former accomplishments. What was lacking in past efforts can now be addressed. Reflected in this new edition is the realization that ethical issues of the world in general and the counseling profession in particular must be examined. If one doubts this, consider the publicity given to the ethical concerns of international alliances, internal government relations, and individual professional relationships—especially our own therapeutic relationships.

This chapter places a high value on ethical judgment and conduct for the ministry and the profession of pastoral counseling. It is an overview meant to challenge the reader to become enlivened with a spirit of concern for ethical principles and issues as applied to pastoral counseling and the mental health profession. Pastoral counseling is a living reality of Jesus' presence in our world. Its contributions, though rooted in an ancient history, are always being renewed for each generation of those called to share in the healing ministry of Jesus. Ethics provides guidelines for the artisans of change as they deal with an increasingly complex set of human issues.

This brief chapter will review pastoral counseling as a ministry so that the reader understands its unique nature and purpose. Flowing from its unique nature, purpose, and professional standards will come a number of ethical concepts to serve as guidelines. It also will be necessary to examine pastoral counseling as a profession in order to clarify the obligations and demands which it shares with other helping disciplines.

THE MINISTRY OF PASTORAL COUNSELING

Pastoral counselors belong to a profession whose history predates its existence as an organization. Pastoral counseling is part of the healing ministry of Jesus. In the New Testament, Jesus is the new Moses, and His ministry is the starting point of all Christian ministries. Actually, the one mission of Jesus encompassed many varied ministries. Jesus was sent by the Father not only to give up His life, but also to preach the good news of salvation—essentially an invitation to change and to have faith. Jesus came so that all may have life and have it abundantly (John 3:16). Jesus spoke of His mission in terms of the liberation process which He proclaimed in His messianic message in Luke's Gospel:

The Spirit of the Lord is upon me because He has chosen me to bring good news to the poor. He has sent me to proclaim liberty to captives and recovery of sight to the blind, to set free the oppressed and announce that the time has come when the Lord will save His people (Luke 4:18–19).

Everything that Jesus did after this "inaugural speech" was a fulfillment of its promises. He did what He promised, and fulfilled in deeds what He voiced. He proclaimed liberty to the captives of sin (Luke 7:36–50) and illusion (Luke 12:11–21), and recovered sight and vision to the physically and spiritually blind (John 9). Jesus freed the oppressed from physical and spiritual paralysis (Luke 5:17–25), from rigid and narrow religious vision (Luke 5:33–39), from guilt (John 8:1–11), from leprosy (Luke 17:11–19), and from suffering (Luke 8:40–50).

The mission of Jesus as detailed above can be divided into four different ministries through which it is achieved. The ministries which have their roots in the Gospel are: ministry in word, ministry of community building, ministry of celebrating, and ministry of healing. What is so noteworthy in the mission of Jesus is the disproportionate amount of time for His healing ministry, namely, helping the burdened and the sick. Properly attuned, pastoral counselors listen to Him saying that people who are well do not need a doctor, but only those who are sick (Matt. 2:17). Another implication is that healing can begin with the creation of an atmosphere. Jesus was with others. In like manner, pastoral counselors invite others to become open to a new healing presence, to examine their scars, and to lance their wounds.

Jesus sent out His disciples with a threefold ministry of teaching, preaching, and healing. The apostolic Church continued the healing ministry of Jesus as reported in nineteen accounts in the Acts of the Apostles. The fathers of the Church continued the same tradition. In nearly every one of the fathers—Justin the Martyr, Iranaeus, Tertullian, Cyprion—there is clear evidence of the belief in exorcisms and the power of the Church to heal. Pastoral counselors participate, through their experience, education, and choice, in continuing the healing and liberating mission of Jesus. It is a ministry which aims at achieving wholeness for the individual, one resulting from a threefold reconciliation with oneself, others, and God. However, before reconciliation can take place, people must be liberated and their pain must be understood as having meaning and purpose.

THE PROFESSION OF PASTORAL COUNSELING

Theoretical Issues

As a profession, pastoral counseling today does not enjoy the time-honored position it has held within the history of the Church. Pastoral counseling is a specific form of individual pastoral care in which ministers utilize the knowledge and skills derived from the contemporary helping professions within a ministerial and theological framework.

Historically, individual pastoral care has been a rich part of the tradition of Christian ministry. Clebsh and Jaekle, in *Pastoral Care in Historical Perspective* (1983), discussed the functions of individual pastoral care under the headings healing, sustaining, guiding, and reconciling. *Healing* entails helping a person to be restored to a condition of wholeness; *sustaining* consists of helping a hurting person to endure; *guiding* involves assisting perplexed persons to make confident choices; *reconciling* seeks to reestablish broken relationships with others and with God. The authors related these four functions to eight periods of Church history from "primitive Christianity" to the present "post-Christendom era." While individual pastoral care has been a part of Christian ministry for some twenty centuries, the effort to reach these goals through the process of pastoral counseling is a twentieth century phenomenon.

Pastoral counseling, as a specific form of pastoral care, attempts to combine insights and techniques derived from the contemporary helping professions with the insights of theology, faith, and ministry. James W. Ewing, in the final chapter of this book, describes the role of pastoral counseling by using the metaphor of a bridge. "Because the field links together religion and behavioral science, and consequently sacred tradition and secular lifestyle, it functions as a structural bridge over the chasms of contemporary compartmentalization of knowledge and professional activity. Those persons attracted to the field usually function with multiple intellectual and professional commitments. At a time when our Western culture is witness to rapid change and fragmentation, pastoral counseling is attempting to bridge such through attention to the integrative and holistic process of human living and knowing."

The goal of training in pastoral counseling is to provide the minister (ordained, vowed religious, lay) with the opportunity to work toward a synthesis that includes: (1) an incorporation of the body of knowledge common to the field of counseling theory and practice; (2) the development of specific counseling skills; (3) an ability to enter into a deep and trustful relationship quickly; (4) an intuitive understanding of how to facilitate therapeutic progress which addresses simultaneously the whole person: physically, intellectually, emotionally, socially, and spiritually; and (5) a clear understanding of one's role as minister.

Accordingly, this twentieth century phenomenon called pastoral counseling has come into its own as a profession. This recognition of its professionalism is evidenced through the publication of the *AAPC Code of Ethics* of the American Association of Pastoral Counselors. Ethics code development is a necessary and essential step in the professionalization of any occupation. A profession such as pastoral counseling requires a code of ethics because society maintains a different relationship with professions than with a business enterprise. As a profession, the underlying notion of pastoral counseling is its proclivity to profess, that is, to claim to have some knowledge, special training, or skill not shared by the nonprofessional. What pastoral counselors profess is clearly outlined in Estadt's definition in the opening chapter of this book: that "A pastoral counselor . . . is a religiously integrated person . . . who approaches others with a sense of mystery . . . along with an ability to enter into communion with others in a therapeutic alliance . . . with the goal of reconciliation and personal religious integration."

Specifically, pastoral counselors profess to fulfill two important functions to those entering a helping relationship; these functions are (1) to enable a person to become free in order to become responsible and (2) to enable a person to deal with pain in its many forms in order to understand the deeper significance it plays in life. It is, however, insufficient for the professional simply to profess in any helping relationship. What is professed must also be believed by the public. Thus, the overriding concern of all professions is the adage *credat emptor*—freely translated as "that the client may believe." This expression is quite different from the more familiar one which governs the sale of goods, *caveat emptor*—"let the buyer beware." Hence, it is of the greatest importance that members of the public believe or trust in the claims made by the professional. This is especially true in a profession such as pastoral counseling where the clients are expected to disclose the most intimate details of their lives, those not ordinarily shared with others.

After reviewing the ethical codes of the American Psychological Association, the American Association of Pastoral Counselors, and the American Association of Counseling and Development, one is struck by the similarity among them. The principles of each code are primarily directed toward ensuring the safety of the public served by the counseling professional. Through ensuring the public's safety, the ethical principles provide a climate or foundation of trust from which helping professionals can build a therapeutic and healing relationship. Hence, the significance of trust in the helping relationship enables one to answer the important question, "Why ethics?" Ethical principles inform the practice of counseling professionals and protect the trust upon which any relationship is based. Conversely, whenever there is a violation of this trust, the public as well as the reputation of the profession is harmed.

Historically, the American Psychological Association (APA) created an ethics committee in 1938; however, a formal ethics code was not adopted until 1953. The first code was developed using a quasi-empirical method. Input from the membership was requested, and this information was used to develop the code. The fact that this code has undergone change and revision through the years indicates how ethics codes must be adaptive to the cultural context and circumstances of the times. The most recent edition was issued in 1981. The most recent American Association of Pastoral Counselors' (AAPC) *Code of Ethics* was adopted by its board of governors on recommendation by the association's ethics committee during the annual convention on April 11, 1986. The association's ethics committee acknowledged the use, with permission, of the *Ethical Principles of Psychologists* in developing its standards and principles. The American Association for Counseling and Development's (AACD)

Ethical Standards was revised by the governing council in March of 1988, and essentially mirrors the content of the previous two codes.

A unique feature of the *AAPC Code of Ethics* is its explicit affirmation that pastoral counselors are committed to a belief in God and in the dignity and worth of each person. Aside from this explicit declaration of a belief in God and the dignity and worth of each individual made in God's image, the *AAPC Code of Ethics* closely parallels the others. While these codes vary in length and specific content, they contain similar themes: to promote the welfare of the consumer, to maintain competence, to protect confidentiality and/or privacy, to act responsibly, to avoid exploitation, and to uphold the integrity of the profession.

In summary, one way to appreciate the full meaning of these various ethical codes is to generalize their content into two broad moral categories:

Care of the Public. Direct care for the public underlies the ethical standards of the American Psychological Association, the American Association of Pastoral Counselors, and the American Association for Counseling and Development. These principles are: *responsibility, moral and legal standards,* and *the welfare of the consumer*. In each of these principles, two related questions are being asked: Did the professional counselor honor the trust of the client? Did the professional counselor take unfair advantage of the client, either intentionally or unintentionally through negligence or ignorance? Whether the lack of care resulting in offensive behavior was intentional or unintentional, the effect on the client or other person is almost always the same.

Care for the Professional's Education and Training. The remaining principles stress concern for the professional's ability and competence to serve the public properly. These include specific discussions of the meaning of professional competence; the ethical issues involved in the making of public statements; the issue of the confidentiality of the professional relationship with clients; the use of various assessment techniques; and, for the APA code, the ethics of the use of animals in experimentation.

Pastoral counseling, as the continuation of the healing ministry of Jesus, enjoys a privileged position among the helping professions. With this privilege comes the obligation to practice this ministry with care. Research amply confirms through clinical experience that whenever we talk about our lives with care, they change. As pastoral counselors, when we care, we do so within the framework of our ministry and of our faith.

Pastoral counseling is in the process of taking its rightful place among the helping professions. It holds a place of honor because it seeks to integrate theology with the behavioral sciences. Pastoral counseling is guided by the spirit of Jesus because it is a ministry done in faith. It is likewise governed by a standard of caring expressed through a code of ethics. The theoretical issues contained in these various codes have been discussed. Their basic content reflects the art of caring. Now, we turn our attention to those practical ethical understandings which flow from the theoretical underpinnings of pastoral counseling. Some recommendations for the future will also be discussed.

Ethical Understandings

1. Pastoral counseling continues the healing ministry of Jesus and so comes under the greatest and most severe sanctions imposed by God spoken through the prophet Ezekiel. Note the adjective *pastoral*. As shepherds, pastoral counselors are called to be not only copilgrims, but also guides for those who are searching for meaning and purpose.

2. Pastoral counselors are mandated to live lives of exemplary conduct. While the meaning as well as the often strict enforcement of ethical principles may make them appear to be synonymous with law, there is one important difference between laws and ethical principles. An important legal principle is the qualifying factor of degree of negligence or intention. Determining a violation of an ethical principle rarely involves consideration of such a qualifying factor. Ethical principles and violations tend to be absolute. This is because of the nature of the population governed by ethical codes, one of well-trained professionals from whom the public demands such exemplary conduct.

3. As members of a helping profession which seeks to establish human relationships and techniques for bringing about personality and behavioral change, pastoral counselors must be eminently aware of those principles which guide the beginning, continuation, and termination of any therapeutic alliance. These principles are clearly delineated in the ethical codes referred to above.

4. Pastoral counselors are not simply counselors with additional training in theology and in the pastoral arts and sciences. Pastoral counselors are mandated to be members in good standing with their sponsoring faith groups. As such, pastoral counselors maintain a vital denominational connectiveness with a religious body.

Pastoral counselors function within a unique context. This context alone gives a correct understanding of what the ministry and profession entails. Pastoral counseling is pastoral because its origin is rooted within the religious ministry of the *cura animarum,* a tradition of care and cure of souls. Accordingly, pastoral counselors derive their authorization to practice this religious ministry from their respective religious bodies or denominations. From this empowerment comes the energy and vitality of the pastoral counseling ministry, a work done in faith within the community of believers.

5. Pastoral counselors frequently serve as ministers in a local congregation. As such they are in a position to counsel parishioners. In this regard, pastoral counselors

would do well to review Principle 7, "Professional Relationships" in the *Ethical Principles of Psychologists,* and Principle III, "Client Relationship and Confidentiality" in the *AAPC Code of Ethics.* Each of these principles speaks of the necessity for avoiding dual relationships with current or former clients. Accordingly, it is recommended that except for grave reasons, a pastor not contract for long-term pastoral counseling with a parishioner.

6. Lastly, an issue which has been surfacing in a number of professional meetings is whether or not pastoral counselors should be certified or licensed as professional counselors. It would seem reasonable that as long as pastors are doing short-term counseling in their parishes, there is no obligation to seek further legitimacy since that counseling is an integral component of the *cura animarum* expected of the pastor by the congregation. However, if a pastoral counselor is doing counseling in a state or private mental health agency, that counselor should receive certification as a professional counselor even though the adjective *pastoral* might be expressed only through an attitudinal presence. In addition, pastoral counselors who are practicing in their parishes and seeing people from the wider community should be regulated by the prevailing laws of certification and licensure in the same way as other professionals since they are offering mental health services to the general public, an activity which is becoming increasingly regulated by the state.

Professional ethics is not an easy issue to treat in so few pages. What has been attempted is to give an overview of pastoral counseling as a ministry and a profession. The practical ethical understandings emerge from the dual nature of this discipline. Since pastoral counseling is dealing with ever-deepening levels of complexity, pastoral counselors would be well advised to engage in further graduate course work to study the implications of the principles discussed in this chapter. In the absence of available course work, collegial discussions with other pastoral counselors, supervisors, and consultants would be beneficial not only to help people to *do* what they believe to be right, but also to help them *decide* what is right.

In conclusion, Micah was an eminently practical man. He exhorted people to act with thoughtfulness as well as to think in terms of their actions. He sounded a call for social justice, and for people and priests alike to reflect on religious ethics. Micah will always be remembered for identifying what God requires of us. "This is what is required of you, to do right, to love goodness, and to walk humbly with your God" (Mic. 6:8).

REFERENCES

Clebsh, W., and C. Jaehle. *Pastoral Care in Historical Perspective.* New York: Jason Aronson, Inc., 1983.
Pius XII. "An Address of His Holiness Pope Pius XII to the Fifth International Congress on Psychotherapy and Clinical Psychology, April 13, 1953." *On Psychotherapy And Religion.* Washington, D.C.: National Catholic Welfare Conference.

RECOMMENDED READINGS

American Association for Counseling and Development. *Ethical Standards*. Washington, D.C.: American Association for Counseling and Development, 1981.

American Association for Marriage and Family Therapy. *Ethical Principles for Family Therapists*. Washington, D.C.: American Association for Marriage and Family Therapy, 1982.

————. *Membership Standards*. Washington, D.C.: American Association for Marriage and Family Therapy, 1982.

————. *Standards on Public Information and Advertising*. Washington, D.C.: American Association for Marriage and Family Therapy, 1982.

American Association of Pastoral Counselors. *AAPC Code of Ethics*. Fairfax, VA: American Association of Pastoral Counselors, 1986.

American Psychological Association. *Ethical Principles of Psychologists*. Washington, D.C.: American Psychological Association, 1981.

Aubrey, R., and M. D'Andrea. "What Counselors Should Know About High Technology," *Counseling and Human Development*, 17(1), 1984, 5–11.

Bentham, J. "An Introduction to the Principles of Morals and Legislation." In W.T. Jones et al (Eds.), *Approaches to Ethics*, 3rd ed. New York: McGraw-Hill, 1977. (Originally published in 1810.)

Berger, M. "Ethics and the Therapeutic Relationship: Patient Rights and Therapist Responsibilities." In M. Rosenbaum (Ed.), *Ethics and Values in Psychotherapy*. New York: Free Press, 1982.

Bergin, A. E. "Psychotherapy and Religious Values," *Journal of Consulting and Clinical Psychology*. 48, 1980, 95–105.

Biggs, D., and D. Blocker. *Foundations of Ethical Counseling*. New York: Springer, 1987.

Burgum, T., and S. Anderson. *The Counselor and the Law*. Washington, D.C.: American Association for Counseling and Development, 1985.

Callis, R. (Ed.). *Ethical Standards Casebook*. Washington, D.C.: American Association for Counseling and Development, 1982.

Corey, G., M. S. Corey, and P. Callanan. *Professional and Ethical Issues in Counseling and Psychotherapy*. Monterey, Calif.: Brooks/Cole, 1979.

Dabner, E. V., and E. S. Daubner. "Ethics and Counseling Decisions," *Personnel and Guidance Journal*, 48(6), 1970, 434–442.

Drane, J. F. "Ethics and Psychotherapy: A Philosophical Perspective." In M. Rosenbaum (Ed.), *Ethics and Values in Psychotherapy*. New York: Free Press, 1982.

Dujovne, B. E. "Sexual Feeling, Fantasies, and Acting Out in Psychotherapy," *Psychotherapy: Theory, Research, and Practice*, 20(2), 1983, 243–50.

Foster, H. M. "The Conflict and Reconciliation of the Ethical Interests of Therapists and Patient," *Journal of Psychiatry Law*, 3(1), 1975, 39–48.

Frankel, M. "Morality in Psychotherapy," *Psychology Today*, 1(4), 1967, 24–30.

Fretz, B. R., and D. H. Mills. "Professional Certification in Counseling Psychology," *Counseling Psychologist*, 9(1), 1980, 2–17.

Fromm, E. *Man for Himself: An Inquiry into the Psychology of Ethics*. New York: Holt, 1947.

Gill, S. J. "Professional Disclosure and Consumer Protection in Counseling," *Personnel and Guidance Journal*, 66(3), 1982, 443–46.

Hare-Mustin, R. T. "Family Therapy May Be Dangerous to Your Health," *Professional Psychology*, 11, 1980, 935–38.

Hart, G. M. *Values Clarifications for Counselors*. Springfield, Ill.: Charles C. Thomas, 1979.

Hogan, R. "Ethical Decision-Making." In F. Chu and S. Trotter (Eds.), *The Madness Establishment*. New York: Grossman, 1974.

Ivey, A. E. "Counseling and Psychotherapy: Toward a New Perspective," *Counseling Psychologist*, 9(2), 1981, 83–98.

Keith-Spiegel, P. "Violation of Ethical Principles Due to Ignorance or Poor Professional Judgement Versus Willful Disregard," *Professional Psychology*, 8, 1977, 288–296.

Keith-Spiegel, P., and G. L. Koocher. *Ethics in Psychology*. New York: Random House, 1985.

Kottler, J. "Ethic Come of Age," *Journal for Specialists in Group Work*, 7(3), 1982, 138–139.

Kottler, J., and R. Brown. *Introduction to Therapeutic Counseling*. Monterey, Calif.: Brooks/Cole, 1985.

Meyer, R. G., E. R. Landis, and J. R. Hays. *Law for the Psychotherapist*. New York: Norton, 1988.

Reich, W. "Psychiatric Diagnosis as an Ethical Problem." In S. Bloch and P. Chodoff (Eds.), *Psychiatric Ethics*. Oxford, England: Oxford University Press, 1981.

Ross, W. (Trans.). *Aristotle's Ethics*. Book I. Chicago: Contemporary Books, 1954.

Serban, G. "Sexual Activity in Therapy: Legal and Ethical Issues," *American Journal of Psychotherapy*, 25, 1981, 76–81.

Siegel, M. "Privacy, Ethics, and Confidentiality," *Professional Psychology*, 10(2), 1979, 249–58.

Snygg, D. "The Psychological Basis of Human Values." In D. Avila, A. Combs, and W. Purkey (Eds.), *The Helping Relationship Source Book*. Boston: Allyn & Bacon, 1972.

Strupp, H. H. "On Failing One's Patient," *Psychotherapy: Theory, Research, and Practice*, 12(1), 1975, 39–41.

————. "Clinical Psychology, Irrationalism, and the Erosion of Excellence," *American Psychologist*, 31(8), 1976, 561–71.

Van Hoose, W. H., and J. A. Kottler. *Ethical and Legal Issues in Counseling and Psychotherapy*, 2nd ed. Washington: Jossey-Bass, 1985.

Woody, R. H., et al. *The Law and the Practice of Human Services*. San Francisco: Jossey-Bass, 1984.

Zemlick, M. J. "Ethical Standards: Cosmetics for the Face of the Profession of Psychology," *Psychotherapy: Theory, Research, and Practice*, 17(4), 1980, 448–53.

Zimpfer, D. "Needed: Professional Ethics for Working with Groups," *Personnel and Guidance Journal*, 50(4), 1971, 14–24.

Zimpfer, D. *Group Work in the Helping Professions: A Bibliography*. Washington, D.C.: American Association for Counseling and Development, 1976.

EPILOGUE

Pastoral Counseling Issues: Current and Future

JAMES W. EWING, PH.D.

Pastoral counseling is rooted in two disciplines of knowledge: religion and behavioral science. While both fields have an identifiable integrity, the interplay between them is difficult to resolve both methodologically and conceptually. By and large, pastoral counseling emerges in its contemporary form as a practice of ministry whose focus is the suffering person seeking healing and wholeness. Pastoral counseling is still in an early stage of development as a discipline that produces its own integral structure under its own terms and methods. However, pastoral counselors have had considerable experience since the 1950s as professional practitioners in ministry and psychotherapy/counseling, which clearly identifies them as a distinct professional group. The most critical current and future issue for pastoral counseling is the shaping of its own discipline which guides the practice of the pastoral counselor and at the same time enhances insight and knowledge of both religion and the behavioral sciences.

A framework which provides criteria for the parameters of the discipline is essential in the task of defining the field. There are five assertions that emerge from the struggles of pastoral counseling practice which furnish such a frame of reference.

The first assertion is the commitment to the power and efficacy of the "new psychology" for the practice of ministry. The fathers and mothers who have given the birthright to pastoral counseling were awed by the capacity for healing and change which Freud, Jung, Adler, Rogers, Sullivan, and Watson discovered in their psychological work. The applications and absorption of this power for ministry was the genius of Boison, Wise, Hiltner, Oates, and others. This commitment has given the pastoral counselor the therapeutic clinical process, the right to claim expertise as a minister and mental health professional, and the basis for pastoral counseling as a clinical discipline.

The second assertion is the commitment to religious institutions, church and synagogue, in a time of ferment and change. The pastoral counselor is convinced of the power and efficacy of religious process and insight. Frustration, alienation, and affection for the religious institutions which the pastoral counselor serves give birth to new forms of ministry which in time will have great impact for ecclesiastical reform. Pastoral counselors are among the forerunners of the reformation of religious institutions in the twenty-first century.

The third assertion is the commitment to theological method based on the inherent authority of human experience. God acts within specific human beings and human institutions. Biblical authority, experiential authority, and the authority of tradition are dialogical. All three stand to each other as mutually corrective and supportive. In the current disarray of theology, pastoral counselors enter the arena as leaders and submit their theological awareness within the ferment of methodological conflict for the sake of healing human pain and suffering.

The fourth assertion is the commitment to participate in the changing political, economic, and social institutions. Personal pain and joy are intricately tied to institutional policies and power. Pastoral counselors participate in the decisions that monitor institutional change, particularly in institutions that are working with health care issues. Change in personality is intricately interwoven with change in institutions. One process cannot be addressed apart from the other.

The fifth assertion is the commitment to nurture the pastoral counselor's internal sense of vocation, call, and imagination. Pastoral counseling is largely a subjective, intuitive, and personal process which encompasses the private, hidden, conflicted, and imaginative dimensions of life. From the wellspring of the self emerge meaning, conviction, and purpose which generate spirit and vision. The preservation of the fragile, sensitive vulnerabilities of human living stimulates the power to risk new imaginative ways of trying things and probing unanswered questions.

These five assertions provide a framework from which to extrapolate projections and to guide the future of pastoral counseling.

One image that helps to describe pastoral counseling/psychotherapy is that of a bridge. Because the field links together religion and behavioral science, and consequently sacred tradition and secular lifestyle, it functions as a structural bridge over the chasms of contemporary compartmentalization of knowledge and professional activity. Those persons attracted to the field usually function with multiple intellectual and professional commitments. At a time when our Western culture is witness to rapid change and fragmentation, pastoral counseling is attempting to bridge such through attention to the integrative and holistic processes of human living and knowing.

Pastoral counseling centers and training programs, which are the unique institutional contributions, are "bridge" institutions between religious and secular ones. These centers have been hewn from the forms of religious communities and the forms of mental health clinics of psychiatry. Their roots are firmly planted in each tradition, and they borrow the practices from each to form a blend which is neither solely religious nor solely secular. This phenomenon has tremendous strengths as well as vulnerabilities. Future development depends upon the capacity to hold in balance such power and weakness. Pastoral counseling centers are in fact established institutions.

This establishment is signaled by publication of such volumes as this book, for persons who have been practicing pastoral counseling and who are involved in the training of pastoral counselors. Establishment is also signaled by the increase in new centers and training programs over the past several years. The American Association of Pastoral Counselors, organized in 1964, has gained sufficient strength to provide professional staff for the guidance, coordination, and organization of this growing phenomenon.

Pastoral counseling is an established clinical art and its institutions are multiplying rapidly. The strength of such establishment is the capacity to fulfill the promise of service and healing to hurting persons. The vulnerability is the ossification of bureaucratic organization which tends to dull the spirit, vision, and service which infected the creativity of the fathers and mothers of the movement. The acceptance and energy of expansion are welcomed. The caution is to avoid the fallacy of fadism.

In the midst of such growth and expansion, the genius will be to keep faithful to the exacting discipline of clinical process and to the perceptive judgments of theological critique. The style of life of the pastoral counseling establishment is to live "in the world" but not be "of the world." The pressures demanded by being a health care institution require living by the rules and regulations of that industry. However, the values that inform the purpose and vision of pastoral counseling remain those of religious institutions. Preservation of the principle that allows formation and *re*formation by the spirit of the religious heritage is essential if a center is to be more than just another mental health clinic or another church. Pastoral counseling is on a risky institutional path, but the risk must be taken for the sake of healing activity.

Training programs emerged as the logical extension of pastoral counseling centers. In the past decade the education of pastoral counselors has moved from the "maverick" to the "orthodox" period.

Most pastoral counselors now receive training in established programs which meet standardized curricular requirements. This training is in contrast to the earlier educational process by which an individual gathered sufficient supervision and counseling experience in an *ad hoc* fashion to qualify for certification.

This shift, too, has its strengths and vulnerabilities. The strength of the established training program is the identification of a distinct educational process which puts together educational content and learning in a unique way. The vulnerability is the discouragement of the spirit and novelty of persons who continue to come to the art in unique and maverick ways.

The genius of pastoral counselor education is the interplay between *academic* learning of ideas, constructs, and organized knowledge with *clinical* learning of practice under supervision. Academic and clinical processes remain in a persistent interacting design. Knowing and doing are always experienced together. Faithfulness to objectivity and subjectivity is the "orthodox" methodological principle of pastoral counselor education.

Delivery of pastoral counseling service and the training of pastoral counselors have moved into the "constantinian stage." Both the power and weakness of this establishment period need to be monitored and critiqued by the spirit and vision of the heritage which has given birth to pastoral counseling.

This volume on pastoral counseling elaborates the accomplishments, structures, issues, and spirit of the field. The religious and laymen and laywomen of the pastoral counseling faculty of the Loyola College graduate program have applied their understanding of the field and share the experience of training others in it. Three general categories are suggested around which to organize many of the specific issues with which pastoral counseling is currently confronted. These are (1) refinement of the establishment position, (2) quantitative and qualitative expansion, and (3) research and development.

REFINEMENT OF THE ESTABLISHMENT POSITION

Refinement of the establishment position includes the issues of a stable economic base, network affiliations with religious and health care institutions, and maintenance of disciplinary standards. The key dynamics of operating from an establishment position are those of leadership and service. Those in pastoral counseling have tended to accentuate a style of dependence and passivity in relationship to religious and medical authority. Moving into the current establishment position, pastoral counselors need to accentuate their accomplishments which enhance both religious and psychotherapeutic activity. Leadership means the capacity to coalesce resources which have been generated in the pastoral counseling field and to put them at the disposal of others. Service means the commitment to maintain the primary values of pastoral counseling to provide healing for hurting persons despite the pressures to compromise such values.

Developing a stable economic base for pastoral counseling is a critical short- and long-term issue. Funding of pastoral counseling activity comes from three sources: contributions from the religious community, payment of fees by persons receiving the service, and reimbursement through health insurance plans. This economic base represents the linkage of pastoral counseling to its basic support communities, which are religious institutions, the persons served, and the health care industry. The establishment position assumes a legitimate claim upon these support communities for funds. Peculiar tensions, however, emerge in pastoral counseling as a consequence of these claims. The basic economic policy of pastoral counseling is that no person is denied service because of lack of economic resources. The sliding fee scale based on family size and income is the standard element in the fee-for-service claim. Although increasing numbers of persons are served by pastoral counselors, the fees received rarely pay for the costs of the service. Supplemental funding to support the sliding fee scale policy is essential.

This supplemental funding is primarily generated from local religious communities and is directly dependent upon the claim that pastoral counseling is ministry, which is organically linked to Churches and synagogues in the community. The balance between the economic independence represented by the fee-for-service claim and the dependence upon the contributory support of pastoral counseling as ministry is frequently precarious.

Protection against this vulnerability is sought through inclusion of pastoral counseling in health insurance plans. The claim of pastoral counseling that it is a part of the health care industry introduces the pressure of competition in the marketplace for the insurance funds. The marketplace is governed by consumer demand and provider supply. Claim upon private and governmental health insurance dollars, which is just emerging in the pastoral counseling movement, makes pastoral counseling activity vulnerable to the economic policies and regulations of the marketplace. A mixture of economic values is generated for the sake of financial stability. The long-term effect upon pastoral counseling because of its peculiar economic base is a sensitive and critical issue.

There is, however, opportunity for economic leadership and service in both ministry and health care which this establishment position creates. In ministry the opportunity is to clarify that money is an integral part of persons' lives through which values, attitudes, and personality dynamics are expressed. While money may have a corruptible influence on the values of serving human need, such corruption can be monitored and corrected. In health care the opportunity is to assure that insurance benefits support the person needing the service and not supply greater profit for the health care professional. The tendency to raise the costs of health service commensurate with the amount of insurance coverage can be modified through a clear commitment of pastoral counseling to establish reasonable compensation for the professional provider regardless of the reimbursement from insurance. This serves both the economic benefit of the person receiving care and adequate coverage of reasonable costs by the pastoral counselor. Such an ethical commitment by pastoral counseling may have some effect on the spiraling costs of mental health care, though it runs counter to the dynamics of profit of the marketplace.

Economic accountability is not only to the value of service, but also to the careful management of financial and personnel resources. In effect, such care is basic stewardship. Pastoral counseling, as a consequence of the establishment position, is developing administrative and management principles uniquely tailored to the service-oriented value of the activity. Training in administration and financial management is occurring so that the maximum utilization of resources in a time of economic scarcity and inflation may be realized.

Network affiliations with religious and health care institutions affirm the establishment position of pastoral counseling. Pastoral counseling is primarily a person-to-person ministry. However, establishment means the institutionalization of the movement so that its resources are visible in the larger context of religious and health care systems.

The role of pastoral counseling in the religious community has been understood as an extension of the local congregation. While this remains true, a larger role has emerged which is the communication of pastoral counseling insights to the very governing and policy structures of the religious institutions themselves. This role has several dimensions, among which are consultation, policy impact, and support. Consultation means the sharing of expertise with Church officials and councils on the many perplexing questions that confront religious institutions today. Policy impact means the influencing of decision making which preserves and enhances the ministry of pastoral counselors themselves. Support means the loyal commitment and critique which comes with the hope and affection for the vitality of religious institutions themselves. Pastoral counseling belongs to religious practice and carries the responsibility to participate in the full life of religious institutions. Though at times withdrawn and isolated from the mainstream of religious life, the pastoral counselor as part of an establishment movement belongs in the thick of church and synagogue activity at local, regional, and national levels. An active network of communication, personal relationships, and informed critique opens the way for pastoral counseling to contribute its learning and insight to the broad context of religious issues.

The role of pastoral counseling in the health care institutions has been understood in varied and ambiguous ways. The primary identification has been with psychiatry and psychology. The scope of health care professions has expanded rapidly in the past few decades. There does exist a loose network which provides a common identification among the plethora of those who supply health care in this country. Pastoral counseling belongs to this network through its claim as a health care profession. This means active relationship to the multitude of professional associations all of whom serve the larger picture of health care service and policy as well as protection of professional self-interest. Pastoral counselors not only stand among their peers in this network, but also enter it from a unique perspective as ministers. A current and long-range issue is the formation of the unique function of pastoral counseling in this network.

Maintenance of disciplinary standards is an essential function of the establishment position. Pastoral counseling has developed specific standards and criteria for persons who claim the right to practice and for centers and training programs that claim the right to be institutions of pastoral counseling. The American Association of Pastoral Counselors was created to function in this area.

The maintenance of standards of pastoral counseling as a discipline of knowledge has no specific mechanism that provides the parameters and controls over the definitions of pastoral counseling. This is primarily an intellectual task which is subject to the methodologies and constructs of the disciplines of religion and behavioral science.

One of the responsibilities of the establishment position is to make the judgments as to what constitutes pastoral counseling. A crucial issue immediately confronting the field is the tension between defining pastoral counseling as primarily psychotherapy and defining it as the range of counseling work conducted by pastors, priests, and rabbis. The focus on psychotherapy narrows the field and provides a specific focus on therapeutic process. The more inclusive focus broadens the definitions and is based on the processes of pastoral practice. The term *pastoral counseling* is used in both ways. This issue is open to considerable discussion over the next few years.

No definitive authority of method or concept has yet emerged that claims a consensus by persons working in the field. The forces that will ultimately determine the consensual authority are subtle and complex. Such standardization comes both from the gradual acceptance of common meaning by the society and from the conscious assertions by the few recognized authorities who are doing the intellectual work. Regulating the process by which this standardization process will occur is beyond the scope of any particular segment of pastoral counseling. The encouragement of this process, however, is the responsibility of persons and institutions that claim the name of pastoral counseling. At this stage the appeal is to all who engage in the activity to be in dialogue with each other for the sake of clear definitions and the stimulation of creative thinking.

Pastoral counseling operating from an establishment position takes the responsibility for its own support, nurture, and regulation, but it does so in the context of all affiliated persons, institutions, and fields. The refinement of this position gathers a cluster of perceived and emergent issues. It calls, however, for capacity to grow in a style of confidence and assertion.

QUANTITATIVE AND QUALITATIVE EXPANSION

The second general category around which to organize specific issues in pastoral counseling—quantitative and qualitative expansion—includes: orderly increase in pastoral counselors, centers, and training programs; the scope of clinical expertise; and the service to persons currently untouched by pastoral counseling.

The key dynamic in the quantitative and qualitative expansion is careful reflection on the assertions within the framework suggested in the first part of this chapter. These five assertions provide the critique for the breadth and depth of pastoral counseling. Commitment to the behavioral sciences, to religious institutions, to a theological method based on human experience, to political, economic, and social change, and to the nurture of the call, vocation, and imagination of pastoral counselors helps to measure the faithfulness to the wider scope of the field.

Orderly growth in the numbers of pastoral counselors, centers, and training programs precipitates the issue of control through certification and accreditation processes. The American Association of Pastoral Counselors is attempting to provide this type of regulatory function, but it is not alone in this attempt. Several other pastoral care organizations established by practitioners in the field and by ecclesiastical bodies are claiming responsibility for this function. A crucial issue, then, is the capacity of all such organizations to intertwine and amalgamate their insights and efforts for the sake of the activity. Efforts by endorsement agencies of the churches and synagogues and the certification organizations of the practitioners to search for such amalgamation gave rise to the Joint Council for Ministries in Specialized Settings, organized in 1979. Whether this effort will be sufficient in light of the rapid growth of the field is yet to be tested. The next decade will reveal the capacity of all interested parties in the field to provide the needed order in the expansion of pastoral counseling.

Quantitative and qualitative expansion is evident in the scope of clinical expertise in pastoral counseling. The issue that is currently preoccupying many pastoral counselors is the integration of religious and pastoral resources into the established concepts and techniques of psychotherapy. The way that such resources lend expanding substance to the processes of diagnosis, treatment, and healing of troubled persons has barely been opened. The pursuit of this type of expansion depends upon the commitments, assumptions, methods, and research which the workers in the field are able to command. Some of this effort is represented in the chapters of this volume.

Expansion also includes increased service to persons barely touched now by pastoral counseling. Pastoral counseling as a practice of psychotherapy has thrived primarily among the middle classes. The poor, the ethnic minorities, children, and the aging are relatively untouched by pastoral counseling. The Churches' work among these populations has been primarily in terms of social welfare. The primary issue for these groups is survival within the minimum standards of human existence. Attention to the psychological welfare based on the traditional forms of psychotherapy has not resulted in much help. The understanding, techniques, and concepts of mental health need investigation and revision if the benefits of pastoral counseling are to reach these groups. The result of such revision not only will be better service, but also will change the understanding of pastoral counseling itself. This type of expansion is occurring in minuscule ways. Encouragement, recognition, and evaluation of these efforts is an issue in pastoral counseling.

RESEARCH AND DEVELOPMENT

Research and development, a third category around which to organize specific issues in pastoral counseling, includes a clear commitment to research, the development of a research methodology uniquely tailored to the integrity of pastoral counseling, and planned coordination and design of research areas predictive of the future directions of the movement.

The key dynamic in research and development is intentional planning to gather the necessary data to test the claims and hypotheses of pastoral counseling. Such research will produce valuable knowledge which will shape the intellectual contributions of pastoral counseling to both religion and behavioral science.

The commitment to invest resources and energy in research is ambivalent among pastoral counselors. Despite some notable exceptions, the pastoral counselor is primarily committed to the service to persons who benefit from the counseling process. This commitment to service is commendable in terms of the practice of ministry, but it often covers the anxiety of inadequacy to do the necessary reflection and hard intellectual work demanded by the discipline. Learning to do pastoral counseling with confidence and control is a long and demanding process. Such professionalization is the most that can be expected from large numbers of pastoral counselors. However, this capacity can be translated into reflective papers and controlled research designs. The profession's expectation of such activities and attention to training in research during the educational process are specific ways in which the commitment of research can be encouraged. Programs that provide for sabbaticals, financial subsidies for concentrated studies, and access to research and grant funds are developmental areas which undergird the commitment to research. Such a commitment to research activity is absolutely essential if pastoral counseling truly is to become a disciplined field with a substantive body of knowledge.

Research methodology has been borrowed primarily from the behavioral sciences. Such empirical knowledge is essential for the pastoral counselor's claim as a mental health professional. Such knowledge is a hallmark of scientific investigation. Such methods have been applied to research in religion with mixed and limited results. Pastoral counseling as an interface field between these two disciplines is struggling for a research methodology which carries authority in both fields. The answer to this issue has not appeared on the current scene but awaits hard intellectual creativity. Development of a viable research methodology based on the integrity of pastoral counseling is an essential issue to the survival and growth of the field.

A first step toward resolving this pressing issue is the coordination of the efforts of those now producing research and reflective publication. The Joint Council on Research sponsored by several pastoral care organizations is a step in this direction. Lacking in this picture, however, is the development of a planning mechanism which provides a systematic design to investigate areas demanding attention. This means the coordination of resources of pastoral counseling centers, theological schools, related disciplines interested in religious and psychological investigation, foundations, appropriate governmental agencies, universities, and publishing houses.

In this chapter an attempt has been made to provide a frame of reference for the parameters of pastoral counseling, a recognition of the movement of pastoral counseling into an establishment position, and suggested categories for organizing specific current and future issues. Commitment, vigor, excitement, and intellect are the essential ingredients which help pastoral counseling to realize the promise envisioned by its founders.

Index